SOMETHING ABOUT THE AUTHOR

SOMETHING ABOUT THE AUTHOR

Facts and Pictures about Contemporary Authors
and Illustrators of Books for Young People

Anne Commire

VOLUME 6

GALE RESEARCH
BOOK TOWER
DETROIT, MICHIGAN
48226

Also Published by Gale

CONTEMPORARY AUTHORS:
A Bio-Bibliographical Guide to
Current Authors and Their Works

(Now Covers More Than 30,000 Authors)

Special acknowledgment is due to the members of the
Contemporary Authors staff who assisted in the preparation of
this volume, and to Gale's art director, Chester Gawronski.

Library of Congress Catalog Card Number: 70-127412
© 1974 by Gale Research Company. All rights reserved.
ISBN 0-8103-0060-5

GRATEFUL ACKNOWLEDGMENT

is made to the following publishers, authors, and artists, for their kind permission to reproduce copyrighted material. ■ **ABELARD-SCHUMAN LTD.** Illustration by Jules Gotlieb from *The Secret Farmyard* by Ruth Epperson Kennell. Copyright ⓒ 1956 by Ruth Epperson Kennell. /Illustration by Juliette Palmer from *A Duck for Keeps* by Helen Kay. Copyright ⓒ 1962 by Helen Kay. Both reprinted by permission of Abelard-Schuman Ltd. ■ **ABINGDON PRESS.** Illustration by Fritz Kredel from *The Silent Storm* by Marion Marsh Brown and Ruth Crone. Copyright ⓒ 1963 by Abingdon Press. /Illustration by Susan Perl from *Watch Out!* by Norah Smaridge. Copyright ⓒ 1965 by Abingdon Press. Both reprinted by permission of Abingdon Press. ■ **ATHENEUM PUBLISHERS.** Illustration by Renate Meyer from *Vicki* by Renate Meyer. Copyright ⓒ 1968 by Renate Meyer. /Illustration by Fuku Akino from *The One-Legged Ghost* by Betty Jean Lifton. Copyright ⓒ 1968 by Betty Jean Lifton. /Illustration by Ray Cruz from *Alexander and the Terrible, Horrible, No Good, Very Bad Day* by Judith Viorst. Pictures copyright ⓒ 1972 by Ray Cruz. /Illustration by Joan Berg from *Aunt America* by Marie Halun Bloch. Copyright ⓒ 1963 by Marie Halun Bloch. /Illustration by William Plummer from *Never Jam Today* by Carole Bolton. Copyright ⓒ 1971 by Carole Bolton. All reprinted by permission of Atheneum Publishers. ■ **THE BOBBS-MERRILL CO., INC.** Illustration by Charles Robinson from *Charlie's World* by Lee Bennett Hopkins. Illustrations copyright ⓒ 1972 by Charles Robinson. /Illustration by Robert Doremus from *Jeff Davis: Confederate Boy* by Lena Young de Grummond and Lynn de Grummond Delaune. Copyright ⓒ 1960 by The Bobbs-Merrill Co., Inc. /Illustration by Harry Lees from *A Book of Heroes* by Dorothy Heiderstadt. Copyright 1954 by The Bobbs-Merrill Co., Inc. All reprinted by permission of The Bobbs-Merrill Co., Inc. ■ **JONATHAN CAPE LTD.** Illustration by Jan Pienkowski from *The Kingdom Under the Sea* by Joan Aiken. Illustrations copyright ⓒ 1971 by Jan Pienkowski. Reprinted by permission of Jonathan Cape Ltd. ■ **CHILDRENS PRESS.** Illustration by Carol Rogers from *Hunters Blaze the Trails* by Edith McCall. Copyright ⓒ 1959 by Childrens Press. Reprinted by permission of Childrens Press. ■ **COWARD, McCANN & GEOGHEGAN, INC.** Illustration by Ib Spang Olsen from *Cat Alley* by Ib Spang Olsen. Illustration and original Danish text copyright ⓒ 1968 by Ib Spang Olsen. /Illustration by Peter Burchard from *The Street of the Flower Boxes* by Peggy Mann. Copyright ⓒ 1966 by Peggy Mann. /Illustration by Rocco Negri from *Androcles and the Lion* by Quail Hawkins. Illustrations copyright ⓒ 1970 by Rocco Negri. All reprinted by permission of Coward, McCann & Geoghegan, Inc. ■ **THOMAS Y. CROWELL CO.** Illustration by William A. Berry from *On Firm Ice* by Carter Wilson. Illustrations copyright ⓒ 1969 by William A. Berry. Reprinted by permission of Thomas Y. Crowell Co. ■ **CROWELL-COLLIER PRESS.** Illustration by Stan Tusan from *Sad Adam-Glad Adam* by Christopher Davis. Copyright ⓒ 1966 by The Macmillan Co. ■ **DELACORTE PRESS.** Illustration by Barbara Cooney from *Snow-White and Rose-Red* by Barbara Cooney. Copyright ⓒ 1965 by Barbara Cooney Porter and Longman Young Books Ltd. /Illustration by Anita Lobel from *Three Rolls and One Doughnut* retold by Mirra Ginsburg. Illustrations copyright ⓒ 1970 by Anita Lobel. /Illustration by Leo and Diane Dillon from *The Ring in the Prairie* by John Bierhorst. Illustrations copyright ⓒ 1970 by Leo and Diane Dillon. All reprinted by permission of Delacorte Press. ■ **J. M. DENT & SONS, LTD.** Illustration by D. J. Watkins-Pitchford from *The Lost Princess* by George MacDonald. Reprinted by permission of J. M. Dent & Sons, Ltd. ■ **DOUBLEDAY & CO., INC.** Illustration by Jacqueline Chwast from *Aunt Bella's Umbrella* by William Cole. Illustrations copyright ⓒ 1970 by Jacqueline Chwast. /Illustration by James Barkley from *Why the Wind God Wept* by Eve Titus. Illustrations copyright ⓒ 1972 by James Barkley. /Illustration by William Sharp from *Twelve Citizens of the World* by Leonard S. Kenworthy. Copyright 1945, by Leonard S. Kenworthy. All reprinted by permission of Doubleday & Co., Inc. ■ **E. P. DUTTON & CO., INC.** Photos by Eva Rappaport from *Banner Forward!* by Eva Rappaport.

son. All reprinted by permission of J. B. Lippincott Co. ■ **LITTLE, BROWN & CO.** Illustration by Trina Schart Hyman from *Favorite Fairy Tales Told in Czechoslovakia* by Virginia Haviland. Illustrations copyright © 1966 by Trina Schart Hyman. /Illustration by Rosemary Wells from *Impossible, Possum* by Ellen Conford. Illustrations copyright © 1971 by Rosemary Wells. Both reprinted by permission of Little, Brown & Co. ■ **MACDONALD & CO., LTD.** Illustration by William Stobbs from *The Adventures of Tom Leigh* by Phyllis Bentley. © 1964 by Phyllis Bentley. Reprinted by permission of Macdonald & Co. Ltd. (London). ■ **THE MACMILLAN CO.** Illustration by Charles Geer from *Wild Geese Flying* by Cornelia Meigs. © 1957 by the Macmillan Co. /Illustrations by Douglas Gorsline from *At the Seven Stars* by John and Patricia Beatty. Copyright © 1963 by John and Patricia Beatty. /Illustration by John Martinez from *Marie Curie: Discoverer of Radium* by Joanne Landers Henry. Copyright © 1966 by John Martinez. /Illustration by Dirk Gringhuis from *Big Mac* by Dirk Gringhuis. Copyright © 1959 by Dirk Gringhuis. All reprinted by permission of The Macmillan Co. ■ **McGRAW-HILL BOOK CO.** Illustration by Roger Duvoisin from *The Happy Lion* by Louise Fatio. Copyright 1954 by Louise Fatio Duvoisin and Roger Duvoisin. Reprinted by permission of McGraw-Hill Book Co. ■ **DAVID McKAY CO., INC.** Illustration by Don Lambo from *The Secret of the Carved Whale Bone* by Arnold Madison. Copyright © 1969 by Arnold Madison. /Illustration by Larry Toschik from *Follow the Honey Bird* by Emily Watson Hallin and Robert Buell. Copyright © 1967 by Emily W. Hallin and Robert K. Buell. Both reprinted by permission of David McKay Co., Inc. ■ **JULIAN MESSNER, INC.** Illustration by Jim Fox from *Inventors in Industry* by Ruby L. Radford. Copyright © 1969 by Ruby L. Radford. /Illustration by Weda Yap from *Willy Wong: American* by Vanya Oakes. Copyright 1951 by Vanya Oakes. Both reprinted by Julian Messner, a division of Simon & Schuster, Inc. ■ **METHUEN & CO., LTD.** Illustration by Richard Leacroft from *The Theatre* by Helen and Richard Leacroft. Copyright © 1958 by Helen and Richard Leacroft. Reprinted by permission of Methuen & Co., Ltd. ■ **WILLIAM MORROW & CO.** Illustration by Tony Chen from *Run, Zebra, Run* by Tony Chen. Reprinted by permission of Lothrop, Lee & Shepard. /Illustration by Leslie Goldstein from *The Devil Cat Screamed* by Verne T. Davis. Copyright © 1966 by Verne T. Davis. Both reprinted by permission of William Morrow & Co. ■ **NATUREGRAPH PUBLISHERS.** Illustration by Laura Louise Foster from *Keer-Loo: The True Story of a Young Wood Duck* by Laura Louise Foster. Copyright © 1965 by Laura Louise Foster. Reprinted by permission of Naturegraph Publishers, Healdsburg, Calif. ■ **W. W. NORTON & CO., INC.** Illustration by Victor G. Ambrus from *High and Haunted Island* by Nan Chauncy. Copyright © 1964 by Nan Chauncy. Reprinted by permission of W. W. Norton & Co., Inc. ■ **S. G. PHILLIPS, INC.** Illustration by Simon Jeruchim from *Edgar Allan* by John Neufeld. Copyright © 1968 by S. G. Phillips, Inc. Reprinted by permission of S. G. Phillips, Inc. ■ **G. P. PUTNAM'S SONS.** Illustration by Ronald Himler from *Glad Day* by Ronald Himler. Copyright © 1972 by Ronald Himler. /Illustration by Robert Quackenbush from *The Boy Who Woke Up in Madagascar* by Robin McKown. Copyright © 1967 by Robin McKown. Both reprinted by permission of G. P. Putnam's Sons. ■ **RAND McNALLY & CO.** Illustration by Jon Nielsen from *Pilgrim Neighbors* by Elvajean Hall. Copyright © 1964 by Rand McNally & Co. /Illustration by Rafaello Busoni from *His Name Was Jesus* by Mary Alice Jones. Copyright 1950 by Rand McNally & Co. /Illustration by Winifred Lubell from *Green is for Growing* by Winifred and Cecil Lubell. Copyright © 1964 by Rand McNally & Co. /Illustration by D. K. Stone from *Christmas Stories Round the World* by Lois S. Johnson. Copyright © 1970 by Rand McNally & Co. All reprinted by permission of Rand McNally & Co. ■ **RANDOM HOUSE.** Illustration by Colette Portal from *The Beauty of Birth* by Colette Portal. Adapted from the French by Guy Daniels. Copyright © 1971 by Colette Portal. /Illustration by George Wiggins from *Mud! Mud! Mud!* by Leonore Klein. Copyright © 1962 by Leonore Klein and George Wiggins. /Illustration by Doris Burn from *Tappy* by Robert Nathan. Copyright © renewed 1966 by Robert Nathan. /Illustration by Marion Holland from *A Big Ball of String* by Marion Holland. Copyright © 1958 by Marion Holland. /Illustration by Imero Gobbato from *The Great Cheese Conspiracy* by Jean Van Leeuwen. Copyright © 1969 by Jean Van Leeuwen Gavril. /Illustration by Robert Lopshire from *Put Me in the Zoo* by Robert Lopshire. Copyright © 1960 by Robert Lopshire. All reprinted by permission of Alfred A. Knopf, Pantheon Books, and Random House, Inc. ■ **ST. MARTIN'S PRESS.** Illustration by Ray Bethers from *How Does It Grow?* by Ray Bethers. Reprinted by permission of St. Martin's Press. ■ **SCHOLASTIC BOOK SERVICES.** Illustration by Tom Eaton from *It's Your World—Don't Pollute It* by Lavinia Dobler. Copyright © 1972 by Scholastic Book Services. /Illustration by Iris Schweitzer from *Dougal Looks for Birds* by Martha Bennett Stiles. Illustrations copyright © 1972 by Iris Schweitzer. /Illustration from *America Fever: The Story of American Immigration* by Barbara Kaye Greenleaf. Copyright © 1970 by Barbara Kaye Greenleaf. All reprinted by permission of Four Winds Press and Scholastic Book Services, a division of Scholastic Magazines, Inc. ■ **CHARLES SCRIBNER'S SONS.** Illustration by Carol Lawson from *Brownjohn's*

Beasts by Allan Brownjohn. Illustrations copyright © 1970 by Macmillan & Co. (London). /Illustration by Leonard Everett Fisher from *Little Calf* by Victor Scheffer. Copyright © 1970 by Victor Scheffer. Both reprinted by permission of Charles Scribner's Sons. ■ **SIMON & SCHUSTER, INC.** Photograph by Myron Wood from *Hollering Sun* by Nancy Wood. Illustrations copyright © 1972 by Myron Wood. Reprinted by permission of Simon & Schuster, Inc. ■ **STECK-VAUGHN CO.** Illustration by Dutz from *Going to the Fair* by Mary Octavia Davis. Copyright © 1968 by Steck-Vaughn Co. Reprinted by permission of Steck-Vaughn Co. ■ **TAPLINGER PUBLISHING CO.** Illustration by Alice Caddy from *Look Down that Winding River* by Ben Lucien Burman. Copyright © 1973 by Ben Lucien Burman. Reprinted by permission of Taplinger Publishing Co. ■ **UNIEBOEK B.V.** Illustration by Rien Poortvliet from *Boris* by Jaap ter Haar. Copyright © 1966 by Van Dishoeck, Van Holkema and Warendorf N.V., Bussum. English translation copyright © 1969 by Blackie & Son Ltd. Reprinted by permission of Unieboek B.V., Bussum—the Netherlands. ■ **THE VANGUARD PRESS, INC.** Illustration by Isadore Seltzer from *No Steady Job for Papa* by Marion Benasutti. Reprinted by permission of The Vanguard Press, Inc. ■ **THE VIKING PRESS, INC.** Illustration by Robert Lawson from *Adam of the Road* by Elizabeth Janet Gray. Copyright 1942 by Elizabeth Janet Gray and Robert Lawson. /Illustration by Lilian Obligado from *There Is a Tide* by Elspeth Bragdon. Copyright © 1964 by Elspeth Bragdon. /Illustration by Barbara McGee from *Jump-Rope Rhymes* by Barbara McGee. Copyright © 1968 by Barbara McGee. /Illustration by Robert Greiner from *Follow My Leader* by James B. Garfield. Copyright © 1957 by James B. Garfield. All reprinted by permission of The Viking Press, Inc. ■ **HENRY Z. WALCK, INC.** Illustration by Richard Lebenson from *The Witch's Brat* by Rosemary Sutcliff. Copyright © 1970 by Rosemary Sutcliff. /Illustration by Fiona French from *The Blue Bird* by Fiona French. Copyright © 1972 by Fiona French. /Illustration by Arnold Spilka from *The Tree and Me* by Michael Sage. Illustrations copyright © 1970 by Arnold Spilka. /Illustration by V. H. Drummond from *The Flying Postman* by V. H. Drummond. Copyright © 1964 by Violet Drummond. Reprinted by permission of Constable Young Books Ltd. All reprinted by permission of Henry Z. Walck, Inc. ■ **FRANKLIN WATTS, INC.** Illustration by Dorothy Marino from *Benjy's Blanket* by Myra Berry Brown. Illustrations copyright © 1962 by Franklin Watts, Inc. /Illustration by F. D. Phillips from *The Ink-Bottle Club Abroad* by Sarah Stafford Smith. Copyright © 1969 by Sarah Stafford Smith. /Illustration by John Hamberger from *Vanishing Wings* by Griffing Bancroft. Copyright © 1972 by Griffing Bancroft. /Illustration by Victoria de Larrea from *Orange October* by Gene Inyart. Copyright © 1968 by Franklin Watts, Inc. /Illustration by Eileen Green from *Jimmy Lane and His Boat* by Frederick Grice. Copyright © 1963 by Oxford University Press. All reprinted by permission of Franklin Watts, Inc. ■ **THE WESTMINSTER PRESS.** Illustration by Lee de Groot from *Miss Tessie Tate* by Jean Horton Berg. Copyright © MCMLXVII by Jean Horton Berg. Reprinted by permission of The Westminster Press. ■ **ALBERT WHITMAN & CO.** Illustration by Laura Bannon from *When the Moon is New* by Laura Bannon. Copyright 1953 by Laura Bannon. /Illustration by Jack Faulkner from *Old Man Riddle* by Carl Memling. Illustrations copyright 1972 by John Faulkner. ■ **WINDMILL BOOKS, INC.** Illustration by Jose and Ariane Aruego from *Milton the Early Riser* by Robert Kraus. Illustrations copyright © 1972 by Jose Aruego.

Illustrations by Rockwell Kent from *Moby Dick* by Herman Melville. Reprinted by permission of The Rockwell Kent Estate. /Illustrations by Elinor Lyon from *The House in Hiding* by Elinor Lyon. Reprinted by permission of the author. /Illustration by Helen V. Stone from "Pable the Potter" in *Presbyterian Life*. Reprinted by permission of the author.

PHOTOGRAPH CREDITS

Phyllis Bentley: Hugh Greaves; Fon W. Boardman, Jr.: Congrat-Butler; Ben Bova: Jay Kay Klein; Edith Brecht: Peel's Studio; Alan Brownjohn: Lindsay Croker; Ben Lucien Burman: Barney Sellers; Mary Chalmers: Norman T. Brecht; Ellen Conford: Charles Fishman; Barbara Cooney: Weston Woods; Harold Courlander: Julian A. Garrett; Deborah Crawford: Willy Ley; V. H. Drummond: Courtesy of Faber & Faber; Mary Lois Dunn: Burl Bell; Erich Fuchs: Foto Rolf Herkner; Mirra Ginsburg: *Newsweek*; John Gordon: Alan Howard; Elizabeth Janet Gray: Bradford Bachrach; Elvajean Hall: William Winston Photo; Molly Costain Haycraft: Courtesy of J. B. Lippincott; Dorothy M. Johnson: Lacy's Studio; Lois Smith Johnson: Glogau; Rockwell Kent: Courtesy of the Rockwell Kent Legacies; Errol Le Cain: Jerry Bauer; Peggy Mann: William Houlton; James Marshall: Andrew Xenios; Robin McKown: Mitchell Studio; Vanya Oakes: Flatte of Hollywood; Edwin A. Peeples: Bob Barrett; Jan Pienkowski: *Evening Echo*; Colette Portal: Julio Silva; Elaine Sommers Rich: Worth; John M. Rosenburg: Fabian Bachrach; Victor B. Scheffer: Wiles and Thomas; James Edward Seidelman: Lexington *Herald-Leader*; Betty Smith: Town and Country Studios; Ruth Hill Viguers: Biennale of Illustrations Bratislava; Carter Wilson: Sissy Krook.

HAZARD ADAMS

ADAMS, Hazard   1926-

PERSONAL: Born February 15, 1926, in Cleveland, Ohio; son of Robert Simeon (a headmaster) and Mary (Thurness) Adams; married Diana Violet White, September 17, 1949; children: Charles Simeon, Perry White. *Education:* University of Washington, Seattle, student, 1943, M.A., 1949, Ph.D., 1953; Princeton University, A.B., 1948. *Office:* Office of the Vice-chancellor, Academic Affairs, University of California, Irvine, Calif.

CAREER: Cornell University, Ithaca, N.Y., instructor, 1952-56; University of Texas, Austin, assistant professor of English, 1956-59; Michigan State University, East Lansing, associate professor, then professor of English, 1959-64; University of California, Irvine, professor and chairman of department of English, 1964-69, dean, school of humanities, 1970-72, vice-chancellor, 1972—. Washington University, St. Louis, Mo., visiting professor, 1959; Trinity College, Dublin, Ireland, Fulbright research scholar and lecturer, 1962-63. *Military service:* U.S. Marine Corps, 1943-45, 1951; became first lieutenant. *Member:* Modern Language Association, American Society for Aesthetics.

WRITINGS: (Editor) *Poems by Robert Simeon Adams*, Bobbs, 1952; *Blake and Yeats: The Contrary Vision*, Cornell University Press, 1955; *The Contexts of Poetry*, Little,

Brown, 1963; *William Blake: A Reading of the Shorter Poems*, University of Washington Press, 1963; *Fiction as Process*, Dodd, 1968; *Poetry: An Introductory Anthology*, Little, Brown, 1968; *The Interests of Criticism*, Harcourt, 1969; *William Blake: Jerusalem, Selected Poems and Prose*, Holt, 1970; *The Truth about Dragons: An Anti-Romance* (School Library Journal book list), Harcourt, 1971; *Critical Theory Since Plato*, Harcourt, 1971; *Lady Gregory*, Bucknell University Press, 1973. Contributor to *Poetry Northwest, Accent, Modern Fiction Studies, Critique*, other professional journals. Member of editorial board, *Studies in Romanticism* and *Blake Studies*.

WORK IN PROGRESS: A novel; *Philosophy of Literary Symbolism.*

ALDON, Adair
See MEIGS, Cornelia Lynde

ALEGRIA, Ricardo E.   1921-

PERSONAL: Born April 14, 1921, in San Juan, Puerto Rico; son of Jose S. and Celeste (Gallardo) Alegria; married Mela Pons (an artist), December 7, 1947; children: Ricardo, Jose Francisco. *Education:* University of Puerto Rico, B.A., 1943; University of Chicago, M.A., 1947; Harvard University, graduate student, 1953-55. *Religion:* Roman Catholic. *Home:* San Jose 101, San Juan, Puerto Rico.

CAREER: University of Puerto Rico, Rio Piedras, associate professor of history, 1947-55, professor of anthropology and history, 1955—, director of archaeological mu-

RICHARD E. ALEGRIA

1

The giant arrived and asked the Princess with whom she was talking. The Princess replied that she was talking with no one—as he could see, there was no one in the room. ■ (From *The Three Wishes* by Ricardo E. Alegria. Illustrated by Lorenzo Homar.)

seum and research center, 1947-55; Institute of Puerto Rican Culture, San Juan, director, 1955—. *Member:* American Anthropological Association (fellow), Society for American Archaeology. *Awards, honors:* Guggenheim Fellow, 1953-55; Doctorate Honoris Causae (Humanities), Catholic University (Puerto Rico), 1971; Doctorate Honoris Causae (Law), New York University, 1971; National Trust for Historic Preservation Award, 1973.

WRITINGS: Historia de nuestros Indios, Puerto Rico Department of Education, 1948; *La Fiesta de Santiago Apostol en Loiza, Puerto Rico,* Coleccion de Estudios Puertorriquenos (Madrid), 1954; *Cuentos folkloricos de Puerto Rico,* Editorial Ateneo (Buenos Aires and Barcelona), 1968; (collector and adaptor) *The Three Wishes* (Puerto Rican folktales for children, translated by Elizabeth Culbert), Harcourt, 1968; *Descubrimiento, conquista y colonizacion de Puerto Rico,* Coleccion de Estudios Puertorriquenos (Madrid), 1969; *El Fuerte de San Jeronimo del Boqueron,* Institute of Puerto Rican Culture, 1969.

WORK IN PROGRESS: Writing on the folklore and history of Puerto Rico and on archaeology of the West Indies, where he did research.

FOR MORE INFORMATION SEE: Horn Book, August, 1969.

ANCKARSVARD, Karin (Inez Maria) 1915-1969

PERSONAL: Surname is pronounced ank-er-sord; born August 10, 1915, in Stockholm, Sweden; daughter of Oscar Emil (a doctor of medicine) and Iris (Forssling) Olson; married Carl M. Cosswa Anckarsvard, January 20, 1940; children: Marie Christine (Mrs. Reinhold Fahlbeck), Marie Cecile, Marie Madeleine, Mikael, Carl Henrik. *Education:* Attended Oxford University, 1934-35; commercial college degree, Stockholm, Sweden, 1936. *Politics:* Conservative. *Religion:* Roman Catholic. *Home:* Skandiavagen 13, Djursholm, Sweden.

CAREER: Secretary of Sveriges Yngre Lakares, 1936-40. *Member:* Catholic Women's League of Sweden (president), Association of Sweden's Authors of Children's Books, Association of Sweden's Authors, Conservative Women's League. *Awards, honors:* Bonnier's childrens' book award, 1958; Ungdomsnytt's Stip.; Swedish State Stip., 1960; Children's Book Choice award, 1963, for *Doktorns Pojk.*

WRITINGS: Bonifacius den Groene, Bonniers, 1952, translation by C. M. Anckarsvard and K. H. Beales published as *Bonifacius the Green,* Abelard, 1962; *Tag Fast Magistern!,* Bonniers, 1955, translation by Annabelle MacMillan published as *The Mysterious Schoolmaster,* Harcourt, 1959; *Tag Fast Spoket!,* Bonniers, 1955, translation by MacMillan published as *The Robber Ghost,* Harcourt, 1961; *Tag Fast Snoegubben!,* Bonniers, 1957, translation by MacMillan published as *Madcap Mystery,* Harcourt, 1962; *Bonifacius och Lill-Bonnie,* Bonniers, 1958, translation by C. M. Anckarsvard and Beales pub-

KARIN ANCKARSVARD

2

... finding the whole business highly interesting, each wanted to make his own personal contribution to the proceedings. ■ (From *Aunt Vinnie's Victorious Six* by Karin Anckarsvard. Illustrated by William M. Hutchinson.)

lished as *Bonifacius and Little Bonnie*, Abelard, 1963; *Varfor just Krabat?*, Bonniers, 1958, translation by Mac-Millan published as *Rider By Night*, Harcourt, 1960; *Liten Roman om Eva*, Bonniers, 1959, translation by MacMillan published as *Springtime for Eva*, Harcourt, 1961; *Foeraeldrafritt Med Faster Lava*, Bonniers, 1960, translation by MacMillan published as *Aunt Vinnie's Invasion*, Harcourt, 1962; *De Sex och faster lava*, Bonniers, 1962, translation by MacMillan published as *Aunt Vinnie's Victorious Six*, Harcourt, 1964; *Jag Vantar Pa Fransiska*, Bonniers, 1962; *Doktorns Pojk*, Bonniers, 1963, translation by MacMillan published as *The Doctor's Boy*, Harcourt, 1965; *Gatan Med Ringen*, Bonniers, 1965, translation by MacMillan published as *The Riddle of the Ring*, Harcourt, 1966; *Svenssons Pojk*, Bonniers, 1966, translation by MacMillan published as *Struggle at Soltuna*, Harcourt, 1968; *Riktiga djuroch naesten riktiga*, Bonnier, 1967. Contributor to *Expressea* (Swedish daily newspaper).

FOR MORE INFORMATION SEE: New York Times Book Review, May 8, 1965; *Third Book of Junior Authors*, edited by de Montreville and Hill, Wilson, 1972.

(Died January 16, 1969)

ARUEGO, Jose 1932-

PERSONAL: Born August 9, 1932, in Manila, Philippines; son of Jose M. (a lawyer) and Constancia (Espiritu) Aruego; married Ariane Dewey (an illustrator), January 27, 1961 (divorced); children: Juan. *Education:* University of the Philippines, B.A., 1953, LL.B., 1955; Parsons School of Design, Certificate in Graphic Arts and Advertising, 1959. *Residence:* New York, N.Y.

CAREER: Village Display Co., New York, N.Y., apprentice, 1959-60; Hayden Publishing Co., New York, N.Y., designer, 1960-62; Mervin & Jesse Levine (fashion advertising agency), New York, N.Y., mechanical boardman, 1963-64; Norman Associates (studio), New York, N.Y., mechanical boardman, 1964-65; Ashton B. Collins, Inc. (advertising agency), New York, N.Y., assistant art director, 1965-68; writer and illustrator of books for children. *Awards, honors:* Outstanding picture book of the year award from *New York Times*, for *Juan and the Asuangs*, 1970, for *The Day They Parachuted Cats on Borneo*, 1971, and for *Look What I Can Do*, 1972; *Look What I Can Do*, *The Chick and The Duckling*, and *A Crocodile's Tale* were Children's Book Council Showcase Titles, 1972, 1973.

JOSE ARUEGO

3

The Creeps next door were still asleep.

So were the Whippersnappers across the way

■ (From *Milton the Early Riser* by Robert Kraus. Illustrated by Jose and Ariane Aruego.)

WRITINGS—Self-illustrated children's books: *The King and His Friends,* Scribner, 1969; *Juan and the Asuangs: A Tale of Philippine Ghosts and Spirits,* Scribner, 1970; *Symbiosis: A Book of Unusual Friendships,* Scribner, 1970; *Pilyo the Piranha,* Macmillan, 1971; *Look What I Can Do,* Scribner, 1971; (with wife, Ariane Aruego) *A Crocodile's Tale,* Scribner, 1972.

Illustrator: Robert Kraus, *Whose Mouse Are You?* (ALA Notable Book), Macmillan, 1970; Kay Smith, *Parakeets and Peach Pies,* Parents' Magazine Press, 1970; Jack Prelutsky, *Toucans Two and Other Poems,* Macmillan, 1970; Charlotte Pomerantz, *The Day They Parachuted Cats on Borneo: A Drama of Ecology* (play), Young Scott Books, 1971; Christina Rossetti, *What Is Pink?,* Macmillan, 1971; Robert Kraus, *Leo the Late Bloomer,* Windmill Books, 1971; Elizabeth Coatsworth, *Good Night,* Macmillan, 1972; (with Ariane Aruego) Robert Kraus, *Milton the Early Riser* (ALA Notable Book) Dutton, 1972; Mirra Ginsburg, *The Chick and the Duckling,* Windmill Books, 1972. Contributor of cartoons to *New Yorker, Look, Saturday Review,* and other magazines.

SIDELIGHTS: Aruego was born in Manila and comes from a family of lawyers and politicians. He holds a B.A. and a law degree from the University of the Philippines, but practiced law for only three months, handling one case—which he lost.

He decided to move to New York City to pursue a boyhood interest in humorous illustration. As a child, he had collected comic books and rented them to his friends. In New York he enrolled in the Parsons School of Design. After his second year at Parsons he spent a summer studying in Europe, where he became interested in doing line drawings. "I discovered that line drawing is a great fulfillment. I drew everything from fire extinguishers to Rodin sculptures to drinking fountains."

His first job after graduating from Parsons was at a Greenwich Village studio, where he pasted feathers on angel wings of mannequins. He was laid off shortly after the Christmas season, and for the next six years he worked for magazines, design studios, and advertising agencies. When he had sold several cartoons to the *Saturday Evening Post* and *Look,* he quit his job and worked for nearly two years as a full-time freelance cartoonist. He then turned to book illustration, where he could expand the antics of the animals he had drawn in many of his cartoons.

Although he has traveled extensively in the United States as a member ambassador for a friendship program, and has toured around the world, Aruego's favorite city is New York. His mural of New York City hangs at the International House on Riverside Drive.

FOR MORE INFORMATION SEE: New York Times Book Review, April 26, 1970, May 2, 1971, May 7, 1972, November 12, 1972; *National Observer,* April 27, 1970; *Library Journal,* May 15, 1970; *Christian Science Monitor,* November 11, 1971; *Horn Book,* June, 1972; *Junior Literary Guild Catalogue,* September, 1972; *Washington Post* "Children's Book World," November 5, 1972.

ELIOT ASINOF

ASINOF, Eliot 1919-

PERSONAL: Surname is accented on first syllable, pronounced *Ace*-in-of; born July 13, 1919, in New York, N.Y.; son of Max and Rose (Tager) Asinof; married Jocelyn Brando (an actress), April 11, 1950 (divorced); children: Martin. *Education:* Swarthmore College, A.B., 1940. *Home:* 255 West End Ave., New York, N.Y. 10023.

CAREER: Professional baseball player with minor league teams owned by Philadelphia Phillies, 1939-41; salesman in men's clothing business in eastern U.S., 1947-50; freelance writer, 1950—. *Military service:* U.S. Army Air Forces, 1942-46; became first lieutenant.

WRITINGS: Man on Spikes, McGraw, 1955; *Eight Men Out,* Holt, 1963; *The Bedfellow,* Simon & Schuster, 1967; *Seven Days to Sunday,* Simon & Schuster, 1968; *The Name of the Game is Murder,* Simon & Schuster, 1968; *People vs. Blutcher,* Viking, 1969; *Craig and Joan* (*School Library Journal* book list), Viking, 1970; *The Ten Second Jailbreak,* Holt, 1973. Also writer of television dramas, motion picture scripts, and magazine articles.

WORK IN PROGRESS: An untitled novel.

SIDELIGHTS: "Writing, to me, is an expression of what I feel and understand about the way we all live. I am constantly experimenting with the form in which to tell my story and make my interpretations. I have shifted from the world of sports where I began as a writer to broader areas of American life, but always concentrated on people, specific people. I find my dramas in their struggles, usually against the power of the so-called Establishment. I do not write for the purpose of entertainment but hope that the reader will be intrigued by the reality of the drama.

"I became a writer in the first place because I felt it was the best way to make a statement about injustice and exploitation. Remembering how great an impact such writers as Sinclair Lewis and Theodore Dreiser had on my impressionistic teenage years, I have tried desperately to emulate them in my impressions of contemporary America."

FOR MORE INFORMATION SEE: Horn Book, August, 1971.

BABBITT, Natalie 1932-

PERSONAL: Born July 28, 1932, in Dayton, Ohio; daughter of Ralph Zane (a business administrator) and Genevieve (Converse) Moore; married Samuel Fisher Babbitt (president of Kirkland College), June 26, 1954; children: Christopher Converse, Thomas Collier II, Lucy Cullyford. Education: Laurel School for Girls, student, 1947-50; Smith College, B.A., 1954. Politics: Democrat. Home: Harding Rd., R.D. 1, Clinton, N.Y. 13323. Agent: Curtis Brown Ltd., 60 East 56th St., New York, N.Y. 10022.

CAREER: Majored in art at college and entered the children's book field as an illustrator. Member: Authors Guild of Authors League of America. Awards, honors: The New York Times listed The Search for Delicious as the best book of 1969 for children ages nine-twelve; Kneeknock Rise was an American Library Association Notable Book, 1970, and a John Newbery Honor Book, 1971; Goody Hall was an Honor Book in the 1971 Children's Spring Book Festival sponsored by Book World and a children's Book Council Showcase title, 1972.

The truth is that Mylo was very much afraid of the dark. ■ (From The Something by Natalie Babbitt. Illustrated by the author.)

WRITINGS—Self-illustrated: *Dick Foote and the Shark* (verse; Junior Literary Guild selection), Farrar, Straus, 1967; *Phoebe's Revolt*, Farrar, Straus, 1968; *The Search for Delicious*, Farrar, Straus, 1969; *Kneeknock Rise* (Junior Literary Guild selection; *Horn Book* honor list; ALA Notable book), Farrar, Straus, 1970; *The Something* (Junior Literary Guild selection), Farrar, Straus, 1970; *Goody Hall* (*School Library Journal* list), Farrar, Straus, 1971; *The Devil's Storybook* (excerpt in *Cricket,* January, February, April, 1974), Farrar, Straus, 1974.

Illustrator: Samuel Fisher Babbitt, *The Forty-Ninth Magician,* Pantheon, 1966; Valerie Worth, *Small Poems,* Farrar Straus, 1972.

Contributor to *Redbook, Publishers Weekly, Horn Book,* and *New York Times Book Review.*

WORK IN PROGRESS: An untitled children's novel about immortality and its possible miseries.

SIDELIGHTS: "As the wife of a college president and mother of three children, I have little enough time for work and none for hobbies except needlework. I write for children because I am interested in fantasy and the possibilities for experience of all kinds before the time of compromise. I believe that children are far more perceptive and wise than American books give them credit for being. I am my own best audience."

FOR MORE INFORMATION SEE: New York Times Book Review, July 2, 1967, November 9, 1969, May 2, 1971; *New Statesman,* November, 1968; *Library Journal,* May 15, 1969, June 15, 1970; *Horn Book,* August, 1969, June, 1970, August, 1971; *Redbook,* December, 1971; *Cricket,* April, 1974.

MARGARET HOPE BACON

BACON, Margaret Hope   1921-

PERSONAL: Born April 7, 1921, in New York, N.Y.; daughter of Norman (an artist) and Myrtle (Hope) Borchardt; married S. Allen Bacon (director of a welfare agency), June 28, 1942; children: Margaret Scattergood, Elizabeth Hope, Peter Farquhar. *Education:* Antioch College, B.A., 1943. *Politics:* Democratic-Independent. *Religion:* Society of Friends. *Home:* 372 East Gowen Ave., Philadelphia, Pa. 19119. *Agent:* John Schaffner, 425 East 51st St., New York, N.Y. 10022. *Office:* American Friends Service Committee, Philadelphia, Pa. 19102.

CAREER: Cooperative League of U.S.A., Chicago, Ill., editorial assistant, based in New York, 1943; *Eastern Cooperator,* New York, N.Y., assistant editor, 1943-44; Springfield State Hospital, Sykesville, Md., psychiatric social worker, 1944-46; Radnor Township School District, Wayne, Pa., part-time director of public relations, 1959-62; American Friends Service Committee, Philadelphia, Pa., director of publicity for Algerian program, 1962-63, director of publicity for international service and affairs, 1964-65, director of press relations, 1965-69, director of information, 1969—. *Awards, honors: Lamb's Warrior* was selected by the Child Study Association one of the Books of the Year, 1970.

WRITINGS: The Quiet Rebels: The Story of the Quaker in America, Basic Books, 1969; *Lamb's Warrior: The Life of Isaac T. Hopper* (juvenile), Crowell, 1970. Contributor of articles, short stories, and poetry to *Saturday Evening Post, Parents' Magazine, Mademoiselle, Better Homes and Gardens, New York Times,* and other publications.

NATALIE BABBITT

WORK IN PROGRESS: A book on Abby Kelley Foster, 19th-century abolitionist and feminist, for Crowell.

SIDELIGHTS: Ms. Bacon went to South Africa for the leader exchange program in the summer of 1964, to the People's Republic of China in May, 1972, and has visited other African and European countries for the American Friends Service Committee. *Hobbies and Other Interests:* Gardening, nature, canoeing, sailing, skiing, reading, the theater.

BAILEY, Matilda
See RADFORD, Ruby L.

BANCROFT, Griffing   1907-

PERSONAL: Born February 18, 1907, in San Diego, Calif.; son of Griffing (a scientist) and Ethel (Works) Bancroft; married Mary Jackson, 1936; married second wife, Jane Eads (a writer and artist), August 22, 1949. *Education:* University of Chicago, Ph.B., 1930. *Politics:* Democrat. *Religion:* None. *Address:* P.O. Box 93, Captiva, Fla. 33924. *Agent:* Julian Bach, Jr., 3 East 48th St., New York, N.Y. 10017.

He tried to come down quietly, but somehow he could not control the fluttering of a wing, which gave him away. ■ (From *Vanishing Wings* by Griffing Bancroft. Illustrated by John Hamberger.)

GRIFFING BANCROFT

CAREER: International News Service, reporter in California and in Washington, D.C., 1933-41; *Chicago Sun,* Chicago, Ill., Washington correspondent, 1941-48; Columbia Broadcasting system, Washington, D.C., commentator, 1948-58. *Wartime service:* Civilian in Psychological Warfare Service, World War II; received Medal of Freedom. *Member:* American Ornithologists' Union, Wilson Ornithological Society, Sanibel-Captiva Conservation Foundation (vice-chairman), Sanibel-Capitiva Audubon Society (vice-president). *Awards, honors:* Christopher Award, 1972, for *Vanishing Wings.*

WRITINGS: (Reviser) William J. Miller, *The Meaning of Communism,* Silver Burdett, 1968; *Snowy: The Story of an Egret* (juvenile), McCall Publishing, 1970; *Vanishing Wings: A Tale of Three Birds of Prey* (Junior Literary Guild selection), Watts, 1972; *The White Cardinal,* Coward, 1973.

WORK IN PROGRESS: Story of the imprinting of a young woodpecker raised in captivity; an account of earlier days of ornithological work and egg collecting.

SIDELIGHTS: "Upon moving to Florida as a free-lance writer, I became alarmed at what man was doing to his fellow creatures on this planet. Against a background of personal field work and research, and the invaluable experience of having engaged in nature study with my father when I was young, I decided to try to recount some of the problems facing our native birds."

FOR MORE INFORMATION SEE: Junior Literary Guild Catalogue, March, 1972; *New York Times Book Review,* May 7, 1972.

BANNON, Laura   d. 1963

PERSONAL: Daughter of James William and Carrie (Freeman) Bannon. *Education:* Western Michigan State College (now Western Michigan University), graduate, two-year course; School of the Art Institute of Chicago, graduate, five-year course. *Home:* 1400 Chicago Ave, Evanston, Ill.

CAREER: Taught in high school at Battle Creek, Mich., for two years; supervised public school art at Mount Clemens, Mich., Port Huron, Mich., and Racine, Wis., while intermittently attending the Art Institute in Chicago; part-time instructor and later director of the Art Institute's Junior School. Exhibited paintings at the International Water Color Show, the American Show, the Chicago Artists' Show, and in smaller galleries. Writer and illustrator of books, all but one juveniles. *Member:* MacDowell Colony, Chicago Society of Artists. *Awards, honors:* Chicago Society of Typographic Arts award, 1944, for *Gregorio and the White Llama; New York Herald Tribune* Spring Book Festival honor award, 1953, for *When the Moon is New;* Friends of American Writers award, 1960, for *Hop-High, the Goat;* Children's Reading Round Table of Chicago Annual Award, 1962.

WRITINGS—Self-illustrated juveniles, except as noted: *Manuela's Birthday in Old Mexico* (Junior Literary Guild selection), Albert Whitman, 1939, new edition, 1943; *Gregorio and the White Llama* (Junior Literary Guild selection), Albert Whitman, 1941; *Red Mittens,* Houghton, 1946; *Patty Paints a Picture* (Junior Literary Guild selection), Albert Whitman, 1946, special edition, E. M. Hale, 1956; *Baby Roo,* Houghton, 1947; *Watchdog* (Junior Literary Guild selection), Albert Whitman, 1948; *Billy and the Bear* (Junior Literary Guild selection), Houghton, 1949.

Big Brother (Junior Literary Guild selection), Albert Whitman, 1950; *Horse on a Houseboat* (Junior Literary Guild selection), Albert Whitman, 1951; *The Best House in the World,* Houghton, 1952; *Mind Your Child's Art* (adult nonfiction), Pellegrini & Cudahy, 1952; *When the Moon Is New: A Seminole Indian Story,* Albert Whitman, 1953; *The Wonderful Fashion Doll,* Houghton, 1953; *Hat for a Hero: A Tarascan Boy of Mexico* (Junior Literary Guild selection), Albert Whitman, 1954; *Burro Boy and His Big Trouble,* Abingdon, 1955; *The Little Sister Doll,* Albert Whitman, 1955; *The Scary Thing,* Houghton, 1956; *Nemo*

Meets the Emperor (illustrated by Katherine Evans), Albert Whitman, 1957; *The Tide Won't Wait: A Nova Scotia Story,* Albert Whitman, 1957; *Jo-Jo, the Talking Crow,* Houghton, 1958; *Whistle for a Pilot,* Houghton, 1959; *Katy Comes Next* (Junior Literary Guild selection), Albert Whitman, 1959.

The Other Side of the World, Houghton, 1960; *Hop-High, the Goat,* Bobbs, 1960; *The Famous Baby-Sitter,* Albert Whitman, 1960; *The Gift of Hawaii* (Junior Literary Guild selection), Albert Whitman, 1961; *Hawaiian Coffee Picker,* Houghton, 1962; *Who Walks the Attic,* Albert Whitman, 1962; *Toby's Friends* (Junior Literary Guild selection), Albert Whitman, 1963; *Little People of the Night,* Houghton, 1963; *The Contented Horse Trader,* Albert Whitman, 1963; *Twirlup on the Moon,* Albert Whitman, 1964; *Make Room for Rags,* Houghton, 1964.

Illustrator: James C. Bowman, *Tales from a Finnish Tupa* (compiled by Margery Bianco from translation by Aili Kolehmainen), Albert Whitman, 1936; James C. Bowman, *Pecos Bill,* Albert Whitman, 1937; Melicent H. Lee and Jung Ho, *Chang Chee,* Harper, 1939; Esther Wood, *Pepper Moon,* Houghton, 1940; May F. McElravy, *Tortilla Girl,* Albert Whitman, 1946; Alice Mary Norton, under pseudonym Andre Norton, *Rogue Reynard,* Houghton, 1947.

LAURA BANNON

SIDELIGHTS: Ms. Bannon was a writer who believed in first-hand knowledge of her subject. For her seventeen regional books, she had lived for as long as eight months in each locality, sketching, painting, and doing research. Her first foreign travel was a trip to Mexico, where she lived with a Japanese family; her friendship with the little daughter of the family resulted in the picture book *Manuela's Birthday*. Another summer she lived in Cusco, Peru, in the Andes, and out of this came *Gregorio and the White Llama*. One summer she lived on a houseboat in the harbor of Sausalito, Calif., which provided the background for *Horse on a Houseboat*. She visited Seminole Indian camps in Florida to write *When the Moon Is New*. On a trip to Nova Scotia she drove out with the fishermen by horse and cart, climbed their ladders, plucked fish from their nets, and found her material for *The Tide Won't Wait*. Ms. Bannon spent eight months in Hawaii, living with families of coffee pickers, following two volcano eruptions, and preparing notes and sketches for two books.

Before she began writing and illustrating her own books, which she also usually designed, Ms. Bannon illustrated a number of children's books by other authors.

FOR MORE INFORMATION SEE: More Junior Authors, edited by Muriel Fuller, Wilson, 1963.

(Died December 14, 1963)

And sometimes, under the trees, the brown roofs of a Seminole Indian camp may be seen. ■ (From *When the Moon Is New* by Laura Bannon. Illustrated by the author.)

■ (From *Why the Wind God Wept* by Eve Titus. Illustrated by James Barkley.)

BARKLEY, James Edward 1941-

PERSONAL: Born April 19, 1941, in New York, N.Y.; son of James Edward (an accountant) and Edith (Santini) Barkley; married Diane Garis, July 8, 1967; children: James, Christine. *Education:* Studied at School of Visual Arts, New York. *Home:* 25 Brook Manor, Pleasantville, N.Y. 10570. *Office:* Our Own Little Studio, 218 Madison Ave., New York, N.Y. 10017.

CAREER: Painter and illustrator; Studio 6, New York, N.Y., president, 1960-64; free-lance illustrator, 1964—; Our Own Little Studio, New York, N.Y., vice-president, 1971—. Parsons School of Design, instructor in advertising illustration, 1970-72. Commissioned to do paintings in Alaska for Department of Parks and in Colorado for U.S. Air Force; designer of air mail stamp for National Park Centennial. *Member:* Society of Illustrators (chairman of national scholarship competition, 1972). *Awards, honors:* Forty-six awards, including Gold Medal Award at Illustrators 10 Show; books he illustrated have been nominated for the Caldecott Medal and John Newbery Award.

ILLUSTRATOR: William H. Armstrong, *Sounder,* Harper, 1969; Jose Maria Sanchez-Silva, *Ladis and the Ant,* translated from the Spanish by Michael Heron, McGraw, 1969; Leslie A. Lacy, *Cheer the Lonesome Traveler: The Life of W. E. B. DuBois,* Dial, 1970; Mary O'Neill, *Winds,* Dial, 1971; Eve Titus, *Why the Wind God Wept,* Doubleday, 1972; *The Minstrele Knight,* Crowell, 1973.

WORK IN PROGRESS: Series of articles and paintings on the national parks.

FOR MORE INFORMATION SEE: Horn Book, October, 1969.

ROBERT BARRY

Not too long on the sides . . .
■ (From *Next Please* by Robert E. Barry. Illustrated by the author.)

BARRY, Robert (Everett) 1931-

PERSONAL: Born October 7, 1931, in Newport, R.I.; son of William Edward (professional golfer) and Emma (Willis) Barry; married Katharina Waetjen (artist), December 28, 1958; children: John Eduard, Christopher Luis. *Education:* Rhode Island School of Design, B.F.A., 1953; Kunstgewerbeschule (Zurich, Switzerland), student of graphic art; Academy of Fine Art (Munich, Germany), student of drawing. *Home:* Cliff Ave., Newport, R.I.

CAREER: Pava Prints, Inc., San Juan, Puerto Rico, partner, 1957-63; Averett College, Danville, Va., instructor in art, 1966-67; Texas Womens University, Denton, Tex., instructor in art, 1967-68; Southeastern Massachusetts University, College of Fine Art, North Dartmouth, Mass., assistant professor, 1968—. Illustrator, series of children's books, United Church Press, Philadelphia, Pa. *Military service:* U.S. Army, 1954-55. *Awards, honors: New York Times* award for book, *Faint George,* 1957; Boys Club of America awards for books, *Faint George,* 1957, and *Next Please,* 1961.

WRITINGS: Faint George, 1957, *Just Pepper,* 1959, *Boo,* 1960, *Next Please,* 1961 (all published by Houghton); *Mr. Willowby's Christmas Tree,* McGraw, 1963; *The Musical Palm Tree,* McGraw, 1965; *Animals Around the World,* McGraw, 1967; *The Riddle of Castle Hill,* McGraw, 1968; *Ramon and the Pirate Gull,* McGraw, 1970.

And very close in the back . . .
■ (From *Next Please* by Robert E. Barry. Illustrated by the author.)

Just a little off the top . . .
■ (From *Next Please* by Robert E. Barry. Illustrated by the author.)

BB
See WATKINS-PITCHFORD, D. J.

BEATTY, John (Louis) 1922-

PERSONAL: Born January 24, 1922, in Portland, Ore.; son of George Shelley (a civil engineer) and Pauline (Kirchhoff) Beatty; married Patricia Robbins (an author), September 14, 1950; children: Ann Alexandra. *Education:* Reed College, B.A., 1943; Stanford University, M.A., 1947; University of Washington (Seattle), Ph.D., 1953. *Home:* 3113 Wendell Way, Riverside, Calif. 92507. *Office:* University of California, Riverside, Calif. 92502.

"I do love the young people, but take care, my lad, that you do not buy trouble, for London is up to the brim with it and evil." ■ (From *At the Seven Stars* by John and Patricia Beatty. Illustrated by Douglas Gorsline.)

JOHN BEATTY

CAREER: University of California, Riverside, associate professor of history and humanities, 1953—. Editorial consultant, Prentice-Hall, Inc. *Military service:* U.S. Army, 1943-45; became staff sergeant; received Silver Star, Purple Heart, Presidential Unit Citation with cluster, Combat Infantryman's Badge. *Awards, honors:* Foundation for Economic Education fellowship; American Philosophical Society grant; Haynes Foundation Fellowship; *At the Seven Stars* named by *New York Times* as one of 1963's one-hundred outstanding books for young people, and *The Royal Dirk* included on similar list in 1966; silver medal of Commonwealth Club of California for *Campion Towers,* best book for young people written by Californians in 1965; Southern California Council on Literature for children and young people best book award, 1966, for *The Royal Dirk.*

WRITINGS—With wife, Patricia Beatty: *At the Seven Stars,* Macmillan, 1963; *Campion Towers,* Macmillan, 1965; *The Royal Dirk,* Morrow, 1966; *A Donkey for the King* (*Horn Book* Honor List), Macmillan, 1966; *The Queen's Wizard,* Macmillan, 1967; *Witch Dog,* Morrow, 1967; *Pirate Royal,* Macmillan, 1969; *King's Knight's Pawn,* Morrow, 1971; *Holdfast,* Morrow, 1972. A comprehensive reading series for Science Research Associates. Contributor to *Horn Book.*

Other writings: (editor with Oliver A. Johnson) *Heritage of Western Civilization: Select Readings,* Prentice-Hall, 1958, 3rd edition, revised and enlarged, two volumes, 1971; *Warwick and Holland: Being the Lives of Robert and Henry Rich,* A. Swallow, 1965. Contributor to *Encyclopedia Americana, Scottish Historical Review, Huntington Library Quarterly,* and *American Libraries.*

WORK IN PROGRESS: A biography of James Hay, first Earl of Carlisle; a biographical guide to 1640 House of Lords; a study of Napoleon's Imperium; with Patricia Beatty, *Master Rosalind.*

SIDELIGHTS: "My hobbies are writing historical novels for young people, watching professional sports (I pitched lefthanded in college), collecting stamps of Canada and Great Britain, and sculpting things like chess pieces in cardboard (the latter more a disease than a hobby). My vocation is university teaching and research in 17th and 18th century English history, although my Ph.D. dissertation was on Napoleon. My fetish is accuracy in fact and tone in all writing." Beatty is competent in French and German, and has traveled in the United States, Canada, the Caribbean, Central America, England, and other parts of Europe.

FOR MORE INFORMATION SEE: *Horn Book,* December, 1971, December, 1972; *Third Book of Junior Authors,* edited by de Montreville and Hill, H. W. Wilson, 1972.

GUNNEL BECKMAN

BECKMAN, GUNNEL 1910-

PERSONAL: Born April 16, 1910, in Falkoeping, Sweden; daughter of John K. (a company director) and Villy (Wiedesheim-Paul) Torulf; married Birger Beckman (a publisher), June 23, 1933; children: Staffan, Björn, Ingar (Mrs. Johan Hirschfeldt), Svante, Suzanne. *Education:* University of Lund, B.M., 1932. *Home:* Alnaesvaegen 8, 17173 Solna, Sweden.

CAREER: Writer for young people. Member (layman) of court of Judicial District of Solna. *Member:* Swedish Authors Association, Amnesty (association for humanizing the treatment of criminals). *Awards, honors:* Bonnier's Prize for best book for young people, 1969, for *Admission to the Feast;* prize of 3,000 kronor from the Literature Fund.

WRITINGS: (Reviser) *Swedish for Tourists* (booklet), 12th edition, Svenska Bokfoerlaget, 1955; *Medan katten var borta* (title means "When the Cat was Away"), Bonnier, 1960; *Unga froken Tova* (title means "Young Miss Tova"), Bonnier, 1961; *Visstgor det ont* (title means "It Hurts—No Doubt"), Bonnier, 1963; *Misstaenkt* (title means "Suspect"), Bonnier, 1965; *Flickan utan namn,* Bonnier, 1967, translation by Anne Parker published as *The Girl Without a Name* (Child Study Association book list), Harcourt, 1970; *Pa galej med farmor* (title means "Out on the Spree with Grandma"), Bonnier, 1968; *Forsok att forsta* (title means "Try to Understand"), Bonnier, 1971, translation by Joan Tate published as *A Room of His Own,* Bodley Head, 1973; *Tre veckor over Liden* (title means "Three Weeks beyond the Proper Time"), Bonnier, 1973, translation by Joan Tate published as *Mia,* Viking, 1974; *Tilltrade till festen,* translation by Joan Tate published as *Nineteen is Too Young to Die* (school edition), Macmillan, in press, published as *Admission to the Feast* (trade edition), Holt, in press.

SIDELIGHTS: "After receiving my B.A., I went into journalism and for eight years edited the two women's pages of a daily newspaper in Gothenburg. In 1933, I married the literature and art critic of the newspaper, who later became the director of a textbook publishing company in Stockholm. After 1943, when we moved to Stockholm, I devoted most of my time taking care of my family (five children)—but I tried to do some free-lance journalism and write two detective stories in collaboration with my husband. For some years I also reviewed children's books for a Stockholm newspaper.

"After my children were grown up, I took an active role in local politics and did some social work in my home town, a municipality just outside Stockholm. For some time I worked as a probation officer and belonged to a panel of lay assessors to the municipal court. I traveled often in Europe and visited the United States in 1965.

"In 1960 I made my debut as a writer of books for children. The first two books were about my own family and my childhood in the twenties. 'Suspect' is a kind of thriller and *The Girl Without a Name* is about a Persian girl adopted by a Swedish couple. 'Out on the Spree with Grandma' is a small book about my first grand-daughter.

14

"No talking, now, Katarina," she said severely, "and Teddy, you really must *try* and hold your pen . . . " ■ (From *The Girl without a Name* by Gunnel Beckman. Illustrated by Borghild Rud.)

Admission to the Feast is my first book for older children. It is about a nineteen-year-old girl who knows that she is going to die. It has been my greatest success until now and is translated into five languages. *A Room of His Own* is about a young country boy coming to Stockholm, his different experiences in a big town, and his contact with an unhappy young girl.

"During the last years I have lectured in schools, etc. on youth problems."

An adaptation of *Admission to the Feast* was presented in four parts on Swedish radio, 1970, Norwegian radio, 1972; an adaptation of *Forsok att forsta* was presented on Norwegian radio, 1972.

FOR MORE INFORMATION SEE: Horn Book, October, 1972.

BELTING, Natalia Maree 1915-

PERSONAL: Born July 11, 1915, in Oskaloosa, Iowa; daughter of Paul Everette and Anna Maree (Hanselman) Belting. *Education:* Coe College, student, 1932-33; University of Illinois, B.S., 1936, M.A., 1937, Ph.D., 1940. *Religion:* Presbyterian. *Home:* R.R. 2, Urbana, Ill. *Office:* 309 Gregory Hall, University of Illinois, Urbana, Ill.

CAREER: University of Illinois, instructor, later assistant professor of history, 1942—, associate professor, 1973—. Supply preacher in rural Presbyterian churches, Illinois. *Member:* Illinois State Historical Society, American Historical Society, American Association of University Women, Delta Zeta, Phi Alpha Theta.

WRITINGS: (With P. E. Belting) *The Modern High School Curriculum,* Garrard, 1940; *Kaskaskia Under the French Regime,* University of Illinois Press, 1948; *Pierre of Kaskaskia,* Bobbs, 1951; *Moon Is a Crystal Ball,* Bobbs, 1952; *In Enemy Hands,* Bobbs, 1953; *Three Apples Fell From Heaven,* Bobbs, 1953; *Cat Tales,* Holt, 1959, published as *King Solomon's Cat: Folk Tales from Around the World,* Rapp & Whiting, 1968; *Indy and Mr. Lincoln,* Holt, 1960; *Verity Mullens and the Indian,* Holt, 1960; *Elves and Ellefolk,* Holt, 1961; *The Long-tailed Bear,* Bobbs, 1961; *The Sun Is a Golden Ear Ring* (ALA Notable book), Holt, 1962; *The Calendar Moon,* Holt, 1964; *The Earth Is on a Fish's Back,* Holt, 1965; *The Stars Are Silver Reindeer,* Holt, 1966; *Christmas Folk,* Holt, 1969; *Winter's Eve,* Holt, 1969; *Summer's Coming In,* Holt, 1970; *Land of The Taffeta Dawn,* Dutton, 1973; *Whirlwind is a Ghost Dancing,* Dutton, 1974; *Our Fathers' Had Powerful Songs,* Dutton, 1974.

WORK IN PROGRESS: Transcribing and editing a dictionary of Illinois language, compiled by Jesuit missionary in 1712 (400-page manuscript).

HOBBIES AND OTHER INTERESTS: Baking, gardening, wood carving, animals, and the Indians of Illinois.

FOR MORE INFORMATION SEE: Horn Book, December, 1969, February, 1970; *Third Book of Junior Authors,* edited by de Montreville and Hill, H. W. Wilson, 1972.

The hallow days of Yule are here.
The nights are long and dark.
A feeble sun scarce warms the day,
And cold congeals the stoutest heart.
■ (From *Christmas Folk* by Natalia Belting. Illustrated by Barbara Cooney.)

NATALIA MAREE BELTING

BENASUTTI, Marion 1908-

PERSONAL: Born August 2, 1908, in Philadelphia, Pa.; daughter of Joseph E. (a builder) and Elvira (Serafini) Gosette; married Frank I. Benasutti (a consulting engineer), August 2, 1930; children: Noel (deceased), Frank J. *Education:* Temple University, special courses. *Politics:* Democrat. *Religion:* Roman Catholic. *Home:* Mt. Vernon 6A3, 885 Easton Rd., Glenside, Pa. 19038. *Agent:* Curtis Brown Ltd., 60 East 56th St., New York, N.Y. 10022.

CAREER: Italian-American Herald (weekly), Philadelphia, Pa., women's editor, 1960-62; National League of American Pen Women (president, Philadelphia branch), Washington, D.C. editor of *Pen Woman,* 1964-68; freelance writer for newspapers and magazines. *Member:* National League of American Pen Women, Philadelphia Art Alliance, Professional Writers' Club of Philadelphia.

WRITINGS: No Steady Job for Papa (novel), Vanguard, 1966. Articles published in magazines, including *McCall's, Mademoiselle, Redbook, American Home,* and *Reader's Digest,* and short stories in *Seventeen, Marriage, Ford Times, Literary Review, Family Weekly* (Great Britain), and Catholic magazines; contributor of features to Philadelphia daily and Sunday newspapers and *Camden Courier-Post;* columnist, "The Feminine View," in *Catholic Star Herald,* Camden, and "Books and Authors," in *Delaware Valley Calendar.*

WORK IN PROGRESS: A cookbook, *With Love Everything Tastes Better; First Wine,* a novel.

SIDELIGHTS: "As far back as 1911, young writers were being advised that 'the art of writing is the art of applying the seat of the pants to the seat of the chair.' That misleading statement has caused more young and beginning writers to come to grief than any other falsely encouraging words ever spoken. It was a long frustrating time before I came to the sad conclusion that *the seat of the pants is not enough.*

After warming my desk chair for a whole year of very hard work, to no avail, I came to the realization that sitting at one's typewriter, perpetrating the same mistakes over and over, was not the way to a successful writing career, and that if a story is returned to you, very quickly and more than twice, the chances are there is something wrong with the story.

Perhaps, I thought despairingly, I should go back to raising petunias, or, for kicks, the night-blooming cereus. I began to sit in that chair, all right, but only to brood, or to look at TV, or to call friends on the telephone. As any writer has learned to his sorrow, any of these devices will devour the bright productive morning hours in huge indigestible chunks. And then where are you? That's exactly where I was. . . .

Human nature being what it is, stubborn, I pulled myself out of the doldrums and began again to write. I batted out stories like mad. Boy met girl in all the most unlikely places but nothing ever came of it. However, I did develop some facility with words and a few good work habits so all was not altogether lost.

Benasutti • No Steady Job For Papa • Vanguard

■ (From *No Steady Job for Papa* by Marion Benasutti. Illustrated by Isadore Seltzer.)

"When, *some five years later,* I began to get encouraging 'letters from editors,' a first thrill as a writer, telling me of the 'charm, warmth, imagery and poetry' of my writing, the loveableness of my characters, assuring me that I had, at long last, *learned to write* I thought that surely now I had arrived.

"One of the most difficult, heartbreaking and almost impossible chores for a beginning writer to do is to attempt to *rewrite* a story in which an editor has expressed interest. He will tell you that he liked your story, *but . . .* And I am telling you that it will be devilish hard, *but*—put the story away and write a new one. For success is not just around the corner and you should not begin to spend that thousand dollars (price recently upped) that will surely be yours from *Ladies' Home Journal.* Let us face it—if the editors do not buy your story it is not because the story is *too good,* it is because, alas, it is not *good enough.* When you've straddled that hurdle, you will have begun to be a pro.

"Now the time has come to apply the seat of the pants to that chair with a vengeance—every day. *Every day.* Write letters, make laundry lists, compose lousy poetry, *anything,* but *write,* until sitting down each morning in that chair becomes as natural as your three-minute egg and as necessary. And perhaps, if you are very lucky, your holy experiment will begin to pay off. The seat of the pants principle will produce results—it will pay off or wear off! But either way, if you are really a writer, you will never give up."

FOR MORE INFORMATION SEE: The Pen Woman, April, 1964; *Horn Book,* February, 1965.

MARION BENASUTTI

BENTLEY, Phyllis (Eleanor) 1894-

PERSONAL: Born November 19, 1894, in Halifax, England; daughter of Joseph Edwin and Eleanor (Kettlewell) Bentley. *Education:* Attended Cheltenham Ladies' College; University of London, B.A., 1914. *Home:* The Grange, Warley, Halifax, Yorkshire, England. *Agent:* A. D. Peters, 10 Buckingham St., London, W.C.2, England.

CAREER: Self-employed novelist. Royal Literary Fund, council and vice-president. *Member:* P.E.N. (vice-president, English centre), Authors Society, Royal Society of Literature (fellow), Halifax Thespians, Halifax Authors' Circle (president), Halifax Antiquarian Society (vice-president). *Awards, honors:* D. Litt., University of Leeds, 1949; O.B.E. (Order of the British Empire), 1970.

WRITINGS: The World's Bane, Unwin, 1918; *Pedagomania,* Unwin, 1918; *Environment,* Sidgwick & Jackson, 1922; *Cat in the Manger,* Sidgwick & Jackson, 1923; *The Spinner of the Years,* Benn, 1928; *The Partnership,* Benn, 1928; *Carr,* Benn, 1929; *Trio,* Gollancz, 1930; *Inheritance,* Gollancz, 1932; *A Modern Tragedy,* Gollancz, 1934; *The Whole of the Story,* Gollancz, 1935; *Freedom Farewell,* Gollancz, 1936; *Sleep in Peace,* Gollancz, 1938; *Take Courage,* Gollancz, 1940; *Manhold,* Gollancz, 1941; *Here Is America,* Gollancz, 1941; *The English Regional Novel,* Allen & Unwin, 1942; *The Rise of Henry Morcar,* Gollancz, 1946; *Some Observations on the Art of Narrative,* Home & Van Thal, 1946; *The Brontes,* Home & Van Thal, 1947; *Life Story,* Gollancz, 1948.

Quorum, Gollancz, 1950; *The Bronte Sisters,* Longmans, for the British Council, 1950; *Panorama,* Gollancz, 1952; *The House of Moreys,* Gollancz, 1953; *Noble in Reason,* Gollancz, 1955; *Love and Money,* Gollancz, 1957; *Crescendo,* Gollancz, 1958; *Kith and Kin,* Gollancz, 1960; *The Young Brontes,* Parrish, 1960; *O Dreams, O Destinations* (autobiography), Gollancz, 1962; *Committees,* Collins, 1962; *Public Speaking,* Collins, 1964; *Tales of the West Riding,* Gollancz, 1965; *A Man of His Time,* Gollancz, 1966; *Ring in the New,* Gollancz, 1969; *The Brontes and Their World,* Thames & Hudson, 1969; *The Pennine Weaver,* Firestone, 1970.

Juvenile: *The Adventures of Tom Leigh,* Macdonald, 1964; *Ned Carver in Danger,* Macdonald, 1967; *Gold Pieces,* Macdonald, 1968, published in America as *Forgery,* Doubleday, 1968; *Sheep May Safely Graze,* Gollancz, 1972; *The New Venturers,* Gollancz, 1973. Various works for the Bronte Society and the British Council. Contributes articles to periodicals, writes plays for children performed on television.

SIDELIGHTS: "My great interest has always been in the history of my own native county, Yorkshire. It has dozens of fascinating stories in its past. I have always loved to walk about the country, especially the very beautiful hills and dales. I write books for children because I want them to know about the past of their own county. When I was a child I lived in an industrial town in Yorkshire, and thought that the county had nothing very exciting in its history. But when I grew up and read about it, I was fascinated. As a child I loved fairy stories and read very many of them, but I cannot write them; I am too close to the people who dwell at my side in my own county, today, to go into fairyland.

"I was able to read very early in my life, and I have devoured books ever since. As a child I loved to play team games, hockey and cricket, and also tennis. I was never very good at games, but I loved them, and I made up my mind when quite young that I should enjoy games and not allow myself to just sit and read, though books were always my passion.

"I was the youngest child of my family; the only girl, with three older brothers. My youngest brother was six years older than myself, but he was always very kind and helpful to me; he taught me to tell the time from the clock, and how to play all sorts of games, halma, draughts, etc. My family is of Yorkshire descent on both sides, and on both sides engaged in the woolen textile industry, for which the West Riding of Yorkshire is famous all over the world.

We had a call from the pedlar. We were sitting at meat when his knock sounded, and I went to open the door. There he stood, spruce and neat as usual, with his bright green suit and his scarlet stockings. ■ (From *The Adventures of Tom Leigh* by Phyllis Bentley. Illustrated by William Stobbs.)

PHYLLIS BENTLEY

"I have been to the U.S.A. several (I think six) times; partly on lecture tours, in which I have been in forty-six states; partly to visit my great friends, my publishers. I have been up in the Adirondacks with them, swam in the lakes, watched beavers at work and deer leap through the bushes in the evening. I have traveled in Italy quite considerably, in France and Germany a little. Although I was born and bred in a town and went away to school at Cheltenham, I love the country dearly, and until recently I went into the country for a walking holiday every year.

Something about the Author

"I live in an old master clothier's house, built about 1672. In my childhood I was very shy and retiring, but when I grew up I began to lecture about literature. People seemed to enjoy this, and I grew happy in contact with them."

HOBBIES AND OTHER INTERESTS: "I have given a great deal of my leisure to the Halifax Thespians, an amateur dramatic society which owns its own theatre and does plays of all kinds."

BERG, Jean Horton   1913-

PERSONAL: Born May 30, 1913, in Clairton, Pa.; daughter of Harry Heber (a manufacturer) and Daisy (Horton) Lutz; married John Joseph Berg (a dentist), July 2, 1938; children: Jean Horton, Julie Joanne Berg Tapp, John Joel. *Education:* University of Pennsylvania, B.S. in Ed., 1935, A.M., 1937. *Religion:* Christian Scientist. *Residence:* Wayne, Pa. *Agent:* McIntosh & Otis, Inc., 18 East 41st St., New York, N.Y. 10017.

CAREER: Teacher of English and Latin in Bridgeville, Del., 1936-38; teacher of creative writing in adult education classes, Radnor Township, Pa., 1966—. Private tutor in Latin. *Member:* Authors Guild, National League of American Pen Women (president of Chester County branch, 1966-68), American Society of Composers, Authors and Publishers, League of Women Voters. *Awards, honors:* Follett Beginning-to-Read Award, 1961; Medallion of Philadelphia, 1963; Alumni Award of Merit, University of Pennsylvania, 1969.

JEAN HORTON BERG

There was an old lady
   named Miss Tessie Tate,
Who'd been roller-skating
   e'er since she was eight.
■ (From *Miss Tessie Tate* by Jean Horton Berg. Illustrated by Lee de Groot.)

WRITINGS—Juvenile books: *Three Mice and a Cat,* Grosset, 1950; *The Jolly Jumping Man,* Grosset, 1950; *The Noisy Clock Shop,* Grosset, 1950; *Baby Susan's Chicken,* Grosset, 1951; *The Playful Little Dog,* Grosset, 1951; *The Big Jump-Up Farm Animal Book,* Grosset, 1952; *Christmas in Song and Story,* Grosset, 1953; *The Traveling Twins,* Grosset, 1953; *It's Fun to Peek,* Grosset, 1955; *The Big Jump-Up Book of Trains, Trucks and Planes,* Grosset, 1955; *Tuggy the Tugboat,* Grosset, 1958.

Pierre, the Young Watchmaker, Bobbs, 1961; *The O'-Leary's and Friends,* Follett, 1961; *The Little Red Hen* (retold), Follett, 1963; *Baby Raccoon,* Grosset, 1963; *The Wee Little Man,* Follett, 1963; *Big Bug, Little Bug,* Follett, 1964; *There's Nothing To Do, So Let Me Be You,* Westminster, 1966; *Miss Kirby's Room,* Westminster, 1966; *Miss Tessie Tate* (Junior Literary Guild selection), Westminster, 1967; *Nobody Scares a Porcupine,* Westminster, 1969.

What Harry Found When He Lost Archie (Child Study Association book list), Westminster, 1970; *Mr. Koonan's Bargain,* Nautilus Press, 1971; *Next Best,* Harper, 1972; *Was She Lost?,* Harper, 1972; *The Green Lady,* Harper, 1972; *Saturday's Friends,* Harper, 1972; *The Cap and the Lamb,* Harper, 1972; *The Right Thing to Do,* Harper, 1972; *One or Many,* Harper, 1972; *All Because of Snow,* Harper, 1972; *Nothing Ever Happens,* Harper, 1972; *The Big Problem,* Harper, 1972.

Other books: *Bright Candle Light* (songs), Pro Art, 1966; (with Russell Stauffer) *Rapid Comprehension Through Effective Reading,* Learn, Inc., 1969; (with Stauffer) *Communications Through Effective Reading,* Learn, Inc., 1971.

Contributor of stories, articles, and poems to *Christian Science Monitor, Highlights for Children, Jack and Jill, Ranger Rick, Today's Girl, Humpty-Dumpty,* and other magazines and newspapers.

WORK IN PROGRESS: A biography of Herman Wrice; an untitled book for teen-agers.

HOBBIES AND OTHER INTERESTS: Tennis (plays several times a week throughout the year), traveling (particularly on cruise ships).

BERRINGTON, John
See BROWNJOHN, Alan

BETHERS, Ray 1902-

PERSONAL: Born April 25, 1902, in Corvallis, Ore.; son of Elmer and Anna (Wells) Bethers; married Peggy Sibley, 1923. *Education:* Studied at University of Oregon, California School of Fine Arts, and at art schools in New York, Paris, London. *Home:* Flat 30, Richmond Ct., Davigdor Rd., Hove 2, Sussex, England.

CAREER: Author-illustrator, formerly residing in Paris, France, now in England. Also designer of type pages, covers, and jackets for most of his books. *Military service:* U.S. Naval Reserve, World War II; became lieutenant commander. *Member:* Dutch Treat Club (New York). *Awards, honors:* Library of Congress purchase prize for wood engraving.

WRITINGS—All self-illustrated: *Pictures, Painters, and You,* Pitman, 1948; *Can You Name Them?: A Pictorial-Information Quiz Book,* Aladdin Books, 1948; *Composition in Pictures,* Pitman, 1949, 3rd edition, 1962; *Perhaps I'll Be a Sailor,* Aladdin Books, 1949; *The Magic of Oil,* Aladdin Books, 1949.

Perhaps I'll Be a Farmer, Aladdin Books, 1950; *Perhaps I'll Be a Railroad Man,* Aladdin Books, 1951; *How Paintings Happen,* Norton, 1951; *From Eye to Camera,* Pitman, 1951; *The Story of Rivers,* Sterling, 1957, revised edition,

It is wonderful to think that a great many of these fruits, nuts and spices have come all the way to you from half the world away. ■ (From *How Does it Grow?* by Ray Bethers. Illustrated by the author.)

Oak Tree Press, 1963; *Photo-Vision,* St. Martin's, 1957; *How to Find Your Own Style in Painting: What Style Is, and How the Kind of a Person You Are Will Influence Your Style,* Hastings House, 1957; *Art Always Changes: How to Understand Modern Painting,* Hastings House, 1958; *Nature Invents, Science Applies,* Hastings House, 1959; *Islands of Adventure,* Hastings House, 1959.

Rivers of Adventure, Hastings House, 1960; *Ships of Adventure,* Constable, 1961, Hastings House, 1962; *What Happens Underground?,* St. Martin's, 1961; *Ports of Adventure,* Constable, 1962, Hastings House, 1963; *What Happens in the Sea?,* Macmillan (London), 1962, St. Martin's, 1963; *How Does It Grow?,* St. Martin's, 1963; *Discoveries: Dinosaurs to Rockets,* Constable, 1963; *The Language of Paintings: Form and Content,* Pitman, 1963; *What Happens in the Sky?,* St. Martin's, 1963; *This Is Our World,* St. Martin's, 1964; *How Did We Get Our Names?,* Macmillan (London), 1966. Former associate editor, *This Week.*

SIDELIGHTS: Bethers is a writer-illustrator in reverse. "Thus I do not write and then illustrate what I have written. But instead [I] use words to fill in what it is not possible to explain in the illustrations. . . . To me there are no single pages in a book, but only facing pages seen as a unit."

RAY BETHERS

BIERHORST, John (William) 1936-

PERSONAL: Born September 2, 1936, in Boston, Mass.; son of John William and Sadie Belle (Knott) Bierhorst; married Jane Byers (a designer of children's books), June 25, 1965; children: Alice Byers Bierhorst. *Education:* Cornell University, A.B., 1958. *Home:* 155 East 47th St., New York, N.Y. 10017.

CAREER: Former concert pianist; became attracted to the study of native American cultures during a botanical field trip to Peru in 1964; subsequently visited pre-Columbian sites in Yucatan and Mexico. *Member:* Friends of the Earth, Nature Conservancy. *Awards, honors: In the Trail of the Wind* was a Children's Book Council Showcase Title, 1972.

WRITINGS—Youth books: (Editor) *The Fire Plume: Legends of the American Indians,* Dial, 1969; (editor) *The Ring in the Prairie: A Shawnee Legend,* originally set down by Henry R. Schoolcraft (Child Study Association book list), Dial, 1970; (editor) *In the Trail of the Wind: American Indian Poems and Ritual Orations,* (ALA Notable Book; Child Study Association book list), Farrar, Straus, 1971.

WORK IN PROGRESS: Songs of the Chippewa, a collection of traditional Indian melodies arranged by Bierhorst for piano and guitar, publication by Farrar, Straus expected in 1974; new translations of the Quetzalcoatl legend, preserved in sixteenth-century Aztec, and of the Mayan prophecy known as Cuceb, both translations to be published as adult books by Farrar, Straus.

HOBBIES AND OTHER INTERESTS: Botany, conservation.

FOR MORE INFORMATION SEE: Horn Book, August, 1971.

At last, unable to restrain himself,
he rushed out and attempted to seize her.
■ (From *The Ring in the Prairie* by John Bierhorst.
Illustrated by Leo and Diane Dillon.)

BISHOP, Curtis (Kent)   1912-1967
(Curt Brandon, Curt Carroll)

PERSONAL: Born Nov. 10, 1912, in Bolivar, Tenn.; son of David (a lawyer) and Ann (Cornelius) Bishop; married Grace Eyres (now a school teacher), June 13, 1940; children: Barry, Burk, Barbee, Brian. *Education:* University of Texas, student, 1933-35. *Politics:* Conservative. *Religion:* Protestant. *Home:* 2705 Bonnie Rd., Austin, Tex.

CAREER: Variously newspaperman, oil field worker, and rodeo announcer, 1935-42; free-lance writer. *Military service:* Served with Foreign Broadcast Intelligence Service in Latin America and Pacific theater. *Awards, honors:* Winner of eleven (out of thirteen) annual awards of Theta Sigma Phi for best juvenile work of the year in Texas.

WRITINGS: Teamwork (short stories), Steck, 1942; *By Way of Wyoming,* Macmillan, 1946; *Sunset Rim,* Macmillan, 1946; *Shadow Range,* Macmillan, 1947; *Lots of Land,* Steck, 1949.

The Lost Eleven, Steck, 1950; *Banjo Hitter,* Steck, 1951; *Saturday Heroes,* Steck, 1951; *Football Fever,* Steck, 1952; *Hero at Halfback,* Steck, 1953; *Larry of Little League,* Steck, 1953; (with wife, Grace Bishop) *Stout Rider,* Steck, 1953; *Fighting Quarterback,* Steck, 1954; *Larry Leads Off,* Steck, 1954; *Goal to Go,* Steck, 1955; *Larry Comes Home,* Steck, 1955; *Dribble Up,* Steck, 1956; *Half-Time Hero,* Steck, 1956; *Little Leaguer,* Steck, 1956; *The Little League Way,* Steck, 1957; *Bar-O Gunsmoke,* Muller, 1958; *Lank of the Little League,* Lippincott, 1958; *The First Texas Ranger,* Messner, 1959.

The Playmaker, Steck, 1960; *Little League Heroes,* Lippincott, 1960; *Sideline Quarterback,* Lippincott, 1960; *Lone Star Leader, Sam Houston,* Messner, 1961; *Rio Grande,* Bouregy, 1961; *Little League Double Play,* Lippincott, 1962; *Rebound,* Lippincott, 1962; *The Big Game,* Steck, 1963; *Lonesome End,* Lippincott, 1963; *Field Goal,* Lippincott, 1964; *Little League Amigo,* Lippincott, 1964; (with Grace Bishop and Clyde Inez Martin) *America: Ideals and Men,* W. S. Benson, 1965; *Little League Stepson,* Lippincott, 1965; *Sideline Pass,* Lippincott, 1965; (with Grace Bishop and Martin) *Trails to Texas,* W. S. Benson, 1965; *Gridiron Glory,* Lippincott, 1966; *Little League Visitor,* Lippincott, 1966; *Fast Break,* Lippincott, 1967; *The Last Outlaw,* Broadman, 1967; *Little League Victory,* Lippincott, 1967; *Little League, Little Brother,* Lippincott, 1968; *Hackberry Jones, Split End,* Lippincott, 1968.

Under pseudonym Curt Brandon: *High, Wide and Handsome,* Dutton, 1950; *Bugle's Wake,* Dutton, 1952.

Under pseudonym Curt Carroll: *The Golden Herd* (novel), Morrow, 1950; *San Jacinto,* Steck, 1957.

Contributor of several hundred stories and articles to magazines. Writer of syndicated column, "This Day in Texas," published in Texas newspapers.

SIDELIGHTS: Motion pictures have been made from five of Bishop's books: one book was adapted for presentation on "Hallmark Playhouse," and one story for television. For material this juvenile author looked into his own activities—he coached Little League teams and other junior sports groups.

(Died March 17, 1967)

BIXBY, William (Courtney)   1920-

PERSONAL: Born June 15, 1920, in San Diego, Calif.; son of Vernon Chamberlain and Courtney (Rudd) Bixby; married Elizabeth L. Knight, 1944; married Susan Babbitt, 1972; children (first marriage): William Jr., Barbara Ruth. *Education:* Virginia Polytechnic Institute, B.S., 1942. *Home and office:* 40 High St., Middlebury, Vt. *Agent:* Collins-Knowlton-Wing, Inc., 60 East 56th St., New York, N.Y.

They had been away from England for over three years. ■ (From *Robert Scott: Antarctic Pioneer* by William Bixby. Sketch by Dr. Edward A. Wilson.)

CAREER: Cowles Magazines, Inc., New York, N.Y., staff writer, 1945-47; Famous Artists School, Westport, Conn., editor-writer, 1947-49; Cowles Magazines, Inc., New York, N.Y., editor-writer, 1949-51; Time Inc., New York, N.Y., associate editor, 1951-53; free-lance writing and teaching in New England, 1953—. *Military service:* U.S. Army, Signal Corps, Air Corps, became first lieutenant; awarded Air Medal, European Theater Campaign. *Awards, honors:* Thomas Alva Edison Foundation Award, 1964, for *The Universe of Galileo and Newton.*

WRITINGS: *The Impossible Journey of Sir Ernest Shackleton,* Atlantic-Little, Brown, 1960 (Junior Literary Guild selection); *The Race to the South Pole,* Longmans, 1961; *Havoc: The Story of Natural Disasters,* Longmans, 1961; *McMurdo, Antarctica,* McKay, 1962; *Skywatchers: The U.S. Weather Bureau in Action* (Junior Literary Guild selection), McKay, 1962; *Waves: Pathways of Energy,* McKay, 1963; *Great Experimenters,* McKay, 1964; *The Universe of Galileo and Newton,* American Heritage Publishing, 1964; *Track of the Bear,* McKay, 1965; *The Forgotten Voyage of Charles Wilkes,* McKay, 1966; *Seawatchers, Oceanographers in Action,* McKay, 1967; *Of Animals and Men: A Comparison of Animal and Human Behavior,* McKay, 1968; *Rebel Genius: The Life of Herman Melville,* McKay, 1970; *Robert Scott: Antarctic Pioneer,* Lippincott, 1970; *A World You Can Live In,* McKay, 1971; *South Street: New York's Seaport Museum,* McKay, 1972; *The Connecticut Guide,* Scribner, in press.

HOBBIES AND OTHER INTERESTS: Collecting American first editions; antiques and sailing.

BLAINE, John
See HARKINS, Philip

BLOCH, Marie Halun 1910-

PERSONAL: Born December 1, 1910, in Komarno, Ukraine; daughter of Rudolf and Sofia (Pelenska) Halun; married Donald Beaty Bloch, 1930; children: Hilary Hopkins. *Education:* University of Chicago, Ph.B., 1935. *Home:* 654 Emerson St., Denver, Colo. 80218. *Agent:* Theron Raines, 244 Madison Ave., New York, N.Y. 10016.

CAREER: U.S. Department of Labor, Washington, D.C., junior economist, 1935-38, 1942-43. Writer of children's books. *Member:* Authors Guild of America, Colorado Authors League, British Society of Authors, Ukrainian Academy of Arts and Sciences in the United States. *Awards, honors: Aunt America* was on master list for William Allen White Award, 1966.

WRITINGS: *Danny Doffer,* Harper, 1946; *Big Steve,* Coward, 1952; *Herbert the Electrical Mouse,* Messner, 1953; *Tunnels,* Coward, 1954; *Dinosaurs,* Coward, 1955; *Tony of the Ghost Towns,* Coward, 1956; *Marya,* Coward, 1957; *Mountains on the Move,* Coward, 1960; *The Dollhouse Story,* Walck, 1961; *The House on Third High,* Coward, 1962; *Look at Dinosaurs,* Hamish Hamilton, 1962; *Aunt America* (ALA Notable Book; *Horn Book* Honor List), Atheneum, 1963; (editor and translator) *Ukrainian Folk Tales,* Coward, 1964; *The Two Worlds of Damyan,*

MARIE HALUN BLOCH

Atheneum, 1966; (editor and translator) *Ivanko and the Dragon,* Atheneum, 1969; *Bern, Son of Mikula,* Atheneum, 1972. Monthly column, reviews of children's books, *Denver Post,* 1950-60.

SIDELIGHTS: "One reason I write for young people is that I remember my own childhood vividly—not events so much as how I felt about things that happened to me, how I felt about different people, what I thought and the ideas I had. Of all my books *Marya* comes closest to that world of the child.

"From my own experience I know that children are good judges of literature, even though they may not always be articulate about their judgments. For human beings are almost instinctively connoisseurs of the story, perhaps because the story satisfies some mysterious human need. So story telling and story listening must be as old as people. Thousands of years ago story tellers must have been as indispensable as the man in the tribe who made good stone hammers or the woman who knew how to cure a sickness by the use of herbs. Sitting in a cave somewhere on a wild winter's night with everyone huddled close around the fire, including the dogs, at their backs the fearsome dark and out there just beyond the mouth of the cave all the rest of the mysterious world, the story teller began, 'Once upon a time, in the long long ago. . . .' And thus wove a spell around the listeners and made them feel warm and strong and able to face the dark again.

"A number of years ago I went back to the town where I was born, in Ukraine. From that and later visits—a profound emotional experience for me, as going home again must be for every human being—came five of my books so far, beginning with *Aunt America*, then *The Two Worlds of Damyan*, two books of Ukrainian folk tales that I translated, and most recently, *Bern, Son of Mikula*. Long before these I wrote *Marya*. It belongs in this same series, for it is the story of an immigrant girl in America—her hard and happy times.

"No matter what the theme or background of my books I always try first of all to tell a good story. But over and above the story itself the reader has every right to expect something more: a new insight into himself, perhaps, a new understanding of other people, an intimate glimpse into a new part of the world or of an unfamiliar aspect of America. A good book, like a good friend, enlarges and enriches one's personal world. This is what I try to do for the reader when I sit down to write a book."

FOR MORE INFORMATION SEE: Horn Book, October, 1969.

BOARDMAN, Fon Wyman, Jr. 1911-

PERSONAL: Born July 28, 1911, in Bolivar, N.Y.; son of Fon Wyman and Lena (Sternberg) Boardman; married Dorothea Reber, 1935 (died, 1971); children: Constance Boardman DeMarco. *Education:* Columbia University, A.B., 1934. *Home:* 16 West 16th St., New York, N.Y. 10011. *Office:* Oxford University Press, 200 Madison Ave., New York, N.Y. 10016.

Lesya stood in front of the mirror in the best room while Mama braided her dark straight hair into two short pigtails. ■ (From *Aunt America* by Marie Halun Bloch. Illustrated by Joan Berg.)

"I get my stories from my own living and my own enthusiasms. For instance, I love the Colorado mountains, where I live in the summers. Out of this love came my books *Tony of the Ghost Towns, The House on Third High, Mountains on the Move,* and *Dinosaurs* as well.

"When my daughter was little she owned a dollhouse furnished partly with antiques and occupied by a very lively and adventuresome family. She kept asking me to write a story about them and I kept saying I would. However, much as I, too, loved the dollhouse and its tenants, for a long time no story came to me. But at last one did and I wrote it and dedicated it to my daughter, because the story was partly about her, too. By that time the dollhouse had been in the attic for a decade and my daughter was away at college. But now her two little girls are enjoying the dollhouse and *The Dollhouse Story*.

FON WYMAN BOARDMAN, JR.

The crossbow was stronger than an ordinary bow and it could fire stone and metal as well as arrows, but it was slow and hard to work. ■ (From *Castles* by Fon W. Boardman, Jr. Illustrated by Frederick T. Chapman. Reprinted by permission of Henry Z. Walck, Inc. Copyright © 1957 by Henry Z. Walck, Inc.

CAREER: Columbia University Press, New York, N.Y., copy writer, 1934-42, advertising and publicity manager, 1942-45, sales promotion manager, 1945-51; Oxford University Press, New York, N.Y., advertising and publicity manager, 1951-60, secretary, 1960-68, vice-president and marketing director, 1968-72. Lecturer in English, Columbia University, 1954-59. *Military service:* U.S. Army, 1943-46; became master sergeant; U.S. Army Reserve, captain in Military Intelligence, retired. *Member:* Publishers' Adclub (secretary, 1952-54, president, 1954-56), Phi Beta Kappa, P.E.N., Columbia University Club, Advertising Club of New York.

WRITINGS: Castles, Oxford University Press, 1957; *Roads,* Walck, 1958; *Canals,* Walck, 1959; *Tunnels,* Walck, 1960; *History and Historians,* Walck, 1965; *Economics: Ideas and Men,* Walck, 1966; *The Thirties,* Walck, 1967; *America and the Jazz Age,* Walck, 1968; *America and the Progressive Era,* Walck, 1970; *The Guilded Age,* Walck, 1972. Contributor: *What Happens in Book Publishing,* edited by Chandler Grannis; *Sales on a Shoestring.* Editor: *Columbia University in Pictures;* general editor of series of twenty-seven guidance books for young people, "Careers for Tomorrow," published by Walck; chairman, editorial advisory board, *Columbia University Forum,* 1958-60.

SIDELIGHTS: "The *Wellsville* (N.Y.) *Daily Reporter* (circulation 5,000) was a testing ground for me as a young man. Between high school and college I worked there for a year and some months, writing all the headlines, deciding what story to play up, covering sports, village government, murders and weddings. It was all tied to writing, and that is what I always wanted to do.

"I was born in Bolivar, a small town in western New York, but before I was old enough to remember anything about it, my family moved to Olean and then to Wellsville, all in the same area. There I remember our house on Pleasant Avenue, which it was. I enjoyed my school years immensely and recall several good teachers who felt a responsibility to me and the taxpayers to teach me their subjects regardless. Good system. I read Tom Swift and G. A. Henty—especially Henty. For sheer enjoyment, the Henty books were the greatest things I ever read. I re-read one of them a few years ago, which was, of course, a mistake.

"My interest in writing began when I was about eleven or twelve and was encouraged by the publication of a poem (on Theodore Roosevelt) in the local newspaper and by winning a D.A.R. contest for a theme which I think must have been about George Washington. After my year with the *Wellsville Daily Reporter,* I went to Columbia, hoping to have my degree in journalism. I was forced to give up that idea, for it would have taken another year of study and the country was in the midst of the Depression. Instead I joined the staff of the Columbia University Press.

"A number of years ago, I was asked to suggest someone who could write a book about castles. 'I'll write a book about castles,' I replied. And so I did and so I became an author. I am firmly convinced that almost any subject can be written on for young people, or adults in a hurry, in understandable but interesting language without talking down. My own reading experience as a child has led me to write as simply and clearly as possible, and to avoid using more and longer words than necessary. I hope that my readers find my books worth the time, either for pleasure received, or in terms of finding the facts they need to know."

HOBBIES AND OTHER INTERESTS: "A trip to England a few years ago confirmed that I'm an Anglophile and so like old castles, roads, tunnels and canals, plus old historians and old economists."

BOLTON, Carole 1926-

PERSONAL: Born January 10, 1926, in Uniontown, Pa.; daughter of Harry M. and Leone (Shomo) Roberts; married John J. Bolton, February 1, 1947; children: Timothy Duke, John Christopher. *Education:* Studied at Ramsey Streett School of Acting, Baltimore, Md., for three years. *Politics:* Democrat. *Religion:* "Former Catholic—now I do not go to church." *Home:* Montville, Me. (R.F.D. 2, Freedom, Me. 04941). *Office:* Thomas Nelson, Inc., 30 East 42nd St., New York, N.Y. 10017.

CAREER: Acted with little theater groups and did office work while attending dramatic school; William Morrow & Co., Inc., New York, N.Y., 1958-64, started as a secretary and became assistant editor of children's books; Meredith Press, New York, N.Y., assistant editor of children's books, 1964-67; Lothrop, Lee & Shepard Co., New York, N.Y., associate editor of children's books, 1967-70; Thomas Nelson, Inc., New York, N.Y., associate editor of children's books, 1972—. *Member:* Authors Guild.

Maddy sometimes wondered if life was really as complicated as men made it out to be, or if they deliberately made it seem that way just to keep women out of their world. ■ (From *Never Jam Today* by Carole Bolton.)

WRITINGS—Books for girls: *Christy,* Morrow, 1960; *The Callahan Girls,* Morrow, 1961; *Reunion in December,* Morrow, 1962; *The Stage Is Set,* Morrow, 1963; *The Dark Rosaleen,* Morrow, 1964; *Never Jam Today* (Junior Literary Guild selection), Atheneum, 1971; *The Search of Mary Katherine Mulloy* (Junior Literary Guild selection), Nelson, 1974.

SIDELIGHTS: "My husband and I moved to Maine in late summer of 1972. We built a small cabin, which we have winterized. We are roughing it—toting our water from a spring, etc. I still go to New York once a month to report at Nelson, but I work and write at home. Someday soon my husband and I hope to raise bees. We are now wintering our first hive and hope to get more."

FOR MORE INFORMATION SEE: *Junior Literary Guild Catalogue,* March, 1971.

BOND, (Thomas) Michael 1926-

PERSONAL: Born January 13, 1926, in Newbury, Berkshire, England; son of Norman Robert and Frances Mary (Offer) Bond; married Brenda Mary Johnson, June 29, 1950; children: Karen Mary. *Education:* Presentation College, student, 1934-40. *Home:* "Fairacre," Farnham Lane, Haslemere, Surrey, England. *Agent:* Harvey Unna, 14 Beaumont Mews, Marylebone High St., London, W1N 4HE, England.

CAREER: Writer. British Broadcasting Corp., London, England, television cameraman, 1954-66. Director, Paddington Productions, Ltd. *Military service:* Royal Air Force, 1943-44, air crew; Army, Middlesex Regiment, 1944-47.

WRITINGS: *A Bear Called Paddington,* Houghton, 1960; *Paddington Helps Out,* Houghton, 1961; *Paddington Abroad,* Collins, 1961, Houghton, 1972; *More About Paddington,* Houghton, 1962; *Paddington at Large,* Houghton, 1963; *Paddington Marches On,* Houghton, 1965; *Here Comes Thursday!,* Harrap, 1966; *Paddington at Work,* Houghton, 1967; *Paddington Goes to Town,* Houghton, 1968; *Thursday Rides Again,* Harrap, 1968, Lothrop, 1969; *Thursday Ahoy!,* Harrap, 1969, Lothrop, 1970; *Parsley's Tail,* B.B.C., 1969; *Parsley's Good Deed,* B.B.C., 1969; *Paddington Takes the Air,* Collins, 1970, Houghton, 1971; *Parsley's Last Stand,* B.B.C., 1970; *Parsley's Problem Present,* B.B.C., 1970; *The Tales of Olga Da Polga* (ALA Notable Book), Penguin, 1971, MacMillan, 1973; *Thursday in Paris,* Harrap, 1971; *Michael Bond's Book of Bears* (anthology), Purnell/Bancroft, 1971; *Michael Bond's Book of Mice,* Purnell/Bancroft, 1972; *Parsley Parade and Parsley the Lion,* Collins, 1972; *The Day the Animals Went on Strike* (picture book), Studio Vista, 1972. Also Author of "The Herbs," thirteen fifteen-minute puppet films, and "The Adventures of Parsley," thirty-two five-minute puppet films. All have been shown on B.B.C. TV and in various other countries. Contributor to British periodicals.

MICHAEL BOND

Things are always happening to me. I'm that sort of bear. ■ (From *A Bear Called Paddington* by Michael Bond. Illustrated by Peggy Fortnum.)

WORK IN PROGRESS: Four "Paddington" picture books for young readers; a sequel to *The Tales of Olga Da Polga.*

SIDELIGHTS: "I believe names and the creation of a character are very important before starting work on a book. The work doesn't come alive otherwise. Paddington started in this way. Living near Paddington Station at the time, I found a toy bear that had been 'left on the shelf unsold' one Christmas Eve. I felt sorry for it and bought it.

"Most of my material is gained from real life experiences and from observation. I often have people say to me 'you're lucky—things happen to you' but in fact, no more happens to me than to anyone else. Being a writer I've trained myself to notice them.

"Although I write mainly children's books I don't write *for* children but more to please myself. If you write *for* children you run the risk of writing down. Although I believe very strongly that children's books are just as important as adult novels (and just as difficult!), I have an ambition to write an adult novel.

"I work mainly from 8:30 to 5:00 but often all hours—like weekends and four o'clock in the morning—much to the disgust of other members of the household. In short, I am a compulsive worker—often with too many ideas chasing too few hours."

Paddington books have been published in Denmark, Sweden, Holland, Germany, Italy, Japan, Poland, and Iceland.

HOBBIES AND OTHER INTERESTS: Motoring, wine, theatre, and gardening.

FOR MORE INFORMATION SEE: Brian Doyle, *The Who's Who of Children's Literature,* Schocken Books, 1968; *Third Book of Junior Authors,* edited by de Montreville and Hill, H. W. Wilson, 1972; *Horn Book,* April, 1973, June, 1973; *Christian Science Monitor,* May 2, 1973.

BOVA, Ben(jamin William) 1932-

PERSONAL: Born November 8, 1932, in Philadelphia, Pa.; son of Benjamin Pasquale and Giove (Caporiccio) Bova; married Rosa Cucinotta, 1953; children: Michael, Regina Marie. *Education:* Temple University, B.S., 1954; Georgetown University, School of Foreign Service, Washington, D.C., certificate, 1955. *Religion:* Roman Catholic. *Office: Analog Science Fiction and Science Fact,* 420 Lexington Ave., New York, N.Y. 10017.

CAREER: Upper Darby News, Upper Darby, Pa., editor, 1954-56; Martin Company, Project Vanguard, Baltimore, Md., technical editor, 1956-58; Physical Science Study Committee, Cambridge, Mass., movie writer, 1958-59; Avco-Everett Research Laboratory, Everett, Mass., technical communications and marketing coordinator, 1960-71; *Analog Science Fiction and Science Fact,* New York, N.Y., editor, 1971—. Lecturer on astronomy, science fiction, rocketry, astronautics, and magnetohydrodynamics. *Member:* National Association of Science Writers, American Association for Advancement of Science, Science Fiction Writers of America, Avco-Everett Fencing Club.

BEN BOVA

WRITINGS: The Star Conquerors, Winston, 1959; *The Milky Way Galaxy,* Holt, 1961; *Giants of the Animal World,* Whitman, 1962; *Reptiles Since the World Began,* Whitman, 1964; *Star Watchman,* Holt, 1964; *The Uses of Space,* Holt, 1965; *The Weathermakers,* Holt, 1967; *Out of the Sun,* Holt, 1968; *The Dueling Machine,* Holt, 1969; *Escape!,* Holt, 1970; *In Quest of Quasers,* Crowell Collier, 1970; *Planets, Life and LGM,* Addison, 1970; *The Fourth State of Matter,* St. Martin's, 1971; *Exiled from Earth,* Dutton, 1971; (with George Lucas) *THX 1138,* Paperback Library, 1971; *The Many Worlds of Science Fiction* (Child Study Association book list), Dutton, 1971; *Starflight and other Improbabilities* (Junior Literary Guild Selection), Westminster, 1973. Contributor to newspapers, magazines and anthologies.

HOBBIES AND OTHER INTERESTS: Fencing, astronomy, anthropology, and history.

FOR MORE INFORMATION SEE: Amazing Science Fiction, June, 1962; *Horn Book,* December, 1969, October, 1971; *Junior Literary Guild Catalogue,* March, 1973.

BRAGDON, Elspeth (MacDuffie) 1897-
(Elspeth)

PERSONAL: Born May 6, 1897, in Springfield, Mass.; daughter of John (headmaster of private school) and Abby (teacher; maiden name Parsons) MacDuffie; married Edwin F. O'Halloran; married Marshall Hurd Bragdon (a race-relations specialist), May 18, 1935; children: John Francis Reynolds (foster son). *Education:* Smith College, A.B., 1920. *Politics:* Independent. *Religion:* Episcopalian. *Home:* 1384 Commonwealth Ave., Boston, Mass. 02134.

ELSPETH BRAGDON

Most of the stones there were old and so covered with lichen that you couldn't read the names cut into them. ■ (From *There is a Tide* by Elspeth Bragdon. Illustrated by Lilian Obligado.)

CAREER: Lowe-Heyward School, Stamford, Conn., teacher, 1920; Pilgrim Press, Boston, Mass., editorial assistant, 1921-22; advertising positions with Filene's, R. H. White, and C. Crawford Hollidge stores in Boston, Mass., May Co., Baltimore, Md., Bloomingdale's and Better Vision Institute, New York, N.Y., 1928-35; taught poetry and writing courses with University of Massachusetts Extension, 1935-39.

WRITINGS—Light verse: *Strange Truth,* Houghton, 1929; *Young Man Beware!,* Houghton, 1932.

Juveniles: *Storytime,* Standard, 1953; *Fairing Weather,* Viking, 1955; *That Jud!* (Junior Literary Guild selection), Viking, 1957; *One to Make Ready* (Junior Literary Guild selection), Viking, 1959; *There is a Tide,* Viking, 1964.

Writer of monthly book review pamphlet for R. W. White, 1929, feature stories for *Springfield Republican,* Springfield, Mass., 1934-36, light verse in *New Yorker* and FPA's "Conning Tower," *New York World,* three pamphlets for Forward Movement of Episcopal Church, 1960-63.

BRANDON, Curt
   See BISHOP, Curtis

BRAYMER, Marjorie (Elizabeth)   1911-

PERSONAL: Born March 21, 1911, in Chicago, Ill.; daughter of Ernest Story and Luella (Lively) Braymer. *Education:* Ohio State University, B.Sci. in Education, 1943; Columbia University Teachers College, M.A., 1944; Stanford University, postgraduate study, 1960-61. *Politics:* Democrat. *Religion:* Congregationalist. *Home and office:* 587 Greer Rd., Palo Alto, Calif. 94303.

CAREER: Editorial work for various motion picture companies and magazines, New York, N.Y., 1930-40; teacher at Sequoia High School, Redwood City, Calif., 1945-66; Addison Wesley Publishing Co., Palo Alto, Calif., editor, 1965-67. National Conference of Teachers of English, National Retired Teachers Association, Archaeological Institute of America, Pi Lambda Theta. *Awards, honors: New York Herald Tribune* Spring Book Festival Honor Book Award, 1960, for *The Walls of Windy Troy;* Vandewater Poetry Prize, Ohio State University, 1943; Morris Fellow in Education, Columbia Teachers College, 1943-44; Newsmaker of Month Award, Redwood City Chamber of Commerce, 1960.

MARJORIE BRAYMER

WRITINGS: (With Evan Lodge) *Adventures in Reading,* Harcourt, 1957, new edition, 1963; *The Walls of Windy Troy* (biography of Heinrich Schliemann; ALA Notable Book), Harcourt, 1960. Has contributed articles on methods of teaching poetry in secondary school to *English Journal;* contributor to *Greek Heritage.*

WORK IN PROGRESS: "A new book addressed to the same age group for whom *The Walls of Windy Troy* was written. Like that book, it reflects my continuing interest in history and mythology and will focus on some of the world's most enduring legends and myths, tracing their pervasive influence on history over the course of time and to the present."

SIDELIGHTS: "My birthplace was Chicago, a good place for a child to learn to iceskate, to swim in Lake Michigan, a few blocks' walk from home, and to make excursions to the Loop, whose bookstores often sponsored lectures by well-known poets and writers. Chicago was then known as a 'writers city,' and a number of famous writers claimed it for their home. Sometimes they would come to the public schools to speak to students in assembly. One of my teachers, on such an occasion, took me onstage to let me greet Carl Sandburg, who had been a guest speaker. Her introduction was this: 'Mr. Sandburg, here is a girl who is going to be a writer, maybe a poet, when she grows up.' Mr. Sandburg, who seemed from where I stood looking up at him to be at least eleven feet tall, leaned down, patted my head, and said, 'How nice. Of course.' That did it. I *had* to be a writer.

After high school I had a year of college before the depression years made it necessary for me, like so many other students, to find a job instead. I went to New York and learned typing and shorthand. Then, after finding the routine of a secretary not to my liking, I worked as a manuscript reader for some of the East Coast offices of Hollywood film studios. At least it had to do with books, even if the actual job of reading plays and books for their possibilities as movie stories was anything but glamourous. It was exacting, hard work, done under constant pressure. In all I spent ten years as a manuscript reader, sometimes freelancing, and occasionally as a publisher's reader.

"One year I took stock. I had written nothing that seemed worthwhile enough to merit publication. The lack of a college degree I felt keenly. And most of all, I knew that I wanted to be a writer myself, not a critic of other people's writing. Rather to my own surprise, I made a firm decision to go back to college and start in again as a student.

"I returned to the Middle West, where college tuition and living expenses were moderate. What I think of now as a four-year adventure in meeting people and challenges began when I enrolled in a small university, then moved later to Ohio State University and studied for a teaching degree. To support myself I took almost any sort of part-time job I could qualify for. It was a merry scramble, but I got my degree, and was given a Fellowship for a year of graduate study at Columbia University. So my path led back to New York for a year.

"It would be misleading to gloss over these years as mere 'adventure' in the sense of having fun. I had to learn to live and eat on an income that dropped as low as $7.50 a week.

One doesn't live lavishly at that figure. But I never regretted leaving the business world for the classroom. I think you will understand why I sometimes counseled my students who asked advice about earning their way through college to consider how costly it was—of one's energy. I believe that having some work experience before college can be just as valuable as the training that college can give. Now that much more aid in the form of federal loans for education is available to them, I am happy that today's students need not face choices as rigorous as mine seemed to me.

"California has been my home since 1945. Writing and research keep my days very full, even though I have officially retired from teaching."

HOBBIES AND OTHER INTERESTS: Archaeology, poetry, music, gardening, and ceramics.

EDITH BRECHT

BRECHT, Edith 1895-

PERSONAL: Born April 7, 1895, in Lancaster City, Pa.; daughter of Milton J. (an educator and public service commissioner) and Mary M. (Wolfe) Brecht. *Education:* Studied at National School of Elocution, Philadelphia, and Millersville State College. *Politics:* Independent. *Religion:* Presbyterian. *Home address:* East Earl Route 1, Lancaster County, Pa. 17519.

CAREER: Writer.

WRITINGS—All children's books: *Ada and the Wild Duck,* Viking, 1964; *Timothy's Hawk,* Viking, 1965; *The Mystery at the Old Forge,* Viking, 1966; *Benjy's Luck,* Lippincott, 1967; *The Little Fox,* Lippincott, 1968. Contributor of poetry and stories to magazines, including *Poetry World, Chatelaine, Toronto Star Weekly, Woman's Day, Ladies' Home Journal, McCall's, Farm Journal, Seventeen,* and others.

WORK IN PROGRESS: Miss Tillie's Garden Plot.

SIDELIGHTS: "I live in a section that is agricultural. The Amish and Mennonites are fine farmers—they are also my friends and neighbors. Living as I do in deep country my door is kept unlocked. Sometimes I will hear it gently open and small soft voices speaking Pennsylvania Dutch. I peep into my living room and discover five little Amish children from three to seven standing there. They have come with a gift of fine, fresh vegetables for me. 'Mother says we can stay fifteen minutes' the oldest who speaks English says—the younger ones speak only Dutch. And so they gather around the television while the oldest asks sweetly, 'Can they see us?' for the people in the picture. The Amish and Mennonites do not have televisions. Any baby appearing on the screen calls forth a loving 'Ah!' I, of course, return the visit and am hailed joyously with: 'Edith cumma!' It is only natural living among them as I do that I should write of them. *Benjy's Luck* and *The Little Fox* are about the Amish.

"After years of living in suburban Philadelphia, I returned to my old bailiwick, Lancaster County; residing with members of my family in an old stone mansion built in 1753 by an early iron master. It was there one night a snowy owl came in a blinding snowstorm to light on a window sill. And a goshawk emptied the dove cote of our fan tails—incidents I used in *Timothy's Hawk* and *The Mystery of the Old Forge.*

"At present I am living alone in a cottage on the edge of a meadow with the Conestoga Creek behind me and the open countryside in my windows. The returning seasons are always an excitement to me—each bird voice, and the opening of wild flowers, old friends to be greeted with warmth. And so I have come to use them as a setting for my stories for children."

Many of Ms. Brecht's stories have been reprinted in Danish and Swedish.

HOBBIES AND OTHER INTERESTS: Out-of-doors (birds, trees, flowers).

BRENNAN, Joseph L(omas) 1903-
(Steve Lomas)

PERSONAL: Born May 26, 1903, in Easton, Pa.; son of Joseph Lomas and Emily (Paulson) Brennan; married Harriet Hunt (sportswear designer), September 22, 1934. *Education:* Attended grade school at West Vernon School, Los Angeles, Calif. *Politics:* Republican. *Home:* The Colony Surf, #1006, 2895 Kalakaua Ave., Honolulu, Hawaii 96815. *Agent:* McIntosh & Otis, Inc., 18 East 41st St., New York, N.Y. 10017.

CAREER: Professional boxer, Los Angeles, Calif., four years; Coca-Cola Co., Los Angeles, Calif., cashier, seven years; Heitler & Brennan, Los Angeles, Calif., partner, seven years; Maren Elwood College, Hollywood, Calif., instructor, two years; free-lance writer in California and Hawaii. *Military service:* U.S. Navy, four years. *Member:* Adventurers Club (Honolulu, Hawaii).

WRITINGS: Tuna Clipper Challenge, Dodd, 1957; *Heart of the Sea,* Dodd, 1958; *A Man Grows Tall,* Messner, 1958; *Call of the Tide,* Messner, 1959; *Thunder on the Beach,* Chilton, 1961; *Waikiki Beachboy,* Chilton, 1962; *Hot Rod Thunder,* Doubleday, 1962; *Fishing Fleet Boy,* Doubleday, 1962; *Pacific Blue,* Washburn, 1962; *The Crimson Angel,* Exposition Press, 1962; *Diamond Head Diver,* Washburn, 1963; *Frog-Suited Fighters* (Literary Guild selection), Chilton, 1964; *Duke of Hawaii,* Ballantine, 1968; *Duke Kahanamoku's World of Surfing,* Grosset, 1968; *World of Surfing,* Angus & Robertson, 1971; *Hawaii's Golden Man,* Hogarth, 1973; *Hawaii's Parker Ranch,* John Day, 1974. Contributor of about 200 pieces to national magazines.

JOSEPH L. BRENNAN

SIDELIGHTS: "Apropos of how I came to write my seventeen published books and the 200-odd magazine stories, I'll confess that it stemmed strictly from an inner urge to share my experiences with others; I've been fortunate in living an extremely active and (I believe) exciting life. In truth, all my books have been based on personal experiences of my own, or of those whom I know personally. I suspect this is a reflection on any genuine creativity to which I'd like to lay claim.

"I was a prodigious reader as a youngster, and early wished that I might someday make my living at writing. Even during the years of my fifty-six fights, I never lost the urge to write. With only a ninth-grade schooling, the odds on making it seemed overwhelming. But, armed with well-studied textbooks on creative writing, I launched into writing only about things I knew. My markets were at first the old-time pulp magazines where I learned my trade. Ultimately, I began hitting the semi-slicks, then finally into the full-length books.

"I directed my writings to people who revel in out-of-door adventure and sports stories. I try to inform as well as entertain. As for my trials and tribulations in this writing business, the work comes hard for me because I keep trying to raise my sights in an effort to make each book a better one than the one preceding it. In fact, I'm a bleeder and a plodder as a writer—careful as a man with a bag of bombs—and my researching is generally a little on the massive side. In connection with the time I put in at writing, I work about eight hours a day here in my tenth-floor apartment on the shore at the foot of Diamond Head.

"I have just finished a history of the fabulous 137-year-old Parker Ranch of Hawaii. It is the largest single cattle kingdom, owned and operated by one man, in all of the United States, and it has a fantastically colorful history. Currently, I'm doing a definitive documentary on the famous *paniolos* (Hawaiian cowboys) of these Islands—a book that has heretofore never been done."

FOR MORE INFORMATION SEE: Adventure Magazine, October, 1955; *El Segundo Herald,* December 27, 1962; *Honolulu Star Bulletin,* January 28, 1964.

BROOKS, Gwendolyn 1917-

PERSONAL: Born June 7, 1917, in Topeka, Kan.; daughter of David Anderson and Keziah (Wims) Brooks; married Henry L. Blakely, September 17, 1939; children: Henry L., Nora. *Education:* Graduate of Wilson Junior College, 1936. *Home:* 7428 South Evans Ave., Chicago, Ill. 60619.

CAREER: Writer. Lecturer at universities, colleges. *Member:* Society of Midland Authors (Chicago). *Awards, honors: Mademoiselle* Merit Award, 1945; National Institute of Arts and Letters grant in literature ($1,000), 1946; Guggenheim fellowships, 1946, 1947; Eunice Tietjens Memorial Prize of *Poetry* Magazine, 1949; Pulitzer Prize in poetry for *Annie Allen,* 1950; Friends of Literature Poetry Award, 1963; Thormod Monsen Literature Award, 1964; fifteen honorary doctorates.

SIDELIGHTS: "I was taken from Chicago to Topeka, Kansas, my mother's home, to be born. A month after my birth my mother and I returned to Chicago, where we have lived ever since. . . .

"I loved poetry very early and began to put rhymes together at about seven, at which time my parents expressed most earnest confidence that I would one day be a writer. At the age of thirteen my poem, 'Eventide,' was accepted and printed by a then well-known children's magazine, *American Childhood*. . . .

"When I was sixteen I began submitting poems to the Chicago *Defender*, a Negro newspaper. Over 75 of these confident items appeared in a variety column of the *Defender* called 'Lights and Shadows.'"

FOR MORE INFORMATION SEE: *American Literature by Negro Authors*, by Herman Dreer, Macmillan, 1950; *Publishers' Weekly*, May 6, 1950; *Saturday Review*, May 20, 1950; *Holiday*, October, 1951; *Portraits in Color*, Pageant, 1962; Haviland and Smith, *Children and Poetry*, Library of Congress, 1969; *Black World*, September, 1971, October, 1971.

These buildings are too close to me.
I'd like to PUSH away.
I'd like to live in the country,
And spread my arms all day.
■ (From *Bronzeville Boys and Girls* by Gwendolyn Brooks. Illustrated by Ronni Solbert.)

WRITINGS: *A Street in Bronzeville*, 1945, *Annie Allen*, 1949, *Maud Martha*, 1953, *Bronzeville Boys and Girls*, 1956, *The Bean Eaters*, 1960, *Selected Poems*, 1962, *In the Mecca*, 1968 (all published by Harper); *Riot*, Broadside Press, 1969; *Family Pictures*, Broadside Press, 1970; *Aloneness* (poetry), Broadside Press, 1971; *Jump Bad*, Broadside Press, 1971; (editor) *A Broadside Treasury*, Broadside Press, 1972; *Report from Part One: An Autobiography*, Broadside Press, 1972.

GWENDOLYN BROOKS

BROWN, Emily
See STERNE, Emma Gelders

BROWN, Marion Marsh 1908-

PERSONAL: Born July 22, 1908, in Brownville, Neb.; daughter of Cassius Henry and Jenevie (Hairgrove) Marsh; married Gilbert S. Brown (a lawyer), 1937 (deceased); children: Paul Marsh. *Education:* State Teachers' College, Peru, Neb., A.B., 1927; University of Nebraska, M.A., 1930; University of Minnesota, postgraduate courses. *Politics:* Republican. *Religion:* Presbyterian. *Home:* 2615 North 52nd St., Omaha, Neb. 68104.

CAREER: Public high schools in Nebraska, teacher of English and speech, 1928-36; State Teachers' College, Peru, Neb., assistant professor of English, 1935-37; Municipal University of Omaha, Neb., associate professor of English, 1953-65, professor, 1965-68. Writer, mainly for teen-agers. *Member:* American Association of University Women (past president, Omaha branch), P.E.O., National Council of Teachers of English, Nebraska Council of Teachers of English, Delta Kappa Gamma, Sigma Tau Delta, Kappa Delta Pi, Nebraska Writers' Guild (past president), Zeta Tau Alpha, Phi Delta Gamma.

MARION MARSH BROWN

"W-a-t-e-r Helen spelled eagerly into Annie's hand." ■ (From *The Silent Storm* by Marion Marsh Brown and Ruth Crone. Illustrated by Fritz Kredel.)

WRITINGS: Young Nathan (Junior Literary Guild selection), Westminster, 1949; *Swamp Fox* (Boys' Clubs of America selection), Westminster, 1950; *Frontier Beacon,* Westminster, 1953; *Broad Stripes and Bright Stars* (Children's Book Club selection), Westminster, 1955; *Prairie Teacher,* Bouregy, 1957; *Learning Words in Context,* Chandler Publishing, 1961; *A Nurse Abroad,* Bouregy, 1963; (with Ruth Crone) *The Silent Storm* (Junior Literary Guild selection), Abingdon, 1963; *Stuart's Landing,* Westminster, 1968; (with Ruth Crone) *Willa Cather: The Woman and Her Works,* Scribner, 1970; *Marnie,* Westminster, 1971. Over two hundred short stories and articles in magazines.

SIDELIGHTS: "As a little girl, I lived on a farm near one of the oldest settlements in Nebraska, it was picturesque, and we never lacked for interesting things to do. There were lovely woods on our farm which gave us wildflowers in spring, gooseberries and wild raspberries in summer, hickory nuts and black walnuts in autumn, and Christmas trees in winter. It had a spring with the coldest water you ever tasted, which formed a pool deep enough for swimming and fed a meandering creek where we waded in summer and skated in winter. In the spreading roots of the old maple trees, we made fairy palaces which we peopled with hollyhock ladies. In the haymow, full of sweet-scented hay, we did acrobatics, burrowed tunnels, discovered nests of baby kittens. On 'Old May,' our white riding horse, we galloped over the hills in summer; on our sleds we skimmed down the same hills in winter.

"Between two big trees in our shady back yard, hung a hammock during the summer months. In it, I lay and read, hour after precious hour, fondling a kitten with the hand that wasn't holding a book. A beautiful collie dog lay curled under the hammock, dozing. Of all the things I loved to do, reading was best. So of course I had to see if I could write things too. When I was ten, I saw my first story in print. It was on the children's page of a Sunday newspaper. I still remember the prize I received for it—a book called *I Wonder Why*.

"That was a good book for me to have, for I wondered 'Why?' about a lot of things then, and still do today, and I believe this is an essential trait for an author to have.

"When I was ready to go to college, I knew there were three things I wanted to do with my life: I wanted to be a wife and mother, I wanted to write, and I wanted to teach. Life has been good to me, for it has granted all three of my wishes and much besides. I went to a small Midwest college, whose grassy campus and red brick buildings under a thousand spreading oaks nestles in the Missouri River Bluffs. Down the 'Big Muddy' we hiked; on her banks we built our campfires. Life was as rich and as unhurried here as it had been on my father's farm. I went out for amateur dramatics and played everything from Jo in 'Little Women' to Kate in 'The Taming of the Shrew.' I gave my first piano recital, wearing my first evening gown. I played tennis. I took all the English and writing courses the college offered. Still I found time to devour shelves of books in the college library.

"During my college years, I began to get a few things published, and this was a big thrill to me, for it was the beginning of the fulfillment of one of my three big wishes. I was graduated from college when I was eighteen and began teaching high school English. I taught in high schools for several years, before completing graduate studies that permitted me to teach in college.

"So it was that I discovered that the supply of really good, interesting books for young teens, particularly the junior high school students, simply was not adequate. I began thinking that perhaps this group of readers would be the group to whom I would devote my writing.

"I met and married an Omaha attorney, and have lived in this Midwest stockyards city ever since. We had one son, who has grown up to be an attorney like his father. During the early years of my married life, I started writing my books for young readers—now numbering ten. After my son was in high school, I went back to teaching, in college. So all three of my wishes were roundly fulfilled.

"I have quit teaching at present in order to devote full time to my writing—and to three adorable small grandchildren. I do a good deal of lecturing and have been on the staff of numerous Writers' Conferences.

"As I am now a widow, I spend considerable time in places other than Omaha, my home base. I can write as well in Gstaad or Singapore or Tucson, as I can in Omaha! I love to see how people live in other parts of the world. I have traveled in all fifty of our United States, in sixteen countries in Europe, and in a half dozen Asian countries. My greatest interest, wherever I go, is people—and people, of course, are the material for the books which I write."

BROWN, Myra Berry 1918-

PERSONAL: Born October 27, 1918, in Minneapolis, Minn.; daughter of Louis (salesman) and Marion (Hosenpud) Berry; married Ned Brown (literary agent), May 2, 1942; children: Lorna, Elizabeth, Jonathan. *Education:* B.A. from University of California (Los Angeles). *Politics:* Democrat. *Religion:* Jewish. *Home:* 21640 Pacific Coast Hwy., Malibu, Calif. 90265.

CAREER: Paramount Pictures, Hollywood, Calif., secretary, 1939-41; A. and S. Lyons, Beverly Hills, Calif., literary agent, 1942-44. Los Angeles County department of mental health, community discussion leader, 1968-70; Los Angeles Council of Girl Scouts, Brownie trainer; active in University of California at Los Angeles Laboratory Elementary School, Family-School Alliance. *Member:* P.E.N., Los Angeles Library Association.

MYRA BERRY BROWN

WRITINGS: *Company's Coming for Dinner*, 1959, *First Night Away From Home*, 1960, *My Daddy's Visiting Our School Today*, 1961, *Flower Girl*, 1961, *Somebody's Pup*, 1961, *Benjy's Blanket*, 1962, *Ice Cream for Breakfast*, 1963, *Birthday Boy*, 1964, *Casey's Sore Throat Day*, 1964, *Amy and the New Baby*, 1965, *Pip Camps Out*, Golden Gate Junior Books, 1966, *Sandy Signs His Name*, 1967, *Best Friends*, Golden Gate, 1967, *Pip Moves Away*, Golden Gate, 1967, *If You Have a Doll*, 1967, *Where's Jeremy?*, Golden Gate, 1968, *Best of Luck*, Golden Gate, 1969 (all published by Watts, except where otherwise noted). Children's Book Reviewer, *Los Angeles Times*, 1960, 1961.

SIDELIGHTS: "I came to write when my youngest child began to read and wished for stories of real family situations. Two daughters had preceded their young brother, so I had much family stuff to draw on. The notion was to provide simple, honest stories for youngsters in which they could see themselves and their own growing-up experiences.

"I have been tutoring children in reading recently and I don't know if I will write more. The times they are a-changin'—and the immediate survival of humanity in this environment is my primary concern."

ALAN BROWNJOHN

"Do you still have to carry that old thing around?" he asked. "Yes, I do," answered Benjy. ■ (From *Benjy's Blanket* by Myra Berry Brown. Illustrated by Dorothy Marino.)

BROWNJOHN, Alan 1931-
(John Berrington)

PERSONAL: Born July 28, 1931, in London, England; son of Charles Henry (a managing printer, retired) and Dorothy (Mulligan) Brownjohn; married Shirley Toulson (a poet), February 6, 1960 (divorced, 1969); children: Steven. *Education:* Merton College, Oxford, B.A., 1953, M.A., 1961. *Politics:* Member of Labour Party. *Religion:* Atheist. *Residence:* London, England.

CAREER: Battersea College of Education, London, England, currently a senior lecturer. Once ran, unsuccessfully, as a Labour candidate for House of Commons. Poet and novelist. Member of Literature Panel, Arts Council of Great Britain. *Member:* Poetry Society (London).

WRITINGS: Travellers Alone (the entire issue of *Artisan 5;* poems), Heron Press (Liverpool), 1954; *The Railings* (poems), Digby Press, 1961; (under pseudonym John Berrington) *To Clear the River* (novel for young people), Heinemann, 1964; *The Lions' Mouths* (poems), Macmillan (London), 1967, Dufour, 1968; *Sandgrains on a Tray* (poems), Macmillan (London), 1969; (with Michael Hamburger and Charles Tomlinson) *Penguin Modern Poets 14,* Penguin, 1969; (editor) *First I Say This* (anthology), Hutchinson, 1969; *Brownjohn's Beasts* (Child Study Association book list), Scribner, 1970; *Warrior's Career,* Macmillan (London), 1972.

As a bear, I am
capable of so
much: running fast, smearing honey,
climbing trees—and an apparent slow
thoughtfulness.
■ (From *Brownjohn's Beasts* by Alan Brownjohn. Illustrated by Carol Lawson.)

WORK IN PROGRESS: A radio play; poems, some for children.

SIDELIGHTS: Brownjohn considers himself "a poet of the mainstream, rather than a traditionalist or *avant-gardist.*" He notes that, as yet, he has traveled extensively only in Scandinavia and that he is an admirer of Swedish civilization. He holds strong left-wing Labour opinions in politics but adds that he is "not an active politician any more." He is a "lover of Faure, Debussy and modern jazz," and a "lover of cats, but would not own one."

HOBBIES AND OTHER INTERESTS: "Table tennis, walking on mountains, running on beaches (can't swim, yet!), books, and people."

FOR MORE INFORMATION SEE: Times Literary Supplement, February 16, 1967; *London Magazine,* March, 1967, October, 1969; *Observer,* March 26, 1967; *Kenyon Review,* Volume 30, number 5, 1968.

BUCKERIDGE, Anthony (Malcolm) 1912-

PERSONAL: Born June 20, 1912, in London, England; son of Ernest George (a bank official) and Gertrud (Smith) Buckeridge; married Eileen Selby, October, 1962; children: Sally, Timothy, Corin. *Education:* Studied at University College, London, 1933-35. *Politics:* Liberal. *Religion:* Church of England. *Home and office:* East Crink, Barcombe Mills, Lewes, Sussex, England. *Agent:* Hughes Massie Ltd., 69 Great Russell St., London W.C.1, England.

CAREER: Schoolmaster at boys' preparatory schools in England, with last teaching post at St. Lawrence College, Ramsgate, Kent, 1945-50; writer of series of radio plays, "Jennings at School," produced by British Broadcasting Corp., starting in 1948, and of Jennings books and other juveniles. *Member:* Society of Authors, Writers' Guild of Great Britain, British Actors' Equity Association.

WRITINGS—"Jennings" series, published in England by Collins: *Jennings Goes to School,* 1950; *Jennings Follows a Clue,* 1951; *Jennings' Little Hut,* 1951; *Jennings and Darbishire,* 1952; *Jennings' Diary,* 1953; *According to Jennings,* 1954; *Our Friend Jennings,* 1955, Penguin, 1967; *Thanks to Jennings,* 1957; *Take Jennings, for Instance,* 1958; *Jennings as Usual,* 1959; *The Trouble with Jennings,* 1960; *Just Like Jennings,* 1961; *Leave It to Jennings,* 1963; *Jennings, of Course!,* 1964; *Especially Jennings!,* 1965; *A Bookful of Jennings,* 1966; *Jennings Abounding,* 1966; *Jennings in Particular,* 1967; *Trust Jennings!,* 1968; *The Jennings Report,* 1969; *Typically Jennings,* 1970; *The Best of Jennings,* 1972; *Speaking of Jennings,* 1973. The "Jennings" books have been translated into twelve languages.

"Rex Milligan" series, published in England by Lutterworth: *Rex Milligan's Busy Term,* 1954; *Rex Milligan Raises the Roof,* 1955; *Rex Milligan Holds Forth,* 1956; *Rex Milligan Reporting,* 1957.

Other books: *A Funny Thing Happened,* Lutterworth, 1953; (editor) *Stories for Boys,* Faber, 1956; (editor) *In and Out of School,* British Book Service, 1958; (editor) *Stories for Boys 2,* Faber, 1965; (contributor) Eric Duthie, editor, *Stirring Stories for Boys,* Odhams, 1966.

ANTHONY BUCKERIDGE

"Jennings is essentially an English-sounding name and for this reason some European translators have adopted instead a name that comes more readily to the lips of their readers. In Germany, Jennings is known as Fredy, in Norway, where he is also the hero of several films, he is called Stompa. In France, they call him Bennett. Thus it seems that, as well as being popular in their own country, Jennings and his friends at Linbury Court have completely won the affection of boys and girls in countries where boarding schools are unknown and school uniforms are unheard of!"

FOR MORE INFORMATION SEE: Geoffrey Trease, *Tales Out of School,* Oxford University Press, 1948; Margary Fisher, *Intent upon Reading,* Brockhampton Press, 1961; John Rowe Townsend, *Written for Children,* Garnet Miller, 1965; Brian Doyle, *The Who's Who of Children's Literature,* Schocken, 1968.

BUCKMASTER, Henrietta

PERSONAL: Daughter of Rae D. (an editor) and Pearl (Wintermute) Henkle. *Education:* Attended Friends Seminary, New York, N.Y., and Brearley School. *Politics:* Liberal. *Religion:* Christian Science. *Agent:* Russell & Volkening, Inc., 551 Fifth Ave., New York, N.Y. 10017.

Author of radio, television and stage plays for young people.

WORK IN PROGRESS: A new title in "Jennings" series; more television and radio plays. Currently writing radio serials for B.B.C. program, "Fourth Dimension."

SIDELIGHTS: "The Jennings stories are comedies about the misadventures of the eleven-year-old hero and his friends at a preparatory school. The trouble with Jennings is the way he ticks—not out loud of course, except when he is being a space rocket in orbit. It is rather that he has his own peculiar way of doing things. Simple matters become complicated to the point of chaos whenever he takes command.

"The humor of the Jennings stories is based upon the logical absurdities of all small boys. As an ex-schoolmaster, I enjoy writing humor set against a background with which I am familiar. If I had been an undertaker instead of a teacher I would write funny stories about funerals!

"The urge to write comedy overtook me when as a small boy I was told to write a story during an English lesson at school. My story was a tragic tale and the writing of it moved me almost to tears—but when the master read it aloud the class rocked with laughter. I was so taken aback that I decided to play for safety and write comedies in future!

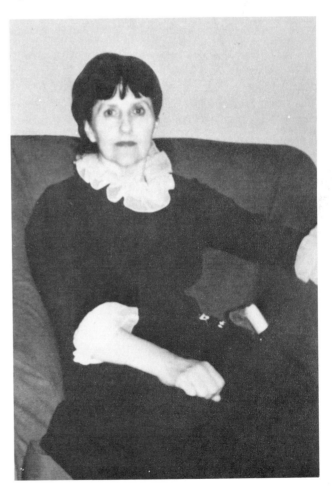

HENRIETTA BUCKMASTER

CAREER: Writer. *Awards, honors:* Ohioana Award in fiction for *Deep River,* 1945; Guggenheim fellowship.

WRITINGS: Let My People Go, Harper, 1941; *Deep River,* Harcourt, 1944; *Bread from Heaven,* Random, 1952; *And Walk in Love,* Random, 1957; *All the Living,* Random, 1962; *Paul: A Man Who Changed the World,* McGraw, 1966; *The Lion in the Stone,* Harcourt, 1968; *The Walking Trip,* Harcourt, 1972.

Children's books: *Lucy and Loki,* Scribner, 1958; *Flight to Freedom,* Crowell, 1958; *Walter Raleigh,* Random, 1964; *The Seminole Wars,* Collier-Macmillan, 1964; *Women Who Changed History,* Collier-Macmillan, 1966; *The Rebel Congressmen,* Scholastic, 1971.

SIDELIGHTS: "I suppose what has prompted the writing of all my books was a concern for people. I was very young when I wrote *Let My People Go* and each day became an extraordinary revelation of the horrors and injustices endured by the black people who were brought here as slaves. And, even more important, their unwillingness to accept bondage, and their own fight against it. Two novels, *Deep River* and *Fire in the Heart,* two nonfiction, *Let my People Go* and *Freedom Bound,* two children's books, *Flight to Freedom* and *Women Who Changed History* have dealt directly with what I learned of these remarkable struggles against indignity and human violation.

"*Bread from Heaven* dealt with another aspect of courage. It's a novel based on a young man I met—sixteen years of age—who had somehow survived eight concentration camps with a remarkable understanding of the qualities that permit survival.

"I found an unexpected theme running through my next three novels, *And Walk in Love, All the Living,* and *The Lion in the Stone.* The first is of Paul the apostle, a spiritual genius, the second of Shakespeare, an imaginative genius, the third of a Secretary General of the United Nations, a moral genius. What distinguished them from other men? What gives them their special kind of courage and indestructability?"

BURMAN, Ben Lucien 1896-

PERSONAL: Born December 12, 1896, in Covington, Ky.; son of Sam and Minna B. Burman; married Alice Caddy (since illustrator of many of his books), September 19, 1927. *Education:* Harvard University, A.B., 1920. *Address:* c/o Taplinger Publishing Co., 200 Park Ave. S., New York, N.Y. 10003.

CAREER: Boston Herald, reporter, 1920; *Cincinnati Times Star,* assistant city editor, 1921; *New York Sunday World,* special writer, 1922; staff contributor, Newspaper Enterprise Association (Scripps-Howard), 1927; war correspondent, Africa and Middle East, 1941. *Military service:* U.S. Army, Field Artillery, World War I; severely wounded at Soissons, France, July, 1918. *Member:* Authors League (formerly on board of directors), P.E.N. (formerly on board of directors), Overseas Press Club, Dutch Treat Club. *Awards, honors:* Southern Authors prize for the most distinguished Southern book of the year for *Blow for a Landing,* 1938; Thomas Jefferson Memorial prize for *Rooster Crows for Day,* 1945; French Legion of Honor for

wartime reporting from Africa, 1947; German Young People's Book Festival prize for *High Water at Catfish Bend,* also chosen by New York Public Library as favorite American book of the year for young people; Dutch Treat Club Gold Medal, 1969, for "distinguished services to American Literature."

WRITINGS: Mississippi, Cosmopolitan Book Corp., 1929; *Steamboat Round the Bend,* Farrar & Rinehart, 1933; *Blow for a Landing,* Houghton, 1938; *Big River to Cross: Mississippi Life Today,* John Day, 1940; *Miracle on the Congo: Report from the Free French Front,* John Day, 1942; *Rooster Crows for Day,* Dutton, 1945; *Everywhere I Roam,* Doubleday, 1949.

Children of Noah: Glimpses of Unknown America, Messner, 1951; *High Water at Catfish Bend,* Messner, 1952; *The Four Lives of Mundy Tolliver,* Messner, 1953; *Seven Stars for Catfish Bend,* Funk, 1956; *It's a Big Country: America Off the Highways,* Reynal, 1956; *The Street of the Laughing Camel,* McGraw, 1959; *It's a Big Continent,*

BEN LUCIEN BURMAN

Something about the Author

River is a beautiful thing. More than that she's a holy thing. Don't need to go to church when you're on the river. ■ (From *Look Down that Winding River* by Ben Lucien Burman. Illustrated by Alice Caddy.)

McGraw, 1961; *The Owl Hoots Twice at Catfish Bend,* Taplinger, 1961; *The Generals Wear Cork Hats,* Taplinger, 1963; *The Sign of the Praying Tiger,* New American Library, 1966; *Blow a Wild Bugle for Catfish Bend,* Taplinger, 1967; *Three from Catfish Bend,* Taplinger, 1967; *Look Down that Winding River,* Taplinger, 1973.

Motion Pictures: "Heaven on Earth," a film version of *Mississippi,* 1929, and *Steamboat Round the Bend,* 1935. Contributor to *Reader's Digest, Saturday Review.*

SIDELIGHTS: "The Novelist is a curious, cud-chewing animal, unlike the rarest found in any zoo. One moment he must have an ear and skin sensitive as the needle of some super-scientific instrument to record the impulses of his fellows; the next, when others would change or misinterpret his writing, he must possess ears of stone and an elephant's skin.

"Perhaps first of all he must have the eyes of the dragonfly, who, I have heard it said, can see in a thousand directions. Without this power to stand watch upon humanity as it goes its way in folly or wisdom, there is nothing. All is without depth, without universality. For the thousand-eyed novelist, the materials of drama are everywhere. But he must not be like the American tourists I have seen so often cruising in state to Casablanca or Algiers, who stop always in the same fashionable hotels and play bridge each night with the same dull companions, then return home thinking they know North Africa. The pursuit of true knowledge requires discomfort. I think it would be very difficult to be a snob and a good novelist. A bus is closer to the people of a country than a train; a buggy or a horse is closer than a bus. Walking is the closest of all. Out of the mosquito bites, the fleas, the hard beds in a tourist court, and all the varied accidents of the road, there gradually emerges a picture of a region, and an understanding of its inhabitants' philosophy.

"The novelist is a creature of many moods and professions, a jack of every trade. With his characters he must be at once doctor, priest, and devil's advocate. He is comedian, tragedian, villain, clown. He must know when to make his audience laugh and when to make it mourn; he must know when the play is ended and it is the hour to go home.

"As he writes and observes he cannot help but become a philosopher, with his own interpretation of the absurb but ever-fascinating pageant that is the human comedy. He need not hope to alter the universe. But he can hold a mirror up to life, so that men may study their reflections and laugh at their childish vanities.

"The mirror he uses may be of many sorts. His hope can be only one—to make the reflection true."

Burman a chronicler of Mississippi life, now has a river light near Baton Rouge named in his honor by the Lighthouse Service of the U.S. Coast Guard. His *Steamboat Round the Bend* was filmed with Will Rogers as its star; *High Water at Catfish Bend* was chosen by Lou Bunin, the puppeteer, for his first full-length motion picture since "Alice in Wonderland." His work has been translated into many languages, including Urdu, Vietnamese, Thai, Burmese, Polish and Czechoslovakian. In World War II Burman was the first correspondent to reach the Free French capital at Brazzaville in French Equitorial Africa. Invalided back to the United States because of anemia, he continued working as a vocal champion of the Free French.

His wife has illustrated sixteen of his books.

FOR MORE INFORMATION SEE: Saturday Review of Literature, October 8, 1949; *New York Herald Tribune Book Review,* November 2, 1953; Edward R. Murrow, *This I Believe,* Simon and Schuster, 1954; *Miami Herald,* May 25, 1958; *St. Louis Post-Dispatch,* May 10, 1972; *New York Times Book Review,* May 13, 1973.

CARROLL, Curt
See BISHOP, Curtis

CHALMERS, Mary (Eileen) 1927-

PERSONAL: Born March 16, 1927, in Camden, N. J.; daughter of Donald Keith and Clarissa (Fox) Chalmers. *Education:* Studied at Philadelphia Museum College of Art for four years, and Barnes Foundation, two years. *Residence:* Haddon Heights, N.J.

WRITINGS—Author and illustrator: *Come For a Walk With Me,* 1955, *Here Comes the Trolley Car,* 1955, *A Christmas Story,* 1956, *A Hat for Amy Jean,* 1956, *George Appleton,* 1957, *Kevin,* 1957, *Throw a Kiss, Harry,* 1958, *Boats Finds a House,* 1958, *The Cat Who Liked to Pretend,* 1959, *Mr. Cat's Wonderful Surprise,* 1961, *Take a Nap, Harry,* 1964, *Be Good, Harry,* 1967 (all published by Harper).

Illustrator: Raymond Bechtle, *Every Day is a World,* Harper, 1957; Dorothy W. Baruch, *I Would Like to Be a Pony and Other Wishes,* Harper, 1959; Charlotte Zolotow, *Big Brother,* Harper, 1960; Ursula Nordstrom, *Secret Language,* Harper, 1960; Joan Heilbroner, *Happy Birthday Present,* Harper, 1961; Charlotte Zolotow, *Three Funny Friends,* Harper, 1961; Betty Boegehold, *Three to Get Ready,* Harper, 1965; *The House of Thirty Cats,* Harper, 1965; Jenny D. Lindquist, *Crystal Tree,* Harper, 1966; Marjorie W. Sharmat, *Goodnight, Andrew, Goodnight, Craig,* Harper, 1969; Ruth Krauss, *I Write It,* Harper, 1970; Syd Hoff, *When Will It Snow?,* Harper, 1971; Nancy Jewell, *The Snuggle Bunny,* Harper, 1972.

SIDELIGHTS: "I suppose I could say that I came to write books for children because I have a sister to whom I have always been very close. When I was in the fifth grade she decided that she would be an artist, so I decided that I would be one too. I went to art school and somewhere in those art school years decided that I would make picture books for small children. That would combine two loves. Books and art.

"For years after art school I took work to publishers. Ursula Nordstrom of Harper & Row told me to write my own story as they never had a manuscript suitable for my work. I wrote book after book but none worked until my sister presented me with a niece.

"That first book was for Susan, in a sense, but it is certainly for all children too. All of my books are for children, not adults. Although, I must say, I am happy if adults like them. I know that some say a children's book is not worth its salt if it isn't really for adults, or at nine years a child should begin reading adult books only. I'm afraid I can't agree.

"But as a writer I'm decidedly lacking. It seems I do, in fact, qualify as an author, since I have written books for children and these books have been published. The simplicity of the picture book is deceptive. A fact, I think, often stated. It is extremely difficult for me to write. Ideas are plentiful, sometimes crowding in on one, pushing each other about. I think all creative people must have this problem. The great trick is deciding what to do and then carrying that idea to a good conclusion. It is decidedly much easier to take someone else's story and make pictures.

"If I am trying to sort out an idea in my mind a good way to help is to do something with one's hands. Nothing too strenuous and nothing that takes thought. I sometimes knit. Long, thin scarves. It must be absolutely quiet. Not even music.

"Surely, everyone writing draws upon their childhood. I know some people in the children's book field who say they have never known any child well. But I have, thanks to my dear sister. And for me there are two other sources from which I draw. Animals and nature. Right now I live with ten cats and two rabbits. Since we are in suburbia, the type of animals must needs be limited. But, really, everything around one is a source of inspiration.

"My second book, *Here Comes the Trolley Car,* was inspired by where I lived at the time. The Baring Street section of Philadelphia. There were the trolley cars, the people who rode in them and the things the trolley passed.

"My two most successful books were initially written for an adult, come to think of it. *A Christmas Story* was a Christmas card sent to Ursula Nordstrom and *Throw a Kiss, Harry* was a thank-you card to Ursula Nordstrom. And, too, Harry was a love letter to all cats and all children everywhere."

FOR MORE INFORMATION SEE: Illustrators of Children's Books: 1946-1956, Horn Book, 1958; *Illustrators of Children's Books: 1957-1966,* Horn Book, 1968; Selma G. Lanes, *Down the Rabbit Hole,* Atheneum, 1971; *Third Book of Junior Authors,* edited by de Montreville and Hill, H. W. Wilson, 1972; *Junior Literary Guild Catalogue,* March, 1973.

CHAPPELL, Warren 1904-

PERSONAL: Born July 9, 1904, in Richmond, Va.; son of Samuel M. (a railway clerk) and Mary L. (Hardie) Chappell; married Lydia A. Hatfield, August 28, 1928. *Education:* University of Richmond, B.A., 1926; studied art at Art Students League, New York, N.Y., 1926-28, Offenbacher Werkstatt in Germany, 1931-32, and Colorado Springs Fine Arts Center, 1935-36. *Politics:* Independent. *Religion:* Protestant. *Home:* James St., Norwalk, Conn. 06850.

CAREER: Designer, graphic artist, and illustrator. Art Students League, member of board of control, 1927-31; instructor at Art Students League, New York, N.Y., 1933-35, at Colorado Springs Fine Arts Center, Colorado Springs, Colo., 1935-36; lecturer at New York University, New York, N.Y. Consultant to Book-of-the-Month Club, 1944—. *Member:* Phi Beta Kappa. *Awards, honors:* Rochester Institute of Technology Goudy Award, 1970; University of Richmond, D.F.A., 1968.

WRITINGS: The Anatomy of Lettering, Loring & Mussey, 1935; *They Say Stories,* Knopf, 1960; *A Short History of the Printed Word: New York Times,* Knopf, 1970. Contributor to *Virginia Quarterly Review, Dolphin, Horn Book* and other periodicals.

Adapter: *The Nutcracker* (music by Tchaikovsky), Knopf, 1958; *The Sleeping Beauty* (music by Tchaikovsky), Knopf, 1961; *Coppelia* (music by Delibes), Knopf, 1965.

MARY CHALMERS

WARREN CHAPPELL

Illustrator: Miguel de Cervantes, *The Adventures of Don Quixote De La Mancha,* Knopf, 1939, new edition, 1960; Sergei Prokofiev, *Peter and the Wolf,* Knopf, 1940; John B. L. Goodwin, *Pleasant Pirate,* Knopf, 1940; Corinne B. Lowe, *Knight of the Sea,* Harcourt, 1941; Julian David, *Three Horses,* Little, Brown, 1942; Elizabeth Yates, *Patterns on the Wall,* Dutton, 1943, new edition, 1953; *Tom Jones,* Illustrated Modern Library, 1943; William Shakespeare, *The Comedies and Tragedies of Shakespeare,* Random House, 1944; Grimm Brothers, *Hansel and Gretel,* Knopf, 1944; Catherine Besterman, *Quaint and Curious Quest of Johnny Longfoot, the Shoe King's Son,* Bobbs, 1947; Edward C. Wagenknecht, editor, *The Fireside Book of Ghost Stories,* Bobbs, 1947; Babette Deutsch, *Reader's Shakespeare,* Messner, 1947; Wagenknecht, *A Fireside Book of Yuletide Tales,* Bobbs, 1948; Catherine Besterman, *Extraordinary Education of Johnny Longfoot in His Search for the Magic Hat,* Bobbs, 1949; *The Complete Novels of Jane Austen,* two volumes, Random House, 1950; Regina Z. Kelly, *Young Geoffrey Chaucer,* Lothrop, 1952; Vincent Sheean, *Thomas Jefferson,* Random House, 1953; Thomas B. Costain, *Mississippi Bubble,* Random House, 1955; Manuel Komroff, *Mozart,* Knopf, 1956; Walter De La Mare, *Come Hither,* Knopf, 1957; Irving Kolodin, *Musical Life,* Knopf, 1958; Charles Perrault, *The Sleeping Beauty,* Knopf, 1961; William Mc-Cleery, *Wolf Story,* Simon & Schuster, 1961; John Updike, *The Magic Flute,* Knopf, 1962; John Updike, *Ring,* Knopf, 1964; Sid Fleischman, *The Ghost in the Noonday Sun,* Little, Brown, 1965; Conrad Richter, *The Light in the Forest,* Knopf, 1966; Kate Douglas Wiggin and N. A. Smith, *The Fairy Ring,* Doubleday, 1967; Paul Delarue, compiler, *French Fairy Tales,* Knopf, 1968; Geoffrey Household, *Prisoner of the Indies,* Little, Brown, 1968; John Updike, *Bottom's Dream,* Knopf, 1969; Charles B. Hawes, *Dark Frigate,* Little, Brown, 1971.

FOR MORE INFORMATION SEE: American Artist, October, 1944; *Sixty-Three Drawings by Warren Chappell,* privately printed, 1955; *Publishers Weekly,* October 1, 1955; *Illustrators of Children's Books: 1946-1956,* Horn Book, 1958; *A Horn Book Sampler,* edited by Norma Fryatt, Horn Book, 1959; Diana Klemin, *The Art of Art for Children's Books,* Clarkson Potter, 1966; *Illustrators of Children's Books: 1957-1966,* Horn Book, 1968; Elinor W. Field, *Horn Book Reflections,* Horn Book, 1969; Diana Klemin, *The Illustrated Book,* Clarkson Potter, 1970; *Horn Book,* October, 1971; *Third Book of Junior Authors,* edited by de Montreville and Hill, H. W. Wilson, 1972.

CHAUNCY, Nan (Masterman) 1900-1970

PERSONAL: Daughter of Charles Edward and Lilla (Osmond) Masterman; married Anthony Chauncy, 1938; children: Heather. *Home:* Chauncy Vale, Bagdad, Tasmania, Australia.

CAREER: Writer. *Member:* Australian Society of Authors, International P.E.N., Writers Fellowship of Australia (former president of Tasmanian branch). *Awards, honors:* Medals for *Devils Hill* as Boys' Clubs of U.S.A. Choice, 1961 and for *Tiger in the Bush,* 1957, *Devils Hill,* 1959, and *Tangara,* 1961, each as best Australian children's book of the year.

NAN CHAUNCY

Summer showed in the depth of the blue sky and in the dazzle on the wave crests as the yacht *Timmari* sped south, running down the east coast of Tasmania before a strong breeze. ■ (From *High and Haunted Island* by Nan Chauncy. Illustrated by Victor G. Ambrus.)

WRITINGS: They Found a Cave, 1949, *World's End was Home,* 1955, *A Fortune for the Brave,* 1956, *Tiger in the Bush,* 1957, *Devils Hill* (ALA Notable Book), 1958, *The Secret Friends* (published in Australia as *Tangara*), 1960, *Half A World Away,* 1962, *The Roaring 40,* 1963, *High and Haunted Island,* Oxford University Press, 1964, *Mathinna's People,* Oxford University Press, 1967, *Lizzie Lights,* Oxford University Press, 1968, *The Lighthouse Keeper's Son,* Oxford University Press, 1969 (all published by Watts except where noted). Scripts for Australian Broadcasting Commission. Contributor to *Wild Life Quadrant,* and other Australian magazines.

SIDELIGHTS: "The valley which is my home is a delight to children. They love the long twisting valley with its steep tree-covered walls, its wild mountain creek, and endless sandstone caves. Here my father—a civil engineer—brought his tribe of six children from England, meaning to clear the bush, plant an orchard (in what was then a great apple growing district) build a home and settle.

"Picture the delight of conventionally brought up children of those days let loose in this wonderland. Everything was a huge adventure, the world full of glorious discoveries. Naturally, the valley, the animals, and the adventures have found their way into my books. . . ."

Ms. Chauncy lived in the home built by her father in Chauncy Vale, which she and her husband turned into a wild life sanctuary. Many of the animals in the sanctuary appeared in her books.

All of Ms. Chauncy's books have been, or are being, translated into thirteen languages and some into Braille. *They Found a Cave* has been made into a film.

FOR MORE INFORMATION SEE: Roger Lancelyn Greer, *Tellers of Tales,* Watts, 1965; *Horn Book,* August, 1969; *Third Book of Junior Authors,* edited by de Montreville and Hill, H. W. Wilson, 1972.

(Died May 1, 1970)

CHEN, Tony 1929-

PERSONAL: Born January 3, 1929, in West Indies; son of Arthur (a merchant) and Marie (Ho Pow) Chen; married Pura DeCastro, 1966; children: Richard, David. *Education:* Art Career School, student, 1949-51; Pratt Institute, B.F.A. (cum Laude), 1955. *Religion:* Roman Catholic. *Home:* 53-31 96th St., Corona, N.Y. 11368.

TONY CHEN

44

What hunter would like to have its head
As a trophy to decorate his wall?
■ (From *Run, Zebra, Run* by Tony Chen. Illustrated by the author.)

CAREER: Newsweek, New York, N.Y., art director, 1961-72; Nassau Community College, Garden City, N.Y., instructor in art, 1972-73. Painter and sculptor, with one-man shows in New York; writer and illustrator of books for children. *Awards, honors:* Awards from Society of Illustrators and from Creativity '71; American Institute of Graphic Arts book award, 1972; Society of Illustrators Award of Excellence, 1972; Creativity Award, *Art Direction Magazine,* 1972; *Honshi* was a Children's Book Showcase Title, 1973.

WRITINGS—Self-illustrated children's book: *Run, Zebra Run,* Lothrop, 1972.

Illustrator: Helen E. Buckley, *Too Many Crackers,* Lothrop, 1962: Isabelle Chang, *Tales From Old China,* Random House, 1969; Herbert H. Wong and Matthew F. Vessel, *Pond Life: Watching Animals Find Food,* Addison-Wesley, 1970; Hannah Johnson, *Hello, Small Sparrow,* Lothrop, 1971; Edith Hurd, *The White Horse,* Harper, 1971; Ruth Dale, *Do You Know a Cat?,* Singer, 1971; Doris Evans, *Breakfast with the Birds,* Putnam, 1972; Aline Glasgow, *Honshi,* Parents' Magazine Press, 1972; *Dakota Sons,* Harper, 1972; Seymour Simon, *The Rockhound Book,* Viking, 1973; Laurence Pringle, *Follow a Fisher,* Crowell, 1973; Applebaum and Cox, *A Not So Ugly Friend,* Holt, 1973; Charlotte Pomerantz, *The Princess and the Admiral,* Addison-Wesley, 1974.

SIDELIGHTS: Much of Chen's painting and sculpture is in private collections.

HOBBIES AND OTHER INTERESTS: Collecting art, especially animal sculpture from diverse cultures.

FOR MORE INFORMATION SEE: American Artist, May, 1972; *New York Times Book Review,* May 7, 1972; *Publishers Weekly,* May 22, 1972.

CHETIN, Helen 1922-

PERSONAL: Born July 6, 1922; daughter of Guy Edward (a physician) and Helen (Collins) Campbell; married Adnan Chetin (a geologist); children: Timur, Sara. *Education:* Attended University of Texas, 1943-45.

CAREER: Stanford University, Stanford, Calif., Institute for Mathematical Studies in the Social Sciences, writer, 1966-71.

WRITINGS: Tales from an African Drum. (Child Study Association book list), Harcourt, 1971; *Perihan's Promise, Turkish Relatives and a Dirty Old Imam,* Houghton, 1973.

WORK IN PROGRESS: Two children's books, *The Story of an Aztec Prince* and *How Far is Berkeley?;* a novel about women: *The Flower of Friendship Fades.*

CHWAST, Jacqueline 1932-

PERSONAL: Surname is pronounced Quast; born January 1, 1932, in Newark, N.J.; daughter of William (a cab driver and landlord) and Lillian (Averman) Weiner; married Seymour Chwast (an artist and designer), December 25, 1953 (divorced); children: Eve Raina, Pamela Ileen. *Education:* Studied at Newark School of Fine and Industrial Art, 1949-52, and at Art Students' League, New York. *Residence:* New York, N.Y.

CAREER: Illustrator of children's books.

WRITINGS—Self-illustrated: *When the Baby Sitter Didn't Come,* Harcourt, 1967; *How Mr. Berry Found a Home and Happiness Forever,* Simon & Schuster, 1968.

Illustrator: Myra Cohn Livingston, *Whispers and Other Poems,* Harcourt, 1958; Myra Cohn Livingston, *Wide Awake and Other Poems,* Harcourt, 1959; Jean L. Latham and Bee Lewi, *The Cuckoo that Couldn't Count,* Macmillan, 1961; Sandol S. Warburg, *I Like You,* Houghton, 1965; Barbara Dana, *Spencer and His Friends,* Atheneum, 1966; Peggy Clifford, *Elliot,* Houghton, 1967; Mary Neville, *The First and Last Annual Pet Parade,* Pantheon, 1968; Sandol S. Warburg, *Hooray for Us,* Houghton, 1970; William Cole, *Aunt Bella's Umbrella,* Doubleday, 1970; Jay Williams, *A Present from a Bird,* Parents' Magazine Press, 1971; Marcia Newfield, *Iggy,* Houghton, 1972; Jean-Jacques Larrea, *Dairy of a Paper Boy,* new edition, Putnam, 1972; Howard E. Smith, Jr., *Play With the Wind,* McGraw, 1972.

■ (From *Aunt Bella's Umbrella* by William Cole. Illustrated by Jacqueline Chwast.)

JACQUELINE CHWAST

WORK IN PROGRESS: Writing and illustrating with cut-paper, *Riches*, a book about two women who want and get too much, for publication by Holt; *Oh Michael*, also for Holt.

SIDELIGHTS: "My intentions in my work are to offer children the feeling that books are a warm, entertaining and enriching place to spend time in. My ideas about my work are changing. Design has become more important. But humor and animation are constant in importance. . . ."

FOR MORE INFORMATION SEE: *Graphis*, Volume 27, 1971/72, January, 1973.

CLARKE, Michael
See NEWLON, Clarke

CLEAVER, Carole 1934-

PERSONAL: Born May 21, 1934, in Ridgewood, N.J.; daughter. of Earl Atherton and Carroll (Amos) Cleaver; married Selden Rodman (a writer), November 7, 1962; children: Carla Pamela, Van Nostrand. *Education:* Rutgers University, student, 1952-53; other courses at Columbia University, Fairleigh Dickinson University, and University of Hawaii. *Politics:* Republican (conservative). *Religion:* Protestant. *Home:* 659 Ramapo Valley Rd., Oakland, N.J. 07436.

CAREER: Mademoiselle, New York, N.Y., assistant beauty editor, 1956-59; *Wyckoff News,* Wyckoff, N.J., editor, 1959-62; free-lance writer and editor. Member of Republican County Committee, Bergen County, N.J., 1956-62.

WRITINGS: (With husband, Selden Rodman) *Horace Pippin: The Artist as a Black American* (juvenile), Doubleday, 1972. Contributor of articles and reviews to *Harper's Bazaar, New Leader,* and other magazines.

WORK IN PROGRESS: A biography of Ben Shahn; a novel entitled *The Keeper of the Clocks.*

FOR MORE INFORMATION SEE: New York Times Book Review, May 7, 1972.

CAROLE CLEAVER

CONFORD, Ellen 1942-

PERSONAL: Born March 20, 1942, in New York, N.Y.; daughter of Harry and Lillian (Pfeffer) Schaffer; married David Conford (an English professor), November 23, 1960; children: Michael. *Education:* Hofstra College (now Hofstra University), student, 1959-62. *Home:* 70 Roy Ave., Massapequa, N.Y. 11758.

WRITINGS: Impossible, Possum (Junior Literary Guild selection), Little, Brown, 1971; *Why Can't I Be William?,* Little, Brown, 1972; *Dreams of Victory* (Junior Literary Guild Selection), Little, Brown, 1973; *Felicia the Critic* (Junior Literary Guild selection), Little, Brown, 1973; *Just the Thing for Geraldine,* Little, Brown, 1974; *Me and the Terrible Two,* Little, Brown, 1974. Contributor of stories and poems to national periodicals, including *Teen, Reader's Digest,* and *Modern Bride.*

SIDELIGHTS: "I have enjoyed writing since I was in the third grade. My first attempts at poetry were to put assigned spelling words into poems instead of simply using each word in a separate and unrelated sentence. I don't think those poems were very good, or even made much sense, but my teacher was pleased with them and encouraged me with praise and enthusiasm.

"I wrote my first book for young children, *Impossible, Possum,* when my own son was four years old. I had been looking for a book for him at the library one day, and didn't like any of the books I found. I thought, 'I can write a better story than some of these.' So I went home and set to work.

"The books I have been writing recently are for older children, ages nine-to-twelve. My ideas and characters for these books (i.e., *Dreams of Victory* and *Felicia the Critic*) come from my own life. My characters are not duplicates of anyone I know, but their personalities, mannerisms and characteristics are derived from those of adults and children I've known myself.

"I really don't know where I get the ideas for my books. Usually the stories develop from the personality of the main character, as in Felicia (the critic) and Victory (the dreamer). When I get an idea for a book, I just jot it down in one sentence, usually, and let it stay in the back of my mind for awhile. If it's a good idea, it usually begins to take shape as a book without my even consciously working at it. And it stays in my mind until I do something about it. (Write it.) If it doesn't keep coming back to me, if it doesn't get bigger and better, it doesn't become a book. For an idea to turn into a book, it has to bother you and haunt you until it forces you to write it.

"When I am not writing (and I only devote two or three hours a day to my writing) I am taking care of my family, including a dog and a cat. I like to cook and bake, play chess, do crossword puzzles, watch old movies on television and read. I love to read, especially mysteries and cookbooks."

FOR MORE INFORMATION SEE: Junior Literary Guild Catalogue, March, 1973; *New York Times Book Review,* June 24, 1973, November 4, 1973; *Horn Book,* December, 1973.

"I don't understand it," she said. "All possums hang by their tails and sleep upside down. Why can't you?" ■ (From *Impossible, Possum* by Ellen Conford. Illustrated by Rosemary Wells.)

ELLEN CONFORD

COONEY, Barbara 1917-

PERSONAL: Born August 6, 1917, in Brooklyn, N.Y.; daughter of Russell Schenck and Mae Evelyn (Bossert) Cooney; married Charles Talbot Porter (a medical doctor), 1949; children: Gretel, Barnaby, Charles Talbot, Phoebe. *Education:* Briarcliff School, graduate, 1934; Smith College, B.A., 1938. *Home and office:* Pepperell, Mass.

CAREER: Free-lance author and illustrator, 1938—. *Military service:* Women's Army Corps, World War II; became second lieutenant. *Awards, honors:* Caldecott Medal for the year's best illustrated book for children, for *Chanticleer and the Fox,* 1958.

WRITINGS—Author and illustrator: *King of Wreck Island,* Farrar & Rinehart, 1941; *The Kellyhorns,* Farrar & Rinehart, 1942; *Captain Pottle's House,* Farrar, 1943; (adapter and illustrator) Chaucer's *Chanticleer and the Fox,* Crowell, 1958; *The Little Juggler,* Hastings, 1961; *Cock Robin,* Scribner, 1965; *Snow White and Rose Red,* Delacorte, 1965; *Christmas,* Crowell, 1967; *Little Prayer,* Hastings, 1967; *Garland and Games and Other Diversions,* Holt, 1969.

Illustrator: Carl Malmberg, *Ake and His World,* Farrar & Rinehart, 1940; Seidlin, *Green Wagons,* Houghton, 1943; Anne Molloy, *Shooting Star Farm,* Houghton, 1946; Lee Kingman, *Rocky Summer,* Houghton, 1948; Child Study Association of America, *Read Me Another Story,* Crowell, 1949; Rutherford Montgomery, *Kildee House,* Doubleday, 1949; Phyllis Krasilovsky, *The Man Who Didn't Wash His Dishes,* Doubleday, 1950; Ruth C. Seeger, *Animal Folk Songs for Children,* Doubleday, 1950; Leonard, *Graymouse Family,* Crowell, 1950; Child Study Association of America, *Read Me More Stories,* Crowell, 1951; Barbara Reynolds, *Pepper,* Scribner, 1952; Miriam E. Mason, *Yours, with Love Kate,* Houghton, 1952; Margaret W. Brown, *Christmas in the Barn,* Crowell, 1952; Ruth C. Seeger, *American Folk Songs for Children,* Doubleday, 1953; Ruth C. Seeger, *American Folk Songs for Christmas,* Doubleday, 1953; Leonard, *Grandfather Whiskers, M.D.,* Crowell, 1953; Lee Kingman, *Peter's Long Walk,* Doubleday, 1953; Margaret G. Otto, *Pumpkin, Ginger and Spice,* Holt, 1954; Helen Kay, *Snow Birthday,* Farrar, Straus, 1955; Louisa M. Alcott, *Little Women,* Crowell, 1955; Kent, *Brookline Trunk,* Houghton, 1955; Catherine S. McEwen, *Away We Go: One-Hundred Poems for the Very Young,* Crowell, 1956; Margaret G. Otto, *Little Brown Horse,* Knopf, 1959.

In the garden grew two rose-bushes, one red and the other white, and because the children were like the roses which grew on the bushes, one was named Snow-White and the other Rose-Red. ■ (From *Snow-White and Rose-Red* by Barbara Cooney. Illustrated by the author.)

Something about the Author

Francis Steegmuller, *Le Hibou et la Poussiquette*, Little, Brown, 1961; Walter De La Mare, *Peacock Pie*, Knopf, 1961; Margaret W. Brown, *Where Have You Been?*, Hastings, 1963; Sarah O. Jewett, *White Heron*, Crowell, 1963; Virginia Haviland, *Favorite Fairy Tales Told in Spain*, Little, Brown, 1963; Field, *Papillot, Clignot et Dodo*, Farrar, Straus, 1964; Hugh Latham, *Mother Goose in French*, Crowell, 1964; Anne Molloy, *Shaun and the Boat*, Hastings House, 1965; Jane Goodsell, *Katie's Magic Glasses*, Houghton, 1965; Samuel F. Morse, *All in a Suitcase*, Little, Brown, 1966; Aldous Huxley, *Crowns of Pearblossom*, Random House, 1967; Alastair Reid and Anthony Kerrigan, *Mother Goose in Spanish*, Crowell, 1968; Edward Lear, *The Owl and the Pussycat*, Little, Brown, 1969; Natalia M. Belting, *Christmas Folk*, Holt, 1969; William Wise, *The Lazy Young Duke of Dundee*, Rand, 1970; Eugene Field, *Wynken, Blynken, and Nod*, Hastings House, 1970; Penelope Proddow, *Dionysus and the Pirates*, Doubleday, 1970; Penelope Proddow, *Hermes, Lord of Robbers*, Doubleday, 1971; Penelope Proddow, *Demeter and Persephone*, Doubleday, 1972; also illustrated Noah Webster, *American Speller*, Crowell; Felix Salten, *Bambi*, Simon & Schuster; Lee Kingman, *Best Christmas*, Doubleday.

BARBARA COONEY

FOR MORE INFORMATION SEE: Illustrators of Children's Books: 1744-1945, Horn Book, 1947; *Illustrators of Children's Books: 1946-1956*, Horn Book, 1958; *More Junior Authors*, edited by Muriel Fuller, H. W. Wilson, 1963; *Newbery & Caldecott Medal Books: 1956-1965*, edited by Lee Kingman, Horn Book, 1965; Diana Klemin, *The Art of Art for Children's Books*, Clarkson Potter, 1966; Jean Poindexter Colby, *Writing, Illustrating and Editing Children's Books*, Hastings House, 1967; *Illustrators of Children's Books: 1957-1966*, Horn Book, 1968; Elinor W. Field, *Horn Book Reflections*, Horn Book, 1969; Lee Bennett Hopkins, *Books Are By People*, Citation Press, 1969; *Horn Book*, October, 1969.

COURLANDER, Harold   1908-

PERSONAL: Born September 18, 1908, in Indianapolis, Ind.; son of David (a primitive painter) and Tillie (Oppenheim) Courlander; married Emma Meltzer, June 18, 1949; children: Erika Courlander Wolfson, Michael, Susan. *Education:* University of Michigan, B.A., 1931. *Home:* 5512 Brite Dr., Bethesda, Md. 20034. *Office:* Voice of America, U.S. Information Agency, Washington, D.C.

CAREER: Farmer in Romeo, Mich., 1933-38; Douglas Aircraft Co., Eritrea (now Ethiopia), historian, 1942-43; U.S. Office of War Information, New York, N.Y., and Bombay, India, editor, 1943-45; U.S. Information Agency, Voice of America, New York, N.Y., editor, 1945-54; U.S. Mission to United Nations, New York, N.Y., press officer, 1954; United Nations, New York, N.Y., writer and editor on *United Nations Review*, 1956-59; U.S. Information Agency, Voice of America, Washington, D.C., senior political analyst, 1960—. *Awards, honors:* Avery Hopwood Award, 1931, 1932; Franz Boas Fund research grant for folklore study in Dominican Republic, 1939; American Council of Learned Societies grants for research in Haiti, 1939, 1940; American Philosophical Society grants for studies in New World Negro cultures, 1946, 1954, 1955; Wenner-Gren Foundation grants for work in United States and West Indian Negro folk music, 1946, 1954, 1955, 1956, 1962, and for work with Hopi Indians, 1971; Guggenheim fellowships for studies in African and Afro-American cultures, 1948, 1955.

WRITINGS: Swamp Mud, Blue Ox Press, 1936; *Home to Langford County,* Blue Ox Press, 1938; *Haiti Singing,* University of North Carolina Press, 1939; *The Caballero,* Farrar & Rinehart, 1940.

The Drum and the Hoe, Life and Lore of the Haitian People, University of California Press, 1960; *Shaping Our Times: What the United Nations Is and Does,* Oceana, 1960; *On Recognizing the Human Species,* One Nation Library, 1960; *Negro Songs From Alabama,* Oak, 1960; *The Big Old World of Richard Creeks,* Chilton, 1962; *Negro Folk Music U.S.A.,* Columbia University Press, 1963; (contributor to monograph) *Religion and Politics in Haiti,* Institute for Cross-Cultural Research, 1966; *The African,* Crown, 1967; *The Son of the Leopard,* Crown, 1974.

Folk tale collections: *Uncle Bouqui of Haiti,* Morrow, 1942; (with George Herzog) *The Cow-Tail Switch, and Other West African Stories,* Henry Holt, 1947; *Kantchil's*

Lime Pit, and Other Stories from Indonesia, Harcourt, 1950; (with Wolf Leslau) *The Fire on the Mountain, and Other Ethiopian Stories,* Henry Holt, 1950; *Ride With the Sun,* Whittlesey House, 1955; *Terrapin's Pot of Sense,* Henry Holt, 1957; *The Hat Shaking Dance, and Other Tales from the Gold Coast,* Harcourt, 1957; *The Tiger's Whisker,* Harcourt, 1959; *The King's Drum,* Harcourt, 1962; *The Piece of Fire, and Other Haitian Tales,* Harcourt, 1964; *Olode the Hunter and Other Tales From Nigeria,* Harcourt, 1968; *People of the Short Blue Corn* (Child Study Association Book list), Harcourt, 1970; *The Fourth World of the Hopis,* Crown, 1971; *Tales of Yoruba Gods and Heroes,* Crown, 1973.

Contributor: *Miscelanea de estudios dedicados a Fernando Ortiz* [Havana], 1955. Contributor of articles to *Saturday Review, Musical Quarterly, New Republic, Journal of Negro History, Opportunity,* and other periodicals.

Albums, compiled and edited from own field recordings: "Cult Music of Cuba," Ethnic Folkways Library, 1949; "Meringues," Folkways Records, 1950; "Drums of Haiti," Ethnic Folkways Library, 1950; "Folk Music of Haiti," Ethnic Folkways Library, 1950; "Folk Music of Ethiopia," Ethnic Folkways Library, 1951; "Songs and

Spider Grandmother spun a web across part of the opening, and to it she attached a thread from her own body. ■ (From *People of the Short Blue Corn* by Harold Courlander. Illustrated by Enrico Arno.)

Dances of Haiti," Ethnic Folkways Library, 1952; "Haitian Piano," Folkways Records, 1952. Compiler and editor of other collections for Ethnic Folkways Library, including "Caribbean Folk Music," "Folk Music, U.S.A.," "African and Afro-American Drums," "Afro-American Folk Music."

WORK IN PROGRESS: An anthology of African and Afro-American oral literature, for Crown.

FOR MORE INFORMATION SEE: More Junior Authors, edited by Muriel Fuller, H. W. Wilson, 1963; *Atlantic,* January, 1968; *Horn Book,* December, 1970.

CRAIG, Mary Francis 1923-
(Mary Francis Shura)

PERSONAL: Born February 27, 1923; daughter of Jack Fant and Mary (Milstead) Young; married Daniel C. Shura, 1943 (died 1959); married Raymond Craig, 1961; children: (first marriage) Marianne, Daniel C., Alice Barrett; (second marriage) Mary Forsha. *Education:* Attended Maryville State College. *Home:* 10 Bayview, Belvedere-Tiburon, Calif. 94920. *Agent:* (Juvenile) Dorothy Markinko, (adult) Patricia Schartle, both McIntosh and Otis, Inc., 18 East 41st St., New York, N.Y. 10017.

HAROLD COURLANDER

CAREER: Free-lance writer. Member: National League of American Pen Women, Theta Sigma Phi.

WRITINGS—All under name Mary Francis Shura: *Simple Spigott*, Knopf, 1960; *The Garret of Greta McGraw*, Knopf, 1961; *Mary's Marvelous Mouse*, Knopf, 1962; *Nearsighted Knight*, Knopf, 1964; *Run Away Home*, Knopf, 1965; *Shoefull of Shamrock*, Atheneum, 1965; *A Tale of Middle Length*, Atheneum, 1966; *Backwards For Luck*, Knopf, 1967; *Pornada*, Atheneum, 1968; *Audhumla and the Blue Valley*, Lothrop, 1969; *The Seven Stone*, Holiday House, 1972.

FOR MORE INFORMATION SEE: *Third Book of Junior Authors*, edited by de Montreville and Hill, H. W. Wilson, 1972.

CRAWFORD, Deborah   1922-

PERSONAL: Born January 16, 1922, in Elizabeth, N.J.; daughter of Edward Choate and Ruth (Pierce) Stonaker; married Andrew W. Crawford, Jr., 1952 (divorced, 1960). *Education:* Took night courses for six years in the 1950's at Columbia University, New York University, and New School for Social Research. *Politics:* Democrat ("usually"). *Religion:* Protestant ("lapsed"). *Home:* 54 West 16th St., New York, N.Y. 10011.

CAREER: Ruthrauff & Ryan, New York, N.Y., advertising copywriter, 1947-49; Grey Advertising, New York, N.Y., copywriter, 1952-54; Book-of-the-Month Club, New York, N.Y., reviewer, 1954—. Researcher for Willy Ley, 1960-69. *Member:* Authors Guild.

WRITINGS—Juvenile: *Pepper! The Story of a Parakeet*, Crown, 1966; *The King's Astronomer, William Herschel*

DEBORAH CRAWFORD

(foreword by Willy Ley), Messner, 1968; *Lise Meitner, Atomic Pioneer*, Crown, 1969; *Four Women in a Violent Time*, Crown, 1970; *Somebody Will Miss Me*, Crown, 1971; *Franz Kafka, Man Out of Step*, Crown, 1973. Contributor to *Magazine of Fantasy and Science Fiction* and *Saint.*

WORK IN PROGRESS: A biography of the science writer, Willy Ley, who died in 1969.

HOBBIES AND OTHER INTERESTS: Classical music, sailing, traveling to Europe and the Caribbean, walking, nature in general and birds in particular.

FOR MORE INFORMATION SEE: *Best Sellers*, April 1, 1970, April 15, 1971; *Library Journal*, May 15, 1970; *Horn Book*, April, 1971, April, 1972, June, 1973.

CROWE, Bettina Lum   1911-
(Peter Lum)

PERSONAL: Born April 27, 1911, in Minneapolis, Minn.; daughter of Burt Francis (a lawyer) and Bertha (an artist; maiden name, Bull) Lum; married Colin Crowe (now with British Diplomatic Service), May 21, 1938. *Education:* Educated privately. *Religion:* Episcopalian. *Agent:* Curtis Brown Ltd., 13 King St., London W.C.2, England.

CAREER: Writer, whose early life was spent shuttling between the United States and the Orient with artist-mother, being much of the time in Peking, China; now resident of New York, N.Y., where husband is British Ambassador to the United Nations. *Member:* Society of Women Geographers, Royal Central Asian Society.

WRITINGS: *Fairy Tales of China*, Dutton, 1959; *The Holiday Moon*, Abelard, 1963; *Fairy Tales from the Barbary Coast*, Muller, 1967; *The Growth of Civilization in East Asia* (juvenile); S. G. Phillips, 1969; *Six Centuries in East Asia: China, Japan and Korea from 14th Century to 1912*, S. G. Phillips, 1973.

Under pseudonym Peter Lum: *Stars in Our Heaven*, Pantheon, 1948; *Fabulous Beasts*, Pantheon, 1951; *Peking 1950-53*, R. Hale, 1958; *The Purple Barrier: The Great Wall of China*, R. Hale, 1960; *Italian Fairy Tales*, Muller, 1963.

SIDELIGHTS: "I came to write because it was something I could do anywhere in a traveling life. I wrote the first book, *Stars in Our Heaven*, because I wanted to interest people in learning to recognize stars and constellations, as I had, by knowing the legends about them. I am always interested in myths and legends. Recently, however, I have been involved in trying to make complicated subjects—such as East Asian history—clear to readers, especially the young, who are unfamiliar with them. It seems important to simplify such subjects, although of course it is even more important to be accurate on facts, dates, etc.

"I write on the typewriter, but very slowly, constantly rewriting, so that the final version is probably the fifth or sixth."

HOBBIES AND OTHER INTERESTS: Far and Middle East, myths and legends, the stars, bird-watching.

By this time the giant had had more than enough of his guest, but he was so afraid of him that he did not know how to get rid of him. ■ (From *Italian Fairy Tales* retold by Peter Lum. Illustrated by Harry and Ilse Toothill.)

CRUZ, Ray(mond) 1933-

PERSONAL: Born June 30, 1933, in New York, N.Y.; son of Ramon (a laborer and construction worker) and Rosaline (Mas-Peralta) Cruz. *Education:* Studied at High School of Art and Design, New York, 1948-51, Pratt Institute, 1951-53, and Cooper Union, 1953-57. *Politics:* "Apolitical." *Home:* 207 West 11th St., New York, N.Y. 10014.

CAREER: Started free-lance illustrating before his graduation from Cooper Union; designed textiles and wallpapers for New Group Studio, 1963, and packaging for cosmetic firms, 1965; has done illustrating for most of the major advertising agencies in New York and for ten book publishers. Work has been exhibited at Society of Illustrators shows, at Doyle, Dane, Benton & Bowles, and McCann-Erickson. *Military service:* U.S. Navy, 1953. *Member:* Society of Illustrators. *Awards, honors:* Honorable mention in Advertising Club of New York annual awards.

ILLUSTRATOR: Carol MacGregor, *Storybook Cookbook,* Doubleday, 1967; Elizabeth Seifert, *White Rose and Ragged Staff,* Bobbs, 1968; Jane Yolen, *Wizard of Washington Square,* World Publishing, 1969; E. M. Preston, *Horrible Hepzibah,* Viking, 1970; Mary Lystad, *Jennifer Takes Over P.S.94,* Putnam, 1971; M. Jean Craig, *Where Do I Belong?,* Four Winds, 1971; Judith Viorst, *Alexander and the Terrible, Horrible, No-Good, Very Bad Day,* Atheneum, 1972; Susan Thorndike, compiler, *The Electric Radish and Other Jokes,* Doubleday, 1973.

WORK IN PROGRESS: Illustrating a group of fairy tales in full color, "a personal project and I do not expect its publication."

HOBBIES AND OTHER INTERESTS: Art history, archaeology, conservation.

FOR MORE INFORMATION SEE: Junior Literary Guild Catalogue, September, 1972; *Horn Book,* June, 1973.

RAY CRUZ

■ (From *Alexander and the Terrible, Horrible, No Good, Very Bad Day* by Judith Viorst. Illustrated by Ray Cruz.)

CUFFARI, Richard 1925-

PERSONAL: Born March 2, 1925, in Brooklyn, N.Y.; married Phyllis Klie, February 18, 1950; children: Richard, Ellen, William, David. *Education:* Pratt Institute, student, 1946-49. *Home and studio:* 1320 East 27th St., Brooklyn, N.Y. 11210.

CAREER: Painter and illustrator; worked for various art studios prior to 1968; free-lance book illustrator, 1968—. *Military service:* U.S. Army, 1943-46; served in Europe. *Member:* Society of Illustrators, American Institute of Graphic Arts. *Awards, honors:* Society of Illustrators "Citation of Merit," 1967-68, 1969-70; *Escape from the Evil Prophecy* was a Children's Book Showcase Title, 1974.

ILLUSTRATOR: Kenneth Grahame, *The Wind in the Willows,* Grosset, 1966; Dorothy Aldis, *Nothing Is Impossible: The Story of Beatrix Potter* (Junior Literary Guild selection), Atheneum, 1969; Cecilia Holland, *The Ghost on the Steppe,* Atheneum, 1969; Alice Marriott, *Winter Telling Stories,* Crowell, 1969; Richard B. Erno, *Billy Lightfoot,* Crown, 1969; Richard O'Connor, *The Common Sense of Tom Paine,* McGraw, 1969.

Gene Smith, *The Winner,* Cowles, 1970; Jesse Stuart, *Old Ben,* McGraw, 1970; Ewan Clarkson, *Halic: The Story of a Gray Seal,* Dutton, 1970; Carla Greene, *Gregor Mendel,* Dial, 1970; T. B. Perara and Wallace Orlowsky, *Who Will Wash the River?,* Coward, 1970; Gunilla B. Norris, *The Top Step,* Atheneum, 1970; Carla Greene, *Before the Dinosaurs,* Bobbs, 1970; Miriam Gurko, *Indian America: The Black Hawk War,* Crowell, 1970; Robert Martin, *Yesterday's People,* Doubleday, 1970; Hans Koningsberger, *The Golden Keys,* Doubleday, 1970; Rosemary Weir, *The Lion and the Rose,* Farrar, Straus, 1970; James Playsted Wood, *The People of Concord,* Seabury, 1970.

T. B. Perara and Wallace Orlowsky, *Who Will Clean the Air?,* Coward, 1971; Eileen Thompson, *The Golden Coyote* (Junior Literary Guild selection), Simon & Schuster, 1971; Nancy Garden, *What Happened in Marston?,* Four Winds, 1971; Sylvia Louise Engdahl, *The Far Side of Evil,* Atheneum, 1971; John L. Hoke, *Ecology,* Watts, 1971; Sophia Harvati Fenton, *Ancient Rome,* Holt, 1971; Elizabeth S. Helfman, *The Bushmen and Their Stories,* Seabury, 1971; Constance Fecher, *The Link Boys,* Farrar, Straus, 1971; Mirra Ginsburg, editor and translator, *The Kaha Bird,* Crown, 1971; Barbara Corcoran, *This is a Recording,* Atheneum, 1971; Kenneth Rudeen, *Jackie Robinson,* Crowell, 1971; Mary Towne, *The Glass Room,* Farrar, Straus, 1971; Robert Froman, *Hot and Cold and Inbetween,* Grosset, 1971; Elizabeth Ladd, *The Indians on the Bonnet,* Morrow, 1971; Edna Barth, *I'm Nobody, Who Are You?,* Seabury, 1971; Harold S. Longman, *Andron and the Magician,* Seabury, 1971.

Franklin Russell, "Pond Trilogy," with titles of *Datra the Muskrat, Corvus the Crow,* and *Lotor the Raccoon,* Four Winds, 1972; Roma Gans, *Water for Dinosaurs and You,* Crowell, 1972; Elizabeth S. Helfman, *Maypoles and Wood Demons: The Meaning of Trees,* Seabury, 1972; Ronald Syme, *Juarez: The Founder of Modern Mexico,* Morrow, 1972; Doris Portwood Evans, *Mr. Charley's Chopsticks,* Coward, 1972; Joseph Claro, *I Can Predict the Future,* Lothrop, 1972; Eth Clifford, *The Year of the Three-Legged Deer,* Houghton, 1972; Mary K. Phelan, *Mr. Lincoln's Inaugural Journey,* Crowell, 1972; Ross E. Hutchins, *The Carpenter Bee,* Addison-Wesley, 1972; Sylvia Louise Engdahl, *This Star Shall Abide,* Atheneum, 1972; Irwin Touster & Richard Curtis, *The Perez Arson Mystery,* Dial, 1972; Touster & Curtis, *The Runaway Bus Mystery,* Dial, 1972; Virginia Lee, *The Magic Moth,* Seabury, 1972; Anne Molloy, *The Years Before the Mayflower,* Hastings House, 1972; Julius Schwartz, *Magnify and Find Out Why,* McGraw, 1972.

Meridel Le Sueur, *Conquistadores,* Watts, 1973; Rosemary Weir, *The Blood Royal,* Farrar, Straus, 1973; Peggy Mann, *My Dad Lives in a Downtown Hotel,* Doubleday, 1973; Sylvia L. Engdahl, *Beyond the Tomorrow Mountains,* Atheneum, 1973; Rosemary Sutcliff, *The Capricorn Bracelet,* Walck, 1973; Martha Bacon, *In the Company of Clowns,* Little, Brown, 1973; Keith Robertson, *In Search of a Sand Hill Crane,* Viking, 1973; D. C. Ipsen, *Eye of the Whirlwind,* Addison-Wesley, 1973; Dale Fife, *Ride the Crooked Wind* (Junior Literary Guild selection), Coward, 1973; Jacqueline Jackson and William Perlmutter, *The Endless Pavement* (Junior Literary Guild Selection), Seabury, 1973; Robert Newman, *The Testing of Tertius,* Atheneum, 1973; Wilma Pitchford Hayes, *Little Yellow Fur,* Coward, 1973; Edward R. Riccuti, *Dancers on the Beach,* Crowell, 1973; Theodore Taylor, *Rebellion Town: Williamsburg, 1776,* Crowell, 1973; Alice Wellman, *Small Boy Chuku,* Houghton, 1973; Lee Kingman, *Escape from the Evil Prophecy,* Houghton, 1973; Andrew J. Offutt, *The Galactic Rejects,* Lothrop, 1973; Janet Townsend, *The Comic Book Mystery,* Pantheon, 1973; *The Story of Pierre de la Verendrye: Fur Traders of the North,* Morrow, 1973; Stella Pevsner, *Call Me Heller, That's My Name,* Seabury, 1973; Betsy Byars, *The Winged Colt of Casa Mia,* Viking, 1973.

■ (From *The Link Boys* by Constance Fecher. Illustrated by Richard Cuffari.)

RICHARD CUFFARI

SIDELIGHTS: "Besides watching my children grow, which is always a source of wonderment, my principal enjoyments are drawing, painting, listening to music and cooking.

"I have always been fascinated by things historical; events, personalities, how people lived and how they looked. I believe that the study of these things help provide insight into the present.

"In illustrating children's books, I have found an outlet for the things that interest me. Conversely, I hope that these interests lend vitality to my drawings and make them of greater use to children.

"I think that working with or for children in any way is a privilege."

FOR MORE INFORMATION SEE: Commonweal, May 21, 1971; *Saturday Review,* May 20, 1972; *Junior Literary Guild Catalogue,* March, 1973; *Publishers Weekly,* April 23, 1973.

DAVIS, Christopher   1928-

PERSONAL: Born October 23, 1928, in Philadelphia, Pa.; son of Edward (a lawyer) and Josephine (Blitzstein) Davis; married Sonia Fogg, June 6, 1953; children: Kirby, Katherine, Emily, Sarah. *Education:* University of Pennsylvania, A.B., 1955. *Agent:* William Morris Agency, 1350 Avenue of the Americas, New York, N.Y.

CAREER: Free-lance writer. University of Pennsylvania, Philadelphia, lecturer in creative writing, 1958-69; Bowling Green State University, Bowling Green, Ohio, lecturer in graduate school of writing, 1970. *Member:* Authors Guild, P.E.N., Phi Beta Kappa. *Awards, honors:* National Endowment for the Arts (fellow), 1967-68; Guggenheim (fellow), 1972-73.

WRITINGS: Lost Summer, Harcourt, 1958; *First Family,* Coward, 1961; *A Kind of Darkness,* Hart-Davis, 1962; *Belmarch,* Viking, 1964; *Sad Adam-Glad Adam* (juvenile), Macmillan, 1966; *The Shamir of Dachau,* 1966; *Ishmael,* 1967; *A Peep into the 20th Century,* Harper, 1971; *The Producer* (nonfiction), 1972. Contributor of poetry, stories, and nonfiction to *The Listener, Tempo de Letteratura, Saturday Evening Post, Der Monat, Esquire, Argosy, Philadelphia Bulletin, Holiday, West, Travel & Leisure,* and *Audience.* Story included in *O'Henry Prize Stories, 1966;* article in *Best Magazine Articles, 1968.*

WORK IN PROGRESS: A novel, *The Sun in Mid-Career.*

SIDELIGHTS: "I am glad to have written a book for children because I enjoyed writing it, which is more than I can say for the novels. When books are made particularly for young people past the age of about twelve, I become uneasy, thinking that perhaps writers should always be writing for everyone and that readers—never mind their age—who love to read should read everything that promises to be good."

CHRISTOPHER DAVIS

[He] winked one eye. He winked the other eye. He winked at a fly. He winked at a bird. He winked at Tommy. ■ (From *Sad Adam-Glad Adam* by Christopher Davis. Illustrated by Stan Tusan.)

DAVIS, Julia 1904-
(F. Draco)

PERSONAL: Born July 23, 1904, in Clarksburg, W.Va.; daughter of John W. and Julia (McDonald) Davis; married Charles P. Healy (deceased). *Education:* Wellesley College, student; Barnard College, B.A., 1922. *Home:* 115 Brookstone Dr., Princeton, N.J. *Agent:* Curtis Brown Ltd., 60 East 56th St., New York, N.Y. 10022.

JULIA DAVIS

CAREER: Author. *Member:* Cosmopolitan Club.

WRITINGS: Sword of the Vikings, Dutton, 1927; *Vaino,* Dutton, 1928; *Mountains Are Free,* Dutton, 1929; *Stonewall,* Dutton, 1930; *Remember and Forget,* Dutton, 1931; *Peter Hale,* Dutton, 1932; *No Other White Men,* Dutton, 1937; *The Sun Climbs Slow,* Dutton, 1940; *The Shenandoah,* Rinehart, 1944; *Cloud on the Land,* Rinehart, 1950; *Bridle the Wind,* Rinehart, 1951; *Eagle on the Sun,* Rinehart, 1956; *Legacy of Love,* Harcourt, 1962; *Ride with the Eagle,* Harcourt, 1962; *The Anvil* (play; produced, 1962), Harper, 1963; *A Valley and a Song,* Holt, 1963; *Mount Up,* Harcourt, 1967.

Under pseudonym F. Draco: *The Devil's Church,* Rinehart, 1951; *Cruise With Death,* Rinehart, 1952.

SIDELIGHTS: "My first book, *Sword of the Vikings,* came about because I was living in Denmark and had a friend who had done some very charming illustrations for these Viking legends. She asked me if I would adapt the tales, which are in Denmark's earliest written history, for American young adults. I did so and signed a contract to produce six more books for Dutton.

George hoped the Indians would not hurt her. When she cried, he shook his head at her. You must not make them mad. ■ (From *A Valley and a Song* by Julia Davis. Illustrated by Joan Berg.)

"I have always found it interesting to go to the sites of the events described in the book whenever possible. For example, before writing my book on Lewis and Clark, I followed as nearly as I could, the route that they took across the continent. This helped make it more real to me, and I believe also, to the readers.

"There is not much more to say about how I write except that the study of history has provided me with a great deal of inspiration and that I am a desperate re-writer. *No Other White Men,* for example, was written seven times before I finally felt it ready for publication."

FOR MORE INFORMATION SEE: Junior Book of Authors, edited by Kunitz and Haycraft, H. W. Wilson, 2nd edition, 1951.

DAVIS, Mary Octavia   1901-
(Dutz)

PERSONAL: Born May 11, 1901, in Castroville, Tex.; daughter of Fletcher (a newspaper publisher and writer) and Roberta Octavia (Hopp) Davis. *Education:* Our Lady of the Lake College, B.A., 1930; additional study at University of Texas; graduate of Famous Writers School, 1966. *Religion:* Roman Catholic. *Home and office:* 125 Adams, San Antonio, Tex. 78210.

CAREER: Primary teacher in San Antonio (Tex.) public schools, 1931-69. Has also been camp counselor, playground director, active in children's theater, and exhibitor in art shows. *Member:* National League of American Pen Women, Poetry Society of Texas, River Art Group, King William Conservation Society, Hondo Art League, Delta Kappa Gamma.

"I'm going to the fair to sell my hats." ■ (From *Going to the Fair* by Mary Octavia Davis. Illustrated by Dutz.)

WRITINGS—Self-illustrated, with illustrations under pseudonym Dutz: *Pinkie*, Steck, 1952; *Rickie*, Steck, 1955; *Mouse Trail*, Steck, 1965; *Going to the Fair*, Steck, 1968. Conductor of poetry page and children's columnist in *Fletcher's Farming;* contributor of poetry to other periodicals.

WORK IN PROGRESS: Six children's books—*Dinkie Doodle Bug, Boss, Sunday Haus, Yanaquana Boy, Bird Boy, Old House, Pump Handle,* and *Lady Bug Stew;* composing songs and dances for children, and adult songs.

SIDELIGHTS: "I began writing when I was nine years old—a sob story on an old paper bag. I still have the story. With parents like mine it was natural to be a writer, artist, and teacher. My first drawing was a cartoon for my father from a magazine. It was pretty bad but he thought it was marvelous—the drawing is now hanging on my studio wall.

"My first studio was in our barn, so I head my business letters 'The Barn Studio.' My coat of arms or special sign is a redheaded woodpecker because I had auburn hair and freckles and that's what kids teased me with—'a redheaded pecker wood.' Great fun."

HOBBIES AND OTHER INTERESTS: Makes character dolls.

"He tried to kill my dad. No cat is going to get away with that." ■ (From *The Devil Cat Screamed* by Verne T. Davis. Illustrated by Leslie Goldstein.)

MARY OCTAVIA DAVIS

DAVIS, Verne T(heodore)   1889-1973

PERSONAL: Born August 14, 1889, in Michigan; son of Theodore Thornton and Mary (De Frienne) Davis; married second wife, Minnie Kathrine Bara, 1937; children: (first marriage) Phyllis Eileen Davis Briody. *Education:* University of Valparaiso, student, 1908-10; International Correspondence School, course in concrete engineering. *Home:* 14152 Lemay St., Van Nuys, Calif. 91405.

CAREER: Carpenter, foreman, and general superintendent of construction, 1916-42, working with U.S. Bureau of Reclamation for ten years, Texas Power and Light, Dallas, 1925-31, and with private firms; Vinnell Co., Inc., Alhambra, Calif., superintendent of construction, 1958-60; then retired from construction work and became full-time writer. *Member:* Masonic Order.

WRITINGS: The Time of the Wolves (junior book), Morrow, 1962; *The Gobbler Called* (junior book), Morrow, 1963; *The Runaway Cattle* (junior book), Morrow, 1965; *The Devil Cat Screamed* (youth book), Morrow, 1966; *The Orphan of the Tundra,* Weybright & Talley, 1968.

WORK IN PROGRESS: Pillows of Stone, an adult western; *The Fountain of Youth,* an adult book.

VERNE T. DAVIS

SIDELIGHTS: "I was born in the Michigan lumber woods in 1889. I taught school two years and worked in a flooring plant and automobile body works for several years. I loved the Michigan woods and spent much time with the birds. I knew all the song birds that came regularly to the nest in the territory around my home.

"Since retiring at the age of seventy-one, I still retain my interest in birds and the squirrels in my back yard; taming the squirrels and teaching them various tricks. I have always read anything I have found about birds and animals."

HOBBIES AND OTHER INTERESTS: Sports, nature.

(Died July 15, 1973)

de GRUMMOND, Lena Young

PERSONAL: Born in Centerville, La.; daughter of William J. Young (a merchant) and Amy (Etienne) Young; married Will White de Grummond (deceased); children: Jewel Lynn (Mrs. Richard K. Delaune), Will White. *Education:* University of Southwestern Louisiana, B.A., 1929; Louisiana State University, M.S., Ph.D., 1956. *Religion:* Protestant. *Office:* School of Library Science, University of Southern Mississippi, Hattiesburg, Miss.

CAREER: Teacher and librarian in Louisiana; Louisiana Department of Education, Baton Rouge, state supervisor of school libraries, 1950-65; University of Southern Mississippi, Hattiesburg, associate professor of library science, 1965—. Deep South Writers Conference, director, 1962-64, president, 1970-72. *Member:* Delta Kappa Gamma, Theta Sigma Phi, National League of American Pen Women, (Crescent City branch; president), Authors Guild, Phi Kappa Phi. *Awards, honors:* Modisette Award for best school library, 1959; Phi Lambda Pi National Award, 1972.

LENA YOUNG de GRUMMOND

Something about the Author

Neck and neck they rode. The air was filled with the noise of the racer's shouts, the thud of the horse's hoofs on the hard dirt, and the cheers of the watching crowd. ■ (From *Jeff Davis* by Lena Young de Grummond and Lynn de Grummond Delaune. Illustrated by Robert Doremus.)

WRITINGS: (With M. S. Robertson) *How to Have What You Want in Your Future,* privately printed, 1959; (with Lynn Delaune) *Jeff Davis, Confederate Boy,* Bobbs, 1960; (with Lynn Delaune) *Jeb Stuart,* Lippincott, 1962; (with Lynn Delaune) *Babe Didrikson,* Bobbs, 1963; (with Lynn Delaune) *Jean Piccard, Balloon Boy,* Bobbs, 1968. Articles in professional journals.

WORK IN PROGRESS: Further biographies, to be written with daughter.

SIDELIGHTS: In 1966, Ms. de Grummond received permission from the librarian of the University of Southern Mississippi Library to found a special collection of contemporary original materials and books related to children's literature. She wrote personal letters to friends and other contacts asking if they cared to help after explaining the purpose. From all over the world, artists and writers responded so eagerly that the collection now contains thousands of items. Author-artist Esphyr Slobodkina even went to Mississippi to make an exciting circus mural in collage along one wall of the library.

In April 1970, at the Children's Book Festival held on the U.S.M. campus each Spring, the collection was named in honor of Ms. de Grummond.

FOR MORE INFORMATION SEE: "Juvenile Miscellany," Summer, 1970, Spring, 1972; *Christian Science Monitor,* April 15, 1972.

DETINE, Padre
See OLSEN, Ib Spang

DIXON, Peter L. 1931-

PERSONAL: Born August 19, 1931, in New York, N.Y.; son of Peter H. and Mary Aline (Jones) Dixon; married Sarah H. Moran (a member of Planned Parenthood staff in Los Angeles), October 27, 1956; children: Pahl, James, Megan (daughter). *Education:* University of Idaho, student, 1950-51; University of California, Los Angeles, B.A., 1968, M.A. in Ed., 1971. *Residence:* Malibu, Calif. *Agent:* Frank Cooper Agency, 9000 Sunset Blvd., Los Angeles, Calif. 90069.

CAREER: Former beach lifeguard and recreation director with Department of Parks and Recreation, Los Angeles, Calif., Systems Development Corp., Santa Monica, Calif., human factors scientist, 1963-67; free-lance writer, 1967—. *Military service:* U.S. Army, 1952-54. *Member:* Writers Guild of America, West.

PETER L. DIXON

62

WRITINGS: Complete Book of Surfing, Coward, 1965, latest revised edition, Ballantine, 1969; *Men and Waves: A Treasury of Surfing,* Coward, 1966; *Where the Surfers Are: A Guide to the World's Greatest Surfing Spots,* Coward, 1967; *The Silent Adventure,* Ballantine, 1967; *Men Who Ride Mountains,* Bantam, 1968; *Soaring,* Ballantine, 1970; (with Laird Koenig) *The Children Are Watching* (novel), Ballantine, 1970; *Ballooning,* Ballantine, 1972; "The Young Adventurers," series of novels with titles, *Wipe Out, Test Run, Silent Flight, Deep Dive, Fire Guard, Fast Snow,* Bowmar, 1972.

Creator of and senior writer for television program, "Sealab 2020." Has written other television shows (such as "The Waltons") and specials and a number of children's programs for various networks. Writer for first two-way interactive cable television program, Qualis Productions, 1973.

WORK IN PROGRESS: Skydiving, for Ballantine; *Freeway,* a novel; a film on asthma for Center Films and La Vinia Hospital, Altadina, Calif.

DOBLER, Lavinia G.   1910-

PERSONAL: Born July 3, 1910, in Riverton, Wyo.; daughter of George Francis (a lawyer and judge) and Grace Louise (Sessions; a pioneer educator) Dobler. *Education:* University of California, Berkeley, A.B., 1933; additional study at University of Puerto Rico, 1934, University of Southern California, 1940-41, Columbia University, 1945-46, New York University (writing classes), 1950-52, University of Cape Coast and Kumasi College (Ghana), University of Ibadan, University at Lagos (Nigeria), 1970-71. *Politics:* Independent. *Home:* 347 East 50th St., New York, N.Y. 10022. *Office:* Scholastic Magazines, 50 West 44th St., New York, N.Y. 10036.

CAREER: Long Beach Press-Telegram-Sun, Long Beach, Calif., reporter, 1928-35; Riverton (Wyo.) public schools, teacher, 1933-35; Santurce, Rio Piedras District, Puerto Rico, supervisor of English, 1935-40; exchange teacher from Puerto Rico to Avenal, Calif., 1940-41; Long Beach (Calif.) public schools, teacher, 1941-44; Scholastic Magazines, New York, N.Y., 1944—, now head librarian of Scholastic Magazines and Book Services. *Member:* Women's National Book Association (secretary), American Association of University Women (vice-president of chapter in Puerto Rico), Authors Guild, Westerners, Order of the Eastern Star, Special Librarians Association (one of the founders of the publishing division), American Library Association, The Forum of Writers For Young People (president, 1960-61, 1971-72), Wyoming Historical Association (charter member). *Awards, honors:* National Librarian award by Dodd, Mead & Co., 1957, for *A Business of Their Own* (book about Junior Achievement); Pittsburgh Honor Book award, 1960, for *Black Gold at Titusville.*

WRITINGS: Glass House at Jamestown, Dodd, 1957; *A Business of Their Own,* Dodd, 1958; *Black Gold at Titusville,* Dodd, 1959; *First American History Book,* Platt, 1960; *Cyrus McCormick,* Bobbs, 1961; *Customs and Holidays Around the World,* Fleet, 1962; *Arrow Book of the United Nations,* Four Winds, 1964; (with William Brown) *Great Rulers of the African Past,* Doubleday, 1965; (with

Edgar W. Toppin) *Holidays Around the World,* Silver Burdett, 1965-67; *Pioneers and Patriots,* Doubleday, 1965; *Lee de Forest: Electronics Boy,* Bobbs, 1965; *The Land and People of Uruguay,* Lippincott, 1965, new edition, 1972; *National Holidays Around the World,* Fleet, 1966; *When Greatness Called,* Noble, 1970; *It's Your World: Don't Pollute It* (Teen Age Book Club selection), Scholastic Book Service, 1972; *Animals at Work,* Scholastic Book Services, 1973.

Compiler: *The Dobler International List of Periodicals for Boys and Girls,* 1960, revised edition (under title *The Dobler World Directory of Youth Publications*), Schulte, 1965; (with Muriel Fuller) *The Dobler World Directory of Youth Periodicals,* Citation, 1970.

Contributor of more than fifty short stories for young people to *Trails for Juniors, World Week, Senior Scholastic, Junior Scholastic, Newstime, News Explorer, World Week, American Junior Red Cross News, News Trails, Vacation Fun,* and other magazines; contributor of twenty articles on children's periodicals to magazines and journals. Author of articles about young people's magazines in professional and trade periodicals.

LAVINIA G. DOBLER

WORK IN PROGRESS: The Green Lizard Mystery, set in St. Lucia, with Peace Corps volunteers as central figures; *National Costumes Around the World; Island in Her Heart,* a book of fiction with Puerto Rico background; *Animals That Have Helped Make History; A Bridge to Cross* (contemporary setting in Wyoming); *Animal Festivals around the World; Symbols of Concern* (with Lee David Hamilton); *Timothy Matlack: Penman of the Declaration of Independence; Frontier Nurse in Wyoming.*

SIDELIGHTS: "My mother and father, each after graduating from universities in Iowa and Nebraska, came to Wyoming to prove up on homesteads, land that the government had opened. So my parents were among the founders of the little town of Riverton, in central Wyoming very close to the snow-covered Wind River Mountains. Daddy was one of the first lawyers and Mother one of the earliest school teachers. Virginia and I were the first twins born in Riverton in the Wind River Indian Reservation. We were baptized by the Episcopal Minister who knew the Indian guide of the Lewis and Clark Expedition. I did my first teaching in Riverton, and not too many years ago, my father's homestead was chosen as the site for a new college, Central Wyoming College. So in memory of my pioneer parents who helped build Riverton, I have given the Grace

STOP POLLUTION. STOP LITTER.
HAVE RESPECT FOR ALL LIVING THINGS.

"IT FELL OFF THAT CAR. WONDER IF THEY KNOW?"

■ (From *It's Your World—Don't Pollute It* by Lavinia Dobler. Illustrated by Tom Eaton.)

Sessions Dobler and George Francis Dobler scholarship (an annual gift). Adjoining the library is the Dobler Room, with an unusual fireplace made from Wyoming jade, moss agates and fossils. These stones were given by the rock hunters of Fremont County.

"Daddy, a member of the State Legislature in 1916, was Chairman of the Judiciary Committee. At that session, the Legislature voted to give the Dobler Twins the privileges of the House. I remember that Virginia and I didn't realize what an honor it was. But it was nice knowing that we could walk up the long stairs of the Capitol to the Legislative Chambers and be greeted by the lawmakers! Since there were no sidewalks in front of our house, we had so much roller skating on the wide cement walks near the Capitol!

"*Glass House at Jamestown* is one of my favorite books. But I like all my books, and consider each character my son and daughter. It is about a real boy, Nathaniel Peacock, who helped to settle Jamestown, Virginia in 1607. He becomes devoted to his pet raccoon, Mattie, and the Indian boy, Tomocomo, and Nat are good friends. Nat wants to become an apprentice in the glass house, and is able to persuade Captain John Smith to let him try. One of Nat's friends is Vicar Hunt, the first Anglican priest to come to America. Vicar Hunt gave Nat *The Book of Common Prayer.* He wrote in the religious book, 'May you always have faith.' I think this is most important for everyone. It is a guide and a truth that everyone can live by—faith in oneself; faith in one's fellowmen; faith in whatever adventure or project you want to accomplish. But you must work for your goal. Do not become discouraged. Have faith! You must believe that you are bigger than anything that can ever happen to you. This will help you in reconciling disappointment and sorrow.

"Another one of my favorite books is *Customs and Holidays Around the World* dedicated to all the boys and girls of the world. So each boy and girl can truthfully say that a book has been dedicated to him or her. Boys and girls of any religion can get information about religious festivals and holidays other boys and girls observe. This gives them an appreciation of a religious holiday that means so much to people of that faith. It is most important that young people have tolerance, understanding and sympathy for others and their beliefs. Then there is hope for peace and good will throughout the world.

"A writer is fortunate if she has a qualified, sympathetic friend who can give guidance and counsel. My good friend and agent is Muriel Fuller, formerly an editor of books for young people. She has always had faith in me and has encouraged me. As a result I have written over thirty books in about fifteen years. I consider writing a skill just as much as training to be a doctor, a lawyer, a teacher, a musician. So if one can study under a skilled, sympathetic teacher, this will help the writer.

"My goal, interestingly enough, is to write one sentence a day. I get that sentence written in my small notebook as I ride on the bus to Fifth Avenue. Then I walk the rest of the way to the Scholastic library. But the important fact is that I have accomplished my goal by 9 a.m. each week-day morning. So I am never frustrated. If one wrote a page a day for one year that would be the equivalent of an adult novel. I am willing to give up all kinds of social life when I

Something about the Author

am involved in writing a book. Sometimes I get eighteen hours of writing done over a weekend. While writing, I am living my book. Being creative seems to fulfill much that I need and crave, and gives me contentment.

"Also I keep thinking, especially when I am writing fiction, that maybe some conversation or observation I have written will help a boy or girl who is troubled or has an unsolved problem. In the past I have used many of the quotations Mother used to give us. In my prize-winning book *A Business of Their Own*, I quoted:

> The heights of great men reached and kept
> Were not attained by sudden flight.
> But they, while their companions slept
> Were struggling upward in the night.

I remember using the above when signing my friends' year-books in 1928, the year my twin and I graduated from Long Beach (Calif.) Polytechnic High School."

DOHERTY, C(harles) H(ugh) 1913-

PERSONAL: Born March 31, 1913, in London, England; son of Edward Henry and Florence (Whittingham) Doherty; married Ruby May Singleton, June 29, 1939. *Educated:* Attended Polytechnic School, London, England, 1924-29. *Home:* 2 Leconfield Ave., London S.W.13, England. *Agent:* Charles Lavell Ltd., 176 Wardour St., London W1V 3AA, England.

C. H. DOHERTY

CAREER: Air Ministry, London, England, draftsman, 1934-36; London County Council, London, England, technical assistant, 1936-40; Ministry of Public Building and Works, London, England, senior engineer, 1940-65, superintending engineer, 1965—. *Member:* Institution of Civil Engineers, Institution of Mechanical Engineers, Institution of Heating and Ventilating Engineers.

WRITINGS—Juvenile: *Brian Decides on Building*, Chatto & Windus, 1960; *Science on the Building Site*, Brockhampton Press, 1962, 2nd edition, 1969; *Science Inside the Building*, Brockhampton Press, 1963; *Science Builds the Bridges*, Brockhampton Press, 1964; *Science and the Tunneller*, Brockhampton Press, 1967; *Tunnels: The Construction, Types and History of Subterranean Transit*, Meredith, 1968; *Bridges*, Hawthorn, 1969; *New Gas for Old: The Story of Natural Gas*, Clifton Books, 1970; *Roads* (adult), Nelson, 1972. Contributor to *World Book Encyclopedia*. Short stories in various publications in Britain and Australia under a pseudonym.

SIDELIGHTS: "As you can see, I am by profession an engineer but my interest in the education of the young engineer and potential engineer and the man of C. P. Snow's 'other culture' makes me think there is a great need for engineers to communicate with 'arts' people and for them to know something of 'science.' Hence I have found myself writing 'science simplified' books both for juniors and adults. This kind of writing is a hobby and 99% perspiration 1% inspiration with the greatest problem how to make the technically complicated easily understood by the unknowledgeable yet interesting, too.

"All art-work of the illustrations in my books has been by others, I providing the basic sketches or sources of material e.g. photographs taken on my travels. As to the actual writing—ball point on paper for my critic, reviser, encourager, checker, typist and partner (all rolled into one wife) to tidy up. How do I come to write them? My agent makes me."

HOBBIES AND OTHER INTERESTS: Caravanning, the gramophone.

FOR MORE INFORMATION SEE: Best Sellers, March 1, 1970; *Times Literary Supplement*, April 16, 1970.

DOMANSKA, Janina

PERSONAL: Born in Warsaw, Poland; daughter of Wladyslaw (an engineer) and Jadwiga (a writer, maiden name, Muszynska) Domanski; married Jerzy Laskowski (a writer), December 22, 1953. *Education:* Academy of Fine Arts, Warsaw, Poland, diploma, 1939.

CAREER: Artist and illustrator. Lived in Italy, 1946-51, teaching at Academy of Fine Arts, Rome, and exhibiting at Roman Foundation of Fine Arts Show and at the International Exposition in Genoa; came to United States in 1952, and exhibited at one-man shows in the New York area, 1957, 1959. Paintings owned by Warsaw's Museum of Modern Art and private galleries in Rome, Italy. *Awards, honors: The Golden Seed* was exhibited in the American Institute of Graphic Arts Children's Book Show, 1962, and received first place certificate from the Printing Industries of Metropolitan New York, 1963; *The Coconut Thieves*

was a prize book in the *New York Herald Tribune* Children's Book Festival, 1964, was listed as one of the notable children's books of 1964 by the American Library Association, and was exhibited in the American Institute of Graphic Arts Children's Book Show, 1964; *If All the Seas Were One Sea* was selected as a Caldecott Honor Book, 1972.

WRITINGS: (Translator from the Polish and illustrator) Maria Konopnicka, *The Golden Seed,* adapted by Catharine Fournier, Scribner, 1962; (translator from the Polish, and illustrator) *The Coconut Thieves,* adapted by Catharine Fournier, Scribner, 1964; (adapter and illustrator) *Why So Much Noise?,* Harper, 1965; (author and illustrator) *Palmiero and the Ogre,* Macmillan, 1967; *Look, There Is a Turtle Flying,* Macmillan, 1968; *The Turnip,* Macmillan, 1969; *Marilka,* Macmillan, 1970; *If All the Seas Were One Sea* (ALA Notable Book; *Horn Book* Honor List; *Library Journal* Book List), Macmillan, 1971; *I Saw a Ship A-Sailing* (*Junior Literary Guild* selection), Macmillan, 1972; *Little Red Hen,* Macmillan, 1973. Drawings have appeared in *Harper's, Reporter,* and other magazines.

Illustrator: Alma K. Reck, *Clocks Tell the Time,* Scribner, 1960; Dorothy Kunhardt, *Gas Station Gus,* Harper, 1961; Natalie Savage Carlson, *Song of the Lop-Eared Mule,* Harper, 1961; Astrid Lindgren, *Mischievous Meg,* Viking, 1962; Aileen Fisher, *I Like Weather,* Crowell, 1963; Mara Kay, *In Place of Katia,* Scribner, 1963; Sally P. Johnson, *Harper Book of Prince's,* Harper, 1964; Ruth Tooze, *Nikkos of the Pink Pelican,* Viking, 1964; Babette Deutsch and Avrahm Yarmolinsky, editors, *More Tales of Faraway Folk,* Harper, 1964; Deutsch and Yarmolinsky, *Steel Flea,* Harper, 1964; Bernice Kohn, *Light,* Coward, 1965; Dorothy Hoge, *The Black Heart of Indri,* Scribner, 1966; Eric P. Kelly, *Trumpeter of Krakow,* Macmillan, 1966; Jerzy Laskowski, *Master of the Royal Cats,* Seabury, 1967; Laskowski, *The Dragon Liked Smoked Fish,* Seabury, 1967; Elizabeth Coatsworth, *Under the Green Willow,* Macmillan, 1971; Edward Lear, *Whizz!,* Macmillan, 1973.

SIDELIGHTS: "I was born in Warsaw, Poland, where I grew up and attended the Academy of Fine Arts. After the Nazi occupation of Poland during World War II, I was shipped to a concentration camp in Germany where my talent for drawing proved my salvation. Several days after my arrival in the camp, my sketches were noticed by a prominent Pole who arranged to have me released in exchange for portraits I painted of his family.

"After the war I studied painting in Italy. Some of my paintings are in the Museum of Modern Art in Warsaw and

"That long-tailed monkey up there in the trees is making so much noise, we can hardly hear ourselves talk. Let's see if we can scare him so much that he will fall down and go away." ■ (From *Why So Much Noise?* by Janina Domanska. Illustrated by the author.)

in private galleries in Rome. When I arrived in the United States I spoke four languages fluently—but not English. I became a textile designer and, as my English improved, began visiting publishers with my drawings.

"I have now illustrated more than thirty children's books in water color and pencil, pen and ink, and etchings and woodcuts. In the basement of my home I operate my own small printing press on which I made the original engravings for *Under the Green Willow* and *If All the Seas Were One Sea.*

"I live in New Fairfield, Connecticut, with my husband, Jerzy Laskowski, who is a bookseller and the author of several children's books."

FOR MORE INFORMATION SEE: New York Times Book Review, April, 1967; *Young Reader's Review,* May, 1967; *Illustrators of Children's Books: 1957-1966,* Horn Book, 1968; *Horn Book,* October, 1969, December, 1970, October, 1971, February, 1973, August, 1973; *Christian Science Monitor,* November 11, 1971; *Top of the News,* April, 1972; *Junior Literary Guild Catalogue,* September, 1972; *Washington Post* "Children's Book World," November 5, 1972; *Third Book of Junior Authors,* edited by de Montreville and Hill, H. W. Wilson, 1972.

JANINA DOMANSKA

MARGOT PATTERSON DOSS

DOSS, Margot Patterson

PERSONAL: Born in St. Paul, Minnesota; daughter of Eugene Northrop (a certified public accountant) and Irene (Watson) Patterson; married John Whinham Doss (a pediatrician), June 7, 1947; children: Richard, Alexander, Jock, Gordon. *Education:* Illinois Wesleyan University, B.A.; graduate study at New School for Social Research and University of Chicago. *Politics:* Democrat. *Religion:* Episcopalian. *Address:* Box 447, Bolinas, Calif. 94924, and 1331 Greenwich St., San Francisco, Calif. 94109. *Office:* San Francisco Chronicle, San Francisco, Calif. 94119.

CAREER: San Francisco Chronicle, San Francisco, Calif., weekly columnist, 1960—. Lecturer at Foothill College, 1972, San Francisco State University, 1973, University of California, 1971—. *Member:* San Francisco Press Club, Sierra Club (life member).

WRITINGS: San Francisco at Your Feet, Grove, 1962; *Bay Area at Your Feet,* Chronicle Publishing, 1970; *Golden Gate Park at Your Feet,* Chronicle Publishing, 1970; *Walks for Children in San Francisco* (juvenile), Grove, 1970. Contributor to magazines.

HOBBIES AND OTHER INTERESTS: Conservation and gardening.

DRACO, F.
See DAVIS, Julia

The view was marvellous up there, and the drover was right; a camel could certainly move! ■ (From *Hamid and the Palm Sunday Donkey* by Mary Drewery. Illustrated by Reginald Gray.)

DREWERY, Mary 1918-

PERSONAL: Born May 9, 1918, in Malpas, Newport, Monmouthshire, England; daughter of Tom and Gladys Violet (Milne) Drewery; married Edgar Dennis Smith (a circuit judge), December 21, 1950; children: Richard George Dennis, John Edgar Pugh. *Education:* Attended Westfield College, University of London, 1936-39. *Religion:* Baptist. *Home:* 20 Furze Lane, Purley, Surrey, England.

CAREER: Writer. Justice of the Peace for the Wallington Petty Sessional Division of South West London. *Member:* Society of Authors, Croydon Writers' Circle (vice-chairman).

WRITINGS—All for young people, unless otherwise noted: *Guide and Observer,* Scout Association, 1955; *The Way to the Stars: First Star,* Scout Association, 1956; *Jungle Lore,* Scout Association, 1957; *Rebellion in the West,* Oliver & Boyd, 1962; *Devil in Print,* Oliver & Boyd, 1963, McKay, 1966; *The Silvester Wish,* Oliver & Boyd, 1966; *A Donkey Called Haryat,* Oliver & Boyd, 1967, published in America as *Hamid and the Palm Sunday Donkey,* Hastings House, 1968; *A Candle for St. Georgios,* Chatto, Boyd, & Oliver, 1969; *Where Four Winds Meet,* Chatto, Boyd & Oliver, 1971; *Window on My Heart* (adult), Hodder & Staughton, 1973. Author of television scripts, "Epilogues," for Southern Television, 1969. Contributor of short stories and articles to *Scout* and other youth magazines.

WORK IN PROGRESS: Life of Pastor Richard Wurmbrand, for Hodder & Stoughton Ltd.

SIDELIGHTS: "Although I had been writing on and off all my life, I had never had anything published until I became a member of the Scout Association in 1942, when I started to contribute occasional articles to 'The Scouter.' After my marriage, my husband (who has been with the Scout movement since 1919), encouraged me to embark on stories and serials for 'The Scout.' My first full-length novel, *Rebellion in the West,* is set in Wales and the Welsh Marshes and arose as a result of a wet summer holiday we spent with my husband's mother in her country home near Ludlow (the starting point of the story). Since then, I have concentrated largely on writing novels for young people, enjoying particularly the setting of my stories in foreign lands. I research the background thoroughly, feeling that the history, legends and traditions of a country all contribute to the nature of its people. My passion for accurate local color has taken me to Jordan, Israel, Greece, Austria, Germany, Belgium, and Finland. My husband and sons join happily in any new writing enterprise and are, I may add, my sternest critics.

"At the same time as writing novels, I am deeply concerned about social and moral problems. In addition to my work as a Justice of the Peace, I seek through the medium of radio, television and occasional hymn-writing to add my small contribution towards achieving a happier world."

HOBBIES AND OTHER INTERESTS: Gardening, theatre, music, foreign travel.

FOR MORE INFORMATION SEE: Books & Bookmen, February, 1968; *Library Journal,* September, 1968; *Young Readers' Review,* December, 1968; *Book World,* March 2, 1969.

MARY DREWERY

On Saturdays they went to the City to shop and on Sundays they went for a joy ride. Nina always sat in the back seat. ∎ (From *The Flying Postman* by V. H. Drummond. Illustrated by the author.)

Something about the Author

DRUMMOND, V(iolet) H(ilda) 1911-

PERSONAL: Born July, 1911, in London, England; daughter of David (an army officer) and Hilda Drummond; married Anthony Swetenham (now a member of London Stock Exchange), December, 1948; children: Julian Pardoe. *Education:* Attended school in Eastbourne, England. *Politics:* Conservative. *Religion:* Church of England. *Home:* 24 Norfolk Rd., London N.W. 8, England.

CAREER: V. H. Drummond Productions Ltd., London, England, chairman, 1960—, producing eighteen cartoon films for British Broadcasting Corp. "Children's Hour," 1963-64; author and illustrator of children's books.

V. H. DRUMMOND

Member: Society of Authors. *Awards, honors:* Kate Greenway Medal of Library Association (British) for most distinguished work in illustration of a children's book for *Mrs. Easter and the Storks,* 1958.

WRITINGS: Phewtus the Squirrel, Oxford University Press, 1939; *Mrs. Easter's Parasol,* Faber, 1944; *Miss Anna Truly,* Houghton, 1945; *Lady Talavera,* Faber, 1946; *Tidgies Innings,* Faber, 1947; *The Charming Taxicab,* Faber, 1947; *Mr. Finch's Pet Shop,* Walck, 1950; *Mrs. Easter and the Storks,* Faber, 1957; *Little Laura's Cat,* Faber, 1961; *Little Laura on the River,* Faber, 1961; *Little Laura and the Thief,* Nelson, 1962; *Little Laura's Best Friend,* Nelson, 1962; *Little Laura and the Lonely Ostrich,* Nelson, 1963; *The Flying Postman,* Walck, 1964; *Miss Anna Truly and the Christmas Lights,* Longmans, 1968; *Mrs. Easter and the Golden Bounder,* Faber, 1970; *Mrs. Easter's Christmas Flight,* Faber, 1972. (All the preceding are illustrated by the author.)

Illustrator: J. K. Stanford, *The Twelfth,* Faber, 1944; T. A. Powell, *Here and There a Lusty Trout,* Faber, 1947; Geoffrey Bles, *The Titles My Own,* Faber, 1952; Arnold Silcord, *Verse and Worse,* Faber, 1952; Eric Partridge, *The Shaggy Dog Story,* Faber, 1953; Barbara Sleigh, *Carbonel King of the Cats,* Bobbs, 1955; Angela Jean, *The Kingdom of the Winds,* Parrish, 1957; Lawrence Durrell, *Esprit de Corps,* Faber, 1957; Barbara Ireson, *Liza and the Helicopter,* Faber, 1958; Alastair Miller, *The Quest of the Catnip Mouse,* Faber, 1967. Also illustrator-writer-producer of "Little Laura" cartoon series for television.

SIDELIGHTS: "I wrote my first children's book, *Phewtus the Squirrel,* for my son then aged four. It was based on a stuffed toy squirrel called Rufus which he mispronounced as 'Phewtus.' My next book was *Mrs. Easter's Parasol,* the idea for which came to me walking with my son in London's Kensington Gardens. This was accepted by Faber who shortly after asked me to illustrate *The Twelfth* and other humorous books.

"I'm told that what success I have had comes in part from the fact that my writing is enjoyed by the grown-up people who read my books to their young children while the latter look at the pictures—and that this enjoyment is passed on to the young.

"In 1963 I drew and produced eighteen films for the 'Children's Hour' on the B.B.C. After the films I decided to concentrate on my watercolor painting and in 1968 held a successful exhibition of my pictures in London. However I decided to write one last children's book for my eldest grandchild in 1968. Since then there have been two more grandchildren and so each has had to have a book written for them. From now on I really intend to concentrate on my painting!"

FOR MORE INFORMATION SEE: Horn Book XXIV, Volume I; *Junior Bookshelf,* October, 1949; *Illustrators of Children's Books: 1946-1956,* Horn Book, 1958; *Illustrators of Children's Books: 1957-1966,* Horn Book, 1968; *Third Book of Junior Authors,* edited by de Montreville and Hill, H. W. Wilson, 1972.

MARY LOIS DUNN

DUNN, Mary Lois 1930-

PERSONAL: Born August 18, 1930, in Uvalde, Tex.; daughter of F. S. (a railroad signal maintainer) and Ruth Alice (Hawkes) Dunn. *Education:* Stephen F. Austin State College (now Stephen F. Austin University), B.A., 1951; Louisiana State University, M.S. in L.S., 1957. *Politics:* "Presently Republican—vote for the man, not the party." *Religion:* Southern Baptist. *Home:* 7555 Katy Freeway, No. 154, Houston, Tex. 77024.

CAREER: Houston Independent School District, Houston, Tex., librarian, 1951—. *Member:* American Library Association, Texas Library Association, Houston Association of School Librarians. *Awards, honors:* Sequoyah Children's Book Award of Oklahoma (determined by vote of children in grades four through nine), 1972, for *The Man in the Box: A Story from Vietnam.*

WRITINGS: The Man in the Box: A Story from Vietnam, McGraw, 1968.

WORK IN PROGRESS: A horse story and a book on motorcycles, both for young people.

DUTZ
See DAVIS, Mary Octavia

EGGENBERGER, David 1918-

PERSONAL: Born July 25, 1918, in Pontiac, Ill.; son of Florian E. (a farmer) and Rose (Huber) Eggenberger; married Lorraine Angstman, August 27, 1943; children: Lynn, April. *Education:* University of Illinois, B.S. in Journalism, 1941. *Politics:* "F.D.R. Democrat." *Religion:* Roman Catholic. *Home:* 8300 McNeil St., Vienna, Va. 22180. *Office:* National Archives, Washington, D.C.

CAREER: Compton's Pictured Encyclopedia, Chicago, Ill., an editor, 1946-57; McGraw-Hill Book Co., New York, N.Y., managing editor and executive editor of encyclopedias, dictionaries, and other reference books, 1957-73; National Archives, Washington, D.C., publications officer, 1973—. *Military service:* U.S. Army, Infantry, 1942-46; became captain; received Bronze Star.

WRITINGS: Flags of the U.S.A., Crowell, 1959, revised edition, 1964; *Dictionary of Battles,* Crowell, 1967.

ELSPETH
See BRAGDON, Elspeth

EVARTS, Hal G. (Jr.) 1915-

PERSONAL: Born February 8, 1915, in Hutchinson, Kan.; son of Hal G. (an author) and Sylvia A. Evarts; married Dorothea Van Dusen Abbott, 1942; children: Mrs. Virginia E. Wadsworth, William A., John V. *Education:* Stanford University, B.A., 1936. *Home:* 6625 Muirlands Dr., La Jolla, Calif. 92037.

CAREER: Set out for Europe after graduation from Stanford and continued on a knapsack trip around the world, 1936-37; worked briefly as screenwriter in Hollywood and reporter for trade journals and newspapers; in 1939 returned to Europe, where he wrote for Paris edition of *New York Herald-Tribune* until France fell to the Nazis; full-time writer of fiction, 1940—. *Military service:* U.S. Army, 1943-45; served in Europe with 89th Infantry Division. *Member:* Western Writers of America, Zeta Psi, Sigma Delta Chi.

WRITINGS—Youth books: *Jim Clyman,* Putnam, 1959; *Treasure River,* Scribner, 1964; *The Talking Mountain,* Scribner, 1966; *Smugglers' Road,* Scribner, 1968; *Mission to Tibet,* Scribner, 1970; *The Pegleg Mystery,* Scribner, 1972; *Big Foot,* Scribner, 1973.

Other fiction: *Ambush Rider,* R. Hale, 1957, Pocket Books, 1971; *Jebediah Smith, Trail Blazer of the West,* Putnam, 1959; *The Secret of the Himalayas,* Scribner, 1962; *Branded Man,* Fawcett, 1965; *Sundown Kid,* Fawcett, 1969; *Man Without a Gun,* Pocket Books, 1972; *The Night Raiders,* Pocket Books, 1972; *The Settling of the Sage,* Pocket Books, 1972; *The Long Rope,* Pocket Books, 1972; *The Man from Yuma,* Pocket Books, 1972; *Fugitive's Canyon,* Pocket Books, 1972.

Contributor of more than one hundred stories to magazines, including *Saturday Evening Post, Collier's, American, Esquire, This Week, Toronto Star Weekly, Liberty, Adventure,* and *Ellery Queen.*

"I was born in a small midwestern town in the heart of the Kansas wheat belt. My boyhood memories of this Norman Rockwell sort of town are tinged with nostalgia for the good old days.

"Life with my father was the most important educative force during my youth. Shortly after I was born, he sold his shoe store in Hutchinson, Kansas, and moved the family to a remote ranch near Cody, Wyoming where we lived for three and a half years. Here, my father raised fur bearing animals (fox and skunk) and wrote to pass the time. By the time of his death seventeen years later, his writing, fiction and nonfiction had appeared in every mass circulation magazine in America.

"My father was a natural-born storyteller, and from childhood I wanted to be a writer too. I often accompanied my father on his wide travels to gather material for stories and articles on camping and hunting trips over much of the West, to Mexico, Alaska, the Florida Keys, New Guinea, and the South Pacific.

"I attended Los Angeles High School and Stanford University where I gave up football after one season on the bench and in my senior year edited the Literary Yearbook. I graduated in 1936 with a B.A. in English.

HAL G. EVARTS

"Ten days after graduation I set out to see the 1936 Olympic Games in Berlin, and wound up taking a knapsack-shoestring trip around the world that lasted fifteen months. I returned to Europe in 1939 and talked myself into a job on the Paris edition of the *New York Herald Tribune* where I remained until the German occupation. I returned for a third time in 1945 as a G.I. to write the history of my 89th Army Infantry Division.

"Since 1940 I have been a full-time freelance fiction writer. Before that I briefly held jobs as a screenwriter in Hollywood, trade journalist, and newspaper reporter. I sold my first article to the *San Francisco Chronicle* for five dollars, my first fiction to the *Toronto Star* for seventy-five dollars. Since then I have published over a hundred magazine stories and twenty-five novels. Some dozen of my stories have appeared on network television.

"My wide variety of personal interests have all, in one way or another, influenced my writing. I particularly value the time I spent knocking about some of the more inaccessible corners of pre-war Asia—Iran, Burma, Indonesia, and three months in western China, and have drawn on this background for many of my stories, and at least three novels. The six summers spent with my family in the Salmon River wilderness area of Idaho, camping, fly fishing, hunting for Indian artifacts, and doing river trips resulted in two novels and a magazine article.

"My primary function as a writer is to entertain. I strive for realism—telling it like it is—and believe that it is possible to write about almost any subject for youngsters if the writer employs good taste, selectivity, and all his skill. My greatest challenge is to write a book that young readers find so enjoyable and meaningful they want to come back for more.

"I enjoy the reassurance of knowing that someone out there is reading my work, and derive the greatest satisfaction when I receive letters from my young readers."

FOR MORE INFORMATION SEE: Young Readers' Review, September, 1968; *Horn Book,* June, 1972.

FAIRFAX-LUCY, Brian (Fulke Cameron-Ramsay) 1898-

PERSONAL: Title since succeeding brother as fifth baronet in 1965 is Major Sir Brian Fulke Cameron-Ramsay-Fairfax-Lucy; born December 18, 1898, in Scotland; son of Sir Henry William Cameron Ramsay-Fairfax (a colonel, British Army) and Ada Christina Lucy; married Honorable Alice Caroline Helen Buchan (an author and daughter of Baron Tweedsmuir), July 29, 1933; children: Edmund John William Hugh, Mary (Mrs. James Scott). *Education:* Attended Eton College, 1912-16, and Royal Military College, Sandhurst, 1916. *Politics:* Conservative. *Religion:* Church of England. *Home:* Charlecote Park, Warwickshire, England; and The Mill, Fossebridge, Cheltenham, England. *Agent:* A. P. Watt & Son, 10 Norfolk St., Strand, London W.C.2, England.

CAREER: Regular officer in the British Army, 1916-33, returning to active duty again, 1939-45; began service with the Queen's Own Cameron Highlanders during World War I (was wounded); stationed on the Northwest Frontier, India, 1919-25, and in Germany, 1926; adjutant of 2nd Cameron Highlanders, 1927-30; aide-de-camp to Lord High Commissioner to General Assembly of Church of Scotland, 1931-33; retired, 1933; steward of National Greyhound Racing Club, 1928-33, stipendiary steward, 1933-36; during World War II served principally as a major with the Cameron Highlanders.

WRITINGS—Children's books: *Horses in the Valley,* Oxford University Press, 1941; *The Horse from India,* Muller, 1944; *Albert: The Adventures of a Farmyard Duck,* Partridge Publications, 1944; *The Cat Did It,* Oxford University Press, 1951; (with Phillipa Pearce) *The Children of the House,* Lippincott, 1968.

WORK IN PROGRESS: His autobiography.

SIDELIGHTS: "I was born with what is generally known as a silver spoon in my mouth. My father was the great-grandson of Sir William Fairfax who fought with General Wolfe at Quebec; later he was made an Admiral and knighted. My mother was an heiress and inherited Charlecote Park on the river Avon. Charlecote is now the property of the National Trust, and nearly all the ten thousand acres we once owned have been sold, but I and my heirs, will be tenants for life of the house and park.

"I was commissioned into the famous Scottish regiment, the Queen's Own Cameron Highlanders. At seventeen, I was the youngest officer serving in the British Army. From then on (having been badly wounded in France in 1918) I served as a regular officer till 1933. I married that year and went on leave from the Army, I studied training race horses and handicapping, besides riding as a successful amateur jockey. I was commissioned to write articles on horseracing which led to a job as racing correspondent for the *Sunday Times* in 1939.

"In September 1939 I was recalled to serve with my regiment, but owing to my severe wounds of 1918 I was passed unfit. I found myself in my little house in Oxfordshire with my wife. I had lost my job as there was to be no racing for the duration of the war.

"I had to earn something to keep us going. How could I do it? As a boy I loved Beatrix Potter's tales, E. Nesbit's books, and above all, *Black Beauty*. I thought then I would love to write something like the latter, as it had given me such pleasure. I wondered then why there were not more books about horses and children so I sat down every day and wrote *Horses in the Valley,* aided and much encouraged by my wife. When it was finished I sent it to six publishers. All turned it down. As a last shot I sent it to the Oxford University Press, and they accepted it, to my great joy. It has become a minor classic, published by the Oxford University Press four or five times. The paperback sold thirty-thousand copies in one day.

"In 1943 my health improved and I applied to return to the Army. After much correspondence I was granted a Medical Board and eventually was passed fit to serve in Great Britain. Once again I was back with the Cameron Highlan-

"Do I have to go first?" Margaret asked. ■ (From *The Children of the House* by Brian Fairfax-Lucy and Philippa Pearce. Illustrated by John Sergeant.)

ders, mostly training recruits. During this period I was often on night duty to turn out Guards at 2 a.m. Sitting in an unheated office wearing a kilt and a great coat I wrote most of the *Horse from India* and *Albert the Duck*. I must admit I had during this period in the Army from 1943-45 many very unpleasant experiences. It seemed that at every place I was stationed we were bombed and I was being moved from one place to another. Then for the third time in these three years I became seriously ill with bronchitis and in April, 1945 I was invalided out of the Army once again.

"My father and mother had died during the war and I inherited quite a large sum of money. So in 1945 I was independent of my Army pay and my writing. I was nearly forty-seven years of age and for the first time in my married life I was able to go to a good restaurant, order what I fancied and buy my wife the things she had longed for for twelve years. Possibly most of all we longed to have a child of our own, and a house of our own. Ten months later my son was born on Victory Day 1945. I shall never forget that ecstasy to have a son born when all Great Britain was celebrating. A daughter was born a little over a year later.

"In 1954 I was cutting down a tree one evening when I suddenly had a great electric pain in my face. It was diagnosed as arthritis in my jaw, and the cartilage was removed. For a year or more I could not eat except through a straw. The agonizing pain never ceased. Finally a surgeon diagnosed the pain not from the jaw but the fifth nerve. He injected it and for one year I was free of pain and wrote the first half of an autobiographical novel, *The Back Stairs*. When the pain returned the surgeon removed the fifth nerve from my brain. The operation was a complete success but I got fluid on the brain. My mind worked day and night. At that period I could have written anything, my imaginative mind was so active.

"Eighteen months later I finished the book but Constable wanted it as a children's book and not as an adult story as I had visualized it, and commissioned Philippa Pearce to adapt it, which she did extremely well, taking it from the original text. It was retitled, *The Children of the House*.

"You might ask, why do I write? The answer is I find it a great escape from the world of reality. I live with my characters during the day and at night I write what they have dictated to me. I am not in any sense a professional writer. I write when I feel like it, but I feel frustrated and dissatisfied with myself if I miss writing, if only a few hundred words each day.

"I write for children because I am very fond of them and animals. I have never been a reader myself and find novels and love stories very boring. I enjoy most, current affairs, history, and memoirs. I have always liked clothes and might have been a designer had I been taught to draw. I have a great reverence for trees, calm seas, and wild flowers. My major blessing is my intense love of my family, of the country, people, and horses."

HOBBIES AND OTHER INTERESTS: All games from cricket to football, and fishing, shooting, and riding; also a love of music and live theatre.

FATIO, Louise

PERSONAL: Born August 18, in Lausanne, Switzerland; daughter of Alfred and Elisa (Chenevard) Fatio; married Roger Antoine Duvoisin (a writer and illustrator of children's books), July 25, 1925; children: Roger (a neurologist), Jacques (an architect). *Education:* Attended boarding school in Basel and College des Jeunes Filles in Geneva. *Address:* P.O. Box 116, Gladstone, N.J. 07934.

CAREER: Began to gather ideas for her own books while helping her husband with his writing for children. *Member:* Authors Guild. *Awards, honors:* The Happy Lion received first prize for a juvenile book from the West German Government, 1956 (it was published in German, 1955).

WRITINGS—All illustrated by her husband, Roger Duvoisin: *The Christmas Forest*, Aladdin Books, 1950; *Anna, the Horse*, Aladdin Books, 1951; *The Happy Lion*, (N.Y. Times best book list), Whittlesey House, 1954, also published in French as *Le Bon Lion*, Whittlesey House, 1960; *The Happy Lion in Africa* (N.Y. Times best book list), Whittlesey House, 1955; *A Doll for Maria*, Whittlesey House, 1957; *The Happy Lion Roars*, Whittlesey House, 1957; *The Three Happy Lions*, Whittlesey House, 1959, also published in French as *Les Trois Bons Lions*, Whittlesey House, 1962; *The Happy Lion's Quest*, Whittlesey House, 1961; *Red Bantam*, Whittlesey House, 1963; *The Happy Lion and the Bear*, Whittlesey House, 1964; *The Happy Lion's Vacation*, McGraw, 1967; *The Happy Lion's Treasure*, McGraw, 1971; *Hector Penguin* (N.Y. Times best book list), McGraw, 1973.

WORK IN PROGRESS: Two children's books, for McGraw.

SIDELIGHTS: "As is the case for most of those who translate their thoughts and beliefs into books—children's books as well as adult books—my books are an extension of my life. Or, I should say, our lives, my husband's and mine, for we have similar backgrounds, share the same tastes, and collaborate on many of our books.

"Our love of people, of nature, our respect for animals which are often expressed in my books, date from our childhood. We spent many summer vacations on farms, my husband in a village of Savoy, I in a French-Swiss one. The need for the full country life not too far from a civilized city led us to settle in New Jersey when we came to America. New Jersey was then a farming land which deserved its name of Garden State.

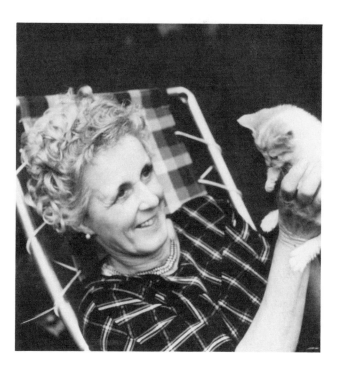

LOUISE FATIO

"Here, in our wood and fields so alive with beautiful animals, wild and domestic, we can forget the bustle, vulgarity, and noise of our industrial age. We even try to keep it away from our books.

"Reading to our sons the books we had read in our childhood, listening to our sons' own inventions, gave us the desire to write children's books of our own. My husband wrote and illustrated his first book for our first son. It was based on drawings the five-year-old boy made and the stories he told about them. Our sons, and even our animals, directly inspired some of the stories made up. *Red Bantam* was the story of one of our Bantam roosters who courageously fought a hawk while a bigger rooster ran off to hide. *A Doll for Marie* was based on the love of our granddaughter for dolls. The Marie of the book was our granddaughter Anne and my husband drew her portrait in his illustrations. *The Happy Lion* was inspired by a true story I read in a French newspaper during one of our trips to France. A friendly, well-fed lion had escaped from a circus which had set up its tent in a small French town. People screamed and ran off in all directions when they saw the good lion stroll through their streets. The lion was saved

The lion just sat down very quietly, for he did not want to miss what was going to happen. ■ (From *The Happy Lion* by Louise Fatio. Illustrated by Roger Duvoisin.)

Something about the Author

when the circus owner brought him back to the circus. I loved that newspaper article.

"Remembrance of childhood impressions, the little dramas and comedies which have been observed in the world around us, personal opinions and ideas, often suggest other stories. This is the case of my book, *Hector Penguin.*

"Although most of these stories have animals as principal actors they never describe actual observations of the animals in our house and land. They are tales in which animals represent various kinds of people as they did in old folk tales and fables. Yet, our dear animals have personalities of their own. To observe their likes and dislikes, the reassuring friendships which grow between some of them, their often astonishingly clever behavior is always interesting and sometimes extremely amusing. This is true not only of our cats and dogs but also of our chickens, ducks, geese, and peacocks. Sometimes, we have written these observations in letters to schools and friends; my husband has been urged, often, to write them into a book.

"My husband and I generally work together on my new ideas for stories. Since he illustrates them this makes it easier to harmonize text and illustrations."

The Duvoisins leave their hillside home to do some extensive traveling every year. Their books have been translated into several languages.

HOBBIES AND OTHER INTERESTS: Growing flowers, the animals on their land, music, reading.

FOR MORE INFORMATION SEE: More Junior Authors, edited by Muriel Fuller, H. W. Wilson, 1963; *Book World,* October 1, 1967; *Young Reader's Review,* November, 1967; *New York Times Book Review,* January 21, 1968; Lee Bennett Hopkins, *Books Are by People,* Citation, 1969; Children's Book Council "Calendar," September-December, 1970; *London Times,* October 18, 1972.

FERMI, Laura 1907-

PERSONAL: Born June 16, 1907, in Rome, Italy; came to U.S., 1939; naturalized, 1944; daughter of Augusto (officer in Italian navy) and Costanza (Romanelli) Capon; married Enrico Fermi (nuclear physicist), 1928 (deceased); children: Nella, Guilio. *Education:* Attended University of Rome, 1926-28. *Home:* 5532 South Shore Dr., Chicago, Ill. 60637.

CAREER: Atomic Energy Commission, Washington, D.C., historian, 1955-56; Massachusetts Institute of Technology, Cambridge, member of staff of Physical Science Study Committee, 1957. Member of board of governors, International House, Chicago, of Air Pollution Control Committee, Chicago, 1960-68, of Northeastern Illinois Metropolitan Area Air Pollution Control Board, 1962-63, of women's board of University of Chicago. Co-founder of Cleaner Air Committee of Hyde Park and Kenwood and of Civic Disarmament Committee (1971). Lecturer. *Member:* Authors Guild, League of Women Voters. *Awards, honors:* Guggenheim Fellowship, 1957; Friends of Literature Prize, 1968.

WRITINGS: (With Ginestra Amaldi) *Alchimia del Tempo Nostro,* Hoepli-Torino, 1936; *Atoms in the Family: My Life With Enrico Fermi,* University of Chicago Press, 1954; *Atoms for the World,* University of Chicago Press, 1957; *The Story of Atomic Energy,* Random, 1961; (co-author) *Galileo and the Scientific Revolution,* Basic Books, 1961; *Mussolini,* University of Chicago Press, 1961; *Illustrious Immigrants,* University of Chicago Press, 1968.

SIDELIGHTS: "I was born and raised in Rome and lived there until I was thirty-one years old. I wrote my first book there, in collaboration with a friend. Both our husbands were physicists, and in the physics department the book came to be known as 'the wives book.' It attempted to explain atoms to persons who were not scientists, and it did rather well. But there was one problem: we wrote our book in 1936, and right after that physicists began making discoveries that changed atomic science.

"Coming to the United States was my greatest adventure. A lot of things changed for me. Although I knew some English, writing was at first out of the question. On the positive side, democracy was much better than Fascism; on the puzzling side, instead of my children going on learning from me, I began learning from them: the English language on a better and more colloquial level, American ways of life, and Americana in all its aspects. At home I talked mostly Italian with my husband and children, and the process of mastering English was painfully slow. Only after ten years in this country could I begin to write again.

"At first it was little stories about visits back to Italy, which were never published but which were liked by friends who encouraged me to go on writing. I had some articles published about war-time experiences in New Mexico, and about science in Italy. And finally my first book in English. I have written six English books in all, and I have worn out a *Collegiate Webster,* a huge *International Webster,* and a *Roget Thesaurus.* Now I use the dictionary and similar aids to solve crossword puzzles and double crostics, not for writing.

"One of the books I enjoyed doing was *The Story of Atomic Energy.* The publisher asked me to do it for the 'Landmark' series, which is for young people. My children were grown by then and I felt out of touch with my future audience. So I hired an eleven-year-old consultant. He used to come whenever I would have a chapter ready for his inspection. I gave him lunch and one dollar for his services. Two things stand out from that collaboration: the boy liked hot dogs stuffed with cheese and peppermint ice cream; and we had once a long discussion about Democritus: I felt that my story should perhaps start in more recent times and that Democritus should be taken off the first chapter. The boy insisted on keeping Democritus and so we did. He seems to have been right: many youngsters wrote me comments and no one complained about Democritus.

"On a different level, my last book was also fun to do. As I studied, interviewed, and talked about the *Illustrious Immigrants* of the thirties and early forties, I realized that our coming to America had been part of a large phenomenon of historical importance, that had depleted Europe of brainpower and had benefited America in many ways. It had also benefited the immigrants themselves, who in this country found great intellectual resources and opportunities. Under these circumstances, and helped by the American traditional hospitality, they became much more productive than they would have been at home. They could make contributions in their many fields of endeavor that helped American culture reach more rapidly the high standards of the postwar times."

FOR MORE INFORMATION SEE: *Atoms in the Family: My Life with Enrico Fermi,* University of Chicago Press, 1954.

FLASH FLOOD
See ROBINSON, Jan M.

FORD, Marcia
See RADFORD, Ruby L.

FOSTER, Laura Louise (James) 1918-

PERSONAL: Born January 25, 1918, in Chillicothe, Ohio; daughter of Ellery Sedgewick (a banker) and Louise (Hoadley) James; married H. Lincoln Foster (now a landscape designer and writer), December 23, 1948; children: Ellery Westwood Sinclair, John Sheldon Sinclair; (stepchildren) H. Rebecca (Mrs. Robert J. Light), Benjamin. *Education:* Attended Chapin School and Bennington College. *Politics:* "Vacillating Republican." *Religion:* Episcopalian. *Home:* Under Mountain Rd., Falls Village, Conn. 06031.

CAREER: Wartime office worker, 1942-46; assistant to husband, teacher of natural history at Vassar Summer Institute, 1949-51; *Lakeville Journal,* Lakeville Conn., assistant editor, 1952-60. Falls Village Board of Education, chairman, 1954-58.

WRITINGS: *Keer-loo: The True Story of a Young Wood Duck,* Naturegraph, 1965; *Keeping the Plants You Pick* (ALA Notable Book), Crowell, 1970.

Illustrator: Boughton Cobb, *A Field Guide to Ferns,* Houghton, 1956; H. Lincoln Foster, *Rock Gardening,* Houghton, 1968; Florence H. Pettit, *How to Make Whirligigs and Whimmy Diddles* (Junior Literary Guild selection; ALA Notable Book), Crowell, 1972.

SIDELIGHTS: "I am primarily a gardener as my husband and I have constructed and maintain—with no outside help—a seven-acre wildflower garden which is visited by between 600-1,000 people a year. I write and draw because I love to, but my New England conscience makes me feel guilty when I do it just for my own pleasure. Thus it's nice to have publishers willing to use my work so that I can feel what I am doing for fun is also useful.

"I think producing books for children is more valuable than producing them for adults because the books I read as a child had the greatest influence on me. It's the old story of bending the twig while it is still supple. If my books open the door for only two or three children into the world of nature which has given me such pleasure, I should be happy.

"My writing and drawing has to be fitted in between my gardening and household chores and sometimes my husband wonders if he is going to have a clean shirt and dinner. Once I am deep in a drawing or sentence it's hard to extract me from the world of imagination."

Ms. Foster does wood carvings of birds (in miniature) as well as botanical drawings. The Fosters have carried on botanical research in the mountains of eastern and western America, France, Switzerland, Great Britain, and the Near East.

FOR MORE INFORMATION SEE: Library Journal, September, 1970. *Horn Book,* October, 1970; *Junior Literary Guild Catalogue,* September, 1972.

LAURA LOUISE FOSTER

Keer-loo now spent a major portion of his day in preening. ■ (From *Keer-Loo: The True Story of a Young Wood Duck* by Laura Louise Foster. Illustrated by the author.)

FRANKLIN, Steve
See STEVENS, Franklin

FRASCONI, Antonio   1919-

PERSONAL: Born April 28, 1919, in Buenos Aires, Argentina; son of Franco and Armida (Carbonai) Frasconi; married Leona Pierce, 1952; children: Pablo, Miguel. *Education:* Came to United States on scholarship to Art Students League, New York, 1945; studied mural painting at The New School for Social Research, 1947. *Home and studio:* 26 Dock Rd., South Norwalk, Conn.

CAREER: Artist. Sometime member of art faculty of The New School, Brooklyn Museum, Vassar College, Atlanta Art Institute, Pratt Institute. Has had 61 one-man shows in the United States, Mexico, Uruguay, Europe. In 1953-54 the Smithsonian Institution, Washington, D.C., circulated a one-man show of his work. Represented in collections of Museum of Modern Art and Metropolitan Museum (New York), Philadelphia Museum, Library of Congress, San Diego Museum, St. Louis Museum, Baltimore Museum, Detroit Art Institute, Honolulu Academy of Art, and other galleries. *Awards, honors:* Twice winner of Inter-American fellowship of Guggenheim Foundation to illustrate poetry of Walt Whitman and Garcia Lorca, 1952-53; National Institute of Arts and Letters grant, 1954; Grand Prix at Venice Film Festival, 1960, for "The Neighboring Shore," a short film with more than one hundred woodcuts illustrating Walt Whitman's poems.

Sun that melts the snow,
Snow that hurts my feet,
why are you bad?
I am not bad;
the Ox is bad
that drinks me.
■ (From *The Snow and the Sun*
by Antonio Frasconi. Illustrated by the author.)

Something about the Author

WRITINGS—All self-illustrated: *12 Fables of Aesop*, Museum of Modern Art, 1954 (newly narrated by Glenway Wescott, 1964); *See and Say*, Harcourt, 1955; *Woodcuts by Antonio Frasconi*, E. Weyhe, 1957; *The House that Jack Built*, Harcourt, 1958; *Birds from My Homeland*, privately published, 1958; *The Face of Edgar Allan Poe*, privately published, 1959; *A Whitman Portrait*, privately published, 1960; *The Snow and the Sun* (ALA Notable Book), Harcourt, 1961; *A Sunday in Monterey*, Harcourt, 1964; *See Again, Say Again*, Harcourt, 1964; *A Bestiary*, Harcourt, 1965; *Kaleidoscope in Woodcuts*, Harcourt, 1968.

Illustrator: Ruth Krauss, *Cantilever Rainbow*, Pantheon, 1965; Pablo Neruda, *Bestiary/Bestiario* (poem), Harcourt, 1965; Louis Untermeyer, *Love Lyrics*, Odyssey, 1965; Walt Whitman, *Overheard the Sun*, Farrar, Straus, 1969; Mario Benedetti, editor, *Unstill Life*, Harcourt, 1969; Isaac B. Singer, *Elijah the Slave*, Farrar, Straus, 1970; Gabriela Mistral, *Crickets and Frogs: A Fable in Spanish and English*, translated by Doris Dana, Atheneum, 1972.

FOR MORE INFORMATION SEE: Print, winter, 1950; *Newsweek*, March 17, 1952, April 5, 1954; *Illustrators of Children's Books: 1946-1956*, Horn Book, 1958; *Horizon*, March, 1961; *Time*, December 20, 1963; *New Republic*, February 29, 1964; *School Arts*, May, 1966; Diana Klemin, *The Art of Art for Children's Books*, Clarkson Potter, 1966; *Illustrators of Children's Books: 1957-1966*, Horn Book, 1968; Diana Klemin, *The Illustrated Book*, Clarkson Potter, 1970; *Graphis 155*, Volume 27, Graphis Press, 1971/72; *Third Book of Junior Authors*, edited by de Montreville and Hill, H. W. Wilson, 1972.

ANTONIO FRASCONI, with son

FRENCH, Fiona 1944-

PERSONAL: Born June 27, 1944, in Bath, England; daughter of Robert Douglas (Lloyd's surveyor), and Mary G. (Black) French. *Education:* Croyden College of Art, N.D.D., 1966. *Residence:* Surrey, England.

CAREER: Psychiatric Hospital, Epsom, Surrey, England, teacher of art therapy, 1967-69; free-lance illustrator, London, England, 1967—. Teacher of design at Wimbledon School of Art. *Awards, honors: The Blue Bird* was a Children's Book Showcase Title, 1973.

WRITINGS—Self-illustrated juveniles: *Jack of Hearts*, Harcourt, 1970; *Huni*, Oxford University Press, 1971; *The Blue Bird*, Walck, 1972; *King Tree*, Oxford University Press, 1973.

SIDELIGHTS: "I intend my books for younger children, and put details in the pictures which might hold their attention even if they cannot read and are 'being-read-to.' The market is from six to nine years old, but maybe younger or older than this, depending on child and parents, etc.

"When I begin a story, it is at first only a vague 'idea,' by no means complete. I continue to think about this idea, sometimes making notes, until I am perfectly sure it will be strong enough for a book. After this I do a great deal of research in museums and libraries, gathering authentic detail that will support the basic idea. Bit by bit the idea grows and changes. After about three months writing and research, and with a much clearer idea of the story, I start to do the pictures. This can take six to nine months. When those are finished the story is rewritten again to link more closely with the pictures. Thus a book can take a year to do.

"I am very influenced by outside material, I treat each book as a new venture, during which I discover information I never knew before. I do not start a book knowing what is going on each page, from cover to cover, but keep other books around me so that I can, at any time, look into them and be informed about details. I never do roughs for finished drawings, but much prefer to redo a 'finished drawing' if it goes wrong. This enables me to keep inspiration alive. Sometimes in the middle of a book, I find I can get so involved, that the picture almost 'draws itself.' This happened with the 'enormous cat' in *The Blue Bird*. But it happens very rarely and in my experience is as good as flying!"

HOBBIES AND OTHER INTERESTS: Collecting "blue and white" china and old editions of children's books.

FOR MORE INFORMATION SEE: Horn Book, October, 1972.

FRICK, C. H.
See IRWIN, Constance Frick

FRICK, Constance
See IRWIN, Constance Frick

Up sprang the cat, enormous and fierce.
He caught the Enchantress in his paws,
and ate her up in one mouthful.

■ (From *The Blue Bird* by Fiona French. Illustrated by the author.)

Something about the Author

■ (From *Journey to the Moon* by Erich Fuchs. Illustrated by the author.)

FUCHS, Erich 1916-

PERSONAL: Born March 16, 1916, in Stuttgart, Germany; son of Friedrich Wilhelm and Maria (Faul) Fuchs; married Hilde Hermann (a master hand weaver), August 30, 1952; children: Andrea, Olaf. *Education:* Kunstgewerbeschule (School of Applied Arts), 1935-37; Staatliche Akademie der Bildende Kuenste (State Academy of Fine Arts), Stuttgart, qualified architect, 1946-48. *Home:* Gruenewaldstrasse 45, Stuttgart, West Germany.

CAREER: State Academy of Fine Arts, Stuttgart, Germany, instructor in weaving, material design, and tapestry weaving, 1949-58; free-lance artist, 1958—. *Military service:* German Army, 1939-45. *Awards, honors:* Fourth prize in modern art competition at Darmstadt, Germany; Primero Graphico die Fiera, Bologna, 1970, for *Moonwalk*.

WRITINGS—Self-illustrated: *Nawai* (Buchpreis selection list), Ellermann Publishers, 1965; *Hier Apollo II*, Ellermann Publishers, 1969, translation published as *Moonwalk: The Story of Apollo II* (Buchpreis selection list), Abelard, 1969; *Journey to the Moon* (*Horn Book* honor list; ALA Notable Book), Seymour Lawrence-Delacorte, 1970; *Wie Arbeitet ein Kernkraftwerk*, Ellermann, 1971, translation published as *What Makes a Nuclear Power Plant Work*, Seymour Lawrence-Delacorte, 1971; *Hier Studio 7*, Ellermann, 1972.

Illustrator: Brothers Grimm, *Vom Fischer und seiner Frau*, Ellermann, 1971.

WORK IN PROGRESS: Junior Atlas.

SIDELIGHTS: "People noticed my artistic ability early in my school years. Painting and drawing were more important to me than were the many academic subjects, so my father had to give up his hope that I would pursue more conventional studies. He thus withdrew me quite early from school and employed me in his goldsmith shop. I was not able to finally realize my ambition to be a free-lance artist until after the end of the war in 1945.

"At first my mode of expression was drawing and the themes were people of the post-war period. In 1945 my pictures were abstract, and in 1948 pure abstract. During this time I created three illustrated books for children, but these were not printed as they were labeled 'too modern.'

"In 1949 I received a position teaching weaving at the State Academy of Fine Arts. While there I married one of my students, Hilde Hermann, who was a tapestry artist. In 1958 my teaching position was unjustly revoked with the explanation that 'Erich Fuchs is too much an artist.' Since this time I have been working as a free-lance artist.

"In 1956 we built a small studio outside the city far from neighbors. In the mornings we slept late and ate a large breakfast amidst stimulating discussions about our work. Not until the afternoon did we begin work, accompanied by coffee and cigarettes. This lasted late into the night.

"When the children were still small, I would tell them stories every night. Everywhere I went I was, and am still today, known as a story teller. Often the story is not yet clear when I begin. However, the best notions come to me during the telling of the story. Fantasy is the starting point of my artistic creation.

"For Christmas, 1963, my children wanted an illustrated book about the stories of Nawai. This book amazed the Ellermann Publishing Company and they printed it. Nawai is a book that should make both modern and more traditional art understandable to children as well as to their parents. The children's book, in my view, is the first art and school book that children get in their hands. I cannot understand when the critics often write 'the book by Erich Fuchs is an art book and therefore more for adults.' I am of the opinion that only the very best is good enough for our children.

"I am not an illustrator. With me the text and pictures appear simultaneously. I try to form both as a unity. It is important to me that the word possess a function just as do the line and the color. In story telling the illustration is the gesture that belongs to the telling. From purely artistic reflections come still further manuscripts for children's books which found no publisher since they were too modern.

ERICH FUCHS

"With regard to my own sketches, I've been working since 1964 on socially critical studies and on sketches in the form of a diary. These allow me to recognize again and again the poor educational system. In addition I've concluded that people in our time, out of ignorance, are afraid of our modern technology, science, and art. In 1969 during the Apollo II shot, I tried to grasp our technical and scientific world with artistic means. I designate the book that grew out of this effort, *Moonwalk,* as an artistic reference book. The reference book demands from me as an artist a dialogue with modern technology and science that permits me to sense today's realities. It is especially the artist, if he is aware of his function in society, who cannot isolate himself from the realities and problems that confront us. The success of my book *Journey to the Moon* proves to me the validity of the course I have entered upon."

FOR MORE INFORMATION SEE: Die Welt, December 9, 1965; *Du-Atlantis,* April, 1966; *Die Zeit,* November 28, 1969; *Durrant's Teachers World* (London), March 29, 1970; *New York Times Book Review,* April 5, 1970; *School Library Journal,* May, 1970.

GARFIELD, James B. 1881-

PERSONAL: Born September 19, 1881, in Atlanta, Ga.; son of Joseph Theodore and Caroline (Bandman) Garfield; married Maudie Sheridan, March 2, 1910 (deceased); married Edith Weil, April 16, 1924 (deceased); children: (second marriage) Caroline Lazarus, Jack Lazarus. *Education:* Educated in Atlanta, where he also studied at Southern Business College. *Politics:* Registered Democrat ("vote the man"). *Religion:* "Believe in all of them." *Home:* 1735 North Western Ave., Los Angeles, Calif. 90027.

CAREER: Became an actor, 1903, and reached Broadway under management of Henry B. Harris of Jesse Lasky Production, 1907; when Harris was lost on the "Titanic," Garfield entered vaudeville with his wife as partner, appearing in original sketch on Pantages and other circuits throughout the United States and Canada; went to Los Angeles in 1930 as a free-lance radio writer and actor, playing in more than 2,500 episodes of soap operas until blindness ended his acting career, 1940; continued to do radio work, 1947-67, broadcasting weekly public service program, "A Blind Man Looks at You," in Los Angeles. Dramatic coach, 1930—; lecturer in public schools, 1957—. Appointed member of California State Board of Guide Dogs of the Blind, 1950, reappointed, 1956, 1960; former secretary, California Council of the Blind. *Military service:* U.S. Army, 1917-20; became sergeant major, 137th Aerial Squadron, American Expeditionary Forces, France.

MEMBER: National Federation of the Blind, California Federation of Chaparral Poets (chapter president, six years; member of state board, 1968), Los Angeles County Club of Adult Blind (president, 1946-63; president emeritus and life member of executive board), Masons. *Awards, honors:* D.O., University of Southern California, 1956, for service to School of Optometry; plaques and other awards for civic service and service to the blind from *Los Angeles Daily News,* 1952, California Council of the Blind, 1963, Active Blind, Inc., 1968, and Mayor of Los Angeles, 1969.

Now he was completely lost . . . [He] tried to feel from which direction the sun was shining by turning his face to feel the heat. ■ (From *Follow My Leader* by James B. Garfield. Illustrated by Robert Greiner.)

WRITINGS: Follow My Leader (youth book), Viking, 1957, latest reprint, 1973; *Visions* (poems), privately-printed limited edition, 1958; *They Like You Better* (youth book), Viking, 1959. Writer of vaudeville sketches and radio scripts. Contributor of stories, poems, and articles to juvenile magazines.

WORK IN PROGRESS: An adult biography; two adult murder mysteries; revising one adult philosophical novel and one juvenile novel.

SIDELIGHTS: Follow My Leader, the story of a blind boy's return to normal living, is in its twelfth printing and has appeared in numerous paperback editions, including editions in New Zealand and Australia. As an actor, Garfield was in practically every large city in the United States. "The theater required and am proficient in British, French, German, Italian, Scotch, Irish, Polynesian and Southern dialects."

GINSBURG, Mirra

PERSONAL: Born in Russia; daughter of Joseph and Bronia (Geier) Ginsburg. *Education:* Attended schools in Russia, Latvia, Canada, and United States. *Home:* 150 West 96th St., New York, N.Y. 10025. *Agent:* Gunther Stuhlmann, 65 Irving Pl., New York. N.Y. 10003.

CAREER: Free-lance editor, and translator from Russian and Yiddish. *Member:* P.E.N. *Awards, honors:* Lewis Carroll Shelf Award, 1972, for *The Diary of Nina Kosterina;* Mildred L. Batchelder nomination, 1973, for *The Kaha Bird,* and 1974, for *The White Ship; The Chick and the Duckling* was a Children's Book Showcase Title, 1973.

WRITINGS—Children's books (editor, adaptor and translator): *The Diary of Nina Kosterina* (young adult; translated only), Crown, 1968; *The Fox and the Hare* (picture book), Crown, 1969; *The Master of the Winds: Folk Tales from Siberia,* Crown, 1970; *Three Rolls and One Doughnut: Fables from Russia* (Child Study Association book list; *School Library Journal* book list), Dial, 1970; *The Kaha Bird: Folk Tales from Central Asia,* Crown, 1971; *One Trick Too Many: Tales about Foxes,* Dial, 1972; *The Chick and the Duckling* (picture book), Macmillan, 1972; *What Kind of Bird is That!* (picture book), Crown, 1972; *Three Kittens* (Junior Literary Guild selection), Crown, 1973; *The Lazies: Tales of the Peoples of Russia,* Macmillan, 1973.

Editor and translator: *The Fatal Eggs and Other Soviet Satire,* Macmillan, 1965; *The Dragon: Fifteen Stories by Yevgeny Zamyatin,* Random House, 1966; *The Last Door to Aiya: Anthology of Soviet Science Fiction,* S. G. Phillips, 1968; *A Soviet Heretic: Essays by Yevgeny Zamyatin,* University of Chicago Press, 1970; *The Ultimate Threshold: Anthology of Soviet Science Fiction,* Holt, 1970.

Translator: Roman Goul, *Azef,* Doubleday, 1962; Vera Alexandrova, *A History of Soviet Literature,* Doubleday, 1963; Mikhail Bulgakov, *The Master and Margarita,* Grove Press, 1967; Mikhail Bulgakov, *Heart of a Dog,* Grove Press, 1968; Mikhail Bulgakov, *Flight* (a play), Grove Press, 1969; Mikhail Bulgakov, *The Life of Monsieur de Moliere,* Funk, 1970; Yevgeny Zamyatin, *We*

MIRRA GINSBURG

86

There was a rabbit in the woods who liked to brag: "I am the bravest beast of all!" he would say. "I have huge paws, huge whiskers, and huge teeth. I'm not afraid of anybody." ■ (From *Three Rolls and One Doughnut* retold by Mirra Ginsburg. Illustrated by Anita Lobel.)

(novel), Viking, 1972; Chingiz Aitmatov, *The White Ship,* Crown, 1972. Other translations include stories by Isaac Bashevis Singer, Isaac Babel, and Zoshchenko, for various anthologies, collections, and magazines; co-translator of Isaac Babel's play, "Sunset," produced in 1966 and 1972.

SIDELIGHTS: "I have loved folk tales since childhood, and have gone on collecting them and delighting in them ever since. I place folk tales among the greatest works of literature. To me, they are a distillation of man's deepest experience into poetry, wisdom, truth, sadness and laughter. The folk tale preserves values that have been largely crushed in the 'modern,' material world. It means truth as opposed to bare fact, wisdom as opposed to mere knowledge, imagination as opposed to sterile, utilitarian (and often destructive) reason. It holds, in all its aspects, the truth about us. And it is play and magic at their purest and most delightful.

"What I try to do in my work, then, is to offer a counterbalance to the merely 'useful,' to extend horizons, to restore dimensions suppressed or eliminated by 'progress.'

"My childhood home in Russia was almost literally in the folktale world: pinewoods and birches, wide fields and meadows rich with wild flowers closely surrounded our small town in Byelorussia. Animals and birds in the woods; animals in the farms and courtyards; gardens and orchards; synagogues and churches; dusty streets turned into muddy puddles after rain, with pigs delightedly wallowing in them and women rinsing wash in rivulets running along the gutter, or in the nearby river; tales of magic and 'superstition'—all these persisted for a long time in the province despite the revolution and, with many other, tragic, things, formed the substance of my earliest years."

HOBBIES AND OTHER INTERESTS: Fiction, especially fantastic and satirical, poetry, cats (big and little), birds, early music, early and primitive art.

FOR MORE INFORMATION SEE: Christian Science Monitor, November 6, 1969, May 2, 1973; *Horn Book,* April, 1971, December, 1971; *Washington Post* ("Children's Book World"), November 5, 1972; *Publishers Weekly,* February 5, 1973.

GITTINGS, Robert (William Victor) 1911-

PERSONAL: Born February 1, 1911, in Portsmouth, Hampshire, England; son of Claude Bromley (a surgeon) and Dora (Brayshaw) Gittings; married Katharine Edith Cambell (a teacher), 1934; married Joan Grenville Manton (an author, writing as Jo Manton), 1949; children: (first marriage) Robert Jr., John; (second marriage) Clare. *Education:* Attended St. Edward's School, Oxford; Jesus College, Cambridge, B.A., 1933, M.A., 1936, Litt. D., 1970. *Home:* Dodds, East Dean, Sussex, England.

CAREER: Jesus College, Cambridge, England, supervisor in history, 1933-40; British Broadcasting Corporation, London, England, writer and producer of literary and historical features, 1940-63; continues to write and broadcast regularly; poet and biographer. Visiting professor of English

literature, Vanderbilt University, summer, 1966, Boston University, 1970, University of Washington, 1972. *Member:* Royal Society of Literature (fellow). *Awards, honors:* Royal Society of Literature award, 1955, for *John Keats: The Living Year, 21 September, 1818, to 21 September, 1819;* W. H. Smith Award, 1968, for *John Keats;* Commander of the Order of the British Empire, 1970.

WRITINGS: John Keats: The Living Year, 21 September, 1818, to 21 September, 1819, Heinemann, 1954; *The Mask of Keats,* Harvard University Press, 1956; (with wife, Jo Manton) *Windows on History,* 4 books, Hulton, 1959-61; *Shakespeare's Rival,* Heinemann, 1960; (editor) *The Living Shakespeare,* Heinemann, 1960, Barnes & Noble, 1968; *This Tower My Prison,* Heinemann, 1961; (with Jo Manton) *The Story of John Keats,* Dutton, 1962; *The Keats Inheritance,* Heinemann, 1964; (with Jo Manton) *Makers of the Twentieth Century,* Longacre Press, 1966; (editor and author of introduction and commentary) *Selected Poems and Letters of John Keats,* Barnes & Noble, 1966; *Matters of Love and Death,* Heinemann, 1968; *John Keats,* Little, Brown, 1968; (editor) *Odes of Keats and Their Earliest Known Manuscripts in Facsimile,* Kent State University Press, 1970; (editor) *Selected Letters of John Keats,* Oxford University Press, 1970; *American Journey: Twenty-five Sonnets,* 1972. (For complete list of writings see *Contemporary Authors,* Volume 25-28.) Also author of *son et lumiere* scripts for St. Paul's and Canterbury Cathedrals.

WORK IN PROGRESS: Research on poetry of Thomas Hardy.

SIDELIGHTS: "I have always been very active in athletic pursuits; but when I was in my early teens, I severely overstrained my back, and had to rest for a year. During this time, someone gave me the complete poems of John Keats. This both began my life long interest in the poet, and started me writing poetry myself. A few years later, my friendship with the playwright, Christopher Fry, stimulated my interest in writing plays as well.

"At college, I studied and taught history, not literature. Many of my narrative poems have to do with historical events, and I have always been drawn to biographical approaches to literature. I suppose I believe that facts, whether treated imaginatively, as in poems, or accurately, as in biography, are generally far more dramatic and interesting than fiction or conjecture.

"I don't think my books are particularly intended *for* any one sort of person; but I hope that, both in poems and prose, they have something to say helpfully about the problems of human nature in general."

HOBBIES AND OTHER INTERESTS: Music, "the English countryside, in which I live," and "traditional sports, *but not* blood-sports."

FOR MORE INFORMATION SEE: Observer Review, March 17, 1968; *New Statesman,* March 22, 1968; *Punch,* April 10, 1968; *New York Times,* July 17, 1968; *Christian Science Moniter,* July 25, 1968; *Book World,* July 28, 1968; *New York Times Book Review,* September 1, 1968; *New Republic,* September 7, 1968; *New York Review,* November 7, 1968.

GLUBOK, Shirley (Astor)

PERSONAL: Born in St. Louis, Mo.; daughter of Yale I. (a merchant) and Ann (Astor) Glubok; married Alfred Tamarin, 1968. *Education:* Washington University, St. Louis, Mo., A.B., Columbia University, M.A. *Religion:* Jewish. *Home:* 59 East 80th St., New York, N.Y. 10021.

CAREER: Author of books on art history and archaeology for young people. Metropolitan Museum of Art, New York, lecturer, 1958—. *Member:* Association of Teachers of Independent Schools (representative), Archaeological Society of America, Lexington Democratic Club, Authors Guild, Triple A Tennis Club, Washington University Archaeological Society. *Awards, honors:* Lewis Carroll Shelf Award, 1963, for *The Art of Ancient Egypt;* Western Writers Association Spur Award, 1971, for *The Art of the Southwest Indians.*

WRITINGS: The Art of Ancient Egypt, Atheneum, 1962; *The Art of Lands in the Bible,* Atheneum, 1963; *The Art of Ancient Greece* (ALA Notable Book), Atheneum, 1963; *The Art of the North American Indian,* Harper, 1964; *The Art of the Eskimo* (ALA Notable Book), Harper, 1964; *The Art of Ancient Rome,* Harper, 1965; *The Art of Africa,* Harper, 1965; (editor) *The Fall of the Aztecs,* St. Martins Press, 1965; *Art and Archaeology,* Harper, 1966; *The Art of Ancient Peru,* Harper, 1966; *The Fall of the Incas,* Macmillan, 1967; *The Art of the Etruscans,* Harper, 1967;

Discovering Tut-ankh-Amen's Tomb (ALA Notable Book), Macmillan, 1968; *The Art of Ancient Mexico,* Harper, 1968; *Knights in Armor,* Harper, 1969; *The Art of India,* Macmillan, 1970; *Discovering the Royal Tombs at Ur,* Macmillan, 1970; *The Art of Colonial America* (Child Study Association book list), Macmillan, 1970; *The Art of Japan* (Child Study Association book list), Macmillan, 1970.

FOR MORE INFORMATION SEE: Horn Book, February, 1970, August, 1972, February, 1973; *Library Journal,* October 15, 1970; *New York Times Book Review,* November 21, 1971, July 2, 1972; *Third Book of Junior Authors,* edited by de Montreville and Hill, H. W. Wilson, 1972; Lee Bennett Hopkins, *More Books by More People,* Chilton, 1973.

GOLDFRANK, Helen Colodny 1912-
(Helen Kay)

PERSONAL: Born October 27, 1912, in New York, N.Y.; daughter of Hyman and Tessie (Herman) Colodny; married Herbert Goldfrank, December 7, 1933; children: Lewis, Deborah, Joan. *Home:* 435 East 87th St., New York, N.Y. 10028.

CAREER: Writer. *Member:* Authors League of America, Pen American Center, National Council of Women, Child Study Association, Women's City Club of New York.

That night Father came home with the smallest dog collar and leash he could find. ■ (From *A Duck for Keeps* by Helen Kay. Illustrated by Juliette Palmer.)

WRITINGS—All under pseudonym, Helen Kay: *Apple Pie for Lewis*, Alladin Books, 1951; *One Mitten Lewis* (Junior Literary Guild selection), Lothrop, 1955; *Snow Birthday* (Junior Literary Guild selection), Farrar, Straus, 1955; *City Springtime*, Hastings, 1957; *Lincoln, A Big Man*, Hastings, 1958; *The Magic Mitt*, Hastings, 1959; *Pony for the Winter* (Junior Literary Guild selection), Farrar, Straus, 1959; *Summer to Share*, Hastings, 1960; *Kendy's Monkey Business*, Farrar, Straus, 1961; *Cats on Pier #56*, Reilly & Lee, 1961; *Abe Lincoln's Hobby*, Reilly & Lee, 1961; *A Duck for Keeps* (Lucky Book Club selection), Abelard, 1962; *How Smart Are Animals?*, Basic Books, 1962; *House of Many Colors*, Abelard, 1963; *The Secrets of the Dolphin*, Macmillan, 1964; *A Stocking for a Kitten*, Abelard, 1965; *Picasso's World of Children*, Doubleday, 1965; *Henri's Hands for Pablo Picasso*, Abelard, 1965; *An Egg Is for Wishing*, Abelard, 1966; *Man and Mastiffs*, Macmillan, 1967; *A Name for Little-No-Name*, Abelard, 1968; *Lion for a Sitter*, Abelard, 1969; *Apron On, Apron Off*, Scholastic, 1969; *Apes*, Macmillan, 1970; *A Day in the Life of a Baby Gibbon*, Scholastic, 1972.

GOLDSTON, Robert (Conroy) 1927-
(James Stark)

PERSONAL: Born July 9, 1927, in New York, N.Y.; son of Philip Henry (a salesman) and Josephine (Conroy) Goldston; married Marguerite Garvey, January 3, 1956; children: Rebecca, Gabrielle, Sarah, Francesca, Maximilian, Theresa. *Education:* Columbia University, student, 1946-53. *Politics:* Unaffiliated socialist. *Religion:* None. *Home and office:* Lista de Correos, Santa Eulalia del Rio, Ibiza, Balearic Islands, Spain. *Agent:* Collins-Knowlton-Wing, Inc., 60 East 56th St., New York, N.Y. 10022.

CAREER: Professional writer, living abroad most of the time, 1953—, ten years in Spain, and two in France and England. *Military service:* U.S. Army, 1945-46; became sergeant. *Awards, honors:* Guggenheim fellowship in fiction, 1957-58.

WRITINGS: The Eighth Day (novel), Rinehart, 1956; *The Catafalque* (novel), Rinehart, 1957; (under pseudonym James Stark) *The Greek Virgin*, Avon, 1959; *A History of Satanism*, Ballantine, 1962; *The Shore Dimly Seen* (novel), Random, 1963; (adapter) *Tales of the Alhambra*, Bobbs, 1963; *The Legend of the Cid* (juvenile), Bobbs, 1964; (adapter) *The Song of Roland*, Bobbs, 1965; *The Last of Lazarus* (novel), Random, 1966; *The Russian Revolution* (juvenile), Bobbs, 1966; *The Spanish Civil War* (juvenile), Bobbs, 1966; *The Life and Death of Nazi Germany* (juvenile), Bobbs, 1967; *Spain* (juvenile), Macmillan, 1967; *The Battle of Bataan* (juvenile), Macmillan, 1967; *The Soviets* (adult nonfiction), Bantam, 1967; *The Rise of Red China* (juvenile), Bobbs, 1968; *The Battle of Manila Bay* (juvenile), Macmillan, 1968; *The Negro Revolution* (ALA Notable Book), Macmillan, 1968; *The Great Depression* (juvenile), Bobbs, 1968; *Barcelona: The Civic Stage* (juvenile), Macmillan, 1969; *London: The Civic Spirit* (juvenile), Macmillan, 1969; *Battles of the Constitution* (juvenile), Macmillan, 1969.

New York: Civic Exploitation (juvenile), Macmillan, 1970; *Suburbia: Civic Denial* (juvenile), Macmillan, 1970; *The Cuban Revolution* (juvenile), Bobbs, 1970; *The Coming of the Cold War* (juvenile), Macmillan, 1971; *The Vietnamese Revolution* (juvenile), Bobbs, 1972; *The Coming of the Civil War* (juvenile), Macmillan, 1972; *The Life and Times of Senator Joe McCarthy* (juvenile), Bobbs, 1972; *The Death of Gandhi* (juvenile), Watts, 1972; *The Siege of the Alcazar* (juvenile), Watts, 1972; *Pearl Harbor!* (juvenile), Watts, 1972; *The Fall of the Winter Palace* (juvenile), Watts, 1972; *The Long March* (juvenile), Watts, 1972; *Our Times: The Sixties* (adult nonfiction), Random House, 1972; *Anarchism* (juvenile), Bantam, in press; *The U.S. and South America* (juvenile), Macmillan, in press; *The War to End Wars* (juvenile), Macmillan, in press; *The Rise and Fall of U.S. Imperialism* (juvenile), Bobbs, in press. Writer of television documentary films, "Sunday in Barcelona," 1958, "Bjorn's Inferno," 1964, and "Running Away Backwards," 1965, for Canadian Broadcasting Corp.

SIDELIGHTS: Goldston observes that the "shocking and growing mindlessness and desperation of American society is a vital, if depressing interest."

FOR MORE INFORMATION SEE: Upptak (Stockholm magazine), spring, 1958, *Horn Book*, August, 1970.

GORDON, John 1925-

PERSONAL: Born November 19, 1925; son of Norman (a teacher) and Margaret (Revely) Gordon; married Sylvia Young, January 4, 1954; children: Sally, Robert. *Education:* Educated in Jarrow and Wisbech, England. *Home:* 99 George Borrow Rd., Norwich, Norfolk NOR 41G, England. *Office: Eastern Daily Press*, Norwich, Norfolk, England.

CAREER: Isle of Ely and Wisbech Advertiser, Wisbech, England, reporter, 1947-51; *Bury Free Press*, Bury St. Edmunds, Suffolk, England, successively chief reporter and sub-editor, 1951-58; *Western Evening Herald*, Plymouth, England, sub-editor, 1958-62; *Eastern Evening News*, Norwich, England, columnist and sub-editor, 1962—. *Military service:* Royal Navy, 1943-47.

WRITINGS: The Giant Under the Snow (junior book), Hutchinson, 1968, Harper, 1970; *The House on the Brink* (suspense novel for young adults), Hutchinson, 1970, Harper, 1971; (contributor) *Young Winter's Tales 2*, Macmillan, 1971.

WORK IN PROGRESS: A novel for young adults.

SIDELIGHTS: "Stories are dreams in disguise. There are dreams hidden in all my stories. They are necessary, but they must remain hidden because they are mine and mean nothing to anybody else. The stories that surround them are meant to make you have similar dreams, your *own* dreams, which will again be secret. Stories are a way of sharing secrets too deep to mention.

"It is because I have to share this kind of feeling with other people that I write stories. And a story, no matter how strange the events in it, must be largely a matter of fact. So the places are real. I was brought up in the Fen Country of England, the eastern part that was once all marshes (or fens), but is now fields of rich black earth that stretch away as flat as the sea from horizon to horizon. It is a place full

It was a cold, bright night . . . [They moved] warily, but once again nothing threatened them as they crossed the city, and they got to the bus station with time to spare. ■ (From *The Giant Under the Snow* by John Gordon. Illustrated by Rocco Negri.)

of stories already. There was a giant killer called Hickathrift; nearer the coast a ghost dog called Old Shuck pads the roads at night; King John is said to have lost his Crown Jewels in the marsh and people still dig for them. I use the places I know. The people become real to me as I write.

"I have a wife and two children, and as our house is too small for me to have a study I have a desk in the corner of one room. But, as it happens, I don't do much of my writing there. I get up early, just before six, and as the kitchen is the place that warms up quickest, I turn on the radiator and work there until everybody comes down. I write in longhand so there's only an exercise book and a pen to remove from the table before the breakfast things take over. I work for the rest of the day as a sub-editor in a newspaper office. My desk in the corner at home is used mainly in the evenings for writing letters.

"I said I use dreams. Dreams reach into strange areas. *The House on the Brink* is a kind of ghost story and it led me into one of the strangest experiences I have had. The house of the title is an actual old house on the brink of an actual river. The 'ghost', a stump of wood that may be a body, is found in the mud of the river and it exerts a powerful influence over the woman who lives in the house.

"I invented everything except the house and the river, and I had not been in the house for fifteen years when I wrote the book and did not revisit it until after the book was published. When I did so I discovered a part of the garden I had not known existed. It was to one side, behind a wall, and stretched away a considerable distance from the house. In the farthest part of it, on the far side of a lawn and almost hidden in the trees, stood a stump. It was very much the shape of the stump I had described in the book but when I went closer I discovered it was stone and not wood. However, at the blunt, rounded top, which in the story contains a skull, there was carved, very faintly and almost worn away by time, the face of a man.

"Everything fitted so close to my story that I went back to the house, which is a showplace open to visitors, and asked about the stump. The custodian told me that it was the shaft of an ancient stone cross that had once stood in the road behind the house, and that seemed to be the end of the matter. She did not know me nor the story I had written, but then she said, 'About a century ago they dredged that old stump from the mud of the river outside.'

"The fens, as I said, are full of stories."

FOR MORE INFORMATION SEE: New Statesman, November, 1968; *Horn Book,* October, 1971; *Signal,* May, 1972.

JOHN GORDON

RON GOULART

GOULART, Ron(ald Joseph) 1933-

PERSONAL: Born January 13, 1933, in Berkeley, Calif.; son of Joseph Silveira and Josephine (Macri) Goulart; married Fran Sheridan (a writer), June 13, 1964; children: Sean, Steffan. *Education:* University of California, Berkeley, B.A., 1955. *Politics:* Democrat. *Religion:* None. *Home:* 87 Olmstead Hill Rd., Wilton, Conn. 06897.

CAREER: Guild, Bascom & Bonfigli (advertising), San Francisco, Calif., copywriter, 1955-57, 1958-60; Alan Alch, Inc., Los Angeles, Calif., consulting copywriter, 1961-63; Hoefer, Dieterich & Brown (advertising), San Francisco, Calif., copywriter, 1967; free-lance writer. *Member:* Mystery Writers of America, Science Fiction Writers of America.

WRITINGS: (Editor and author of introduction) *The Hardboiled Dicks* (anthology), Sherbourne, 1965; *Line Up Tough Guys,* Sherbourne, 1966; *The Sword Swallower* (novel), Doubleday, 1968; *The Assault on Childhood* (nonfiction), Sherbourne, 1969; *After Things Fell Apart* (novel), Ace, 1970; *Broke Down Engine* (short stories), Macmillan, 1971; *What's Become of Screwloose?* (ALA Best Young Adult book list), Scribner, 1971; *Gadget Man* (novel), Doubleday, 1971; *Death Cell* (novel), Beagle, 1971; *If Dying Was All* (novel), Ace, 1971; *Hawkshaw* (novel),

Doubleday, 1972; *Too Sweet to Die* (novel), Ace, 1972; *Wildsmith* (novel), Ace, 1972; *The Chameleon Corps* (short stories), Macmillan, 1972; *Cheap Thrills: An Informal History of the Pulp Magazines* (nonfiction), Arlington, 1972; *Plunder* (novel), Beagle, 1972; *The Same Lie Twice,* (novel), Ace, 1973; *Shaggy Planet* (novel), Lancer, 1973; *A Talent for the Invisible* (novel), DAW, 1973; *An American Family* (nonfiction), Warner, 1973; *Cleopatra Jones* (novel), Warner, 1973; *The Tin Angel* (novel), DAW, 1973. Stories anthologized in more than thirty collections, including *Best Detective Stories, Spectrum 4,* and *Year's Best Science Fiction.* Magazine contributions also include nonfiction and humor.

WORK IN PROGRESS: Several novels; another collection of science fiction stories for Scribner; a history of newspaper adventure comic strips for Arlington.

GOULD, Lilian 1920-

PERSONAL: Born April 19, 1920, in Philadelphia, Pa.; daughter of Reuben Barr (an executive) and Lilian Valentine (Scott) Seidel; married Irving Gould (owner of an advertising agency), November 16, 1944; children: Mark, Scott, Paul, John. *Education:* Charles Morris Price School of Journalism, A.A., 1938; twenty years later resumed studies in evening classes at University of Pennsylvania. *Politics:* "Mildly liberal." *Religion:* Episcopalian. *Home:* 117 Sugartown Rd., Devon, Pa. 19333. *Agent:* Lurton Blassingame, 60 East 42nd St., New York, N.Y.

MEMBER: Women's International League for Peace and Freedom, Friends' Peace Committee, Philadelphia Children's Reading Round Table.

WRITINGS: Our Living Past (juvenile), Lippincott, 1969.

WORK IN PROGRESS: A book on the evolution of behavior, titled *Hunters, Women, and War;* a juvenile novel laid in Africa, *Spear Over the Sacred Tree.*

SIDELIGHTS: "I am deeply concerned with the education of young people, specifically that they learn about themselves and their world: the physical and cultural development of their own species as it emerged from lower animals. This includes the origin of instinct and behavior, the causes of violence, the process of learning, the significance of sexual differences, and much more—most of which is overlooked in school. Ecology, genetics, anthropology, ethology, and related subjects could well be introduced four or five years before college, but only if it is brought within reach. This, I think, is a *writer's* job rather than a specialists's; and that is the reason why, even though I had no scientific training, I undertook to lead the young reader (and his teacher) through the maze of current theory.

"I live, and have lived for the past twenty-three years, in a large, turn-of-the-century, white frame house in Devon, Pa., which is on the Main Line of Philadelphia. With my husband, it was here and, earlier, in Bryn Mawr that I have raised our four sons.

"Philadelphia is my city; it is where I was born and lived the few years before my parents moved to the Main Line. My mother, grandmother, and great-grandmother were

92

born there, too. My grandfather was manager of Philadelphia's Bellevue-Stratford Hotel for over a quarter of a century; my great-grandfather supplied the bronze for the statue of William Penn that sits atop City Hall. Although I attended suburban public schools, I went to college in the city and then worked there—in advertising agencies mostly, because that is one way a person can write and get paid for it. I was secretary, copywriter, production manager and Jill-of-all trades in the world of advertising. That is, until I married an art director and settled down with Spock, Gesell, and Freud on one hand and children on the other. I had a lot to learn about children.

"I was writing, and getting together in the evenings with other house-bound housewives who wrote. Short stories and poetry were my specialty because their length suited the amounts of time I had available. (I would still rather write poetry than anything else.) Publication was not my aim then; I was sharpening the tools of my craft, and nothing hones word precision as well as does the writing of poetry. Then, twenty years after I left college, I was enrolling at the University of Pennsylvania—evening classes only—and commuting the twenty miles on a regular basis. It was at Penn's Writers' Workshop that Christopher Davis urged me to write for publication, to 'send stuff out'; also to 'stay home and write.' And so I ceased being the perennial course-taker I had become.

LILIAN GOULD

"But what to write? The short story market is limited; more so the poetry market. The answer was there in the form of a class I was asked to teach at a Friends' First Day School. I was no teacher; only one of the parents. Nor was I a Quaker; only a long-standing attender at the Friends' Meeting. But no matter, for the course was to be the *Old Testament,* subtitled *The Beginnings of Our Religion.* By this time I understood children pretty well, but I had a lot to learn about the subject of this course. The children were fifth and sixth graders—uncommonly precocious youngsters: inquisitive, sceptical, challenging, and chatty. I was nervous, clutching my only textbook: the new translation of the *Torah.* We started with that and got no further; nor was there anything in the traditional Christian Sunday School material that would help. It was the old *Genesis* vs. Darwinism controversy.

"So the class and I learned together, with teacher one short step ahead of students. We learned about evolution, about creation. And I filled notebooks with their questions about how it all began. In those two years we went from the birth of the planet to the invention of cuneiform writing, pausing at fossils, dinosaurs, mammals, monkeys, and the beliefs of primitive man. Not only were those classes an unexpected success with the children, but out of my jumble of notes a book was born. Then began the four years' research into religion, plus anthropology, paleontology, biology, genetics, physics, geophysics and other unfamiliar territory. I delved into the writings of Father Teilhard, Arthur Koestler, Julian Huxley, Rene Dubos, Konrad Lorenz, Theodosius Dobzhansky, and anyone else who had a theory about man. All of them had different (and differing) ideas about human evolution. Still, I got most of it together in my head and wrote a book for young people. One reviewer says that *Our Living Past* conveys, unlike other books on evolution, excitement and wonder. If so, that is because I was taught by children to ask the *how* and *why* of things as they are."

GRAY, Elizabeth Janet 1902-
(Elizabeth Gray Vining)

PERSONAL: Born October 6, 1902, in Philadelphia, Pa.; daughter of John Gordon (a businessman) and Anne Moore (Iszard) Gray; married Morgan Vining, January 31, 1929 (deceased). *Education:* Bryn Mawr College, A.B., 1923; Drexel Institute School of Library Science, B.S., 1926. *Politics:* Independent. *Religion:* Society of Friends. *Address:* Kendal at Longwood, Box 194, Kennett Square, Pa. 19348. *Agent:* Curtis Brown Ltd., 50 East 56th St., New York, N.Y. 10022.

CAREER: Tutor to the Crown Prince of Japan, 1946-50. Vice-president of trustees of Bryn Mawr College, 1951-71. *Member:* Authors League, P.E.N. Club (New York). *Awards, honors:* Constance Lindsay Skinner award; American Women's Eminent Achievement award; Distinguished Daughter of Pennsylvania; Third Order of the Sacred Crown, Japan; Newbery Medal for book, *Adam of the Road,* 1943; *Herald Tribune* Spring Festival award for book, *Sandy,* 1945; fourteen honorary degrees, including Litt.D., Tufts College, 1952, Litt.D., Lafayette College, 1956, D.Ed., Rhode Island College of Education, 1956, and L.H.D., Haverford College, 1958.

Adam had never been so frightened in all his life. He had never before been on the wrong side of the law. ■ (From *Adam of the Road* by Elizabeth Janet Gray. Illustrated by Robert Lawson.)

Something about the Author

ELIZABETH JANET GRAY

WRITINGS: Meredith's Ann, Doubleday, 1929; *Tilly-Tod,* Doubleday, 1929; *Meggy MacIntosh,* Doubleday, 1930; *Tangle Garden,* Doubleday, 1932; *Jane Hope,* Viking, 1933; *Beppy Marlowe of Charles Town,* Viking, 1936; *Young Walter Scott,* Viking, 1938; *Penn,* Viking, 1938; *Contributions of the Quakers,* Davis, 1939; *The Fair Adventure,* Viking, 1940; *Anthology with Comments,* Pendle Hill, 1942; *Adam of the Road,* Viking, 1942; *Sandy,* Viking, 1945; (under name Elizabeth Gray Vining) *Windows for the Crown Prince,* Lippincott, 1952; *The World in Tune,* Harper, 1954; *The Virginia Exiles,* Lippincott, 1955; *Friend of Life: The Biography of Rufus M. Jones,* Lippincott, 1958; *The Cheerful Heart,* Viking, 1959; *Return to Japan,* Lippincott, 1960; *I Will Adventure,* Viking, 1962; *Take Heed of Loving Me,* Lippincott, 1963; *Flora: A Biography,* Lippincott, 1966, published in England as *Flora MacDonald,* Bles, 1967; *I, Roberta,* Lippincott, 1967; (under name Elizabeth Gray Vining) *Quiet Pilgrimage* (autobiography), Lippincott, 1970; (under name Elizabeth Gray Vining) *The Taken Girl,* Viking, 1972.

FOR MORE INFORMATION SEE: Junior Book of Authors, edited by Kunitz and Haycraft, H.W. Wilson, 1934, 2nd edition, 1951; *Newbery Medal Books: 1922-1955,* edited by Miller and Field, 1955; *Horn Book,* December, 1970, December, 1972.

GREENLEAF, Barbara Kaye 1942-

PERSONAL: Born July 1, 1942, in New York, N.Y.; daughter of Louis C. (a builder) and Alice (Ginsburg) Kaye; married Jonathan W. Greenleaf (an advertising executive), July 29, 1965; children: Caroline Kaye, Catherine Kaye. *Education:* Vassar College, B.A., 1963. *Home:* 5 Birch Grove Dr., Armonk, N.Y. 10504.

CAREER: Grolier, Inc., New York, N.Y., assistant editor of *New Book of Knowledge,* 1963-64; *New York Times,* writer, 1964-66. *Member:* League of Women Voters.

WRITINGS: America Fever: The Story of American Immigration (Child Study Association book list), Four Winds, 1970; *Forward March to Freedom: The Story of A. Philip Randolph* (Child Study Association book list), Grosset, 1971. Contributor to *Newsday, Bride and Home, Bride's Magazine,* and other publications.

WORK IN PROGRESS: A novel; short stories.

SIDELIGHTS: "I write because it's the most interesting thing I can think of to do—also, it's the only thing I do well. I wrote *America Fever* because I wanted to correct the impression that all immigrants either became millionaires in this country or paraded about constantly in quaint costumes. The truth is that most newcomers did not even reach the middle class, their children did. Moreover, most immigrants did not come for religious freedom but for economic gain. I loved working on the book, especially the times when I read about the immigrants' personal experiences.

BARBARA KAYE GREENLEAF

Irishmen fleeing the potato famine often sailed to England because the short trip over there cost less than a dollar. Others went to the United States and Canada. ■ (From *America Fever: The Story of American Immigration* by Barbara Kaye Greenleaf.)

"I wrote the A. Phillip Randolph biography because I feel he is the most important, unsung black hero in American history. He made great advances against job discrimination not only for blacks but for all working Americans. Meeting Mr. Randolph was a great thrill after doing so much research into his life—he was like a character stepping out of an epic!

"Right now I am working on a novel, a love story. I closet myself away (literally, since I work in what once was a walk-in closet) four days a week for five hours at a time. I put the baby on the floor next to me and take her advice on all artistic matters. Since this is my first novel I am finding that there are many skills I must learn, things that never came up in nonfiction writing, such as character development, transition, description and dialogue. It is a great challenge.

"To anyone who is considering becoming a writer I advise reading, reading, and more reading, everything from the printing on cereal boxes to *War and Peace.*"

GRICE, Frederick 1910-

PERSONAL: Born June 21, 1910, in Durham, England; son of Charles Oliver and Mary Jane (Hewitt) Grice; married Gwendoline Simpson, April 8, 1939; children: Gillian (Mrs. C. G. Clarke), Erica (Mrs. N. Johnson). *Education:* King's College, University of London, B.A. (honors); Hatfield College, University of Durham, D.Th.P.T. *Religion:* Anglican. *Home:* 91 Hallow Rd., Worcester, England.

CAREER: City of Worcester Training College, Worcester, England, head of English department, 1946—. *Military service:* Royal Air Force, 1941-46; became flight lieutenant.

WRITINGS: Folk Tales of the North Country, Drawn from Northumberland and Durham, Thomas Nelson, 1944; *Folk Tales of the West Midlands,* Thomas Nelson, 1952; *Folk Tales of Lancashire,* Thomas Nelson, 1953; *Night Poem, and Other Pieces,* Peter Russell, 1955; *Aidan and the Strolling Players,* Duell, 1960 (published in England as *Aidan and the Strollers,* J. Cape, 1960); *The Bonny Pit Laddie,* Oxford University Press (London), 1960, published in America as *Out of the Mines: The Story of a Pit Boy,* Watts, 1961; *The Moving Finger,* Oxford University Press (Toronto), 1962, published in America as *The Secret of the Libyan Caves,* Watts, 1963; *Rebels and Fugitives,* Batsford, 1963, Norton, 1964; *A Northumberland Missionary,* Oxford University Press, 1963; *Jimmy Lane and His Boat,* Watts, 1963; *The Rescue* [and] *The Poisoned Dog* (two tales), Watts, 1963; *Bill Thompson's Pigeon,* Oxford University Press (London), 1963, Watts, 1968; *A Severnside Story,* Oxford University Press, 1964; (with Dora Saint) *The Lifeboat Haul* [and] *Elizabeth Woodcock* (the former by Grice, the latter by Saint), Oxford University Press, 1965; *The Luckless Apple,* Oxford University Press, 1966; *The Oak and the Ash,* Oxford University Press, 1968; *Dildrum, King of the Cats, and Other English Folk Stories* (includes "Dildrum, King of the Cats," "Black Vaughan," "The Magic Ointment," "The Iron Gates," "The Boy and the Fairies," "The Three Rivers," "The Pedlar of Swaffham," and "The Well at the World's End"), Watts, 1968; *The Courage of Andy Robson,* Oxford University Press, 1969; *The Black Hand Gang,* Oxford University Press, 1971; *Young Tom Sawbones,* Oxford University Press, 1972. Author of textbooks for slow readers. Contributor to periodicals and to British Broadcasting Corp. feature and poetry programs.

SIDELIGHTS: "I was born in the North of England, in the far north, within hearing distance of the bells of Durham Cathedral. My father, who was a miner, worked in a small colliery a few miles out of Durham. I always think that I had the best of three worlds: the world of the pit village with its strikes, lock-outs, evictions and accidents, and the warm company of a close-knit neighborly community; the world of the beautiful mediaeval city of Durham where I went to school, a city of fine architecture and novel traditions of piety and erudition; and the world of the austerely beautiful and unspoilt countryside that encircled the colliery village, merging into the lonely dales to the west, and the borderland moors of Northumberland to the North.

"The first book I wrote was a simple collection of North Country legends and folk tales. Some I had been told by my father, some by other acquaintances, some I had encountered in old histories. I was interested in them because they seemed to embody something of the spirit of the land which was the mainspring of my inspiration. The most popular of my stories is 'The Bonny Pit Laddie,' which is set in my native colliery village, and incorporates much of the personal history of my own family, especially my grandmother and my uncles, and draws heavily upon the vicissitudes of the mining community of Durham.

"The variety of my interests, and in particular my interest in English literature (for the greater part of my working life I have lectured on this to college students) has prompted me to investigate other themes such as the fortunes of strolling players in the early nineteenth century (*Aidan and*

Something about the Author

the Strolling Players), the lives of the railway navvies who built the British railways in the mid-nineteenth century *(Young Tom Sawbones),* etc., but I think I write best and most authentically about the north, and the north of a generation or more ago. Certainly these are the stories to which children respond most vividly.

"I do not write with children in the forefront of my mind. Rather I write about children, and the adult world as seen through the eyes of children. I have little difficulty in remembering what the world looked like in my pre-adolescent years; and I think I am helped by the fact that in general I distrust over-wrought writing, and prefer a simpler less involved style.

"I write a great deal of poetry, mainly for my own satisfaction, and my mentors in this field are, in the main, those whose view-point and style are relatively umcomplicated—Wordsworth, Hardy, R. S. Thomas and Robert Frost. Though I have great sympathy with avant-garde writers and avant-garde artists I learn from them rather than seek to imitate them. I tend—and this is a weakness in my

Jimmy Lane lived with his uncle and aunt, Mr. and Mrs. Lane. They lived in a little house in a town on the River Severn. ■ (From *Jimmy Lane and His Boat* by Frederick Grice. Illustrated by Eileen Green.)

work—to shy away from the contemporary scene, and to retreat to the past of my own boyhood, or to a past that resembles that of my early years.

"For detail I tend to draw heavily upon my own commonplace books. For more than thirty years I have kept voluminous notes of incidents, places, conversations etc. I find life very fascinating and feel impelled to record whatever happens to me. My books usually grow out of these multifarious records."

FOR MORE INFORMATION SEE: Books and Bookmen, July, 1968, June, 1969.

GRINGHUIS, Dirk
See GRINGHUIS, Richard H.

GRINGHUIS, Richard H.   1918-
(Dirk Gringhuis)

PERSONAL: Born September 22, 1918, in Grand Rapids, Mich.; son of Leonard J. and Ruth (Perry) Gringhuis; married Helen Lees, 1941; children: Richard Lees. *Education:* Studied at Greason School of Painting, 1937, American Academy of Art, 1938-40, Grand Central Art School, 1942. *Home and office:* 1707 Mt. Vernon, East Lansing, Mich. *Agent:* Marilyn E. Marlow, Curtis Brown Ltd., 60 East 56th St., New York, N.Y. 10022.

FREDERICK GRICE

Most people said it couldn't be done. No bridge could stand the strong winds and the grinding ice . . . ■ (From *Big Mac* by Dirk Gringhuis. Illustrated by the author.)

Something about the Author

CAREER: Free lance advertising artist, Grand Rapids, Mich., 1942-44; Fideler Co., Grand Rapids, Mich., illustrator, 1945-47; Hope College, Holland, Mich., art director, 1947-51; free lance author and illustrator, East Lansing, Mich., 1952—; Michigan State University Museum, East Lansing, staff artist, 1964—, curator of exhibits, 1964—, associate professor of education, 1971—. Michigan Naval Militia, commander; Michigan Council of Arts, councilman. Writer, producer, teacher, weekly television program, "Open Door to Michigan." Lecturer at book fairs, schools, libraries. *Member:* Company of Military Collectors and Historians, Authors Guild, Midwest Museums Conference, Michigan Museum Association.

WRITINGS—Author and illustrator: *Tuliptime*, Whitman, 1949; *Here Comes the Bookmobile*, Whitman, 1950; *The Young Voyageur*, Whittlesey House, 1956; *The Eagle Pine*, McKay, 1959; *Big Mac*, Macmillan, 1960; *Rock Oil to Rockets*, Macmillan, 1961; *The Big Hunt*, Dial, 1962; *The Big Dig*, Dial, 1962; *Saddle the Storm*, Bobbs, 1962; *Of Cabbages and Cattle*, Dial, 1962; *In Scarlet and Blue*, Dial, 1963; *Of Fish and Ships and Fishermen*, Whitman, 1964; *From Tall Timber*, Whitman, 1964; *Mystery at Skull Castle*, Reilly & Lee, 1964; *Open Door to the Great Lakes*, Duell, Sloan & Pearce, 1966; *Stars on the Ceiling*, Meredith, 1967; *Giants, Dragons and Gods*, Meredith, 1968; *Lore of the Great Turtle*, Mackinac Island State Park Comm., 1970; *The Great Parade*, Hillsdale Press, 1971; *Let's Color Michigan*, Hillsdale Press, 1971; *Michigan's Indians*, Hillsdale Press, 1972; (with J. Alan Holman) *Mystery Mammals of the Ice Age*, Hillsdale Press, 1972; *Were-*

RICHARD H. GRINGHUIS

Wolves to Will-of-the-Wisps, Mackinac Island State Park Comm., 1973. Art editor, *Children's Health Bulletin*, 1952-66.

SIDELIGHTS: "While my writing, illustrating and painting did not begin until 1947, my boyhood was filled with the works of Pyle and Wyeth, the writings of Ernest Thompson Seton and others. Christmas to me was to have a book under the tree, the thicker and more exciting the better. This love for the romantic and the adventures finally led me into a series for various publishers of works on my own state, Michigan. Now with twenty-eight published and the twenty-ninth ready to illustrate, I find that over half of these have dealt with Michigan's colorful past from the Woddland Indian, my all time favorite, to the French and British periods. In this vein I have been fortunate in doing many large historic murals of these early times as well. Now with a full time position at the Michigan State University Museum, I find that my free-lance must be done on weekends. But the interest is still there and I hope to produce at least one new book each year for many years to come.

"Why do I write and illustrate for children? Because, 'my people,' the eight-to-twelve group particularly, offer enthusiasm and honesty not found too often in the world of big people."

HALE, Linda (Howe) 1929-

PERSONAL: Born January 8, 1929, in Providence, R.I.; daughter of George Locke (an architect and writer) and Elizabeth (Parker) Howe; married Edward Everette Hale (a lawyer), August 15, 1953 (divorced, 1969); children: Nina, Eliza, Ellen, Thomas Edward, George Hale. *Education:* Studied art at Carnegie Institute of Technology, 1946-47; Barnard College, B.A., 1951. *Home:* 1100 West Plumb Lane, Reno, Nev.

CAREER: Viking Press, New York, N.Y., reader of Junior Books, 1952-55; Pinon Gallery, Reno, Nevada, partner, 1963-66; Nevada Art Gallery, Reno, Nev., director, 1967-68; presently teaching at University of Nevada as graduate student in English department. *Member:* Marin Society of Artists (California), Nevada Artists Association.

WRITINGS: (And Illustrator) *The Glorious Christmas Soup Party*, Viking, 1962.

WORK IN PROGRESS: Children's stories.

SIDELIGHTS: "*The Glorious Christmas Soup Party* came from living in an isolated part of California and missing the bustle of a family. The animals, except for the pig, were all residents of the ranch, including the mice. The story almost wrote itself and I mistrusted this, so I put it away for six months, went over it again and mailed it off. I think I had been thinking so much about that the story and pictures came very easily. There was the notion of sharing, and of parents loving their children even when they were cross with them. But mostly, surrounding those ideas, was that of the importance of people together."

HOBBIES AND OTHER INTERESTS: Reading, chess, painting, movies, cooking.

HALL, Elvajean

PERSONAL: Born May 30, in Hamilton, Ill.; daughter of Nelson (a clergyman) and Nellie Jean (Hyer) Hall. *Education:* Oberlin College, A.B.; University of Wisconsin, graduate study; Columbia University, B.S. *Politics:* Independent Republican. *Religion:* Protestant. *Home:* 233 Commonwealth Ave., Boston, Mass. 02116. *Office:* Division of Program, 88 Chestnut St., West Newton, Mass. 02161.

CAREER: Milwaukee University School, Milwaukee, Wis., teacher and librarian, 1937-42; Jackson (Mich.) public schools, school library supervisor, 1942-44; Stephens College, Columbia, Mo., onetime head librarian; Newton (Mass.) public schools, supervisor of School Library Services, 1946—. Library consultant, Chung Chi College, The Chinese University of Hong Kong, 1962-63, lecturer in children's literature, University College, Dublin, summers, 1967-69. *Member:* American Library Association, National Education Association, American Association of School Librarians, Women's National Book Association (president of Boston chapter, 1957-59; national secretary, 1959-61), National League of American Pen Women (president of Boston branch, 1970-72), Association for Supervision and Curriculum Development, New England School Library Association, Massachusetts School Library Association, Delta Kappa Gamma, Kappa Delta, Boston Authors Club (board of directors, 1972-73).

Chickens seemed a priceless gift to the Indians. ■ (From *Pilgrim Neighbors* by Elvajean Hall. Illustrated by Jon Nielsen.)

ELVAJEAN HALL

WRITINGS: Books to Build On, Bowker, 1954, 2nd edition, 1957; *Land and People of Argentina,* Lippincott, 1960, new edition, 1972; *Pilgrim Stories,* Rand, 1962; *Land and People of Norway,* Lippincott, 1963, new edition, 1973; *Pilgrim Neighbors,* Rand, 1964; *The Volga: Lifeline of Russia,* Rand, 1965; *Land and People of Czechoslovakia,* Lippincott, 1966, revised edition, 1972; *Hong Kong* (Junior Literary Guild selection), Rand, 1967; (with Charles Mozley) *The Psalms,* Watts, 1968; (with Calvin L. Criner) *Picture Map Geography of Eastern Europe,* Lippincott, 1968; (with Mozley) *The Proverbs,* Watts, 1970; (with Robert J. Houlehen) *The Battle for Sales,* Lippincott, 1973; *Jobs in Marketing and Distribution,* Lothrop, 1974. Contributor of articles to educational and library journals, and reviews to library journals; has had sixty-five cartoons published over the years.

WORK IN PROGRESS: Several other books.

SIDELIGHTS: "I wrote my first book when I was in the fourth grade. It was part of the language arts program of the Elmhurst, Illinois public schools. This was a happy year and my life centered around the book which I wrote, illustrated and bound by hand. I still treasure my 'masterpiece'—after all these years. In eighth grade I wrote a weekly column for the 'Lake Forester,' the local paper where we were then living. In high school I had a weekly column called 'Seen about School' in the school newspaper. I won an essay contest in which the thirty-one high schools of the Chicago metropolitan area competed, and the prize was a week's trip to Washington, D.C. where I met the winners from other parts of the United States. I think it is very important for a child to take part in as many writing activities as possible when still a child. Writing is like a tree; it puts down roots.

"Children often ask me if I have been to all the places I write about. The answer is yes. When I was doing my book on Hong Kong, I had a six-month sabbatical leave to go to Hong Kong to act as adviser to the library program in the new Chinese University. I lived at Chung Chi College, in a Chinese girls' dormitory only twelve miles from the frontier with China. From my bedroom window on a hillside, I looked down on an old-fashioned Chinese farm that had all the scents and noises of the country. I watched the planting, weeding and harvesting of rice. This was an experience I shall never forget.

"I have hiked many miles across the mountains of Hong Kong and the tiny villages nestled in hidden valleys. Most people think of Hong Kong as a tourist attraction, I see it as the most beautiful and fascinating place I have ever been, with its sophisticated cities and over 900 tiny country villages in the mountains.

"When planning for my book, *The Volga,* I visited Russia and drove 2,000 miles through the country, actually seeing the Volga and waving to the Russian tourists who make the Volga river boat trip the experience of their lifetime. In preparation for *Czechoslovakia* and *Eastern Europe,* I followed the course of the Danube which is a ribbon of water tying them together. When working on my book on Norway, I arranged to live in the home of a Norwegian educator. I was shipwrecked going to the Arctic but managed to get on the next ship north. I have sat in the President's box at the Opera House in Buenos Aires as the guest of the official family. I have traced the course followed by the Argentine hero San Martin as he crossed the Andes and made his way north to Lima, Peru and then Gayaquil, Ecuador, where he met with Bolivar to decide who would be 'top man' in the South American attempt to overthrow Spanish control.

"I have climbed Mt. Kilimanjaro (well, not quite to the top), and have flown up the Rift Valley of Africa which is a giant geological fault starting in the Middle East and petering out in Mozambique. From the air it looks like a tremendous river with 'banks' sometimes 1,500 feet high. In anticipation of my books on the Biblical psalms and proverbs, I visited several of the important excavations in the Middle East.

"I have hiked in the Fiji Islands and have been toasted in 'Kava' by a native chieftain surrounded by all the men of his tribe. On my five mile return to my hotel, the chief sent an escort to take me on a short-cut along the palm-bordered beach. When my escort asked me if I would like a drink, he shinnied fifty feet or more up a cocoanut palm, hacked off two cocoanuts, and cut off their tops. We then had the local equivalent of a 'coke'—a drink of fresh cocoanut milk which looks and tastes like sweetened cow's milk.

"I could go on and on and on and on. . . ."

Ms. Hall has been to Hong Kong (3 times), Japan (5), Korea (2), Philippines (3), Taiwan (2), Ireland (7), Norway (5), British Isles (32), and has visited, at least once, every country of Europe except Albania.

HOBBIES AND OTHER INTERESTS: Freighter travel, researching for books, and taking colored films to use in her lectures to school and community groups. Also enjoys bicycle riding and cartooning.

HALLIN, Emily Watson 1919-

PERSONAL: Born October 4, 1919, in Fort Smith, Ark., grew up in Colorado; married Clark Ossell Hallin (a pilot), August 16, 1952 (lost on flight in West Africa, 1969); children: Daniel, Diane, Brian. *Education:* University of Missouri at Kansas City, A.B. (cum laude), 1939. *Religion:* Protestant. *Home:* 13861 Cicerone Lane, Los Altos Hills, Calif. 94022.

CAREER: Publicist and public relations representative, Pratt & Whitney Aircraft and Chance Vought Aircraft, 1942-52; free-lance writer, 1952—. Stanford University, Stanford, Calif., international studies staff, 1967—.

WRITINGS—Juveniles: *Wild White Wings,* McKay, 1965; *Follow the Honey Bird,* McKay, 1967; *Moya and the Flamingoes,* McKay, 1969. Contributor to *Coronet, Sunset, American Illustrated,* United Press International Newsfeatures, *Guideposts,* and to juvenile, aviation and trade magazines and newspapers.

SIDELIGHTS: "For many years, I was a reporter and editor, writing stories about airplanes. One of these articles concerned a jet airplane which crashed after colliding with a whistling swan. I grew curious about this bird who could fly so high, and who migrated all the way from the Arctic circle to California each year. I began to write about birds.

"My husband was a pilot, and until he was lost on a flight in Africa, he helped me to trace the birds' migration routes and to see the world as a bird might see it."

EMILY WATSON HALLIN

There was an earth-shaking crack, and Ori felt himself hurled hard to the ground. A small brownish bird with white tail feathers cheeped in alarm and brushed its wings shakily against his face. ■ (From *Follow the Honey Bird* by Emily Watson Hallin and Robert Buell. Illustrated by Larry Toschik. Reprinted by permission of David McKay Co., Inc.)

"Our family has been privileged to live and travel in many parts of the world and to study the customs and languages of many peoples. We lived for some time in both Japan and Saudi Arabia, and among our most memorable experiences were riding in a helicopter over the mountains of Japan, camping out in a desert sandstorm, and skin-diving in the coral gardens of the Red Sea.

"Because I have been a reporter, I like to write about something I have actually seen and investigated, and on which I have done considerable research. *Follow the Honey Bird* was written after I had traveled near Mount Kilimanjaro in Kenya and Tanzania. The boys, Riko and Ori, are modeled after two young Masai cattle herders who gave my children a spear. *Moya and the Flamingoes* was written after I had studied the flamingoes on the lakes in the Rift Valley of Africa. The characters were drawn from some Kikuyu boys who were selling baskets there.

"I am at present doing research for a fourth book about birds. During this research, my daughter, Diane, and I, traveled to Midway Island in the middle of the Pacific to observe the Albatross, or 'Gooney Bird.' In studying birds, I am constantly struck by the many species of birds which

must live in regions remote from and unattractive to men in order to survive. I hope to convey something in my books which will give human beings a better knowledge of the habits of birds and will make it easier for birds to survive in our world. I feel that children are the best audience for this message, because they have a longer time to do something about it than we adults.

"I live in an apricot orchard on a hill where there are many birds, including bluejays, humming birds, owls, and a mockingbird who can croak like a frog. I also have a white cat, Linus, whose hobby is sleeping. Between naps, he displays a unique feature: he has one blue eye and one yellow eye."

HAMMER, Richard 1928-

PERSONAL: Born March 22, 1928, in Hartford, Conn.; son of Morris Harry (in advertising) and Mildred (Chaimson) Hammer; married Nina Ullman (engaged in cardiac research), November 27, 1955; married Arlene Nadel (actress), November 24, 1970; children: (first marriage) Joshua I., Anthony G. *Education:* Syracuse University, A.B., 1950; Trinity College, Hartford, Conn., M.A., 1951; Columbia University, graduate student, 1951-53. *Politics:* Democrat. *Religion:* Jewish. *Home:* 1155 North La Cienaga Blvd., West Hollywood, Calif. 90069. *Agent:* Harold Matson Co., Inc., 22 East 40th St., New York, N.Y. 10016.

CAREER: National Broadcasting Co., New York, N.Y., news assistant, 1952-53; *Barron's Weekly,* New York, N.Y., associate editor, 1954-59; *Fortune,* New York, N.Y., associate editor, 1959-63; *New York Times,* New York, N.Y., editorial staff, 1963-72. *Member:* Society of Magazine Writers (vice-president, 1965), Authors League of America, PEN. *Awards, honors:* Academy Award for Best Documentary Short Subjects, 1971, for "Interviews with My Lai Veterans"; nominated for National Book Award and Pulitzer Prize, 1972.

WRITINGS: Between Life and Death (nonfiction), Macmillan, 1969; *One Morning in the War: The Tragedy at Son My* (nonfiction), Coward-McCann, 1970; *The Court Martial of Lt. Calley* (nonfiction), Coward, 1971; (with Martin A. Gosch) *Lucky: The Life and Times of Charles "Lucky" Luciano* (nonfiction), Little, Brown, 1973. Author-narrator of film, "Interview with My Lai Veterans." Contributor to *Playboy, New York Times Magazine, New York Times Book Review, Look, Harper's, Nation, Midstream, Life International,* and other periodicals.

WORK IN PROGRESS: The Real Story of Organized Crime in America, to be published by Playboy Press in 1974; *Bucksbaum's Revenge,* a novel.

HARKINS, Philip 1912-
(John Blaine, a joint pseudonym)

PERSONAL: Born September 29, 1912, in Boston, Mass.; son of E. F. Harkins; married Anita Nash, 1953; children: Joan, Arthur Dodge, Abbie Dodge. *Education:* Attended public and private schools in Boston, then University of Grenoble, 1931-32, and School of Political Science, Paris, 1932-33. *Address:* P.O. Box 142, Paget 6, Bermuda.

CAREER: Traveled on his own in North Africa and Europe after finishing high school; reporter, and semi-pro hockey player.

WRITINGS—Mainly junior books: *Coast Guard, Ahoy!*, Harcourt, 1943; *Bomber Pilot*, Harcourt, 1944; *Lightning on Ice*, Morrow, 1946; *Touchdown Twins*, Morrow, 1947; *The Big Silver Bowl*, Morrow, 1947; *Southpaw from San Francisco*, Morrow, 1948; *Punt Formation*, Morrow, 1949; *Son of the Coach*, Holiday House, 1950; *Knockout*, Holiday House, 1950; *Double Play*, Holiday House, 1951; (with Paul D. Harkins) *The Army Officers Guide*, McGraw, 1951; *Center Ice*, Holiday House, 1952; *Road Race*, Crowell, 1953; *Blackburn's Headhunters*, Norton, 1955; *Young Skin Diver*, Morrow, 1956; *Game, Carol Canning!*, Morrow, 1953; *Breakaway Back*, Morrow, 1959; *The Day of the Drag Race*, Morrow, 1960; *Fight Like a Falcon*, Morrow, 1961; *Argentine Road Race*, Morrow, 1962; *Where the Shark Waits*, Morrow, 1963; *No Head for Soccer*, Morrow, 1964; (with Harold Leland, under joint pseudonym John Blaine), *Danger Below*, Grosset, 1968.

Blackburn's Headhunters was filmed as "Surrender—Hell," 1958.

FOR MORE INFORMATION SEE: More Junior Authors, edited by Muriel Fuller, H. W. Wilson, 1963.

HARRIS, Christie (Lucy Irwin) 1907-

PERSONAL: Born November 21, 1907, in Newark, N.J.; has lived in Canada since 1908; daughter of Edward (a farmer) and Matilda (Christie) Irwin; married Thomas Arthur Harris (a Canadian immigration officer), February 13, 1932; children: Michael, Moira (Mrs. Donald Johnston), Sheilagh (Mrs. Jack Simpson), Brian, Gerald. *Education:* Provincial Normal School, Vancouver, British Columbia, permanent teachers' certificate, 1925; University of British Columbia, summer, 1925. *Religion:* Church of England. *Residence:* Vancouver, British Columbia, Canada; and Anderson Valley, Calif. *Agent:* McIntosh & Otis, Inc., 18 East 41st St., New York, N.Y. 10017.

CAREER: Teacher, British Columbia, Canada, 1926-32; free-lance writer for Canadian Broadcasting Corp. radio, 1936—. *Member:* Authors League of America. *Awards, honors:* First award in educational radio and television competitions at Columbus, Ohio, for school radio series, "Laws for Liberty," produced by Canadian Broadcasting Corp; Canadian Association of Children's Librarians "Book of the Year" Medal and Pacific Northwest Booksellers' Award, 1967, for *Raven's Cry;* British Columbia Librarians' award for "British Columbia's Best in Children's Literature," 1972; Canadian Authors' Association, Vicky Metcalf Award for Children's Books, 1973.

WRITINGS: Cariboo Trail, Longmans, Green, 1957; *Once Upon a Totem*, Atheneum, 1963; *You Have to Draw the Line Somewhere*, Atheneum, 1964; *West With the White Chiefs*, Atheneum, 1965; *Raven's Cry*, Atheneum, 1966; *Confessions of a Toe-Hanger*, Atheneum, 1967; *Forbidden Frontier*, Atheneum, 1968; *Let X Be Excitement*, Atheneum, 1969; (with daughter, Moira Johnston) *Figleafing Through History: The Dynamics of Dress*, Atheneum, 1971; *Secret in the Stlalakum Wild* (Junior Literary

Guild selection), Atheneum, 1972; (with husband, Tom Harris) *Mule Lib*, McClelland & Stewart, 1972; *Once More Upon a Totem*, Atheneum, 1973. Radio scripts include several hundred school programs, twelve adult plays, juvenile stories, women's talks. Women's editor, *A S & M News*.

SIDELIGHTS: "I simply cannot help writing. When I was a busy young mother with five children, an inconvenient old house in the country, and no help, I still turned out a steady stream of words. And sold them. Every little domestic disaster became a humor sketch for the Canadian Broadcasting Corporation . . . or else a note in that little red book that later became a gold mine of ideas about the way children think and speak.

"Three of my books are case histories of my children, written with their very active help; all three have been widely reviewed as both 'funny' and 'very sane.' *You Have to Draw the Line Somewhere* is a case history of my fashion artist daughter; *Confessions of a Toe-Hanger* is a humorous case history of her not-so-talented sister; *Let X be Excitement* is a humorous case history of the brother who became an aeronautical research engineer and test pilot. I use my family as characters and technical advisers because they won't sue me or charge me."

CHRISTIE HARRIS

"I'm very interested in pioneer times in Western Canada; and the fact that the Early Canadian West was so different from the Early American West lets me do my junior historical novels from an unusual angle. And since I clearly remember living in a log house on a homestead in western Canada, I have a feeling for the early West. And I find I'm a little inclined to model my pioneer characters on my own parents, and old neighbors I remember. I'm very inclined to get the idea for pioneer stories in some of the little-read old journals observant people kept. Some point interests me, and I go on to the 'What if. . . .?'

"I find I have a special feeling for the young people who were children of a Hudson's Bay Company father and an Indian mother. Their sudden humiliation at the time of our Gold Rush, and the activism some of them engaged in are naturals for sparking a story. Several of my books have featured such young rebels.

"The Northwest Coast Indians especially interest me; and I've been fortunate enough to get into many remote villages and to make friends with old Indians who will tell me things I can't find out in libraries and archives. I've found it a real challenge to take their tragic history, their magnificent culture, and their fascinating legends; and then make it all real and understandable to today's young people. I had a Canada Council grant to go back to the Northwest, where I had lived for four years, to do field research for *Raven's Cry*."

Ms. Harris' daughter, Moira, has illustrated three of her books: *Figleafing through History, Confessions of a Toe-Hanger*, and *You Have to Draw the Line Somewhere*.

FOR MORE INFORMATION SEE: *Profiles*, Canadian Library Association, 1971; *Junior Literary Guild Catalogue*, March, 1972; *Horn Book*, June, 1973.

HASKELL, Arnold L(ionel)   1903-

PERSONAL: Born July 19, 1903, in London, England; son of Jacob S. (a banker) and Emmy (Mesritz) Haskell; married Vera Saitzoff, July 4, 1926 (deceased); married Vivienne Marks, 1970; children: Francis, Stephen, Helen (Mrs. B. Mecs). *Education:* Attended Westminster School, London, England; Trinity Hall, Cambridge, M.A. (with honors), 1926. *Politics:* Liberal. *Religion:* Roman Catholic. *Home:* Beechwood House, Widcombe Hill, Bath, Somerset, England.

CAREER: William Heinemann Ltd., London, England, member of editorial staff, 1927-32; toured America with Russian Ballet, 1933-34; *Daily Telegraph*, London, England, dance critic, 1935-38; *Melbourne Herald* and *Sydney Daily Telegraph*, Melbourne and Sydney, Australia, guest critic, 1936-37; lecturer in Australia, 1938-39; lecturer for British Council in European countries, 1950-51, 1953-55; lecturer, and student of ballet in Union of Soviet Socialist Republics, 1960, 1962. Adviser to Dutch government on formation of national ballet company, 1954; Varna International dance competition, vice-president of jury, 1964. Royal Ballet School, director, 1947-68, governor, 1957—; Trent Park Training College, governor, 1953-58, 1961; Bath University, member of the court, 1971. *Member:* Royal

Academy of Dancing (vice-president), Garrick Club, Savile Club, Chelsea Arts Club. *Awards, honors:* Chevalier de la Legion l'Honneur, 1950; Commander, Order of the British Empire, 1958.

WRITINGS: *The National Ballet*, A. & C. Black, 1943, 2nd edition, 1947; *Going to the Ballet*, Phoenix House, 1950 (published in America as *How to Enjoy Ballet*, Morrow, 1951); *Ballet, 1945-1950*, Longmans, Green, for the British Council, 1951; *A Picture History of Ballet*, Hulton, 1954, revised edition, 1957; (translator) Serge Lifar, *History of Russian Ballet from Its Origins to the Present Day*, McGraw, 1954.

The Wonderful World of Dance, Garden City Books, 1960 (published in England as *The Story of Dance*, Rathbone, 1960, revised edition Macdonald & Co., 1969); *The Beauty of Ballet*, Pitman, 1961; *The Russian Genius in Ballet: A Study in Continuity and Growth*, Pergamon, 1963; *Ballet Retrospect*, Batsford, 1964, Studio Books 1965; *What Is Ballet?*, MacDonald, 1965; *Ballet Russe: The Age of Diaghilev*, Weidenfeld & Nicolson, 1968 (For complete list of writings see *Contemporary Authors*, Vol. 5-8.) Editor of *Ballet Annual*, A. & C. Black, 1947-63.

Contributor to *Encyclopaedia Britannica, Chambers's Encyclopaedia*, and *Annual Register*. Contributor to *British Journal of Aesthetics*.

SIDELIGHTS: "Ever since the success of *Balletomania* (Simon & Schuster, 1934), I have been known as a writer on ballet and it is difficult to escape from this label. I am interested in a wide number of subjects—travel, art, fa-

ARNOLD L. HASKELL,
from the painting by Paul Wyeth, R.B.A.

The precision line of the chorus and, lower, solo dancer Juliet Prowse.
■ (From *The Wonderful World of Dance* by Arnold L. Haskell. Photo by Tom Hustler.)

miliar nursery objects. In fact, people interest me and dancing is perhaps the original manifestation of man as an artist.

"I have written both for children and adults but I do not make a sharp distinction. My best audience is in the fifteen plus range. As a lecturer I have long been aware of the fact that you cannot bluff the fifteen plus listeners with jargon as you can so many adults. You have to prove yourself with every lecture and every new book. It is a challenge I enjoy.

"As director of the Royal Ballet School, I taught English and some history and I feel that this experience has been of real value to me as a writer. A great headmaster once said to me, 'With Children you need to explain things two or three times, with adults at least seven, their minds are so cluttered.' I have found this true as I have also had much experience in adult education.

"I think that this over-discussed question of the 'generation gap,' as it is called, is greatly exaggerated. It only occurs when older people make themselves ridiculous by making tremendous efforts in trying to be young, fail in the effort and are annoyed. I am content to be old, it has many privileges, and I readily admit that there are many things I cannot understand. However, the sympathy is there. I remember my youth, even my childhood and have always kept in contact with young people. I have found that they accept me as I am." Haskell is bilingual in French and English.

HOBBIES AND OTHER INTERESTS: Collecting sculpture, especially that of Rodin, Maillol, Dalou, Carpeaux, and Epstein (collection exhibited at Bristol Art Gallery, 1963), also collector of paediatric antiques; travel in eastern Europe.

HAVILAND, Virginia 1911-

PERSONAL: Born May 21, 1911, in Rochester, N.Y.; daughter of William J. and Bertha (Esten) Haviland. *Education:* Cornell University, B.A., 1933. *Politics:* Democrat. *Office:* Children's Book Section, Library of Congress, Washington, D.C. 20540.

CAREER: Boston (Mass.) Public Library, began 1934, children's librarian, 1941-48, branch librarian, 1948-52, reader's adviser for children, 1952-63; Library of Congress, Washington, D.C., head of Children's Book Section, 1963—. *Horn Book* (magazine), associate editor, 1952-63, reviewer, 1952—; Simmons College, School of Library Science, lecturer, 1957-62; Trinity College, lecturer, 1969—. Newbery-Caldecott Award Committee (American Library Association), chairman, 1953-54; *New York Herald Tribune* Children's Spring Book Festival Awards, judge, 1955-57; *Book World*, Children's Spring Book Festival Awards, judge, 1969; National Book Awards, judge, 1969; International Hans Christian Andersen Award, member of jury, 1959—, president of jury, 1972 and 1974. Representative of American Library Association at European conferences of International Board on Books for Children and International Federation of Library Associations. Hewins Lecturer at New England Library Association.

MEMBER: International Board on Books for Children (executive board), International Federation of Library Associations (executive committee), American Library Association (chairman of Children's Library Association, 1954-55; chairman of book evaluation committee, 1962-63), National Council of Administrative Women in Education, District of Columbia Library Association, Washington Children's Book Guild.

WRITINGS: Travelogue Storybook of the Nineteenth Century, Horn Book, 1950; *William Penn, Founder and Friend*, Abingdon, 1952; "Favorite Fairy Tales" series, Little, Brown, 1959—, comprising *Favorite Fairy Tales Told in England*, 1959, . . . *in France*, 1959, . . . *in Germany*, 1959, . . . *in Ireland*, 1961, . . . *in Norway*, 1961, . . . *in Russia*, 1961, . . . *in Scotland*, 1963, . . . *in Spain*, 1963, . . . *in Poland* (ALA Notable Book), 1963, . . . *in Italy*, 1965; *Ruth Sawyer*, Walck, 1965; *Favorite Fairy Tales Told in Sweden*, 1966, . . . *in Czechoslovakia*, 1966, . . . *in Japan*, 1967; (with William Jay Smith) *Children and Poetry*, Library of Congress, 1970; *Favorite Fairy Tales Told in*

Greece (Child Study Association book list), Little, Brown, 1970; *Favorite Fairy Tales Told in Denmark,* Little, Brown, 1971; (compiler) *The Wide World of Children's Books,* Library of Congress, 1972; *Children's Books of International Interest,* American Library Association, 1972; *A Fairy Tale Treasury,* Coward, 1972; *Told in India,* Little, Brown, 1973; *Children and Literature: Views and Reviews,* Scott, Foresman, 1973. Contributor to *Horn Book, Wilson Library Bulletin,* and other library journals.

SIDELIGHTS: "My earliest writing for publication was *on demand:* articles related to children's books and reading—like my 'Children and Their Friends the Authors' which the Boston Public Library published in 1946 in its quarterly then called *More Books.* Next was my Caroline M. Hewins Lecture which was published as a book, *The Travelogue Storybook of the Nineteenth Century.* Children's books and writing about children's literature I also did later on request, probably because I was too busy with library programs to have enough of that idle time for pondering which is necessary for the development of ideas.

VIRGINIA HAVILAND

[The King] called his son-in-law and asked what had happened to him on his journey and where he had stopped. ■ (From *Favorite Fairy Tales Told in Czechoslovakia* by Virginia Haviland. Illustrated by Trina Schart Hyman.)

"I often protested that I should not write just because I was asked to—and I said this to the editor whose request led to my writing *William Penn.* But inevitably when I got into the writing, I found that I enjoyed it.

"In 1948, when I was pursuing Frederic Melcher's suggestion for my contribution to the lecture series on the history of children's books, I dug around in nineteenth-century review media where children's books received sustained critical attention. It was the beginning of a deep interest in old children's books, which had started when I studied children's literature with the famous librarian Alice M. Jordan and is continuing now in a fascinating project with rare books of the eighteenth and nineteenth centuries.

"In the mid-1950's I began to edit and compile—and sometimes also to translate, as from the French and German—collections of folk tales which were intended to enable very young children to read fairy tales. I was again pushed by a publisher, Helen Jones, the children's book editor at Little, Brown. She well understood the library boom in requests for volumes of tales for the small children captivated then by a series of fairy-tale dramatizations—a demand that could not be satisfied by the fatter volumes in relatively small print. Again I found my interests broadening, for this field is wide and fascinating. My delight in searching for tales grew immensely as my series of 'Favorite Fairy Tales' lengthened. Travel abroad every year has furthered it, too, for I have found some of the help I needed—as in Japan where I met librarians, storytellers, and writers who know their folk tales well.

"So indeed one step has led to another, always with that push I needed, into the international children's book world as well as at home. Research and writing has filled my life to the brim, for I have never stopped reviewing children's books for the *Horn Book Magazine* (I've worked with three editors there, from the end of 1951) and I have not interrupted my full-time library work. I've just had my tenth birthday with the Children's Book Section at the Library of Congress, where I came from the Boston Public Library to establish a new center for reference and research in children's literature."

FOR MORE INFORMATION SEE: Horn Book, February, 1970, June, 1970, June, 1971, October, 1972, December, 1972, February, 1973, April, 1973; *Top of the News,* January, 1972; *New York Times Book Review,* October 8, 1972; "The Calendar," May-August, 1973.

HAWKINS, (Helena Ann) Quail   1905-

PERSONAL: Born March 29, 1905, in Spokane, Wash.; daughter of Heinrich Gutherz (a fruit broker) and Helen Rich (Lyon) Hawkins. *Education:* University of California, Berkeley, student, 1927. *Politics:* Democrat. *Religion:* Episcopalian. *Home:* 1404 Glendale Ave., Berkeley, Calif. 94708.

CAREER: Bookseller in Spokane, Wash., 1923-26, and Berkeley, Calif., 1926-29; *Publisher's Weekly,* New York, N.Y., staff, 1929-30; Sather Gate Bookshop, Berkeley, Calif., sales staff, 1931-34, head of children's department, 1934-54, head of adult and juvenile departments, 1952-54; University of California Press, Berkeley, assistant sales and promotion manager, 1954-61; Sather Gate Bookshop, consultant on library services and book fairs, 1961-1970. Literary agent briefly in 1940's. Lecturer to teachers, librarians, and writers on children's books; former story lady, reading from children's books over KPFA-FM, for a year.

WRITINGS: (With V. W. von Hagen) *Quetzal Quest,* Harcourt, 1939; (with V. W. von Hagen) *The Treasure of the Tortoise Islands,* Harcourt, 1940; (compiler) *Prayers and Graces for Little Children,* Grosset, 1941, revised edition (under title *A Little Book of Prayers and Graces*), Doubleday, 1952; *Who Wants an Apple?,* Holiday, 1942; *A Puppy for Keeps,* Holiday, 1943; *Don't Run, Apple!,* Holiday, 1944; *Too Many Dogs,* Holiday, 1946; *Mark, Mark, Shut the Door,* Holiday, 1947; *The Best Birthday,* Doubleday, 1954; *Mountain Courage,* Doubleday, 1957; *The Aunt-Sitter,* Holiday, 1958; *Androcles and the Lion,* Coward, 1970.

Contributor to *Encyclopaedia Britannica,* 1963. Also contributor to *Publisher's Weekly, Woman's Home Companion, Elementary English.*

WORK IN PROGRESS: A book on Alfred the Great, *The King Who Burned the Cakes;* a mystery story for girls, *San Francisco Secret.*

SIDELIGHTS: "Have only a small creative talent, but I have worked hard to make each book as good as I possibly could. . . . If an idea strikes me as good I'll work on it off and on until it is publishable—sometimes years later. *Who Wants an Apple?* was written first in 1929 and published in 1942.

"I write unfashionable books—but children seem to like them. Since retirement I have done volunteer lecturing or rather talking with children in the Oakland, Calif. public schools. Their enthusiasm is very rewarding."

FOR MORE INFORMATION SEE: Horn Book, February, 1971.

QUAIL HAWKINS

In splendor the emperor of all Rome entered to sounds of music and shouts from the admiring crowd. ■ (From *Androcles and the Lion* by Quail Hawkins. Illustrated by Rocco Negri.)

HAYCRAFT, Howard 1905-

PERSONAL: Born July 24, 1905, in Madelia, Minn.; son of Julius Everett (a lawyer, legislator, and district judge) and Marie (a teacher; maiden name, Stelzer) Haycraft; married Molly Randolph Costain (daughter of author Thomas B. Costain), October 9, 1942. *Education:* University of Minnesota, A.B., 1928. *Religion:* Episcopalian. *Office:* H. W. Wilson Co., 950 University Ave., Bronx, N.Y. 10452.

CAREER: University of Minnesota Press, Minneapolis, staff member, 1928; H. W. Wilson Co. (publishers of reference works and indexes for libraries), Bronx, N.Y., promotional and editorial work, 1929-34, member of board of directors, 1934—, assistant secretary of firm, 1934-39, vice-president, 1940-52, president, 1953-67, chairman of board, 1967—. Forest Press, Inc., member of board of directors, 1951-68 (president, 1961-62). U.S. War Department, specialist, associated with publication of "G.I. Guides," 1942; President's Committee on Employment of the Handi-

Something about the Author

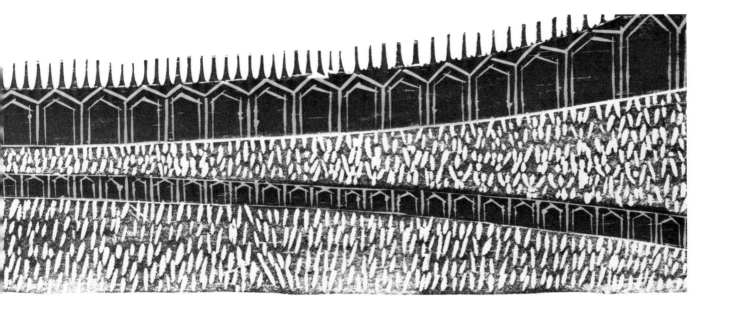

capped, member, 1963—. *Military service:* U.S. Army, Special Services, 1942-46; became major; received Army Commendation Medal. *Member:* Mystery Writers of America (president, 1963), Players Club, Dutch Treat (N.Y.), Kappa Sigma. *Awards, honors:* Edgar Allan Poe Award ("Edgar") for criticism, Mystery Writers of America, 1947; Outstanding Achievement Award, University of Minnesota, 1954; first recipient of Sir Francis Campbell Medal and citation, American Library Association, 1966, for outstanding contributions to library service for the blind.

WRITINGS: Murder for Pleasure: The Life and Times of the Detective Story, Appleton, 1941; *Books for the Blind & Physically Handicapped: A Postscript and an Appreciation,* Library of Congress, 1965, 4th revised edition, 1972.

Editor: (And author of introduction) Arthur Conan Doyle, *The Boys' Sherlock Holmes,* Harper, 1936, new edition, 1961; *The Boys' Book of Great Detective Stories,* Harper, 1938; *The Boys' Second Book of Great Detective Stories,* Harper, 1940; *Crime Club Encore,* Doubleday, 1942; *The Art of the Mystery Story* (critical essays), Simon & Schuster, 1946; (and author of introduction) *Fourteen Great Detective Stories,* Modern Library, 1949; (with John Beecroft) *Treasury of Great Mysteries,* two volumes, Simon & Schuster, 1957; (with John Beecroft) *Ten Great Mysteries,* Doubleday, 1959; (and author of introduction) *Five Spy Novels,* Doubleday, 1962; (with John Beecroft) *Three Times Three* (mystery story collection), Doubleday, 1964; (and author of introduction) Arthur Conan Doyle, *Sherlock Holmes' Greatest Cases* (large print), Watts, 1967; (with Beecroft) *A Treasury of Great Mysteries,* Doubleday, 1969.

Editor, "Wilson Authors Series": (With Stanley Kunitz and W. C. Hadden) *Authors of Today and Yesterday,* 1933, 2nd edition, 1934; (with Kunitz, Hadden, and others) *The Junior Book of Authors,* 1934, 3rd edition, 1956; (with Kunitz) *British Authors of the Nineteenth Century,* 1936; (with Kunitz) *American Authors, 1600-1900,* 1938; (with

Kunitz) *Twentieth Century Authors,* 1942, *First Supplement,* 1955; (with Kunitz) *British Authors Before 1800,* 1952.

Mystery critic for *Harper's,* 1941-42, and *Ellery Queen's Mystery Magazine,* 1946-48; contributor to other magazines. Editorial consultant, Doubleday Mystery Guild, 1948-61.

SIDELIGHTS: "My lifelong interest in mystery and detective stories began at the age of about ten, when I discovered a copy of *The Adventures of Sherlock Holmes* in the home of a relative and devoured it at one sitting. From that day on I have been an avid and appreciative reader of this form of fiction, and in the 1930's I approached the publishing firm of Harper with the idea of a *Boys' Sherlock Holmes,* to be made up of specially selected Holmes stories, together with a special informative introduction. Harpers liked the idea, and it was followed by *The Boys' Book of Great Detective Stories,* a collection of outstanding detective short stories by various authors, with informative introductions to the individual tales; and by *The Boys' Second Book of Great Detective Stories,* of the same nature. My intention in compiling these volumes was to introduce young readers to this form of fiction and thus to share with them the pleasure I had enjoyed for so many years myself. I am happy to say that all of these volumes have been continuously in print for well over thirty years, and that I continue to receive letters about them from young readers of both sexes.

"In doing research for these books in various libraries, I discovered that no adequate history of the detective story existed, and I determined to write one myself. After several years of work, nights, weekends, and holidays (for I continued my full-time employment with the New York firm of H. W. Wilson Co., publishers of indexes and reference works for libraries) my history was finally finished and was published with the title *Murder for Pleasure.* After a four-year stint in the army during World War II, it seemed logical to follow up *Murder for Pleasure* with a collection of some fifty-two critical essays about the mystery-detective story; this was published as *The Art of the Mystery Story.* I also reviewed mystery stories for *Harper's Magazine* and *Ellery Queen's Mystery Magazine.* These various activities led in due course to an affiliation (again in my 'leisure' time) with the Doubleday Mystery Guild and to the compilation (usually with the late John Beecroft, editor of the Literary Guild) of a number of anthologies of mystery and detective novels and short stories.

"Meanwhile back at the H. W. Wilson Co.—in addition to various corporate duties—I was involved with Stanley Kunitz (who was later to receive the Pulitzer Prize for poetry) in the compilation of a number of biographical reference books known as the 'Wilson Authors Series'. Best known of this series to young readers, of course, is *The Junior Book of Authors.*

"In the 1960's I became a temporary legal user of 'Talking Books' (recorded books supplied by the government without charge to blind and certain physically handicapped persons) and this experience led to a lasting interest in the problems of the blind and handicapped, especially in the field of reading. My brochure *Books for the Blind and Physically Handicapped* has been published for free distribution, available on request, by the Library of Congress and is now in its fourth edition."

FOR MORE INFORMATION SEE: John L. Lawler, *The H. W. Wilson Company: Half a Century of Biographical Publishing,* University of Minnesota Press, 1950; *Saturday Review,* February 3, 1951; *Current Biography,* February, 1954; *New York Times,* February 25, 1968.

MOLLY COSTAIN HAYCRAFT

HAYCRAFT, Molly Costain 1911-

PERSONAL: Born December 6, 1911, in Toronto, Ontario, Canada; daughter of Thomas B. (a writer) and Ida (Spragge) Costain; married Howard Haycraft (now chairman of board of publishing firm of H. W. Wilson Co. and author), October 9, 1942. *Education:* Attended Ogontz School for Girls. *Residence:* Hightstown, N.J. *Agent:* Curtis Brown Ltd., 60 East 56th St., New York, N.Y. 10022.

CAREER: Otto K. Liveright (literary agent), New York, N.Y., assistant, 1935-37; *Saturday Review of Literature,* New York, N.Y., secretary to Amy Loveman, 1937-39; Curtis Brown Ltd. (literary agents), New York, N.Y., assistant in magazine department, 1939-42. Author. Mercantile Library Association, director, 1960—, secretary, 1965—. *Member:* Cosmopolitan Club (New York, N.Y.).

WRITINGS: Queen Victoria, Messner, 1956; *First Lady of the Theatre–Sarah Siddons,* Messner, 1958: *Too Near the Throne,* Lippincott, 1959; *The Reluctant Queen,* Lippincott, 1962; *The Lady Royal,* Lippincott, 1964; *My Lord Brother: The Lion Heart,* Lippincott, 1968; *The King's Daughters,* Lippincott, 1971; *Countess Carrots,* Lippincott, 1973.

WORK IN PROGRESS: Royal Lovers, a novel about King Alexander III and Queen Margaret of Scotland.

SIDELIGHTS: "I began writing late, having seen as a literary agent, how much heartbreak can be in store for a writer. Once started, I've never looked back! The lives of the kings, queens, and princesses of England are an inexhaustible source of readable stories. Before I stop, I hope to have a novel set in each century from the Eleventh to the Nineteenth—the only one I've skipped so far is the Fifteenth." Ms. Haycraft researches her books on trips abroad, mainly in England.

HOWARD HAYCRAFT

HEIDERSTADT, Dorothy 1907-

PERSONAL: Born October 8, 1907, in Geneva, Neb.; daughter of Charles Alden and Florence (Kilmer) Heiderstadt. *Education:* University of Kansas, A.B., 1936; Simmons College, B.S. in L.S., 1937. *Home:* 3028 Sheley Rd., Independence, Mo. 64052.

CAREER: Public library, Kansas City, Mo., children's librarian, 1930-36; public library, Bethlehem, Pa., children's supervisor, 1937-42; public library, Kansas City, Mo., branch librarian, 1942-65, reference librarian, 1966-67, branch librarian, 1967-70, retired, 1970. *Member:* Authors Guild of America, Oklahoma Historical Society, Phi Beta Kappa.

WRITINGS: A Book of Heroes, Bobbs, 1954; *Indian Friends and Foes,* McKay, 1958; *To All Nations,* Nelson, 1959; *A Bow for Turtle,* McKay, 1960; *Knights and Champions,* Nelson, 1960; *Ten Torchbearers,* Nelson, 1961; *Frontier Leaders and Pioneers,* McKay, 1962; *Lois Says Aloha,* Nelson, 1963; *More Indian Friends and Foes,* McKay, 1963; *Marie Tanglehair,* McKay, 1965; *Stolen by the Indians,* McKay, 1968; *Painters of America,* McKay, 1970.

SIDELIGHTS: "I have always loved to write. I think it began when I was in the third or fourth grade and the teacher wrote word lists on the board. We were supposed to write sentences using the words. We were always very bored with this exercise, and wrote dumb sentences like, 'She ran quickly,' etc. Then one day the teacher read a poem to us, the one about the blind men and the elephant. You know how it goes: each blind man touches the elephant: one gets hold of its ear and says the elephant is like a fan; another gets hold of the tail and thinks the elephant is built like a rope, and so on. As I looked at the word list that day, the creative artist awoke in me and I decided to use the words in interesting sentences about the blind men and the elephant. The teacher was pleased, and read my sentences aloud to the class, and this bit of fame was very nice, but the thing I remembered with joy, and have experienced over and over as I write, was the delight of that first moment when I said to myself, 'I will write about the blind men and the elephant.'

"An English history book I studied in the sixth grade influenced me. I loved it, and read it from cover to cover many times, and even decided to write a history of my own. That Christmas my parents gave me a desk, but the desk was not the place I selected for writing my book. It was up in an apple tree in our backyard; there I could get away from my sisters and the neighbor kids. Something else must have interfered, however, for when I got past the warriors who painted themselves with woad, and the chariots with knives on the wheels, I quit. But I still loved the book which had inspired this; all the history of England was told in hero stories in that book.

"There were lots of good story-tellers in our family. One of them was my mother, and I was the most avid listener she had. As she went about her work, sewing, cooking, ironing, she told me stories, mainly about her childhood. One of her grandmothers had been an Indian Agent in Oklahoma, and Mom visited her and played with the Indian children, and how I loved those stories about the Indians and about Great-Grandma's little dog Kelley and her cream-colored horse Terrapin which was given to her by the Indians and wouldn't let anyone except her ride him!

"Well, all this—the joy of writing and an interest in hero stories and Indians—went into the books I have written since, mostly volumes of hero stories and biographies of Indians. I think you need to love to write, and you need to have special interests. You need to be able to work hard and be persistent. It isn't easy to sell a manuscript, but I think you can if you keep trying. After you sell the manuscript, there's a lot of hard work ahead. If you write mostly nonfiction, as I do, your facts must be right, your dates must be exact; your editor goes over them, and you have to go over them, too, and verify them. Sometimes your editor questions something you say, and you have to prove you are right by quoting the source of your information. Nobody takes your word for it, you have to prove it. All this is very character-building and teaches you to be patient and to get along with people, especially editors. I don't believe it would be possible to do it if you didn't have, down in your heart to buoy you up, the joy of writing!"

HOBBIES AND OTHER INTERESTS: Travel, photography, reading.

DOROTHY HEIDERSTADT

The leaders of Valencia expected no mercy. But again the Cid showed himself just and good. They were told to till their fields and return to ways of peace. ■ (From *A Book of Heroes* by Dorothy Heiderstadt. Illustrated by Harry Lees.)

HENRY, Joanne Landers   1927-

PERSONAL: Born February 24, 1927, in Indianapolis, Ind.; daughter of Delver Harold (an electrical engineer) and Octavia (Greene) Landers; married Earl Henry (now a market gardener), October 11, 1958; children: David, Katherine. *Education:* University of Rochester, B.A., 1948. *Religion:* Protestant. *Residence:* Eden, N.Y.

CAREER: Bobbs-Merrill Co., Inc. (publishers), Indianapolis, Ind., editorial assistant, 1951-55; Oxford University Press, New York, N.Y., school and library consultant, 1955-58; Bobbs-Merrill Co., Inc., children's book editor, 1958; free-lance writer for children, 1958—. Eden Free Library Board, vice-president, 1965-66.

WRITINGS: George Eastman: Young Photographer, Bobbs, 1959; *Elizabeth Blackwell: Girl Doctor,* Bobbs, 1961; *Andrew Carnegie: Young Steelmaker,* Bobbs, 1966; *Marie Curie: Discoverer of Radium,* Macmillan, 1966; *Bernard Baruch: Boy from South Carolina,* Bobbs, 1971.

SIDELIGHTS: "I've had a life-long interest in children's books, but it never occurred to me to try to write one until Bobbs suggested that I keep up my interest, after my marriage, by writing instead of editing. Since American history was my major in college, writing biographies was a natural choice for me to make.

"To me history is filled with wonderfully exciting stories that can be brought into focus and made meaningful through biographies for young readers. I do not write to teach or preach, but to awaken in children an appreciation of history and real-life drama, which many times can be far more thrilling than any tale of fiction. I write because I am enthusiastic about my subjects and my audience and I'd like to bring the two of them together with a book.

"In doing research on my subjects I examine every possible source, so that my view of the subject and the resulting book will be scrupulously accurate. Also, I write from personal observation of locale whenever possible; I wrote *George Eastman* after living in Rochester for four years; *Elizabeth Blackwell* after visiting various parts of New York State; *Andrew Carnegie* after a trip to Scotland; *Bernard Baruch* after a trip through South Carolina; *Marie Curie* after a week's stay in Paris."

HOBBIES AND OTHER INTERESTS: Playing chamber music (cello), gardening, and working as a volunteer in the local school library.

JOANNE LANDERS HENRY

112

She had so longed for Paris that now she wanted to see as much of it as she could. ■ (From *Marie Curie* by Joanne Landers Henry. Illustrated by John Martinez.)

HILL, Ruth A.
See VIGUERS, Ruth Hill

HILLERMAN, Tony 1925-

PERSONAL: Born May 27, 1925; son of August Alfred (a farmer) and Lucy (Grove) Hillerman; married Marie Unzner, August 16, 1948; children: Anne, Janet, Anthony, Monica, Stephen, Daniel. *Education:* Oklahoma State University, student, 1943; University of Oklahoma, B.A., 1946; University of New Mexico, M.A., 1966. *Politics:* Democrat. *Religion:* Roman Catholic. *Home:* 2729 Texas N.E., Albuquerque, N.M. 87110. *Agent:* Ann Elmo Agency, Inc., 52 Vanderbilt Ave., New York, N.Y. 10017.

CAREER: Borger News Herald, Borger, Tex., reporter, 1948; *Morning Press-Constitution,* Lawton, Okla., city editor, 1948-50; United Press International, political reporter in Oklahoma City, Okla., 1950-52; bureau manager in Santa Fe, N.M., 1952-54; *New Mexican,* Santa Fe, N.M., political reporter, later editor, 1954-63; University of New Mexico, Albuquerque, assistant to the president, 1963-66, chairman of department of journalism, 1966—. *Military service:* U.S. Army, 1943-45; received Silver Star, Bronze Star, and Purple Heart. *Member:* Sigma Delta Chi, Phi Kappa Phi, Albuquerque Press Club.

WRITINGS: The Blessing Way (ALA Notable Book), Harper, 1970; *The Fly on the Wall,* Harper, 1971; *The Boy Who Made Dragonfly,* Harper, 1972; *Dance Hall of the Dead,* Harper 1973; *The Great Taos Bank Robbery,* University of New Mexico Press, 1973. Contributor to *True, New Mexico Quarterly,* and other periodicals.

WORK IN PROGRESS: The text of a David Muench photography book on New Mexico, to be published by the Portland Art Center.

SIDELIGHTS: Film rights to *Dance Hall of the Dead* have been optioned to Bob Banner Associates, Inc., with the author contracted for the screenplay. The novel is based on the Zuni Reservation and concerns, as did *The Blessing Way,* the beliefs and values of modern Indians. Hillerman, who had Indians as playmates and friends, says that he is interested in what can be done, in the literary sense, with the contrast of cultures.

FOR MORE INFORMATION SEE: Library Journal, February 1, 1970, June 15, 1970; *New Yorker,* May 23, 1970; *Variety,* August 19, 1970.

. . . the toy looked very little like the butterfly he had promised his sister. Instead he had created a wonderful creature, like none before him had ever seen. ■ (From *The Boy Who Made Dragonfly* by Tony Hillerman. Illustrated by Laszlo Kubinyi.)

HIMLER, Ronald 1937-

PERSONAL: Born October 16, 1937, in Cleveland, Ohio; son of Norbert and Grace (Manning) Himler; married Ann Danowitz, June 18, 1972; children: Daniel, Anna. *Education:* Cleveland Institute of Art, Diploma, 1960; further study at Cranbrook Academy of Art, 1960-61, and New York University, 1968-70. *Residence:* New York, N.Y.

CAREER: General Motors Technical Center, Warren, Mich., technical sculptor (styling), 1961-63; artist and illustrator, 1963—. Toy designer and sculptor for Transogram Co., New York, N.Y., 1968, and Remco Industries, Newark, N.J., 1969. *Awards, honors:* Books he illustrated, *Baby* and *Rocket in My Pocket*, received American Institute of Graphic Arts awards, 1972.

WRITINGS: (Compiler and illustrator) *Glad Day*, Putnam, 1972.

Illustrator: Carl A. Withers, *Rocket in My Pocket,* new edition (Himler did not illustrate original edition), Science Research Associates, 1972; Fran Manushkin, *Baby,* Harper, 1972; Elizabeth Winthrop, *Bunk Beds,* Harper, 1972; Robert F. Burgess, *Exploring a Coral Reef,* Macmillan, 1971; Millicent Brower, *I'm Going Nowhere,* Putnam, 1972; Charlotte Zolotow, *Janey,* Harper, 1973; Marjorie Weinman Sharmat, *Morris Brookside, a Dog,* Holiday House, 1973; Tom Glazer, *Eye Winker, Tom Tinker, Chin Chopper,* Doubleday, 1973; Dorothy Kunhardt, (design) *Lucky Mrs. Ticklefeather, and Other Funny Stories,* Golden Press, 1973; Fran Manushkin, *Bubblebath,* Harper, in press; William C. Grimm, *Indian Harvest,* McGraw, in press; Robert Burch, *Hut School and the Wartime Homefront Heroes,* Viking, in press; Paul Showers, *Moonwalker,* Doubleday, in press; Ann Himler, *Guardian of the Forest, Keeper of the Trees,* Harper, in press.

FOR MORE INFORMATION SEE: New York Times Book Review, June 25, 1972, November 12, 1972.

Such a lot to do, dear,

Such a lot to see!

How we ever can get through

Fairly puzzles me.

Hurry up and out, dear,

Then—away! away!

In and out and round about,

Here's another day!

W. Graham Robertson

■ (From *Glad Day* by Ronald Himler. Illustrated by the author.)

CORINNE K. HOEXTER

HOEXTER, Corinne K.   1927-

PERSONAL: "O" in surname is silent; born November 3, 1927, in Scranton, Pa.; daughter of Edward D. (a manufacturer) and Aimee Helen (Rosenfelder) Katz; married Rolf Hoexter (an engineer), December 25, 1955; children: Vivien, Michael Frederic. *Education:* Wellesley College, B.A. (with high honors in English), 1949; University of Chicago, M.A., 1950. *Residence:* Englewood, N.J.

CAREER: Experiment in International Living, Putney, Vt., promotion assistant, 1950-51; *Parents' Magazine,* New York, N.Y., editorial assistant, 1951-53; Magazine Management, New York, N.Y., associate editor, 1953-54; Pines Publications, New York, N.Y., associate editor, then managing editor, 1954-57; J. J. Little & Ives, New York, N.Y., picture editor, 1957-59; *Art News Annual,* New York, N.Y., managing editor, 1959-60. Active in Englewood Social Service Federation and other civic and urban projects in the area. *Member:* Chinese Historical Society of America, League of Women Voters, National Association for the Advancement of Colored People, Englewood Nature Association, Phi Beta Kappa, Stuyvesant Yacht Club, Chatham Yacht Club (Chatham, Mass.). *Awards, honors:* Fulbright fellowship at University of Bologna, 1953.

WRITINGS: (With Ira Peck) *A Nation Conceived and Dedicated,* Scholastic Book Services, 1970; *Black Crusader: Frederick Douglass* (Child Study Association book list), Rand, 1970. Contributor to *Scholastic Scope.*

WORK IN PROGRESS: A book on personalities involved in the early history of the Chinese in America.

SIDELIGHTS: "I can remember always intending to be a writer—as a child, I used to spin out endless novels in my head, then entertain my friends on the front porch, or my sister in bed, with them. I have always been a voracious reader and many of my favorite books were histories or historical novels. Often I wove historical people and 'old unhappy far-off things and battles long ago' into the stories I told.

"Since history was always so real to me and threw so much light on our own world and problems, I felt it could be equally real to other young people today, not something 'dry and dusty.' I have tried to show the historical people in my books as people, after all, struggling with many of the same problems we face today, involved in the old and continuing human battle against injustice. At the same time I have tried to show individuals in relation to the great events and movements of history.

"Beyond history, my major interests as a writer are in literature and the arts, in urban problems and in nature and ecology. For recreation I enjoy reading, playing the piano and family singing and chamber music, modern dance, sailing, skiing, ice skating, walking in the city and hiking in the country. I'm also fond of travel and visiting places of historical and artistic interest. I enjoy concerts, theatre, art museums, etc. I spent a summer in Italy as a student and have toured Scotland, England, France, Italy and Denmark. I have been in Puerto Rico, the Virgin Islands and California, especially San Francisco, major location of my next book. I often spend the summer at Eastham on Cape Cod. I speak and read fluent French, passable Italian and Spanish, and minimal German and Hebrew.

"In our small city of Englewood and the nearby metropolis, New York, my family and I have been interested in a variety of urban problems (as indicated by organizational and civic activities listed above). Our chief project at the moment is preserving a beautiful piece of wild land on the west slope of the Palisades, one of the last in Englewood, and turning it into a nature center for the benefit of the whole city."

HOGARTH, Jr.
See KENT, Rockwell

HOLISHER, Desider   1901-1972

PERSONAL: Born February 2, 1901, in Budapest, Hungary; son of Leopold (a goldsmith-jeweler) and Anna (Weiner) Holisher; married Myra Zlatogorsky, December 25, 1928; children: Leo. *Education:* University of Berlin, M.Econ., 1926; Berlin Photography Academy, student, 1927-28. *Religion:* Jewish. *Home:* 611 West 111th St., New York, N.Y. 10025.

CAREER: Reporter Feature Syndicate, Berlin, Germany, feature writer and photo editor, 1929-33; Rome correspondent for European newspapers and magazines, 1933-38; writer, photographic illustrator, and teacher in United States, 1938-72. Sometime instructor in pictorial arts and photography at Rutgers University, and City College, New York.

WRITINGS: *Roma Centro Mondiale,* Andrea Scattini (Rome), 1937; *The Eternal City—Rome of the Popes,* Ungar, 1943; *The House of God,* Crown, 1946; *Pilgrims Path—The Story of Plymouth,* Stephen-Paul Publishers, 1947; *Capitol Hill—The Story of Congress,* Schuman, 1952; *The Synagogue and Its People,* Abelard, 1955; *Growing Up in Israel,* Viking, 1963.

Collaborator, doing photographic parts of the books: (With William Bridges) *Big Zoo,* Viking, 1941; (with Clarence W. Hall) *Protestant Panorama,* Farrar, Straus, 1951; (with Theodore McClintock) *Animal Close-Ups,* Abelard, 1958.

Author of over three hundred illustrated articles and photostories in periodicals in the United States and Europe; American magazines include *National Geographic, Life, Action, Pic, This Week, Popular Photography;* also contributed to publications of the U.S. Army Civil Affairs Division for Europe.

SIDELIGHTS: As an accredited correspondent in Rome, 1933-38, Holisher was the first newspaperman permitted to photograph the daily life and activities within the Vatican State. His illustrated articles went to magazines and newspapers in Switzerland, France, England, Netherlands, Austria, and Hungary, and were republished throughout Europe.

(Died August 11, 1972)

MARION HOLLAND

HOLLAND, Marion 1908-

PERSONAL: Born July 7, 1908, in Washington, D.C.; daughter of Maurice Crowther (a zoologist) and Lola (Davis) Hall; married Thomas W. Holland (an economist), 1939; children: Barbara, Nicholas, Judith, Rebecca, Andrew. *Education:* Swarthmore College, A.B., 1929. *Home:* 4100 Rosemary St., Chevy Chase, Md. 20015. *Agent:* McIntosh & Otis, Inc., 18 East 41st St., New York, N.Y. 10017.

CAREER: Author and illustrator of children's books. *Member:* Authors Guild, Children's Book Guild (Washington, D.C.; past president). *Awards, honors:* Boys' Clubs of America Junior Book Award for *Billy's Clubhouse.*

So I got a big bump
On the top of my head.
And it made a big lump.
And I sat there and said . . .
■ (From *A Big Ball of String* by Marion Holland. Illustrated by the author.)

Something about the Author

WRITINGS—Self-illustrated, except as noted: *Billy Had a System,* Knopf, 1952; *Billy's Clubhouse,* Knopf, 1955; *No Children, No Pets,* Knopf, 1956; *A Tree for Teddy,* Knopf, 1957; *A Big Ball of String,* Random House, 1958; *Muggsy* (not self-illustrated), Knopf, 1959; *No Room for a Dog* (not self-illustrated), Random House, 1959; *The Secret Horse,* Little, Brown, 1960; *Teddy's Camp-Out,* Knopf, 1963; *Casey Jones Rides Vanity,* Little, Brown, 1964.

WORK IN PROGRESS: Research on background for a book laid in the 1850's.

SIDELIGHTS: "I did a little illustrating for a children's magazine, which requires reading a story in manuscript carefully. (Too often it is possible to conclude that the illustrator did not read the story at all.) Sometimes I thought I could have improved on a story, which I mentioned to an editor who said, 'If you think it's so easy to write a children's story, why don't you run home and write one?' So I ran home and wrote one, which the editor accepted. As I had a house full of children at the time, it turned out that paper and a typewriter are less vulnerable to accidents than all the paraphernalia an illustrator needs; you can still read a page of type with a little grape jelly on it, but grape jelly on a picture means doing the whole thing over."

HOWARTH, David   1912-

PERSONAL: Born July 18, 1912, in London, England; son of Osbert J. R. and Eleanor (Paget) Howarth; married Nanette Smith; children: Clare, Virginia, Stephen, Joanna. *Education:* Cambridge University, B.A., 1933. *Home:* Brasted, Kent, England. *Agent:* Curtis Brown Ltd., 60 East 56th St., New York, N.Y. 10022.

CAREER: Baird Television Co., London, England, researcher, 1933-34; British Broadcasting Corp., London, England, assistant talks editor, 1934-40, war correspondent, 1939-40; free-lance writer. *Military service:* Royal Naval Volunteer Reserve, World War II; became lieutenant commander.

WRITINGS: Across to Norway, Sloane, 1952; *Thieves' Hole,* Rinehart, 1954; *We Die Alone,* Macmillan, 1955; *Sledge Patrol,* Macmillan, 1958; *D-Day,* McGraw, 1959; *The Shadow of the Dam,* Macmillan, 1961; *The Desert King: Ibn Saud and His Arabia,* McGraw, 1964; *Panama,* McGraw, 1966; *Waterloo,* Atheneum, 1968; *Trafalgar,* Atheneum, 1969; (editor) *Great Escapes* (Child Study Association book list), David White, 1969. Writer of serials and articles appearing in *Saturday Evening Post, Harper's,* and in British periodicals.

HULTS, Dorothy Niebrugge   1898-

PERSONAL: Born September 6, 1898, in Brooklyn, N.Y.; daughter of Frank Bernard (an insurance broker) and Mary (Spink) Niebrugge; married Charles Voorhees Hults (a physician), February 22, 1938 (died, 1971); children: Marjory Hults Negus (stepdaughter). *Education:* Wellesley College, B.A., 1921; Pratt Institute Library School, M.L.S., 1951. *Politics:* Republican. *Religion:* Protestant. *Home:* 1801 Dorchester Rd., Brooklyn, N.Y. 11226.

CAREER: Brooklyn (N.Y.) Public Library, children's librarian, 1922-24, 1926-38, 1949-60. *Member:* Long Island Historical Society, Brooklyn Botanic Garden, Garden Club of Flatbush (vice-president, 1970-71), Brooklyn Wellesley Club (president, 1944-46), Mardi Club (president, 1963-65), Women's Guild Flatbush-Tompkins Congregational Church (president, 1966-68).

WRITINGS: New Amsterdam Days and Ways, Harcourt, 1963.

SIDELIGHTS: "I have never aimed to be a star, but rather, hoped to contribute to the beauty and accord in the community where I lived as opportunities arose.

"I majored in music and literature in college. I liked children and books and became a children's librarian. I resigned when I married a doctor because I had a lot to learn about smoothly running a home with doctor's offices and becoming a stepmother, but, later, I combined homemaking and librarianship.

DOROTHY NIEBRUGGE HULTS

As the people grew richer and built larger houses, they also filled them with more beautiful objects. ■ (From *New Amsterdam Days and Ways* by Dorothy Niebrugge Hults. Illustrated by Jane Niebrugge.)

"When TV arrived upon the scene, the non-visual library story hours lost their popularity. It was then that I took up puppetry, both making puppets and giving and adapting the shows. The stories came alive and the shine in children's eyes was my reward.

"There was a great need for a suitable book on the life of the early Dutch settlers as every New York school child has assignments on this subject. None of the books were adequate. Since I have a Dutch maiden name and my husband was descended from the early Dutch settlers, I had a natural curiosity to discover what these long ago people were like. Upon retiring, I devoted my time to studying available books and looking into their original sources (translated into English). It was a fascinating experience and the information I gathered delights adults as well as children.

"My sister, Jane Niebrugge, is a commercial artist and I believe that her illustrations greatly enhanced the popularity of the book. She has put people in the quaint streets, people doing all sorts of things and enjoying themselves."

HOBBIES AND OTHER INTERESTS: Oil painting of landscapes, boats, and flowers, also puppeteering and music.

GENE INYART

INYART, Gene 1927-

PERSONAL: Pronunciations are Na-*mo*-vich and In-*yart*; born July 11, 1927, in Olney, Ill.; daughter of Ernest William (a retailer) and Pauline (Martin) Inyart; married Stanley B. Namovicz, Jr. (now a personnel specialist), October 3, 1959; children: Susan, Catherine, Matthew, Daniel. *Education;* University of Michigan, B.A. (with distinction), 1949; Catholic University of America, M.S. in L.S., 1963. *Religion:* Roman Catholic. *Home:* 333 Lincoln Ave., Takoma Park, Md. 20012.

CAREER: Public Library of District of Columbia, Washington, D.C., children's librarian, 1950-53, chief of Schools Division, 1953-57, chief of Extension Department, 1957-60. *Member:* American Library Association. *Awards, honors:* Franklin Watts Juvenile Fiction Award, 1959, for *The Tent under the Spider Tree.*

WRITINGS: The Tent under the Spider Tree, Watts, 1959; (with E. H. Gross) *Childrens Service in Public Libraries: Organization and Administration,* American Library Association, 1963; *Susan and Martin,* Watts, 1965; *Jenny,* Watts, 1966; *Orange October,* Watts, 1968; *Rabbit Girl?,* Sea Cliff, 1974.

Let's see now. What should it be? Poem, play, or story? ■ (From *Orange October* by Gene Inyart. Illustrated by Victoria de Larrea.)

SIDELIGHTS: "I read voraciously, garden sporadically, houseclean with great reluctance, cook enthusiastically, and spend much of the time when I should be writing gazing out the window at the finches and titmice on the bird feeder. In my writing I care more about my characters than my plots and concentrate on interpersonal relationships—how people react one to another and how they feel about themselves and others. I rewrite a great deal (very slowly) and am part owner (with my husband and four children) of a Schipperke dog named Barque, two gerbils named Plum and Pickle, a hermit tree crab named Ernie, and a nameless guppy."

IRWIN, Constance Frick 1913-
(C. H. Frick, Constance Frick)

PERSONAL: Born May 11, 1913, in Evansville, Ind.; daughter of Herman Christian (physician) and Minnie (Lauenstein) Frick; married William Robert Irwin (professor of English, University of Iowa), June 15, 1954; children: William Andrew (stepson), *Education:* Indiana University, A.B. (with distinction), 1934, M.A., 1941; Columbia University, B.S. in L.S. (with high honors), 1947. *Home:* 415 Lee St., Iowa City, Iowa.

CAREER: Reitz High School, Evansville, Ind., librarian, 1937-42, 1947-54; Evansville College (now University of Evansville), Evansville, Ind., librarian, 1946; Columbia University Press, New York, N.Y., book editor, 1947; University of Iowa, Iowa City, instructor in library science, 1961-63, assistant professor, 1963-67. *Military service:* U.S. Naval Reserve, 1942-45, became lieutenant commander. *Member:* American Library Association, Authors Guild, National League of American Pen Women, Phi Beta Kappa, Delta Kappa Gamma, Pi Lambda Theta, Alpha Chi Omega, Junior League. *Awards, honors:* Midland Booksellers Association, Black Hawk Award, 1964, and Ella Victoria Dobbs Award for Published Research, 1965, both for *Fair Gods and Stone Faces.*

WRITINGS: The Dramatic Criticism of George Jean Nathan, Cornell University Press, 1943; *Tourney Team,* Harcourt, 1954; *Five Against the Odds,* Harcourt, 1955; *Patch,* Harcourt, 1957; *Jonathan D.,* Lothrop, 1959; *The Comeback Guy,* Harcourt, 1961; *Fair Gods and Stone Faces,* St. Martins, 1963; *Gudrid's Saga,* St. Martin's Press, 1974.

SIDELIGHTS: "Why do I write? Because I have to; it's a compulsion. Perhaps it's because I'm interested in people, curious about individuals and how they relate to others and why. Yet to tell a living person's story exactly as it happened seems to me an invasion of privacy. So in fiction books I blend the experiences of others and invent. I watch and wonder—wonder why certain people do what they do and how they might react in a given situation. Out of these musings come the plots. The plots aren't fully charted in advance. They develop as characters grow and point the way.

"I'm also interested in the almost forgotten people of the past, those the history books have ignored. They too deserve their day in the sun.

"The sound of the language interests me too, especially the rhythm of a sentence. Sometimes a single perfect word excites me, not a word strung together from fragments of Latin but a word that has color and flair and conciseness.

"Some of you know me as C. H. Frick, author of sports books for boys. I wrote about boys because when I was growing up there were three boys in our home, my brother and two cousins. I shared their sports, their other interests, their troubles and pleasures. Later, as a high school librarian, it was my privilege to be acquainted with succeeding generations of young people.

"I have written under my married name, Irwin, as well as my maiden name, Frick. I have written for adults as well as children, running the gamut from a picture book to a scholarly book and stopping off at several levels between to write fiction and also nonfiction on various subjects because I like the stimulus of change. So much of interest lies about us. I want to feel free to roam, not be confined to one age level or one subject. I want to grow as a person as well as, hopefully, helping readers to grow. Growth requires stimulation as a body requires food."

CONSTANCE FRICK IRWIN

JACKSON, Caary
See JACKSON, C. Paul

JACKSON, C(aary) Paul 1902-
(Caary Jackson; pseudonyms: O. B. Jackson, Colin Lochlons, Jack Paulson)

PERSONAL: Born 1902, in Urbana, Ill., son of Caary and Goldie (Harding) Jackson; married Orpha Cook, 1922; children: Betty Jackson Soudek, Paul L., William L., Mae L. *Education:* Western Michigan University, A.B., 1929; University of Michigan, M.A., 1943. *Home:* 1825 Neptune Dr., Englewood, Fla. 33533.

CAREER: Teacher in Van Buren County (Mich.) schools, 1922-27, Kalamazoo (Mich.) public schools, 1929-51; full-time writer of books for boys, 1951—.

WRITINGS: All Conference Tackle, 1947, *Tournament Forward,* 1948, *Rose Bowl All-American,* 1949, *Rookie First Baseman,* 1950, *Rose Bowl Line Backer,* 1951, *Dub Halfback,* 1952, *Clown at Second Base,* 1952, *Little Leaguer's First Uniform,* 1952, *Giant in the Midget League,* 1953, *Spice's Football,* 1955 (all published by Crowell); *Bud Plays Junior High Football,* 1957, *Two Boys and a Soap Box Derby,* 1958, *Little League Tournament,* 1959, *Bud Plays Junior High Basketball,* 1959.

Bud Baker, T-Quarterback, 1960, *World Series Rookie,* 1960, *Bullpen Bargain,* 1961, *Pro Hockey Comeback,* 1961, *Bud Baker, Racing Swimmer,* 1962, *Pro Football Rookie,* 1962, *Tommy, Soap Box Derby Champion,* 1963, *Little Major Leaguer,* 1963, *Chris Plays Small Fry Football,* 1963 (all published by Hastings); *How to Play Better Baseball,* Crowell, 1963; *Pee Wee Cook of the Midget League,* 1964, *Super Modified Driver,* 1964, *Bud Plays Senior High Basketball,* 1964; *Fullback in the Large Fry League,* 1965, *Minor League Shortstop,* 1965, *Senior High Freestyle Swimmer,* 1965, *Rookie Catcher with the Atlanta Braves,* 1966 (all published by Hastings); *Bantam Bowl Football,* Hastings, 1967; *Bud Baker, High School Pitcher,* Hastings, 1967; *Tim, the Football Nut,* Hastings, 1967; *Hall of Fame Flankerback,* Hastings, 1968; *How to Play Better Basketball,* Crowell, 1968; *Second Time Around Rookie,* Hastings, 1968; *Big Play in the Small League,* Hastings, 1968; *Pennant Stretch Drive,* Hastings, 1969; *Baseball's Shrine,* Hastings, 1969; *Stepladder Steve Plays Basketball,* Hastings, 1969; *Pass Receiver,* Hastings, 1970; *Rose Bowl Old Pro,* Hastings, 1970; *Bud Baker, College Pitcher,* Hastings, 1970; *Tom Mosely, Midget Leaguer,* Hastings, 1971; *Halfback,* Hastings, 1971; *Fifth Inning Fadeout,* Hastings, 1972; *Eric and Dud's Football Bargain,* Hastings, 1972; *How to Play Better Football,* Crowell, 1972.

Under name Caary Jackson: *Shorty Makes the First Team,* 1950, *Shorty at Shortstop,* 1951, *Shorty Carries the Ball,* 1952, *Shorty at the State Tournament,* 1955, *Buzzy Plays Midget League Football,* 1956, *Stock Car Racer,* 1957, *The Jamesville Jets,* 1959, *A Uniform for Harry,* 1962, *Seashores and Seashore Creatures,* Putnam, 1964, *Midget League Catcher,* 1966, *Haunted Halfback,* 1968 (all published by Follett, unless otherwise noted).

Under name Caary Jackson, with wife, Orpha B. Jackson: *Star Kicker,* 1955, *Hillbilly Pitcher,* 1956, *Basketball Clown,* 1956, *Puck Grabber,* 1957, *Freshman Forward,* 1959, *The Short Guard,* 1961, *High School Backstop,* 1963, *No Talent Letterman,* 1966 (all published by McGraw).

Under pseudonym O. B. Jackson: *Basketball Comes to North Island,* McGraw, 1963; *Southpaw in the Mighty League,* McGraw, 1965.

Under pseudonym Colin Lochlons: *Stretch Smith Makes a Basket,* Crowell, 1949; *Squeeze Play,* Crowell, 1950; *Three and Two Pitcher,* Crowell, 1951; *Triple Play,* Crowell, 1952; *Barney of the Babe Ruth League,* Crowell, 1954.

Under pseudonym Jack Paulson: *Fourth Down Pass,* John C. Winston, 1950; *Match Point,* Westminster, 1956; *Side Line Victory,* Westminster, 1957.

SIDELIGHTS: "Lots of people think of a writer as somebody different, I suppose. All the writers I know, including myself, do not think we are different than run-of-the-mill people. Certainly there is nothing 'highbrow' or aloof about Jackson.

The old familiar butterflies fluttered as Bud selected a bat. ■ (From *Bud Baker: High School Pitcher* by C. Paul Jackson. Illustrated by Frank Kramer.)

"I wrote short stories for pulp magazines before I wrote books, chiefly because I always enjoyed reading sports stories. My first book was written more because an editor wrote that 'while Jackson writes on-field action well done enough to create an illusion of the reader being there, I doubt that he can motivate a book-length manuscript.' Such a challenge has always been like waving a red cloth in front of a bull. I vowed that I would write a book, get it published and send the first copy to that so-and-so. I wrote the book—*All Conference Tackle*—and have had more than seventy others published since, but I never sent so-and-so a copy.

"I enjoy writing and I especially enjoy knowing through fan letters and librarians and teachers that a certain amount of entertainment is brought to young readers by books I write. I hope the Man Upstairs continues to grant me the privilege of writing for a long, long time yet."

C. PAUL JACKSON

JACKSON, O. B.
See JACKSON, C. Paul

JAMES, Dynely
See MAYNE, William

JAMES, Josephine
See STERNE, Emma Gelders

JANE, Mary Childs 1909-

PERSONAL: Born September 18, 1909, in Needham, Mass.; daughter of Henry Thomas and Grace (Dyer) Childs; married William S. Jane, 1937; children: Stephen, Thomas. *Education:* State Teachers College, Bridgewater, Mass., B.S., 1931. *Religion:* Congregationalist. *Home:* Pump St., Newcastle, Me. 04553.

CAREER: Teacher in Pippapass, Ky., 1931-32, Chester, Mass., 1932-35, Needham, Mass., 1935-37. Author of juvenile mystery novels. *Member:* Poetry Fellowship of Maine (president, 1945-46). *Awards, honors:* Boys' Clubs of America gold medal, 1967, for *Ghost Rock Mystery.*

WRITINGS: Mystery in Old Quebec, 1955, *Ghost Rock Mystery,* 1956, *Mystery at Pemaquid Point,* 1957, *Mystery at Shadow Pond,* 1958, *Mystery on Echo Ridge,* 1959, *Mystery Back of the Mountain,* 1960, *Mystery at Dead End Farm,* 1961, *Mystery Behind Dark Windows,* 1962, *Mystery*

He flashed the beam around the pasture in every direction but there was nothing to be seen. ■ (From *The Ghost Rock Mystery* by Mary C. Jane. Illustrated by Raymond Abel.)

by Moonlight, 1963, *Mystery in Longfellow Square,* 1964, *Indian Island Mystery,* 1965, *Dark Tower Mystery,* 1966, *Mystery on Nine Mite Marsh,* 1967, *Mystery of the Red Carnations,* 1968, *The Rocking Chair Ghost,* 1969, *Mystery in Hidden Hollow,* 1970 (all published by Lippincott.) Co-editor, *Interior of a Question Mark* (poetry collection), Colby College Press, 1959.

SIDELIGHTS: "Places give me the starting idea for my books, as a rule, and the settings of my stories are usually places I have found exciting or interesting when I've vacationed there.

"I love hiking, camping, picnicing, and all outdoor kinds of pleasure. Reading is, of course, my *first* love, and while I'm extremely fond of poetry, both to read and write, and philosophy, and current serious nonfiction, I am also given to relaxing with a murder mystery two or three evenings a week. I loved mysteries from the time I first read Mary Roberts Rinehart's *The Circular Staircase* at age twelve—yes, and before that, when I read Augusta Huell Seaman's children's mysteries.

"As a teacher, I felt that getting children to read was the most important thing I could do, and I could often start a slow reader, one who found no fun in books, to reading by giving him a good juvenile mystery and getting him started on it—and thus 'hooked.' That's why I write mysteries: *I hope to lure children into becoming readers.* Other writers with greater artistic skill and talent may write books that these children will love later—but first, we have to get them to enjoy books.

"*Mystery of the Red Carnations* is woven around a favorite theme of mine—that life can and should be adventurous. Mysteries often fill that need for 'something exciting to happen'—but I hope they may also enliven imaginations so children gain a truer idea of what adventure really is.

"My husband and I have had wonderful chances to travel across this country and in England, and the six weeks in England took me to the homes (birthplaces, etc.) of many long-loved authors. *Something about the Author?*—finding *that* out has always constituted adventure for me."

MARY CHILDS JANE

JENNISON, C. S.
See STARBIRD, Kaye

JOHNSON, Dorothy M(arie) 1905-

PERSONAL: Born December 19, 1905, in McGregor, Iowa; daughter of Lester Eugene and Louisa (Barlow) Johnson. *Education:* Montana State University (now University of Montana), B.A., 1928. *Home:* 2309 Duncan Dr., Missoula, Mont. *Agent:* McIntosh & Otis, Inc., 18 East 41st St., New York, N.Y. 10017.

CAREER: Gregg Publishing Co., New York, N.Y., magazine editor, 1935-44; Farrell Publishing Corp., New York, N.Y., magazine editor, 1944-50; *Whitefish Pilot,* Whitefish, Mont., news editor, 1950-53; Montana State Press Association, secretary-manager, 1953-67; University of Montana, Missoula, assistant professor of journalism, 1953-67. *Awards, honors:* Spur Award, Western Writers of America,

DOROTHY M. JOHNSON

1956; University of Montana Alumni Association Distinguished Service Award, 1961; Litt.D., University of Montana, 1973.

WRITINGS: Beulah Bunny Tells All, Morrow, 1942; *Indian Country,* Ballantine, 1953; *The Hanging Tree,* Ballantine, 1957; *Famous Lawmen of the Old West* (juvenile), Dodd, 1963; *Greece: Wonderland of the Past and Present* (juvenile), Dodd, 1964; *Farewell to Troy* (juvenile), Houghton, 1964; *Some Went West* (juvenile), Dodd, 1965; *Flame on the Frontier* (short stories), Dodd, 1967; *Witch Princess,* Houghton, 1967; *Warrior for a Lost Nation: A Biography of Sitting Bull,* Westminster, 1969; *Montana* (juvenile), Coward, 1970; *Western Badmen* (juvenile), Dodd, 1970; *The Bloody Bozeman,* McGraw, 1971; (with R. T. Turner) *The Bedside Book of Bastards,* McGraw, 1973. Contributor of stories and articles to magazines. A number of stories anthologized, adapted for radio and television presentation.

SIDELIGHTS: "My stories have been translated into German, Spanish, Italian, Indonesian, Urdu, Polish and something that is either Russian or Czechoslovakian—it looks queer and my name comes out Johnsonova."

Ms. Johnson is an honorary member of the Blackfeet tribe in Montana, with the Indian name of Kills-Both-Places, and honorary police chief of Whitefish, Montana. The motion pictures "The Hanging Tree," Warner Bros., 1959, "The Man Who Shot Liberty Valance," Paramount, 1962, and "A Man Called Horse," 1972, are all based on her stories.

JOHNSON, Lois S(mith)

PERSONAL: Born in Parkersburg, W. Va.; daughter of Robert Bruce (a minister) and Carrie E. (Smith) Smith; married George Virgil Johnson, June 29, 1920 (deceased); married Bernard C. Becker, October 16, 1971; children: Janet Elizabeth (Mrs. Russell Little), William Bruce (deceased). *Education:* Marietta College, student, 1912-14; Colorado College, A.B., 1916; graduate work at San Jose State College, 1930, and University of California, Berkeley, 1935-38. *Religion:* Baptist. *Home:* 4164 Palisades Rd., San Diego, Calif. 92116.

CAREER: Elementary school teacher in Colorado Springs, Colo., 1916-18; junior high school teacher in Springfield, Ohio, 1918-20; elementary and high school teacher in Monterey, Calif., 1930-43; American National Red Cross, Washington, D.C., 1943-59, editor of Junior Red Cross periodicals, 1946-59. Consultant, American National Red Cross Office of International Relations, 1960. *Member:* Women's National Press Club, Women's National Book Association, Children's Book Guild (president, 1954-55), P.E.O. Sisterhood, Phi Beta Kappa.

WRITINGS: Christmas Stories Round the World (Child Study Association book list), Rand, 1960, deluxe edition, 1970; *Happy Birthdays Round the World,* Rand, 1963; *Happy New Year Round the World,* Rand, 1966; *What We Eat: The Origins and Travels of Foods Round the World,* Rand, 1969. Contributor of articles and short stories to magazines.

"The eldest of five children in a minister's family, I grew up in various parts of the United States. From my birthplace we moved to New York City, where my schooling began. My growing-up years through the junior year of high school were spent in El Paso, Texas. My high school work was completed at the Academy of Marietta College, when my father returned to his first pastorate in Parkersburg. My first two years of college were taken at Marietta College in Ohio; then, when my father received a 'call' to a church in Denver, I transferred to Colorado College, where I received an A.B. degree, cum laude, and a Phi Beta Kappa key, besides having fun in dramatics, glee club, sorority, and other campus activities.

"My interest in people, in travel, and in international affairs, began at an early age. From childhood, our home was a gathering place for returning missionaries, whose stories of their experiences in foreign lands were always fascinating to me. At one point in my teaching days, my classes included children from a cross-section of countries—Italy, Spain, Portugal, Sicily, Mexico, Japan, China. It was never a problem to put on international programs. At one time, I was brought into close contact with the Japanese Americans in the high school as sponsor for their Japanese-American Club.

"My work with the American Red Cross during World War II brought me into contact with a different kind of concern. My first A.R.C. assignment was serving as counselor to groups of A.R.C. overseas workers on their way to ports of embarkation. At the close of the war, I was asked to become editor of the two youth magazines—*Journal* for high school students, and the *News* for elementary schools. This position I held for thirteen years. Each issue of the magazines carried news of A.R.C. activities in other countries, as well as stories of children in other lands. A Spanish edition of the *News*, intended particulary for the children in Puerto Rico was started while I was editor. Through Red Cross field trips, my horizons were further widened by assignments to Canada and other countries of the world, as well as to schools in various parts of this country. After my retirement I served as program consultant in the Office of International Relations, preparing program materials for Chapter use, and planning travel schedules for international visitors.

"Writing on international subjects then was a natural for me after my retirement. My desire to write goes back to a newspaper contest I entered when I was about ten years old, in which my story was awarded first prize. Encouragement to write was given me all during my growing-up years by my parents who surrounded their children with good reading material, and were ever ready to give advice on my writing efforts, and by understanding teachers who offered helpful criticism.

"From my travels, I was fortunate in being able to gather first-hand information for my 'Round the World' books. From my Red Cross experiences, I became acquainted with many people from foreign countries, whose help in furnishing information I needed in the preparation of my books was invaluable. While living in Washington, D.C., I found the Embassies most willing to give me whatever information I needed. Upon completion of my work, they

Each time Erika passed the window she peeked out. But she could see nothing—only a thick blanket of snow covering the quiet street. ■ (From *Christmas Stories Round the World* by Lois S. Johnson. Illustrated by D. K Stone.)

LOIS S. JOHNSON

were also most helpful in checking the facts so that we could be sure what I had written was absolutely correct."

Mrs. Johnson traveled to Hawaii and Japan, 1956; British Isles and northern Europe, 1958; around the world, 1960-61; Bahamas, 1962; Bermuda, 1964; Greece and southern Europe, 1966; nine countries of Europe, 1969. All of her original manuscripts, proofs, etc., are in repository at the library of Southern Mississippi University.

JONES, Mary Alice

PERSONAL: Born in Dallas, Tex.; daughter of Paul and Mamie (Henderson) Jones. *Education:* University of Texas, B.A., 1918; Northwestern University, M.A., 1922; Yale University, Ph.D., 1932; University of Edinburgh,

postdoctoral study, 1955. *Politics:* Independent. *Religion:* Methodist. *Home:* Apartment 908, 3415 West End Ave., Nashville, Tenn. 37203. *Office:* Rand McNally & Co., Box 7600, Chicago, Ill. 60680.

CAREER: The Methodist Church, Nashville, Tenn., editor of children's publications, 1922-25; also free-lance writer of church school curriculum materials, 1923-45; International Council of Religious Education (now National Council of Churches), Chicago, Ill., director of children's work, 1930-45; Rand McNally & Co., Chicago, Ill., editor of children's books, 1945-51; The Methodist Church, Board of Education, Nashville, Tenn., director of children's work, 1951-64; Rand McNally & Co., consulting religious book editor, 1964—. Visiting professor at Northwestern University, Yale Divinity School, Duke University, Iliff School of Theology, Garrett Theological Seminary, and other seminaries; special lecturer at Duke University, McMurry College, Southern Methodist University, and elsewhere; member of faculty at summer schools of religious education. Member of White House Conference on Children, 1940, 1950, 1960, and of White House Conference on Education, 1955. Church posts include membership on General Assembly of National Council of Churches and on executive board of United Council of Church Women. *Member:* Authors League of America, League of Women Voters, American Association of University Women, Wesleyan Service Guild, Theta Sigma Phi, Pi Beta Phi.

*WRITINGS—*Adult: *Training Juniors in Worship,* 1930; *The Church and the Children,* 1932; *The Faith of Our Children,* Abingdon, 1935; *Guiding Children to Christian Growth,* Abingdon, 1949; *The Christian Faith Speaks to Children,* Abingdon, 1965.

Juveniles: (Editor) *My Own Book of Prayers: For Boys and Girls,* 1938, *Old Testament Stories,* 1939, *Stories of the Christ Child,* 1940, *Jesus and His Friends,* 1940, *Bible Stories of the Creation,* 1941, new edition, 1967, (editor) *First Prayers for Little Children,* 1942, *Tell Me About God,* 1943, new edition, 1968, *Tell Me About Jesus,* 1944, new edition, 1968, *Tell Me About the Bible,* 1945, *Tell Me About Prayer,* 1948, *Friends of Jesus,* 1948, *Bible Stories for Little Children,* 1949 (all published by Rand).

His Name Was Jesus, 1950, *Bible Stories,* 1952, *Tell Me About Heaven,* 1952, *My First Book About Jesus,* 1953, *Bible Stories: Old Testament,* 1954, *Stories of the Christ Child,* 1954, *Prayers and Graces for a Small Child,* 1955, *God Is Good,* 1955, *Tell Me About Christmas,* 1958, (editor) *Ten Commandments for Children,* 1958, *God Speaks to Me* (poems), 1961; *The Lord's Prayer,* 1964, *Tell Me About God's Plan for Me,* 1965, *God's Church is Everywhere,* 1965, *Know Your Bible,* 1965, *Me Myself and God,* 1969, *Friends are for Loving,* 1970, *Bible Stories: God's Work in Man's Life,* 1973 (all published by Rand).

Writer of curriculum materials for Presbyterian, Methodist, and Congregational church schools. Contributor to a dozen periodicals, among them *Child Study, Parents' Magazine, Christian Century,* and *Baptist Leader.*

SIDELIGHTS: Twenty-two million copies of her children's books have been sold, with translations in eight languages. *Hobbies and other interests:* Reading mystery stories ("the ones with refined, cultivated murderers—not gangsters"), world travel.

FOR MORE INFORMATION SEE: Hearthstone, November, 1958; *International Journal of Religious Education,* December, 1963; *More Junior Authors,* edited by Muriel Fuller, H. W. Wilson, 1963.

MARY ALICE JONES

For a long time he sat quietly. ■ (From *His Name was Jesus* by Mary Alice Jones. Illustrated by Rafaello Busoni.)

KATZ, Fred(eric Phillip)   1938-

PERSONAL: Born September 23, 1938, in Rochester, N.Y.; son of Benjamin N. and Rose (Kaufman) Katz; married Elsa Szold, July 30, 1961; children: Jeffery, Stephen. *Education:* University of Michigan, B.A., 1960. *Politics:* Democrat. *Religion:* Jewish. *Home:* 5918 Briarwood Lane, Peoria, Ill. 61614. *Agent:* Don Gold, William Morris Agency, 1350 Avenue of the Americas, New York, N.Y. 10019. *Office:* Szold's, Inc., 2201 Southwest Adams, Peoria, Ill. 61602.

CAREER: *Sport,* New York, N.Y., member of staff, 1961-71, as managing editor, 1968-71; Szold's, Inc. (department store), Peoria, Ill., assistant vice-president, 1971—. Member of board of directors, Neighborhood House and Peoria Symphony, 1972—. *Military service:* U.S. Army Reserve, 1961-68, with active duty, 1960-61; became captain. *Member:* Society of Magazine Writers (president, 1968-70).

WRITINGS: *Art Arfons: Fastest Man on Wheels,* Thomas Nelson, 1965; *American Sports Heroes of Today,* Random House, 1970; (editor) *The Glory of Notre Dame,* Bartholomew House, 1971.

KAY, Helen
See GOLDFRANK, Helen Colodny

KENNELL, Ruth E(pperson) 1893-

PERSONAL: Surname is pronounced Kenn-*ell*; born September 21, 1893, in Oklahoma City, Okla.; daughter of Julius (a farmer) and Sara Ellen (Seeger) Epperson; married Frank Risley Kennell (a teacher), July 7, 1917 (deceased); children: James Epperson, David Epperson. *Education:* University of California, Berkeley, student, 1913. *Politics:* Democratic Party. *Religion:* Unitarian Universalist. *Home:* 1646 Madrono Ave., Palo Alto, Calif. 94306. *Agent:* Ruth Cantor, 156 Fifth ave., New York, N.Y. 10010.

CAREER: Richmond (Calif.) Public Library, children's librarian, 1914-17; American Colony Kuzbas, Kemerovo, Siberia, librarian and secretary, 1922-24; International Library, Moscow, Soviet Union, reference librarian, 1925-27; secretary and guide to Theodore Dreiser on his Russian tour, 1927-28; Newspaper Enterprise Association (N.E.A.; a syndicate), correspondent in Moscow, Soviet Union, 1930-32; writer of children's books and short stories, 1931-58, and lately, of nonfiction. Correspondent for *Nation* in American Colony Kuzbas and later Moscow, 1922-31. Active in China and Russian war relief work, 1941-45. *Member:* Women's International League for Peace and Freedom (literature chairman of Palo Alto branch, 1965-71), League of Women Voters, Civic League (Palo Alto).

WRITINGS—Juvenile fiction, except as noted: *Vanya of the Streets,* Harper, 1931; *Comrade One-Crutch,* Harper, 1932; *That Boy Nikolka and Other Tales of Soviet Children* (first published serially in *Story Parade,* 1943), Russian War Relief, Inc., 1945; *Adventure in Russia: The Ghost of Kirghizia,* Messner, 1947; *The Secret Farmyard,* Abelard, 1956 (text edition with *Teacher's Guide*), Houghton, 1968; *Dreiser and the Soviet Union 1927-1945: A Personal Chronicle* (adult nonfiction), International Publishers, 1969.

One of her short stories, "Lisa's Song," has been included in six collections and school readers, 1942-71; other stories originally published in *Story Parade* and *Child Life* have been reprinted in *Invitation to Reading,* Harcourt, 1945, *Youth Replies I Can,* Knopf, 1945, *Story Parade Yellow Book, Story Parade Star Book,* and in texts. Writer of short stories and serials for church school papers published by Methodist Book Concern, 1932-42, and stories for Junior Red Cross magazines, 1940-45, and other juvenile periodicals.

WORK IN PROGRESS: A book about the American Colony Kuzbas, Kemerovo, Siberia, for International Publishers.

SIDELIGHTS: "My mother came from Ohio and my father from Nebraska with their parents in the 'eighties when the cry was: 'Go West!' They met and married in Kansas. In 1889, they joined the race, in a covered wagon, to stake claims in Cherokee Strip, part of the Indian Territory in Oklahoma, which was not yet a state. I was born when our sod house had been replaced by a frame house. Papa died when I was seven and my mother took me, my sister and two brothers to live in Oklahoma City.

"I attended grade and high school there. During my first year in high school, I won first prize in a story contest and was launched on my writing career. In my junior year I won a gold medal given by the Women's Club for 'excellence in composition.' I also wrote stories for the monthly school paper on which I was art editor. At that time I was undecided about my career—writer or artist. I am glad I chose to be a writer. I prefer to express my ideas and ideals in articles and stories.

"I finished my senior year in high school after we moved to California. At the University of California in Berkeley I took a course in library methods, and later became children's librarian in the Richmond Public Library. I held a weekly story hour, which not only versed me in children's literature, but also in the art of story-telling. My flair for drawing found expression in posters for the children's room. Those were happy years.

The hens, their plumage gleaming white in the gathering dusk, slipped into the coop one by one. The last to go in was Queen Elizabeth. She moved with stately leisure, once more the ruler of the roost. ■ (From *The Secret Farmyard* by Ruth Epperson Kennell. Illustrated by Jules Gotlieb.)

"After I married and had a baby son, my husband and I joined a group for technical aid to Russia after the Revolution. As members of the American Industrial Colony Kuzbas, we left our baby boy with his grandmother and went with a group to a mining town in Western Siberia on a two-year contract. I was correspondent for *The Nation,* and served as secretary and librarian in the offices. During our two years in Kemerovo, the Colony members had renovated the run-down coal mines and finished the chemical plant. Being the only coke ovens not in the Nazi invaders' hands during their occupation of industrial centers in World War II, both the coal mines and chemical plant played a major role in the defeat of our common enemy. Today, Kuzbas is one of the greatest industrial centers in the Soviet Union.

"After more than two years in Kemerovo, I went to Moscow where I worked in an international library. I also wrote prefaces to Russian editions of American novels. Grandma Kennell brought my little son to Moscow and he stayed with me in the hotel for foreign workers while his father was teaching English at the Technological Institute in Tomsk, Siberia. When the famous American novelist, Theodore Dreiser, came to Moscow as guest of the Soviet Union, I acted as his secretary and interpreter on his 77-day tour of the country.

"Returning home after an absence of more than five years, I wrote my first book for children, *Vanya of the Streets,* about a Russian boy made an orphan and homeless during World War I and the famine and pestilence which followed. It was beautifully illustrated by a Russian artist and was so well received that my publisher asked me to write another book about Russian children. *Comrade One-Crutch* tells the story of another orphan who had lost a leg during the war, and was adopted by our Colony. The same Russian artist illustrated that book. Another story, *That Boy Nikolka,* tells about a boy whose bravery helped the defenders of Moscow during World War II. 'The Village Treasure' tells of another brave Russian boy during the siege of Stalingrad, and is included in a collection of stories about young heroes in our Allied countries during World War II, *Youth Replies I Can.* My last book about Russian children is *Adventure in Russia* whose hero was left an orphan in World War II and was sent with other orphans from the besieged city of Leningrad to a sanitarium in Central Asia where he has many adventures."

FOR MORE INFORMATION SEE: American Mercury, April, 1932; (biographical comment by H. L. Mencken) *Youth Replies I Can,* Knopf, 1945.

RUTH E. KENNELL

KENT, Rockwell   1882-1971
(Hogarth, Jr.)

PERSONAL: Born June 21, 1882, in Tarrytown Heights, N.Y.; son of Rockwell (a lawyer and mining engineer) and Sara (Holgate) Kent; married Kathleen Whiting, 1909; married Frances Lee, 1926; married Shirley Johnstone, 1940; children: (first marriage) Rockwell, Kathleen Kent Finney, Clara Kent Pearce, Barbara Kent Carter, Gordon. *Education:* Attended Episcopal Academy of Connecticut; attended Horace Mann School, Columbia University (architecture), 1901-04; studied art under William M. Chase, Hayes Miller, Robert Henri, Abbott H. Thayer. *Home:* Au Sable Forks, N.Y. 12912. *Agent:* H. Keith Thompson, Jr., P. O. Box 254, Wall Street Station, New York, N.Y. 10005.

CAREER: Architect, carpenter, contractor, dairy farmer, artist, and writer. Kent first exhibited as a painter at the National Academy of Design in 1905; after that his work (as a wood-engraver, lithographer, and illustrator, as well as painter) was shown widely in America and in Europe. He is represented in New York's Metropolitan Museum, the Chicago Art Institute, in other museums in the United States and in The Hermitage (Leningrad) and the Pushkin Museum (Moscow). Illustrator of many books, including his own, the works of Shakespeare, *The Bridge of San Luis Rey, Moby Dick, Beowulf, The Canterbury Tales, Leaves of Grass, Paul Bunyan, Faust, The Decameron,* and *Candide.*

MEMBER: International Workers Order (former president), Artists Union of United Office and Professional Workers, United Brotherhood of Carpenters and Joiners (CIO), Dairy Farmers Union of the Northeast, United States Farmers Association, International Longshoreman's and Warehouseman's Union (honorary), Academy of Fine Arts (Soviet Union; honorary), National Institute of Arts and Letters. *Awards, honors:* $28,000 Lenin Peace Prize, 1967.

■ (From *Moby Dick* by Herman Melville. Illustrated by Rockwell Kent.)

WRITINGS: Wilderness, Putnam, 1920, Modern Library, 1930; *Voyaging Southward from the Strait of Magellan,* Putnam, 1924, revised edition, 1968; *N by E* (Literary Guild selection), Brewer & Warren, 1930, Harcourt, 1933; (with bibliography and list of prints by Carl Zigrosser) *Rockwelkentiana,* Harcourt, 1933; *Salamina,* Harcourt, 1935; (editor) *World-Famous Paintings,* Wise, 1939, 2nd edition, 1947; *This Is My Own,* Duell, Sloan & Pearce, 1940; *A Northern Christmas* (most of text and illustrations taken from *Wilderness*), American Artists Group, 1941; *On Earth Peace,* American Artists Group, 1942; *It's Me O Lord* (autobiography), Dodd, 1955; *Of Men and Mountains,* Asgaard Press, 1959; *Greenland Journal,* Obolensky, 1962; *Voyaging,* Grosset, 1968; *After Long Years: Being a Story of Which the Author, for a Change, is not the Hero,* Asgaard Press, 1968; *Rockwell Kent: The Early Years,* Bowdoin College, Museum of Art, 1969.

Books of drawings, monologues, incidental writings, illustrations: *The Seven Ages of Man,* privately published, 1918; *Alaska Drawings,* Knoedler & Co., 1919; *The Bookplates and Marks of Rockwell Kent,* Random, 1929; Herman Melville, *Moby Dick,* Random House, 1930; *A Birthday Book,* Random, 1931; *Beowulf,* Random House, 1932; Chaucer, *Canterbury Tales,* Covici Friede, 1934; *How I Make a Woodcut,* Esto, 1934; *Saga of Gisli,* Harcourt, 1936; Shakespeare, *Complete Works,* two volumes, Doubleday, 1936; *Later Bookplates & Marks of Rockwell Kent,* privately published, 1937; *Forty Drawings Done by Rockwell Kent to Illustrate the Works of William Shakespeare,* Garden City, 1937; Esther Shephard, *Paul Bunyan,* Harcourt, 1941; *Rockwell Kent,* American Artists Group, 1945; *The Mad Hermit* (seven drawings for *Wilderness*),

Asgaard Press, 1955; Voltaire, *Candide,* Barron, 1963. Contributor of articles to popular magazines. Editor, *Creative Art.* Contributing editor, *Colophon.*

WORK IN PROGRESS: Continuation of autobiography; a collection of articles and letters.

SIDELIGHTS: "I was sent to school, and then another school, and then to college. One school I didn't like, so I ran away. Latin I didn't like, so they tried to break me. My teachers gave up." After flirting with architecture, Kent spent ten years wandering and painting. In 1916, he wanted to go to Alaska to paint the mountains, sea, and wilderness, so he had himself incorporated as Rockwell Kent, Inc. He sold shares to his friends and with the proceeds lived for a year with his eight-year-old son on Fox Island, not 400 miles south of the Arctic Circle. When his Alaskan paintings were exhibited in 1920, they sold so well the shares paid a twenty-per-cent dividend and Kent bought back his stock in himself.

In the thirties, Kent became world renowned not only for his paintings but also for his political beliefs. "When I was a young fellow I was very much disturbed by there being some people with lots of money and lots of people with no money. I thought a lot about it and I read a lot about it, so that when I voted for the first time, I voted Socialist. I'm still disturbed by the fact that there are some people with a lot of money and a lot of people with no money and a few million with no jobs, and that the world is rich in resources and that people are starving to death, and that all the people in the world want to live and yet a good part of the time they're busy killing each other." Because of his political stand, Kent found himself ignored as an artist in the fifties and sixties; questioned by the McCarthy Senate hearings on Communism; and denied a passport by the State Department on the suspicion he was a Communist. In the latter case, Kent sued and won in the United States Supreme Court in a landmark decision. He commented: "I'm an American who doesn't want his corns stepped on."

As an artist, Kent seldom relied on cross-hatching in his drawings. His control of parallel-line shading is evident in all his work. Art critic, James Huneker, referred to him as an "athlete of the brush." "Kent's paintings, watercolors, lithographs and woodcuts often depicted the stark and rugged aspects of nature—bleak and icy mountains and lonely shacks and frozen wastes," wrote Alden Whitman in the *New York Times.* "They reflected his adventurous life in Maine, Greenland, Arctic Alaska, and Tierra del Fuego at the tip of South America and in wilderness areas of this country. His style was distinctive, vigorous and simple, yet his people were portrayed with the subtle compassion of one who knew their secrets."

Wrote David Preiss: "Although he liked children, he never illustrated a book intended primarily for them. Indeed, a trait far ahead of its time, he made very little distinction between youth and seniority, for he kept the idealism, the agility, and the virility of youth throughout his life." "Life has always been, and God help me, always will be so exciting," said Kent, "that I'll want to talk about it. I rate even my being an artist and a writer by being heart and soul a revolutionist. I think that the ideals of youth are fine, clear

ROCKWELL KENT (ca. 1932)

and unencumbered; and that the real art of living consists in keeping alive the conscience and sense of values we had when we were young.''

FOR MORE INFORMATION SEE: New Republic, May 4, 1927; *Time,* September 20, 1937, March 22, 1971; Sharon Brown, editor, *Present Tense,* Harcourt, 1941; *American Book Collector,* summer, 1964; *Esquire,* January, 1967; *Illustrators of Children's Books: 1957-1966,* Horn Book, 1968; Diana Klemin, *The Illustrated Book,* Clarkson Potter, 1970; *New York Times,* March 14, 1971; *Newsweek,* March 22, 1971; *Antiquarian Bookman,* May 17, 1971; *American Artists,* November, 1972.

(Died March 13, 1971)

Arturo Toscanini, now recognized as the greatest conductor of this generation... ■ (From *Twelve Citizens of the World* by Leonard S. Kenworthy. Illustrated by William Sharp.)

CAREER: Friends Select School, Philadelphia, Pa., assistant to headmaster, 1934-36; Brunswick School, Greenwich, Conn., social studies teacher, 1936-38; Friends Central School, Philadelphia, Pa., head of social studies department, 1938-42; Friends International Center, Berlin, Germany, director, 1940-41; United Nations Educational, Scientific, and Cultural Organization, secretariat, 1946-48; Brooklyn College, Brooklyn, N.Y., 1949—, now professor of education. Chairman of International-Intercultural Education Committee of the Association for Childhood Education. *Member:* Tau Kappa Alpha, National Council for the Social Studies, Association for Supervision and Curriculum Development. *Awards, honors:* Van Loan Essay Contest, winner; Citizen of Paris Award.

WRITINGS: Introducing Children to the World, Harper, 1956; *Twelve Citizens of the World,* Doubleday, 1956; *Leaders of New Nations,* Doubleday, 1960; *Profile of Nigeria,* Doubleday, 1961; *Profile of Kenya,* Doubleday, 1962; *Guide to Social Studies Teaching,* Wadsworth, 1962, new edition, 1973; *Three Billion Neighbors,* Ginn, 1965; *Background Papers for Social Studies Teachers,* Wadsworth, 1966; *Social Studies for the Seventies: In Elementary and Middle Schools,* College Xerox, 1973.

KENYON, Ley 1913-

PERSONAL: Born May 28, 1913, in London, England; son of Arnold Kingsley (a company director) and Margaret (Jolly) Kenyon. *Education:* Attended Marylebone Grammar School; Central School of Arts and Crafts, London, England, student, 1931-34. *Home:* 37 Cranley Gardens, London S.W.7, England. *Agent:* Martin Forrest, The Handly Management, 51 Church St., Boston, Mass. 02116.

CAREER: Artist, with war drawings in collection of Na-

KENWORTHY, Leonard S. 1912-

PERSONAL: Born March 26, 1912; son of Murray S. and Lenora (Holloway) Kenworthy. *Education:* Earlham College, A.B., 1933; Columbia University, A.M., 1935, Ed.D., 1948. *Home:* 2676 Bedford Ave., Brooklyn, N.Y. *Office:* Brooklyn College, Brooklyn, N.Y. 11210.

tional Gallery; professional aqualung diver and underwater photographer, participating in the Costeau underwater archaeological excavations in the Mediterranean, and in British Research Divers' Expedition to the Red Sea, 1965. Commonwealth lecturer for J.Y. Cousteau (of the French Navy) Group, showing films made by Cousteau and himself, in England, continental Europe, Africa, and Near and Far East. *Military service:* Royal Canadian Air Force, 1940-45; became squadron gunnery leader; awarded Distinguished Flying Cross. *Member:* Chelsea Arts Club, British Sub-Aqua Club. *Awards, honors:* Winston Churchill Memorial Trust Fellowship, 1971.

WRITINGS: Pocket Guide to the Undersea World, Collins, 1957; *Tauch Mit!,* Albert Muller, 1958; *Discovering the Undersea World,* Sterling, 1962; *Aqualung Diving,* Geo. Allen, 1971.

WORK IN PROGRESS: A fifty-minute documentary film and commentary on Aldabra, an island in the Indian Ocean famous for its unique animal and bird life.

SIDELIGHTS: An authority on aqualung diving, Kenyon was invited to Buckingham Palace in 1960 to teach the Duke of Edinburgh to dive.

C. CLE. KINNEY

KINNEY, C. Cle(land) 1915-

PERSONAL: Born December 15, 1915, in Victoria, B.C., Canada; son of C. Robert (an engineer) and Jane (Cleland) Kinney; married Jean Stout Brown (now an advertising consultant and author), June 10, 1960; children: Gwen Kinney Bates, Peter, Thomas, Charles; (stepchildren) Susan Brown Fisher, Dina Brown Anastasie. *Education:* Massachusetts School of Art, student, 1931-35. *Politics:* Democrat. *Religion:* Episcopalian. *Home and studio:* Box 222, Gaylordsville, Conn. 06755.

CAREER: Artist, writer. Water colors exhibited at one-man show in New York, N.Y., photographs in other shows.

WRITINGS—All with wife, Jean Kinney: *What Does the Tide Do?,* Young Scott, 1965; *What Does the Sun Do?,* Young Scott, 1965; *What Does the Moon Do?,* Young Scott, 1965; *How to Get 20 to 90% Off on Everything You Buy,* Parker, 1966; *21 Kinds of American Folk Art and How to Make Each One,* Atheneum, 1971; *57 Tests that Reveal Your Hidden Talents,* Hawthorn, 1972. (For complete list of writings see *Contemporary Authors,* Volume 11-12).)

SIDELIGHTS: "My wife and I do many books for children, and here is how we work. As collaborators, we decide on a basic approach for a book. This we discuss with a publisher and get a contract. Then we go 'on location' (to Cape Cod to do a book about the tide, Mt. Rainier to do a book about the clouds, Arizona to do a book about the sun, etc.). There we do research and sketch preliminary illustrations. When we return to Connecticut, my wife does most of the writing and I do all of the illustrations for the finished book."

KLEIN, Leonore (Glotzer) 1916-

PERSONAL: Born September 4, 1916, in New York, N.Y.; daughter of Isidor (teacher) and Sadie (April) Glotzer; married Joseph M. Klein (chairman, high school English department), April 1, 1939; children: Judith Anne, Robert Morris, *Education:* Barnard College, B.A., Wellesley College, M.A.; Columbia University, M.S. in L.S., 1964. *Home:* 7 Barbara Lane, Hartsdale, N.Y. 10530.

CAREER: Long Island City High School, Long Island, N.Y., librarian, 1950-52; Bryant High School, Astoria, N.Y., librarian, 1952-54; Florida Southern College, Lakeland, Fla., reference librarian, 1954-59; public schools, Pleasantville, N.Y., librarian, 1959-62; public schools, White Plains, N.Y., librarian, 1962—.

WRITINGS: The Happy Surprise, Grosset, 1952; *Guess What?* Grosset, 1953; *Project Book for Boys and Girls,* Grosset, 1956; *What Would You Do If?,* Young Scott Books, 1956; *Brave Daniel* (Junior Literary Guild selection), Young Scott Books, 1958; *Arrow Book of Tricks and Projects,* Scholastic, 1960; *Mud, Mud, Mud,* Knopf, 1962; *Henri's Walk to Paris,* Young Scott Books, 1962; *Run Away John,* Knopf, 1963; *Tom and the Small Ant,* Knopf, 1965; *The Arrow Book of Project Fun,* Scholastic 1965; *What Is an Inch?,* Harvey, 1966; *Huit Enfants et un Bebe,* Abelard, 1966; *How Old is Old?,* Harvey, 1967; *Too Many*

Parents, Knopf, 1968; *Just Like You,* Harvey House, 1968; *Just a Minute,* Harvey House, 1969; *Silly Sam,* Scholastic Book Services, 1969; *"D" Is for Rover,* Harvey House, 1970; *Only One Ant,* Hastings House, 1971.

SIDELIGHTS: "Writing began with me when I was six years old and wrote 'An Ode to the Chicken Pox', but my fate as a children's author was sealed when I became a counselor at a children's camp and, every night, told my eight year olds a running story that began on July 4th and ended on August 20th, the last day of camp.

"From then on, ideas arrived in my mind from many sources. I wrote *Mud, Mud, Mud* when I was living in Florida where the rain mixed with the sand and disappeared, instead of turning into the gooey, delicious mud of New York State. *Henri's Walk to Paris* and *Huit Enfants et un Bebe* (Eight Children and One Baby) were both based on Jewish folk stories I'd heard many times. I wrote *"D" Is for Rover* for my granddaughter who would soon begin to learn her alphabet and *Only One Ant* was very important to me because, when I wrote it, I was beginning to worry that boys and girls and grown men and women were no longer caring as much as they used to about people and animals and insects.

"If there is time for quiet and thinking, I can let the various ideas for stories that arrive in my head simmer for awhile to see if these ideas make a pattern or form a story. Many do not and I must forget them. Some get written but never

Sylvia Abercrombie brought mud into the house on her hands and left some on the walls. ■ (From *Mud! Mud! Mud!* by Leonore Klein. Illustrated by George Wiggins.)

published. For every story of mine that has been published, I've written two that were not.

"I am happiest writing in bed with lots of folded paper around me that I make into little books. In this way I can imagine a picture for every page of words that I write. Now that I'm a grandma, I should be getting new ideas from the stories I tell my grandchildren when I visit them or they visit me.

"When I am not functioning as a librarian in a junior high school, I like to travel and look at birds, especially at tiny warblers that are hard to see but are beautifully colored if you can catch a sight of them in your bird glasses. Sometimes I like to fish, but I think soon that I won't fish anymore and let the fish I might have caught swim in the small amount of unpolluted water that is left."

KOCH, Dorothy (Clarke) 1924-

PERSONAL: Born October 8, 1924, in Ahoskie, N.C.; daughter of David Arthur (a minister) and Agnes (Jones) Clarke; married William Julian Koch (now a professor, University of North Carolina), November 28, 1947; children: Patricia, Jean, Deborah, David. *Education:* Meredith College, B.A., 1947; attended University of Geneva, 1971; University of North Carolina, M.Ed., 1972. *Religion:* Episcopalian. *Home:* 401 Clayton Rd., Coker Hills, Chapel Hill, N.C.

CAREER: Free-lance writer for children. Instructor in writing for juveniles. *Member:* North Carolina Writers Group.

WRITINGS: I Play at the Beach, 1955, *Gone Is My*

LEONORE KLEIN

I am glad those little animals
Left their shells for me.
■ (From *I Play at the Beach* by Dorothy Koch. Illustrated by Feodor Rojankovsky.)

Something about the Author

DOROTHY KOCH

Goose, 1956, *When the Cows Got Out,* 1958, *Let It Rain,* 1959, *Monkeys Are Funny That Way,* 1962, *Up the Big Mountain,* 1964 (all published by Holiday).

HOBBIES AND OTHER INTERESTS: Tennis, golf, gardening, designing clothes, dancing, landscape design.

LACY, Leslie Alexander 1937-

PERSONAL: Born in 1937, in Franklin, La.; son of Nathaniel Lenard (a physician) and Lillie Lacy. *Education:* Attended private schools in the South before going to New England to college; University of Southern California, M.A.; also attended University of California, Berkeley, and University of Ghana. *Home:* Apt 508, 3200 16th St. N.W., Washington, D.C. 20010.

CAREER: Active with political groups embracing "explicit socialist alternatives to capitalism" while a law student in California, where he eventually joined the Afro-American Association; went to Africa in 1962 and spent four years studying and teaching at University of Ghana, Legon; returned to United States after Ghana's President Kwame Nkrumah was deposed in 1966.

WRITINGS: (Contributor) Gwendolyn Carter, editor, *Politics in Africa,* Harcourt, 1966; (contributor) LeRoi Jones and Larry Neal, editors, *Black Fire,* Morrow, 1968; *Black Africa on the Move* (juvenile), Watts, 1969; (contributor) John Henrik Clark, editor, *Malcolm X,* Macmillan, 1969; *Cheer the Lonesome Traveler; The Life of W.E.B. Du-Bois,* (young adult book), Dial, 1970; *The Rise and Fall of a Proper Negro* (autobiography), Macmillan, 1970; (author of introduction) Wole Soyinka, *The Interpreter,* Macmillan, 1970.

LADER, Lawrence 1919-

PERSONAL: Born August 6, 1919, in New York, N.Y.; son of Ludwig and Myrtle (Powell) Lader; married Joan Summers, 1961; children: Wendy Summers. *Education:* Harvard University, A.B., 1941. *Politics:* Democrat. *Home and office:* 51 Fifth Ave., New York, N.Y. 10003. *Agent:* Roberta Pryor and Phyllis Jackson, International Famous Agency, 1301 Avenue of the Americas, New York, N.Y. 10019.

CAREER: American Broadcasting Company, New York, N.Y., press department, 1942; *Coronet* Magazine, New York, N.Y., contributing editor, 1946-47; *Glamour* Magazine, New York, N.Y., feature editor, 1953; New York University, New York, N.Y., adjunct associate professor of journalism, 1968-72; free-lance writer, 1941—. *Military service:* U.S. Army, 1942-46, attaining rank of lieutenant. *Member:* Society of Magazine Writers (president, 1958, vice-president, 1957), National Association for Repeal of Abortion Laws (chairman, 1969—), Yorkville Democratic Club (director of information, 1959-64), Harvard Club (New York).

WRITINGS: The Margaret Sanger Story, Doubleday, 1955; *The Bold Brahmins: New England's War Against Slavery (1830-63),* Dutton, 1961; *Margaret Sanger* (juvenile), Crowell, 1969. (For complete list of writings see *Contemporary Authors,* volume 1-4.) Contributor of some 300 articles to *Look, Reader's Digest, This Week, American Heritage, McCall's, New Yorker, New Republic, Good Housekeeping, Redbook,* and other magazines.

HOBBIES AND OTHER INTERESTS: Collecting contemporary art, mainly Italian.

LANGSTAFF, John (Meredith) 1920-

PERSONAL: Born December 24, 1920, in New York, N.Y.; son of B. Meredith and Esther Knox (Boardman) Langstaff; married Nancy Woodbridge, 1948; children: Carol, John, Gerry, Deborah. *Education:* The Choate School, diploma, 1939; attended Curtis Institute of Music, 1940-41; Juilliard School of Music, 1946-49; Columbia University, 1949-51. *Home:* 9 Burlington St., Lexington, Mass. 02173. *Office:* Young Audiences of Massachusetts, 74 Joy St., Boston, Mass.

CAREER: Musician; started as boy soprano soloist, Grace Church, New York, and with Bretton Woods Boy Singers. Has given concerts throughout United States and abroad, appearing as soloist with National Symphony, New York Philharmonic, Montreal Symphony, Little Orchestra Society, Minneapolis Symphony; makes recordings and appearances on radio and television, including a music series for British Broadcasting Corp. and a series of book programs for National Broadcasting Co. Artist-lecturer for Association of American Colleges; former head of the music department, Potomac School, McLean, Va. and Shady Hill School, Cambridge, Mass.; presently on faculty of School of Education, Simmons College, Boston, Mass. *Military service:* U.S. Army, Infantry, for four years; became first lieutenant; received Purple Heart, Gold Star.

MEMBER: American Guild of Musical Artists, Actors Equity, International Folk Music Council, Country Dance Society of America (governing board), Urban League, "Philosophers-Kings" Club (Washington, D.C.). *Awards, honors:* Caldecott Prize for *Frog Went A-Courtin'*, 1956; recognition by National Federation of Musicians for presenting outstanding American music abroad, 1959.

WRITINGS: *Frog Went A-Courtin'*, 1955, *Over In the Meadow*, 1957, *On Christmas Day In the Morning!*, 1959, *The Swapping Boy*, 1960, *Ol' Dan Tucker*, 1963, *Hi! Ho! The Rattlin' Boy: And Other Folk Songs for Group Singing*, Harcourt, 1969, (with Nancy Langstaff) *Jim Along, Josie* (ALA Notable Book; *Horn Book* Honor List), 1970, *Gather My Gold Together*, Doubleday, 1971; *The Golden Vanity*, 1972, *Soldier, Soldier Won't You Marry Me?*, Doubleday, 1972, *Saint George and the Dragon*, Athe-

Frog went a-courtin', he did ride,
Sword and pistol by his side.
■ (From *Frog Went a-Courtin* retold by John Langstaff. Illustrated by Feodor Rojankovsky.)

Something about the Author

JOHN LANGSTAFF

neum, 1973, *The Two Magicians*, Atheneum, 1973, *Shimmy, Shimmy, Coke-A-Pop!*, 1973, (all published by Harcourt, unless otherwise noted).

Recordings for children: *Hello World!* (with Little Orchestra Society and Mrs. Franklin D. Roosevelt), RCA Victor; *Singing Games for Children*, His Master's Voice; *American Ballads and Folk Songs*, Tradition; *Songs for Singing Children*, and *Let's Make Music with John Langstaff*, Conversa-phone.

Other recordings: *John Langstaff Sings*, Capitol; *Recital of Purcell-Dowland Songs*, Renaissance; *Contemporary Ballad Poetry*, Jupiter.

HOBBIES AND OTHER INTERESTS: Camping, hiking, morris dancing, modern art, poetry, and brass rubbings.

FOR MORE INFORMATION SEE: Newbery and Caldecott Medal Books: 1956-1965, edited by Lee Kingman, Horn Book, 1965; *Horn Book*, December, 1969, December, 1970, April, 1972, June, 1972, December, 1973; *Christian Science Monitor*, November 11, 1971, May 2, 1973; *Third Book of Junior Authors*, edited by de Montreville and Hill, H. W. Wilson, 1972.

LATHAM, Frank B(rown) 1910-

PERSONAL: Born October 20, 1910, in Belington, W.Va.; son of George Robert (a cabinetmaker) and Winifred (Brown) Latham; married Lucille Smith, September 4, 1937; children: Linda Jean. *Education:* West Virginia Institute of Technology, A.B., 1933; Northwestern University, B.S. (journalism), 1934. *Residence:* Carmel, N.Y. *Office: Reader's Digest*, 380 Madison Ave., New York, N.Y. 10017.

CAREER: Transradio Press, Chicago, Ill., news editor, 1934-35; Scholastic Magazines, New York, N.Y., associate editor, then managing editor, 1935-45; *Look*, New York, N.Y., senior editor, 1945-71; Reader's Digest General Books, New York, N.Y., editorial work on *Encyclopedia of American History*, 1972—. *Member:* Authors Guild of the Authors League of America, Deadline Club of Sigma Delta Chi (New York; vice-president, 1968-70). *Awards, honors:* Named Alumnus of the Year, West Virginia Institute of Technology, 1950.

WRITINGS—All for young people, except as noted: (With N. V. Carlisle) *Miracles Ahead* (adult), Macmillan, 1945; *Jed Smith, Trail Blazer*, American Book Co., 1954; *Nathaniel Greene, Fighting Quaker*, American Book Co., 1955; *The Law or the Gun: The Mormons at Far West*, American Book Co., 1956; *Abraham Lincoln*, Watts, 1968; *The Dred Scott Decision*, Watts, 1968; *Lincoln and the Emancipation Proclamation*, Watts, 1968; *The Trial of John Peter Zenger*, Watts, 1969; *The Rise and Fall of Jim Crow*, Watts, 1969; *The Great Dissenter: Justice John Marshall Harlan*, Cowles, 1970; *Jacob Brown and the War of 1812*, Cowles, 1971; *The Panic of 1893*, Watts, 1971; *F.D.R. and the Supreme Court Fight*, Watts, 1972; *American Justice on Trial*, Watts, 1972; *The Transcontinental Railroad*, Watts, 1973.

WORK IN PROGRESS: Serving as consultant and researcher on television program on the Constitution and the Supreme Court.

FRANK B. LATHAM

The man waded in the water while they worked so the beaver would not smell them and be scared away. ■ (From *Jed Smith* by Frank B. Latham. Illustrated by William Hutchinson.)

138

"My interest in history began at seven when I saw and heard my grandfather, a Union colonel in the Civil War and member of the House during the impeachment of Andrew Johnson, pacing the floor and cussing about that event; he was tossed out of the Republican party for voting against the impeachment of Johnson. During school days I was greatly influenced by reading John G. Neihardt's *Song of the Indian Wars,* and Stephen Vincent Benet's *John Brown's Body. . . .* The most valued testimonial I ever received (unsolicited and not influenced [I hope] by ties of blood) came from my daughter who said: 'Gee, if you had been writing history when I was in school, I'd have liked it much more!' "

LEACROFT, Helen (Mabel Beal)   1919-

PERSONAL: Born September 27, 1919, in Leicester, England; daughter of Gerald and Emma (Wilkinson) Beal; married Richard Leacroft (architect, illustrator, author), July 27, 1940; children: Joanna Mary, Robert. *Education:* Attended Loughborough Girls High School; Royal Academy of Dramatic Art, diploma, 1935, and City of Leicester Training College. *Home:* Keven Lodge, 21, Station Road, Countesthorpe, Leicester, England.

CAREER: Actress, teacher, authoress. Fosse School, Leicester, England, senior mistress. B.B.C., Midland region, broadcast plays. Girl Guide Association, county of Leicestershire, drama adviser.

WRITINGS: (All with Richard Leacroft) *The Buildings of Ancient Egypt,* Penguin, 1954, revised and enlarged edition, Young Scott Books, 1963; *Churches and Cathedrals,* Penguin, 1957; *The Theatre,* Roy Publishers, 1958; *Early Architecture in Britain,* Methuen, 1960; *Historic Houses of Great Britain,* Penguin, 1962; *The Buildings of Ancient Greece,* Young Scott Books, 1966; *The Buildings of Ancient Rome,* Young Scott Books, 1969; *The Buildings of Ancient Man,* Young Scott Books, 1973; *The Buildings of Ancient Mesopotamia,* Young Scott Books, 1974. Contributor to *Britannica Junior.*

WORK IN PROGRESS: The Buildings of Byzantium.

SIDELIGHTS: Richard Leacroft is an architect; he also trained as a scene designer at the London Theatre Studio. Helen Leacroft studied at the Royal Academy of Dramatic Art, and it was while they were working in the theatre that they met and married.

"We started to write books together for young people in 1948. Our work is essentially a partnership; we are both concerned, in the first instance, with all the necessary research involved before the ideas which we have can be turned into illustrations and text. Whenever possible we visit the places on which our books are based and see for ourselves the sites and buildings of the ancient civilizations about which we write. We have traveled in Canada and the United States, Egypt, Greece, Italy and Turkey as well as the British Isles.

"The first step towards turning the remains which we see into material for books is to take photographs, as in many cases our reconstructions are prepared on traces overlaying a photograph of the actual remains, so that you may compare the reconstruction with the original if you are lucky enough to visit the sites. Reference is made, whenever possible, to the original excavation reports. We have to record all our information in note form before we can start work on the actual book.

"We are both full-time teachers and our books therefore have to be prepared in our spare time, in the evenings, at weekends and during the holidays. We have many discussions as to the ways in which the drawings, which Richard does, and the text, which I do, shall be presented. Sometimes these discussions can be quite heated, but we usually manage to agree in the end.

"We live in a village some six miles from Leicester; which is an important city in the middle of England. Both our children are now grown-up. Robert is a sound engineer at the B.B.C., while Joanna is in charge of the fashion department at the Southfields College of Further Education. We have two grandchildren, Amanda and Victoria, who both like to sit by Grandpa and 'help' him with his drawings."

LEACROFT, Richard (Vallance Becher) 1914-

PERSONAL: Born July 16, 1914, in London, England; son of John F. and Nance (Alcock) Leacroft; married Helen Beal, July 27, 1940; children: Joanna Mary, Robert. *Education:* Attended Imperial Service College, Windsor; School of Architecture, Northern Polytechnic, London, England; School of Architectural Association, London, England, honours diploma, 1935; London Theatre Studio. *Home:* Keven Lodge, 21, Station Road, Countesthorpe, Leicester, England.

CAREER: Architect, lecturer, illustrator, author. City of Leicester Polytechnic, Leicester, England, with responsibility for the history of architecture and human studies, school of architecture. Stage scene designer and theatre design consultant. *Member:* Society of Industrial Artists, Society for Theatre Research. *Awards, honors:* Royal Institute of British Architects, Athens Bursary, 1954, for the study of Greek theatres; R.I.B.A., Rose Shipman Studentship, 1960, for study of experimental theatres in United States and Canada.

WRITINGS: The Theatre and You (pamphlet), Army Bureau of Current Affairs, 1946; *Civic Theatre Design,* Dobson, 1949; *Building a House,* Penguin, 1949.

With Helen Leacroft: *The Buildings of Ancient Egypt,* Penguin, 1954, revised edition, Young Scott Books, 1963; *Churches and Cathedrals,* Penguin, 1957; *The Theatre,* Roy Publishers, 1958; *Early Architecture in Britain,* Methuen, 1960; *Historic Houses of Great Britain,* Penguin, 1962; *The Buildings of Ancient Greece,* Young Scott Books, 1966; *The Buildings of Ancient Rome,* Young Scott Books, 1969; *The Buildings of Ancient Man,* Young Scott

[Acting] could be very humiliating. The actors had their revenge, however, when the audience was particularly rustic; in one instance they made a point of answering each other with speeches from different plays so that the whole performance made complete nonsense. ■ (From *The Theatre* by Helen and Richard Leacroft. Illustrated by Richard Leacroft.)

Something about the Author

Books, 1973; *The Development of the English Playhouse,* Methuen, 1973; *The Buildings of Ancient Mesopotamia,* Young Scott Books, 1974. Contributor to *Encyclopaedia Britannica, Britannica Junior,* and to professional journals.

WORK IN PROGRESS: The development of the classical theatre.

SIDELIGHTS: See Leacroft, Helen.

FOR MORE INFORMATION SEE: Plays and Players, September, 1973.

Le CAIN, Errol (John) 1941-

PERSONAL: Surname is pronounced LeeCane; born March 5, 1941, in Singapore; son of John and Muriel (Kronenburgh) Le Cain. *Education:* Attended St. Joseph's Institution, Singapore. *Politics:* Liberal. *Religion:* Roman Catholic. *Home and office:* 80 Grove Park Terrace, London W.4, England. *Agent:* Eva Morris, 19 Russell St., London W.1, England.

CAREER: Richard Williams Studios, London, England, designer and animator, 1964-69; involved with animation

The princess now had a beautiful green cabbage for a head, and the heads of the maids had become marrows, tomatoes, carrots and peas. They were the finest vegetables imaginable, but vegetables they were. ■ (From *The Cabbage Princess* by Errol Le Cain. Illustrated by the author.)

sequences for television commercials and motion pictures, including "The Spy with a Cold Nose," "Gawain and the Green Knights," "Prudence and the Pill," "Casino Royale," "The Charge of the Light Brigade," and "The Last Valley"; also did a sequence for the Broadway musical, "The Apple Tree." Writer and illustrator of children's books. *Awards, honors:* Top Ten Best Award from *Amateur Cine World,* 1963, for cartoon, "Victoria's Rocking Horse."

WRITINGS—Self-illustrated juveniles: *King Arthur's Sword,* Faber, 1968; *The Cabbage Princess,* Faber, 1969; (retold) *The White Cat,* Faber, 1973.

Illustrator: Anthea Davies, *Sir Orfeo,* Faber, 1970; *Rhymes and Verses of Walter de la Mare,* Faber, 1970; *The Faber Book of Songs for Children,* Faber, 1970; Rosemary Harris, *The Child in the Bamboo Grove,* Faber, 1971; *Cinderella,* Faber, 1971; *The Rhyme of the Ancient Mariner,* Arcadia Press, 1971; Daphne du Maurier, *My Cousin Rachel,* Heron Books, 1971; Daphne du Maurier, *The House on the Strand,* Heron Books, 1971; *Let's Find Out about Halloween,* Watts, 1971; Helen Cresswell, *The Beachcombers,* Faber, 1971; *Early Britain,* Watts, 1972; Herman Wouk, *The Caine Mutiny,* Heron Books, 1972; Kathleen Abell, *King Orville and the Bullfrogs,* Little, Brown, 1972; Anthony Lewis, *The Dragon Kite,* Holt, 1972; Rosemary Harris, *The King's White Elephant,* Faber, 1973; Rosemary Harris, *The Lotus and the Grail,* Faber, 1974; John Keats, *The Eve of St. Agnes,* Arcadia Press, 1974.

ERROL LE CAIN

SIDELIGHTS: "I suppose that when I tell a story, I prefer to draw the pictures first and then explain it. I really do my books to please myself, and if they can communicate my feelings and please children, then I am *really* overjoyed. Writing comes very hard to me."

Born in Singapore, Le Cain spent his childhood in the Far East, traveling extensively to Japan, Hong Kong, Saigon and living five years in India. He acquired a fascination for the myths and legends of these countries and of the 'exotic west,' which resulted in *King Arthur's Sword.*

At the age of fourteen he made an animated film, entitled 'The Enchanted Mouse,' on a borrowed 8mm cine camera and at fifteen made a second attempt, 'The Goatherd,' this time on 16mm. This film so impressed Pearl & Dean's Asian representative that it resulted in his coming to London to work in their advertising studios.

FOR MORE INFORMATION SEE: Times Literary Supplement, April 16, 1970; *Graphis,* Vol. 27, 1971/72; *She,* October, 1972.

LEE, Mildred   1908-

PERSONAL: Born February 19, 1908, in Blocton, Ala.; daughter of Dallas Powell and Aeolian (Spear) Lee; married James Henry Hurstwood Scudder (now a lands acquisition agent), May 10, 1947; children: Barbara Lee Schimpff DuLac, Robert Donald Schimpff, Jane Powell Scudder. *Education:* Bessie Tift College, student, 1925-26; additional courses at Troy Normal College, Columbia University, New York University, and University of New Hampshire. *Religion:* United Liberal. *Home:* 1361 52nd Ave. N., St. Petersburg, Fla. 33703.

CAREER: Free-lance writer. *Member:* St. Petersburg Council on Human Relations. *Awards, honors:* Child Study Association Children's Book Award, 1964, for *The Rock and the Willow;* Austrian National Award and Alabama Association Award, 1971, for *The Skating Rink.*

WRITINGS: The Invisible Sun, Westminster, 1946; *The Rock and Willow* (ALA Notable Book), Lothrop, 1963; *Honor Sands,* Lothrop, 1966; *The Skating Rink* (Junior Literary Guild Selection; *Horn Book* Honor List), Seabury, 1969; *Fog* (ALA Notable Book), Seabury, 1972; *Sycamore Year,* Lothrop, 1974. Contributor of short stories to *Ladies' Home Journal, Redbook, Tanager.*

WORK IN PROGRESS: A junior novel, *Sycamore Year.*

SIDELIGHTS: "Why do I write? Because I have to. Why do I have to? Some great yearning I suppose, compels me toward the form of communication most natural and pleasing to me.

"I began writing when I was a child. Actually, before I could adequately manage the mechanics of writing I was creating in my own queer way—which was to 'read' my own inventions from the covers of any book that pleased my sense of touch, sight—and yes, smell, for I used to punctuate my 'reading' with sticking my nose to the edge of the pages for the sheer joy of smelling the book! I do not recall that I ever did this 'reading' to myself; it was always to my younger brother and sister and made a nice combination of entertaining them and myself at the same time. Where it came from I cannot imagine, but some part of it must have been imitative—I greatly loved the world of books and quite easily identified it with my own.

"My father was a Baptist minister and we lived in a succession of small southern towns that scarcely ran to cultural pursuits. Right through high school I never lived in one single town that boasted a public library. I can't recall the school libraries as having any bearing on my education at all. It is wonderful to me now to see that, wherever I go, there is a library on however modest a scale.

"The books I loved when I was a pre-teenager were those we got for birthdays and Christmases. We had volumes of fairy tales, of course, but I did not care so much for fantasy. With the teens, came some rather light-weight romantic novels that bowled me over. I wept and rejoiced and suffered in turn as I was supposed to with the rather melodramatic characters in their likewise situations. I can't recall having had any particular guidance and certainly no severe restrictions. Often my taste left much to be desired, but slowly it formed. I learned good from mediocre, went away to college and got acquainted with a library along with other new experiences. I had begun writing by then, really putting words on paper, and had been for several years.

"I get my characters from real people, of course, but never in their entirety. A bit here and there, from this person—maybe even a forgotten one about whom something may float up from the mists of subconscious—or from a member of my family. Anywhere and everywhere, but most of all out of my own head."

FOR MORE INFORMATION SEE: Third Book of Junior Authors, edited by de Montreville and Hill, H. W. Wilson, 1972; *Horn Book,* February, 1973.

MILDRED LEE

Le SUEUR, Meridel 1900-

PERSONAL: Surname is pronounced Le Sewer; born February 22, 1900, in Murray, Iowa; daughter of Arthur and Marion Le Sueur; husband deceased; children: Rachel Le Sueur, Deborah Le Sueur. *Education:* "My education was to live and travel below ground and on the surface and above ground in the Midwest. I did not finish high school; was a drop out before the first world war. There have always been drop outs." *Politics:* "My politics is that of life." *Religion:* "My religion, the world." *Home:* 1653 Victoria S., St. Paul, Minn. 55118.

CAREER: Writer since the age of fifteen ("or perhaps earlier"). Instructor in writing courses at University of Minnesota. *Awards, honors:* Second prize in Work Progress Administration (WPA) writing contest in the 1940's (Richard Wright was the first-prize winner).

WRITINGS: Annunciation, limited edition, Platen Press, 1935; *Salute to Spring and Other Stories,* International Publishers, 1940; *North Star Country,* Duell, Sloan & Pearce, 1945; *Little Brother of the Wilderness: The Story of Johnny Appleseed,* Knopf, 1947; *Nancy Hanks of Wilderness Road: A Story of Abraham Lincoln's Mother,* Knopf, 1949; *Sparrow Hawk* (story of an Indian boy), Knopf, 1950; *Chanticleer of Wilderness: A Story of Davy Crockett,* Knopf, 1951; *The River Road: A Story of Abraham Lincoln,* Knopf, 1954; *Crusaders* (biography of her parents), Blue Heron, 1955; *Corn Village: A Selection,* Stanton & Lee, 1971; *The First Book of the Conquistadores,* Watts, in press; *The First Book of the Mound Builders,* Watts, in press. Work included in *American Folkways,* edited by Erskine Caldwell. Contributor to magazines and newspapers through the years.

WORK IN PROGRESS: A book of poems about Indian women, *Changing Woman;* a long narrative of Demeter and Persephone; a book on Robert Emmet, Irish patriot, researched in Dublin.

SIDELIGHTS: "I am very much interested in illuminating areas of history which have been in the dark. I have taken literally hundreds of tapes of Northwest farmers and workers. I love to write for the New People as I call the young of today—their minds are open, pure and alive."

Meridel Le Sueur retained her maiden name after marriage, and both daughters use her surname. "This was and is a kind of matriarchy," she notes. She lives part of the year in the Southwest, pursuing an interest in the Pueblo and Hopi Indians.

LIFTON, Betty Jean

PERSONAL: Born June 11, in New York, N.Y.; daughter of Oscar and Hilda Kirschner; married Robert Jay Lifton (professor of psychiatry, Yale University), March 1, 1952; children: Kenneth Jay, Karen. *Education:* Barnard College, B.A., 1948. *Home:* Rimmon Road, Woodbridge, Conn. *Agent:* Marilyn Marlow, Curtis Brown, 60 East 56th St., New York, N.Y. 10022.

It was the most magnificent cedar they had ever seen, although the mountain was covered with them. It rose regally above the others, as if it were their natural leader. ■ (From *The One-Legged Ghost* by Betty Jean Lifton. Illustrated by Fuku Akino.)

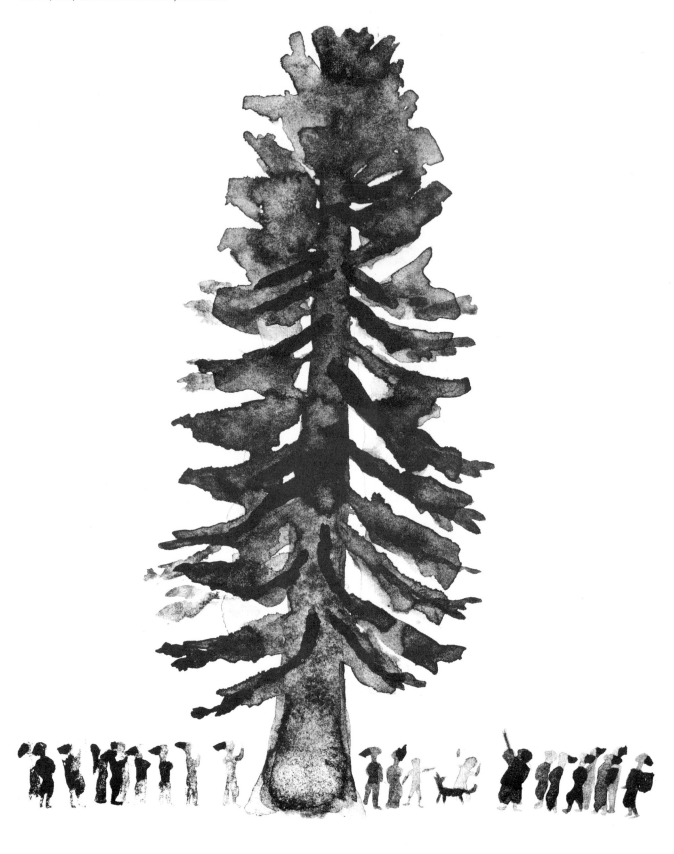

Something about the Author

BETTY JEAN LIFTON

CAREER: Free-lance writer of books for children. *Awards, honors: New York Herald Tribune* award for *Kap the Kappa*, 1960, *Return to Hiroshima*, 1970; *Children of Viet Nam* was nominated for the National Book Award, 1973.

WRITINGS: *Joji and the Dragon*, Morrow, 1957; *Mogo the Mynah*, Morrow, 1958; *Joji and the Fog*, Morrow, 1959; *Kap the Kappa*, Morrow, 1960; *The Dwarf Pine Tree*, Atheneum, 1963; *Joji and the Amanojaku*, Norton, 1965; *The Cock and the Ghost Cat*, Atheneum, 1965; *The Rice-Cake Rabbit*, Norton, 1966; *Many Lives of Chio and Garo*, Norton, 1966; *Taka-Chan and I*, Norton 1967; *The One-Legged Ghost*, (Junior Literary Guild selection), Atheneum, 1968; *Kap and the Wicked Monkey*, Norton, 1968; *The Secret Seller*, Norton, 1968; *Return to Hiroshima* (Junior Literary Guild selection), Atheneum, 1970; *A Dog's Guide to Tokyo*, Norton, 1970; *The Mud Snail Son*, Atheneum, 1971; *The Silver Crane*, Seabury, 1971; (with Thomas C. Fox) *Children of Viet Nam*, Atheneum, 1972; *Goodnight, Orange Monster*, Atheneum, 1972. Contributor to newspapers and periodicals. Writer for children's theatre: "Moonwalk," City Center, New York, 1970.

SIDELIGHTS: "I live in an old colonial house in Woodbridge, Connecticut, with my husband, and my young son and daughter. When I am not working on children's books, I write adult plays which are produced in summer stock, or magazine articles related to my travels."

Believing that a children's writer has a commitment to the world of children in life as well as in literature, Ms. Lifton has a Korean child with the Foster Parent Plan and is helping a group of children, The Folded Crane Club, in Hiroshima, who are working for peace.

Her interest in the Far East, out of which grew her Japanese legends, *The Dwarf Pine Tree, The Cock and the Ghost Cat* and *The One-Legged Ghost*, began when she and her husband went to Japan to live in 1952. They spent from 1952 to 1954 in Tokyo, then from 1960 to 1962 in Tokyo, Kyoto and Hiroshima, and also lived in Hong Kong from 1954 to 1956. It was during these years that the folk lore of southeast Asia, and the legends, art, and folkcrafts that are a part of Japanese culture became highly important to her.

FOR MORE INFORMATION SEE: *New York Times Book Review* "Children's Book Section," May 2, 1971; *Horn Book*, June, 1971, August, 1971, December, 1971; *Washington Post* "Children's Book World," November 5, 1972; *Third Book of Junior Authors*, edited by de Montreville and Hill, H. W. Wilson, 1972.

LIST, Ilka Katherine 1935-
(Ilka List Maidoff)

PERSONAL: Born November 22, 1935, in Orange, N.J.; daughter of Albert (an engineer) and Phyllis (Carrington) List; married Jules Maidoff, August 28, 1959 (divorced, August, 1967); children: Lee David, Jonah Asher, Natasha Katherine. *Education:* Studied at Cornell University, 1953-54, Reed College, 1954-55, and University of St. Andrews, 1956-57. *Home:* R.F.D. 3, Dover Foxcroft, Me. 04426. *Agent:* Marilyn Marlow, Curtis Brown Ltd., 60 East 56th St., New York, N.Y. 10022. *Gallery agent:* Dick Eyen, 205 East 60th St., New York, N.Y.

CAREER: Brooklyn Friends School, Brooklyn, N.Y., high school teacher of art, women's studies, and contemporary values, 1969-72; City University of New York, New York, N.Y., art specialist, Workshop Center for Open Education, 1972—; professional sculptor exhibiting in group shows at Environment Gallery, New York, N.Y. *Member:* New York Society of Women Artists. *Awards, honors:* Yaddo fellowship, 1972; *Questions and Answers about Seashore Life* was a Children's Book Showcase Title, 1972.

WRITINGS—For young people: (Under name Ilka List Maidoff; self illustrated) *Let's Explore the Shore*, Obolensky, 1962; *Questions and Answers About Seashore Life*, Four Winds, 1971.

WORK IN PROGRESS: *Woodlands*, for Crowell; *Values*, a teen-age book, for Pantheon; a book on the beach, for Putnam.

ILKA KATHERINE LIST

SIDELIGHTS: "I have become very interested in the ecology of the woodland. . . . I live on a farm now after thirteen years in the city with the children, four horses, four milking goats, two calves, two dogs, etc. I have always been interested in the human figure and in animal forms. . . . I am starting a series of studies for fountains, and am working on woman's relationship to herself (and others)."

LOBEL, Anita (Kempler) 1934-

PERSONAL: Born June 3, 1934 in Cracow, Poland; married Arnold Lobel, 1955; children: Adrianne, Adam. *Education:* Pratt Institute, B.F.A.

CAREER: Author and illustrator of books for children. *Awards, honors: Book World* Children's Spring Book Festival Award, 1973, for *Little John; A Birthday for the Princess* was a Children's Book Showcase Title, 1974.

WRITINGS—all self-illustrated: *Sven's Bridge,* 1965, *The Troll Music,* 1966, *Potatoes, Potatoes,* 1967, *The Seamstress of Salzburg,* 1970, *Under a Mushroom* (Child Study Association book list), 1971, *A Birthday for the Princess,* 1973 (all published by Harper).

Illustrator: Paul Kapp, *Cock-A-Doodle-Doo! Cock-A-*

Doodle-Dandy!, Harper, 1966; Meindert de Jong, *Puppy Summer,* Harper, 1966; F. N. Monjo, *Indian Summer,* Harper, 1968; Alice Dalgliesh, *The Little Wooden Farmer,* Macmillan, 1968; Benjamin Elkin, *The Wisest Man in the World,* Parents' Magazine Press, 1968; Barbara Borack, *Someone Small,* Harper, 1969; Doris Orgel, *Uproar,* McGraw, 1970; *Three Rolls and One Doughnut: Fables from Russia,* edited by Mirra Ginsburg, Dial, 1970; Benjamin Elkin, *How the Tsar Drinks Tea,* Parents' Magazine Press, 1971; Theodore Storm, *Little John,* retold by Doris Orgel, Farrar, Straus, 1972; John Langstaff, *Soldier, Soldier, Won't You Marry Me,* Doubleday, 1972; Cynthia Jameson, *One for the Price of Two.*

SIDELIGHTS: Ms. Lobel was born in Poland, has lived in Stockholm, and came to the United States in 1952. "Having lived close to much peasant art as a child, I have always been interested in the decorative arts. It is hard for me to leave any white surface alone. I embroider clothes whenever I can and have also designed needlepoint tapestries."

FOR MORE INFORMATION SEE: Illustrators of Children's Books: 1957-1966, Horn Book, 1968; Lee Bennett Hopkins, *Books Are by People,* Citation Press, 1969; *Horn Book,* February, 1971; *Publishers Weekly,* May 17, 1971; Selma G. Lanes, *Down the Rabbit Hole,* Atheneum, 1971; *Third Book of Junior Authors,* edited by de Montreville and Hill, H. W. Wilson, 1972.

ANITA LOBEL

They all drive home together. ■ (From *Small Pig* by Arnold Lobel. Illustrated by the author.)

LOBEL, Arnold (Stark) 1933-

PERSONAL: Born May 22, 1933, in Los Angeles, Calif.; son of Joseph and Lucille (Stark) Lobel; married Anita Kempler, 1955; children: Adrianne, Adam. *Education:* Pratt Institute, B.F.A., 1955.

CAREER: Author and illustrator of books for children. *Awards, honors:* Caldecott Honor Book award, 1971, for *Frog and Toad Are Friends* and 1972, for *Hildilid's Night; Frog and Toad Are Friends* was a National Book Award finalist, 1971; *Book World* Spring Book Festival Award, 1972, for *Frog and Toad Together; Hildilid's Night,* 1972, *On the Day Peter Stuyvesant Sailed into Town, Frog and Toad Together, Seahorse,* 1973, and *The Clay Pot Boy,* 1974, were Children's Book Showcase Titles; Christopher Award, 1973, for *On the Day Peter Stuyvesant Sailed into Town; Frog and Toad Together* was a Newbery Honor Book, 1973.

WRITINGS: A Zoo for Mister Muster, 1962, *Prince Bertram the Bad,* 1963, *A Holiday for Mister Muster,* 1963, *Lucille,* 1964, *Giant John,* 1964, *The Bears of the Air,* 1965, *Martha, the Movie Mouse,* 1966, *The Great Blueness and Other Predicaments,* 1968, *Small Pig,* 1969, *Frog and Toad Are Friends* (ALA Notable Book; *Horn Book* Honor List), 1970, *Ice-Cream Cone Coot and Other Rare Birds,* Parents' Magazine Press, 1971, *On the Day Peter Stuyvesant Sailed into Town* (ALA Notable Book), 1971, *Frog and Toad Together* (ALA Notable Book), 1972 (all published by Harper, except where otherwise noted).

ARNOLD LOBEL

Illustrator: Fred Phleger, *Red Tag Comes Back,* Harper, 1961; Susan Oneacre Rhinehart, *Something Old, Something New,* Harper, 1961; Peggy Parish, *Let's Be Indians,* Harper, 1962; Millicent E. Selsam, *Terry and the Caterpillars,* Harper, 1962 (translated by Pura Belpre, *Teresita y Las Orugas,* Harper, 1969); Betty Baker, *The Little Runner of the Longhouse,* Harper, 1962; Millicent E. Selsam, *Greg's Microscope,* Harper, 1963; Charlotte Zolotow, *The Quarreling Book,* Harper, 1963; Mildred Myrick, *The Secret Three,* Harper, 1963; Nathaniel Benchley, *Red Fox and His Canoe,* Harper, 1964; Miriam Young, *Miss Suzy,* Parents' Magazine Press, 1964; Phil Ressner, *Dudley Pippin,* Harper, 1965; Millicent E. Selsam, *Let's Get Turtles,* Harper, 1965; Charlotte S. Zolotow, *Someday,* 1965; Lilian Moore, *The Magic Spectacles and Other Stories,* Parents' Magazine Press, 1966; Nathaniel Benchley, *Oscar Otter,* Harper, 1966; Millicent E. Selsam, *Benny's Animals, and How He Put Them in Order,* Harper, 1966; Andrea DiNoto, *The Star Chief,* Macmillan, 1967; Peggy Parish, *Let's Be Early Settlers with Daniel Boone,* Harper, 1967; Nathaniel Benchley, *The Strange Disappearance of Arthur Cluck,* Harper, 1967; Mildred Myrick, *Ants Are Fun,* Harper, 1968; Edward Lear, *The Four Little Children Who Went Around the World,* Macmillan, 1968; *The Comic Adventures of Old Mother Hubbard and Her Dog,* Bradbury, 1968; Lilian Moore, *Junk Day on Juniper Street,* Parents' Magazine Press, 1968; Judith Viorst, *I'll Fix Anthony,* Harper, 1969; Nathaniel Benchley, *Sam, the Minuteman,* Harper, 1969.

Jack Prelutsky, *Terrible Tiger,* Macmillan, 1970; Laura Cathon, *Tot Botot and His Flute,* Macmillan, 1970; Cheil Duran Ryan, *Hildilid's Night,* Macmillan, 1971; Sulamith Ish-Kishor, *The Master of Miracles,* Harper, 1971; Brothers Grimm, *Hansel and Gretel,* Delacorte, 1971; Miriam Young, *Miss Suzy's Easter Surprise,* Parents' Magazine Press, 1972; Robert A. Morris, *Seahorse,* Harper, 1972; Paula Fox, *Good Ethan,* Bradbury, 1973; Cynthia Jameson, *The Clay Pot Boy,* Coward, 1974.

SIDELIGHTS: "It is a kind of pleasant omnipotence that I feel at the drawing board. There is a little world at the end of my pencil. I am the stage director, the costume designer, and the man who pulls the curtain. If I'm in the mood, I can admit to being despotic, too, for when a character is not behaving as I would wish him to he can be quickly dismissed with a wave of my eraser. This is certainly part of the joy of making books for children."

HOBBIES AND OTHER INTERESTS: Painting, music, theatre, "and just plain reading."

FOR MORE INFORMATION SEE: Young Readers' Review, October, 1966, February, 1969; *National Observer,* November 4, 1968; *Illustrators of Children's Books: 1957-1966,* Horn Book, 1968; *Horn Book,* August, 1969, October, 1970, April, 1971, December, 1971, June, 1972, December, 1972; Lee Bennett Hopkins, *Books Are by People,* Citation Press, 1969; *Saturday Review,* May 10, 1969, May 20, 1972; *Publishers Weekly,* May 17, 1971, February 26, 1973, February 25, 1974; Selma G. Lanes, *Down the Rabbit Hole,* Atheneum, 1971; *Graphis 155,* volume 27, 1971/72; *Third Book of Junior Authors,* edited by de Montreville and Hill, H. W. Wilson, 1972; *Top of the News,* April, 1972; *New York Times Book Review,* May 7, 1972, April 22, 1973; *Junior Literary Guild Catalogue,* March, 1973.

NORMAN LOBSENZ

LOBSENZ, Norman M(itchell) 1919-

PERSONAL: Born May 16, 1919, in New York, N.Y.; son of Philip N. (a painter) and Mabel (Karpe) Lobsenz; married Margery Darrell (an editor), January 17, 1953 (deceased); married Dorothea Harding (editorial researcher), May 23, 1969; children: (first marriage) Michael Lewis, James Elliot, George Philip. *Education:* New York University, B.S., 1939; Columbia University, Graduate School of Journalism, M.S., 1940. *Religion:* Quaker. *Home:* 300 West End Ave., New York, N.Y. 10023.

CAREER: Newsday (daily newspaper), Nassau County, N.Y., assistant city editor, 1940-43; British Information Services, New York, N.Y., news editor, 1943-44; U.S. Office of War Information, New York, N.Y., news editor, 1944-45; *New York Daily Mirror,* New York, N.Y., copy editor, 1945-46; *Quick,* New York, N.Y., managing editor, 1950-53; Hillman Periodicals, New York, N.Y., editorial director, 1955-56; free-lance writer, 1946-50, 1956—. Editorial consultant, Ziff-Davis Publishing Co., Western Publishing Co., and Ideal Publishing Co., New York, N.Y. *Member:* Society of Magazine Writers, Overseas Press Club. *Awards, honors:* Family Service Association of America national first prize for writings in field of family life; American Dental Association, first prize for medical writing.

WRITINGS: Emergency!, McKay, 1958; *The Insect World,* Golden Press, 1959, revised edition, 1962; *The First Book of West Germany,* Watts, 1959, revised edition, 1972; *The First Book of National Parks,* Watts, 1959, revised edition, 1966; *The First Book of National Monuments,* Watts, 1959, revised edition, 1968; (with Thelma Keitlen) *Farewell to Fear,* Bernard Geis Associates, 1960; *The First Book of Ghana,* Watts, 1960, revised edition, E. Ward, 1966; *Golden Book Picture Atlas of the World,* Volume V, *Africa,* Golden Press, 1960; *Is Anybody Happy?,* Doubleday, 1962; *Writing as a Career,* Walck, 1963; *First Book of East Africa,* Watts, 1965; *The Boots Adams Story,* Phillips Petroleum Co., 1965; *First Book of the Peace Corps,* Watts, 1968; *First Book of Denmark,* Watts, 1970. (For complete list of writings see *Contemporary Authors,* Volume 9/10.) Writer of documentary films and television scripts. Contributor of about 500 articles to *Reader's Digest, Redbook, Good Housekeeping, McCall's, Look, Ladies' Home Journal,* other national magazines.

LOCHLONS, Colin
See JACKSON, C. Paul

LOMAS, Steve
See BRENNAN, Joselp L.

LOPSHIRE, Robert (Martin) 1927-

PERSONAL: Born April 14, 1927, in Sarasota, Fla; son of Roy Howard and Dorothy (DeLaGrange) Lopshire; married Jane Haller Ingalls, October 21, 1946 (divorced); children: Robert Martin, Jr., Howard Clyde, Terri Jane, Victoria Anne. *Education:* Attended Vesper George School of Art, Boston, Mass., 1946-47, and School of Practical Art, Boston, Mass., 1947-48. *Address:* Box 107, R.D. 2, Cochranville, Pa. 19330.

CAREER: Free-lance artist and illustrator, Philadelphia, Pa., 1948-54, Boston, Mass., 1954-56, New York, N.Y., 1956-59; Random House, New York, N.Y., creative art director, 1959-61; owner of advertising agency, Sergeantsville, N.J., 1961-64. Consultant art director for companies in New York; paintings in private collections, and permanent display, U.S. Pentagon, Air Force Collection; presently serves as public relations director for the Academy of Model Aeronautics on a part-time basis. *Military service:* U.S. Coast Guard, 1944-45, served in Pacific theatre; Air Sea Rescue, 1945-46, combat photographer; awarded invasion awards. *Awards, honors:* Numerous painting awards for realistic still life and landscapes.

WRITINGS—All self-illustrated: *Put Me in the Zoo,* Random, 1961; *How to Make Flibbers,* Random, 1964; *Beginner's Guide to Building and Flying Model Airplanes,* Harper, 1967; *I Am Better Than You!,* Harper, 1968; *It's Magic?,* Macmillan, 1969; *Radio Control,* Macmillan, 1973. Contributor to *Model Airplane News.*

Illustrator: *Ann Can Fly,* Random House; Kin Platt, *Big Max,* Harper, 1965; Betty Baker, *Pig War,* Harper, 1969; Richard Margolis, *Wish Again, Big Bear,* Macmillan, 1972; Bernard Wiseman, *Little New Kangaroo,* Macmillan, 1973.

WORK IN PROGRESS: Miniature Aircraft: A Beginner's Guide; The Right Spot; We the Oversigned; Wheels, Wheels, Wheels.

SIDELIGHTS: "I came to write my first book because, at the time, I was employed as creative art director on the 'Beginner Book' project at Random House, the first of the truly planned assaults on young minds. After struggling through eight zillion God-awful manuscripts, I nobly decided that I could do at least as well, and slipped one into the pile. Banzaii! *Put Me in the Zoo* was accepted, and my silly career was launched as a kiddie-book type. I intended the first, and most of the following, for the people of my own intelligence level—six year olds.

Oh! They would put me
in the zoo,
if they could see
what I can do.
■ (From *Put Me in the Zoo* by Robert Lopshire. Illustrated by the author.)

ROBERT LOPSHIRE
by Robert Lopshire

"I derive my fantastically witty and sensitive tomes from my equally soggy brain after one hell of a lot of blood, sweat, and aspirin. I normally get my best thoughts from politicians' speeches, minority group protests, an hour in the bathroom, or a long drive in my car. I find the latter the most truly productive and rely on it when the others fail. (*Put Me in the Zoo* is little more than a politicians wail of claims, and, very frankly, more honest than any I've heard to date.)

"It takes me a year to write a book and illustrate it, mainly because I am never satisfied with the product unless I can nit pick it to death, being absolutely sure that all we six-year olds can really understand it. In that I am still old-fashioned enough to believe that every story must have a moral, this is a point always welded in, albeit badly at times.

"Personally, I weep over Lassie stories; curse profoundly at stupid drivers, lady shoppers, hippies, Dr. Spock, most of television, and all politicians; find most people at parties dull and insipid; ponder at length the mentality of American labor when I buy yet another shoddy 'Made in America' gizzmo; prefer to talk to women, tire of American males 'shop talk;' despise mini skirts on tubby women, love the same on svelte young things; love all kinds of music, but

hate rock and roll and the big 'put on' it represents; dislike TV and all the false values it places before the masses as 'gospel,' likewise the TV biz of setting up any actor, news spieler, or garbage truck driver, as an authority on almost anything . . . etc., etc. In other words, I am perhaps a bit of a cube, but one honestly fed up with sensationalism for the sake of sales. I owned an ad agency once, and am perhaps more finely attuned than most, and therefore a bit more nasty about the whole silly mess. Growf!

"In conclusion, I am 6 feet 3 inches, my hands drag on the ground when I walk, I'm surly, and deep down . . . I'm shallow."

HOBBIES AND OTHER INTERESTS: Radio-controlled model aircraft, antiques, archery, architecture, painting, woodworking, and helping young people gain an interest in sports and hobbies.

LOWENSTEIN, Dyno 1914-

PERSONAL: Born November 29, 1914, in Berlin, Germany; son of Kurt and Mara (Kerwel) Lowenstein; married Tilde Hoffman, February 1, 1924; children: Steven, Karin, Tim. *Education:* Sorbonne, University of Paris, diploma statistician. *Home:* 63-42 110th St., Forest Hills, N.Y. *Office:* 175 Fifth Ave., New York, N.Y. 10010.

CAREER: Pictograph Corp., New York, N.Y., director, 1950—. *Military service:* U.S. Army, Office of Strategic Services, 1942-45; became lieutenant.

WRITINGS: Pictographs and Graphs, Harper, 1952; *Money* (for young adults), Watts, 1963; *First Book on Graphs,* Watts, 1969. Also illustrator of school texts for Watts, Holt, Globe, and others.

LUBELL, Cecil 1912-

PERSONAL: Born June 6, 1912, in Leeds, England; son of Joseph (a tailor) and Jennie Rachel (Samuel) Lubell; married Winifred A. Milius (now an artist-illustrator), September, 1939; children: David, Stephen. *Education:* Harvard University, B.A., 1933, M.A., 1935. *Residence:* Croton-on-Hudson, N.Y. *Office: American Fabrics,* 24 East 38th St., New York, N.Y. 10016.

CAREER: Men's Reporter (trade magazine), editor, 1945-50; menswear stylist and design consultant in New York, N.Y., 1950-57; *Argosy* (magazine), New York, N.Y., menswear columnist, 1955-57; Institute for Motivational Research, Croton-on-Hudson, N.Y., promotional director, 1958-59; *American Fabrics* (quarterly textile journal), New York, N.Y., editor, 1960-73; writer of children's books.

WRITINGS—All juveniles, with wife, Winifred Lubell: *The Tall Grass Zoo,* Rand McNally, 1960; *Up a Tree,* Rand McNally, 1961; *Rosalie, the Bird Market Turtle,* Rand McNally, 1962; *Green is for Growing,* Rand McNally, 1964; *In a Running Brook,* Rand McNally, 1968; *A Zoo for You: Some Indoor Pets and How to Keep Them,* Parents' Magazine Press, 1970; *Birds in the Streets: The City Pigeon Book,* Parents' Magazine Press, 1971; *Clothes Tell a Story: From Skin to Space Suits,* Parents' Magazine

Press, 1971; *Picture Signs and Symbols,* Parents' Magazine Press, 1972; *By the Seashore,* Parents' Magazine Press, 1973; *To Market, To Market,* Parents' Magazine Press, 1974.

WORK IN PROGRESS: "Textile Design Source Books," sixteen volumes to be published by Van Nostrand, beginning 1975-70.

SIDELIGHTS: "I find that writing for children is both easier and more difficult than writing for adults. Easier because they are usually shorter than adult works. More difficult because there are no short cuts with words. Nothing can be taken for granted. Everything must be self-explanatory. For me, the challenge I set myself is to write in blank verse to an iambic beat. It reads well aloud and is not too obviously 'poetry.' A good exampe of what I do is our book, *By the Seashore.* It almost satisfies me."

FOR MORE INFORMATION SEE: Lee Bennett Hopkins, *Books Are by People,* Citation, 1969.

LUBELL, Winifred 1914-

PERSONAL: Born June 14, 1914, in New York, N.Y.; daughter of Lester and Elsa Milius; married Cecil Lubell (a writer and editor), 1938; children: David, Stephen. *Education:* Studied at Art Students' League, New York, 1933-35, and Duncan Phillips Museum School, Washington, D.C., 1936. *Home:* 101 North Highland Pl., Croton-on-Hudson, N.Y. 10520.

CAREER: Artist, and designer and illustrator of children's books; has had one-man show of drawings and prints in New York; woodcuts have been exhibited in New York, Philadelphia, Boston, and Dallas. Formerly taught art to children.

WRITINGS—Self-illustrated: *Here Comes Daddy,* W. R. Scott, 1945.

Illustrator and collaborator with husband, Cecil Lubell: *The Tall Grass Zoo,* Rand, 1960; *Up a Tree* (Junior Literary Guild selection), Rand, 1961; *Rosalie: The Bird Market Turtle,* Rand, 1962; *Green Is for Growing* (Junior Literary Guild selection), Rand, 1964; *In a Running Brook,* Rand, 1968; *A Zoo for You,* Parents' Magazine Press, 1970; *Birds in the Street,* Parents' Magazine Press, 1971; *Clothes Tell a Story,* Parents' Magazine Press, 1971; *Picture Signs and Symbols,* Parents' Magazine Press, 1972; *By the Seashore,* Parents' Magazine Press, 1973.

Illustrator and collaborator with others: (With I. P. Miller)

But there are many plants that are not green,
And do not need the sun to help them grow.
■ (From *Green is for Growing* by Winifred and Cecil Lubell. Illustrated by Winifred Lubell.)

The Stitchery Book: Embroidery for Beginners, Doubleday, 1965; (with Dorothy Sterling) *Fall Is Here* (Junior Literary Guild selection), Doubleday, 1966; (with Dorothy Sterling) *The Outer Lands,* Doubleday and Natural History Press, 1967; (with Söphia A. Boyer) *Gifts from the Greeks: Alpha to Omega,* Rand, 1970.

Illustrator: Millicent Selsam, *See Through the Sea,* Harper, 1955; Millicent Selsam, *See Through the Forest,* Harper, 1956; Dorothy Sterling, *The Story of Caves* (Junior Literary Guild selection), Doubleday, 1956; Millicent Selsam, *See Through the Jungle,* Harper, 1957; Millicent Selsam, *See Through the Lake,* Harper, 1958; Millicent Selsam, *See Up the Mountain,* Harper, 1958; Aylesa Forsee, *Louis Agassiz: Pied Piper of Science,* Viking, 1958; Millicent Selsam, *The Birth of an Island,* Harper, 1959; Dorothy Sterling, *Creatures of the Night,* Doubleday, 1960; Mary Stuart Graham, under name Mary Stuart, *The Pirate's Bridge* (Junior Literary Guild selection), Lothrop, 1960; Dorothy Sterling, *Caterpillars,* Doubleday, 1961; Dorothy Sterling, *Ellen's Blue Jays,* Doubleday, 1961; Jay Williams, *I Wish I Had Another Name,* Atheneum, 1962; Dorothy Sterling, *Spring Is Here!,* Doubleday, 1964; Marion Garthwaite, *The Twelfth Night Santons,* Doubleday, 1965; Marguerite M. Miles and others, *Qui Est La?'* Prentice-Hall, 1966; Jean Craighead George, *The Moon of the Mountain Lion,* Crowell, 1968; William Wise, *Nanette, the Hungry Pelican,* Rand, 1969.

WINIFRED and CECIL LUBELL

152

Illustrator and scripwriter for four filmstrips "Mathematics for Children" issued by Hudson Photographic Industries.

SIDELIGHTS: "As an illustrator of nature books, the biggest challenge I face is how to make my animals or plants look alive, not pinned to a board, not stiff dead specimens. For this, photographs or 'scientific' drawings, no matter how brilliantly done, can only be supplements to careful observation of the living creature or plant.

"For me the key problem is to understand the articulation of the plant or the animal. How is it joined? How do the parts fit together? How are the legs of the lizard different from the legs of the pigeon, or the hamster? How do the wings of the damselfly join its thorax?

"Always my hope is to sum up in a drawing the concentrated essence of a creature or a plant, to project it almost like a caricature. Colette puts it so beautifully. She writes: 'After all, there is only *one* creature.'"

FOR MORE INFORMATION SEE: Lee Bennett Hopkins, *Books Are by People*, Citation, 1969; *Children's Book Council Bulletin*, January-April, 1972.

LUM, Peter
See CROWE, Bettina Lum

LYNCH, Patricia (Nora)   1900-1972

PERSONAL: Born June 7, 1900, in Cork City, Ireland; daughter of Timothy Patrick (a businessman) and Nora (Lynch) Lynch; married Richard Michael Fox (an author), October 31, 1922 (deceased). *Education:* Educated at convent school, and at secular schools in Ireland, Scotland, England, and Belgium. *Residence:* Dublin, Ireland. *Address:* c/o J. M. Dent & Sons Ltd., Aldine House, 10-13 Bedford St., London W.C.2, England.

CAREER: Author of children's books, 1925—. *Christian Commonwealth*, London, England, staff member, writing feature stories, and other articles, 1918-20. *Member:* P.E.N. (Dublin; delegate to P.E.N. Congress in Vienna), Irish Women Writers' Club. *Awards, honors:* Silver Medal, Aonac Tailtean, for *The Cobbler's Apprentice;* London Junior Book Club annual award, for *The Turf-Cutter's Donkey;* Irish Women Writers' Club annual award, for *Fiddler's Quest.*

WRITINGS: *The Green Dragon*, Harrap, 1925; *The Cobbler's Apprentice*, Harold Shaylor, 1930; *The Turf-Cutter's Donkey: An Irish Story of Mystery and Adventure*, Dent, 1934, Dutton, 1935; *The Turf-Cutter's Donkey Goes Visiting: The Story of an Island Holiday*, Dent, 1935, published in America as *The Donkey Goes Visiting: The Story of an Island Holiday*, Dutton, 1936; *King of the Tinkers*, Dutton, 1938; *The Turf-Cutter's Donkey Kicks Up His Heels*, Dutton, 1939; *The Grey Goose of Kilnevin*, Dent, 1939, Dutton, 1940.

Fiddler's Quest, Dent, 1941, Dutton, 1943; *Long Ears*, Dent, 1943; *Knights of God: Stories of the Irish Saints* (Children's Book Club selection), Hollis & Carter, 1945,

Regnery, 1955, new edition published as *Knights of God: Tales and Legends of the Irish Saints*, Bodley Head, 1967, Holt, 1969; *Strangers at the Fair and Other Stories*, Browne & Nolan, 1945; *A Story-Teller's Childhood* (autobiographical), Dent, 1947, Norton, 1962; *The Mad O'Haras*, Dent, 1948, published in America as *Grania of Castle O'Hara*, L. C. Page & Co., 1952; *Lisbeen at the Valley Farm, and Other Stories*, Gayfield Press, 1949.

The Seventh Pig, and Other Irish Fairy Tales, Dent, 1950, new edition published as *The Black Goat of Slievemore, and Other Irish Fairy Tales*, 1959; *The Dark Sailor of Youghal*, Dent, 1951; *The Boy at the Swinging Lantern*, Dent, 1952, Bentley, 1953; *Tales of Irish Enchantment*, Clonmore & Reynolds, 1952; *Delia Daly of Galloping Green*, Dent, 1953; *Orla of Burren*, Dent, 1954; *Tinker Boy*, Dent, 1955; *The Bookshop of the Quay*, Dent, 1956; *Fiona Leaps the Bonfire*, Dent, 1957; *Shane Comes to Dublin*, Criterion, 1958; *The Old Black Sea Chest: A Story of Bantry Bay*, Dent, 1958; *Jinny the Changeling*, Dent, 1959; *The Runaways*, Basil Blackwell, 1959.

Sally from Cork, Dent, 1960; *Ryan's Fort*, Dent, 1961; *The Golden Caddy*, Dent, 1962; *The Turf-Cutter's Donkey*, Dent, 1962; *The House by Lough Neagh*, Dent, 1963; *Holiday at Rosquin*, Dent, 1964; *The Twisted Key, and Other Stories*, Harrap, 1964; *Mona of the Isle*, Dent, 1965; *The Turf-Cutter's Donkey Goes Visiting*, Dent, 1965; *The Kerry Caravan*, Dent, 1967; *Back of Beyond*, Dent, 1967.

"Brogeen" series; all published by Burke Publishing, except as indicated: *Brogeen of the Stepping Stones*, Kerr-Cross Publishing Co., 1947, *Brogeen Follows the Magic Tune*, 1952, Macmillan (New York), 1968, *Brogeen and the Green Shoes*, 1953, *Brogeen and the Bronze Lizard*, 1954, Macmillan (New York), 1970, *Brogeen and the Princess of Sheen*, 1955, *Brogeen and the Lost Castle*, 1956, *Cobbler's Luck* (short stories), 1957, *Brogeen and the Black Enchanter*, 1958, *The Stone House at Kilgobbin*, 1959, *The Lost Fisherman of Carrigmor*, 1960, *The Longest Way Round*, 1961, *Brogeen and the Little Wind*, 1962, Roy, 1963, *Brogeen and the Red Fez*, 1963, *Guests at the Beech Tree*, 1964.

WORK IN PROGRESS: A book with Isle of Man background, for Dent; another "Brogeen" book for Burke Publishing Co.

SIDELIGHTS: Her fantasies, most of them based in Ireland, have reached children of many lands. In French editions, Brogeen (a leprechaun) has been renamed Korik, a creature of Bregon folklore. Eight books have been translated into French, four into Gaelic, five into Dutch, others into German, Swedish, and Malay. *Brogeen and the Little Wind* was dramatized in six installments for the British Broadcasting Corporation "Children's Hour," and *The Mad O'Haras* was dramatized for a television series; other stories have been adapted for radio and issued in Braille.

FOR MORE INFORMATION SEE: *Junior Bookshelf*, March, 1943, March, 1949; Patricia Lynch, *A Story-Teller's Childhood*, Dent, 1947; *Times Literary Supplement*, May 25, 1967; *Library Journal*, July, 1969, May, 1970; *Books and Bookmen*, February, 1970.

(Died September, 1972)

LYON, Elinor 1921-

PERSONAL: Born August 17, 1921, in Guisborough, Yorkshire, England; married Peter Wright (a schoolmaster), April 19, 1944; children: Roger, Jane, Michael, Mary. *Education:* Educated at Headington School, Oxford, England, 1934-38, St. George's School, Montreux, Switzerland, 1939, and Lady Margaret Hall, Oxford, 1940-41 (university studies interrupted by the war). *Home:* 2 Horton Crescent, Rugby, Warwickshire, England.

CAREER: Writer for young people, 1949—. *Military service:* Women's Royal Naval Service, 1942-44.

WRITINGS: Hilary's Island, Hodder & Stoughton, 1948, Coward, 1949; *Wishing Water-gate,* Coward, 1949; *The*

■ (From *The House in Hiding* by Elinor Lyon. Illustrated by the author.)

House in Hiding, Coward, 1950; *We Daren't Go a-Hunting,* Hodder & Stoughton, 1951; *Run Away Home,* Viking, 1953; *Sea Treasure,* Hodder & Stoughton, 1955; *Dragon Castle,* Hodder & Stoughton, 1956; *The Golden Shore,* Hodder & Stoughton, 1957; *Daughters of Aradale,* Hodder & Stoughton, 1957; *Rider's Rock,* Hodder & Stoughton, 1958, Follett, 1968; *Cathie Runs Wild,* Hodder & Stoughton, 1960, Follett, 1968; *Carver's Journey,* Hodder & Stoughton, 1962 (published in America as *The Secret of Hermit's Bay,* Follett, 1967); *Green Grow the Rushes,* Brockhampton Press, 1964, Follett, 1967; *Echo Valley,* Brockhampton Press, 1965, Follett, 1967; *The Dream Hunters,* Brockhampton Press, 1966, Follett, 1967; *Strangers at the Door,* Brockhampton Press, 1967, Follett, 1969; *The Day That Got Lost,* Brockhampton Press, 1968; *The Wishing Pool,* Brockhampton Press, 1970.

SIDELIGHTS: "I've been making up stories for as long as I can remember, and I began writing them down as soon as I could write at all. My early attempts were mostly sentimental nonsense, but they gave me practice in forming sentences, which is always useful.

"After writing a large number of stories that might have appealed to romantic and retarded adolescents—but to nobody else—I set out to write a story for children, *Hilary's Island.* This expressed one of my strongest childhood desires—to be a boy instead of a girl—and it was accepted by Hodder & Stoughton. Since then I have written eighteen more books, mostly for ten-to-fourteen year olds, but lately more for the eight-to-ten age group. For the first twelve I did my own illustrations, mainly in black and white silhouettes.

ELINOR LYON

"There's no method about my writing; I do it in spasms when I feel in the mood and have some uninterrupted spare time. Most of the plot works itself out while I'm doing housework or mending or something equally mindless, and when I come to write it down it usually comes out as I want it the first time, though sometimes I have to revise words and phrases that don't sound right. There has to be some strong interest or feeling to start me off on a new plot, and the setting is nearly always the wild places where I've spent holidays, often Scotland or Wales, and for which I feel homesick while I live in flat Midland country.

"My characters come from memories of my childhood, or people I've met, or the sort of people I've wanted to be, with numerous details supplied—consciously or subconsciously—from my experiences with my own family of four children.

"What I always hope to achieve is an exciting story, well written and not too far-fetched, involving strong feelings and life-like characters who develop with the story. Easier said than done!"

MADISON, Arnold 1937-

PERSONAL: Born November 28, 1937, in Bayport, N.Y.; son of Arnold Alfred (a lithographer) and Jeanette (Tonder) Madison. *Education:* State University of New York College at Plattsburgh, B.Sc., 1958. *Home:* R.D. 3, Swart Hill Rd., Amsterdam, N.Y. 12010.

CAREER: Public school teacher in Bethpage, N.Y., 1958-68; writer for young people. Actor at Wingspread Summer Theatre, Colon, Mich., 1957, and director of community theater productions; St. Davids' Writers Conference, instructor, summers, 1970, 1971. *Member:* Mystery Writers of America (chairman, juvenile awards committee, 1970), Authors League of America, Forum of Writers for Young People. *Awards, honors: Danger Beats the Drum* was runner-up for Edgar Allan Poe (Edgar) Award of Mystery Writers of America as best juvenile mystery of 1966.

WRITINGS: Danger Beats the Drum, Holt, 1966; *Think Wild!,* Holt, 1968; *The Secret of the Carved Whale Bone,* McKay, 1969; *Vandalism: The Not-So-Senseless Crime* (Child Study Association book list), Seabury, 1970; *Drugs and You,* Messner, 1971; *Fast Break to Danger,* Pyramid, 1972; *Vigilantism in America,* Seabury, 1973; *Treasure Hunting as a Hobby,* Hawthorn, 1974. More than thirty-five serials, stories and articles published in juvenile and adult periodicals.

WORK IN PROGRESS: A nonfiction investigation aimed for young adult readers.

SIDELIGHTS: "What can you say about a 36-year-old author of books for children and young adults? That he enjoys reading mysteries as well as nonfiction books—especially books on the theatre. That he has a student pilot's license and has had many happy hours in a Cessna 150. That he likes to attend high school basketball games and spends days and nights during the summer swimming in water: salt or fresh.

"I know that all fiction writing in some way reflects upon an author's life experiences but I have never purposely put anything I did into my books. *Danger Beats the Drum* was set on an Adirondack Lake. I spent my college years in the Adirondacks. Then—the hero, Bob, had a thing to get straightened out about him and his father, and I, too, had problems in that area. Perhaps the most autobiographical of my books was *Think Wild!* The things that the boys did, my friends and I did when we were the age of Ted and Jeff. *The Secret of the Carved Whale Bone* was written after I had visited Sag Harbor, New York, which is an old whaling port. The pleasant little town had such an aura of history about it, that I came away with an urge to write a mystery placed in such a setting. As I say in my introduction to *Vandalism,* the most fascinating part of the research for the book were the informal talks I had with teenagers about times that they or their friends had engaged in vandalistic acts. The boys and girls were so open and honest that I couldn't help admiring them though I could not condone some of the things they had done.

"*Drugs and You* was a harrowing experience. The day I visited Odyssey House in New York City will not be forgotten. The adult leaders of the facility deserve all the support they can get. And, the youngsters in their Teenage House were superb human beings. They had come face-to-face with their own demons and were struggling to over-

ARNOLD MADISON

The box-like structure hung over the water's edge and gave a perfect view of the bay. ■ (From *The Secret of the Carved Whale Bone* by Arnold Madison. Illustrated by Don Lambo. Reprinted by permission of David McKay Co., Inc.)

come fierce obstacles. Other research for the book was not quite as uplifting. Newspaper articles from all over the country arrived, detailing so many deaths or crimes connected with drug addiction that at times I thought the whole social problem was insurmountable. But in a way that made me more determined to do a good job. There was a NEED for the book.

"As for *Fast Break to Danger,* I finally had a chance to write about my favorite sport—basketball. And the setting for the book was the new section of New York State I had just moved to. So I guess there is plenty of *me* in my books.

"Other than writing, I'm a normal type guy. I enjoy outgoing people, being an introvert myself, and hate hypocrisy and bigotry in any form. I am a colossal failure when it comes to manipulating anything mechanical. Though I generally don't care for science-fiction, there is a story by Ray Bradbury I enjoy—'The Telephone.' In the story the electrical system takes on a life of its own and dominates the world. The theme strikes a responsive chord in me because in my daily battles with anything mechanized, I have had definite feelings that the inanimate objects were actively plotting against me.

"I operate at an equally low level in social settings. I'm the sort of guy whose name you forget even while you're talking to me. Arnold Madison will never be remembered for a witty remark he made at a party. But that's all right. Maybe, in some small way, I'll be remembered as an author."

MAIDOFF, Ilka List
    See LIST, Ilka Katherine

DAVID MALCOLMSON

156

MALCOLMSON, David 1899-

PERSONAL: Born January 27, 1899, in El Paso, Tex.; son of James Waddell and Katherine Malcolmson; married Esther Van Doren, 1923; children: Molly Malcolmson Gustin. *Education:* University of Illinois, B.S., 1920, A.B., 1921. *Politics:* Liberal, usually Democrat. *Home:* 491 Mesa Rd., Santa Monica, Calif.; and Potomac, Ill. *Agent:* Shirley Collier Agency, 1127 Stradella Rd., Los Angeles, Calif., 90024; Marie Rodell, 145 East 49th St., New York, N.Y. 10017.

CAREER: Hart, Schaffner & Marx, Chicago, Ill., labor manager, 1922-24; University of California, extension lecturer in creative writing, 1927-30; operator of grain farm, Potomac, Ill., 1942—. *Military service:* U.S. Marine Corps, 1918-19; became gunnery sergeant. *Member:* Tau Beta Pi, Phi Beta Kappa, Tau Kappa Epsilon.

WRITINGS: Ten Heroes, Duell, Sloan & Pearce, 1941; (with Lila Lofberg) *Sierra Outpost,* Duell, Sloan & Pearce, 1941; *Yipe,* Atlantic-Little, Brown, 1956; *London: The Dog Who Made the Team,* Duell, Sloan & Pearce, 1963; *Farm Dog,* Atlantic-Little, Brown, 1963. Contributor of stories and articles to *Saturday Evening Post, Coronet, Harper's Bazaar, Blue Book, Golden Book, American Home,* and other magazines.

WORK IN PROGRESS: A story, in iambic pentameter, about the lives and loves of the ten digits, called *Ten Fingers on the Stars.*

SIDELIGHTS: "*Yipe* is a true story about a dog. Though there are no children in it, I came to write it because of a little girl. One night I found her crying. 'I don't want Carolyn to make a war on Mommy,' Cathy cried. Her older sister had been quarreling with her mother all day long.

"So *Yipe* had to be written, for Yipe too had a quarrelsome daughter. After *Yipe* became an Atlantic book it was reprinted for school children as a Cadmus book and children write me letters. 'I like best,' many have written, 'the war between Yipe and Tuffy.' Believe it or not, they liked having the mother win."

Sierra Outpost has been optioned by Walt Disney Productions to be made into a television series.

MANGIONE, Jerre 1909-

PERSONAL: Born March 20, 1909, in Rochester, N.Y.; son of Gaspare (a house painter and paperhanger) and Giuseppina (Polizzi) Mangione; married Patricia Anthony (an artist), February 18, 1957. *Education:* Syracuse University, B.A., 1931. *Home:* 1901 Walnut St., Philadelphia, Pa. 19103. *Agent:* Russell and Volkening, Inc., 551 Fifth Ave., New York, N.Y. 10017. *Office:* Department of English, University of Pennsylvania, Philadelphia, Pa. 19104.

CAREER: Time, New York, N.Y., staff writer, 1931; Robert M. McBride & Co. (publishers), New York, N.Y., book editor, 1934-37; Federal Writers Project, Washington, D.C., national coordinating editor, 1937-39; U.S. Immigration and Naturalization Service, Washington, D.C., and Philadelphia, Pa., special assistant to commissioner, 1942-48, editor-in-chief of official publication, *Monthly Review,* 1945-47; writer for advertising and public relations offices, including N. W. Ayer & Son, Inc., and Columbia Broadcasting System Television, New York, N.Y., and Philadelphia, Pa., 1948-61; University of Pennsylvania, Philadelphia, director of freshman composition, 1961-65, director of writing program, 1965—, professor of English, 1968—. Visiting lecturer, Bryn Mawr College, 1967-68; visiting professor, Trinity College (Rome campus), summer, 1973.

MEMBER: Authors Guild of the Authors League of America, Institute of Contemporary Art (board, 1964—), National Council of Teachers of English, Conference on College Composition and Communication, American Association of University Professors, P.E.N., America-Italy Society (board, 1959—), Philadelphia Art Alliance (chairman, literary arts committee, 1958-61), Pi Delta Epsilon. *Awards, honors:* Yaddo creative writing fellowship, 1939, 1944, 1946, 1962, 1964, 1968, 1972; Guggenheim fellowship, 1945; MacDowell Colony creative writing fellowship, 1957, 1958, 1959, 1960, 1964, 1967, 1971; Fulbright research fellowship in Sicily, 1965; Friends of the Rochester Public

JERRE MANGIONE

Library award, 1966, for *Night Search;* Rockefeller Foundation research grant, 1968-69; American Philosophical Society research grant, 1971; title of *Commendatore* for contributions to literature from the Republic of Italy, 1971; Athenaeum Literary Award, 1972.

WRITINGS: Mount Allegro, Houghton, 1943, 2nd edition (with introduction by Dorothy Canfield Fisher), Knopf, 1952, 3rd edition, Hill & Wang, 1963, 4th edition, Crown, 1972; *The Ship and the Flame,* Current Books, 1948; *Reunion in Sicily,* Houghton, 1950; *Night Search,* Crown, 1965; *Life Sentences for Everybody* (satiric fables), Abelard, 1965; *A Passion for Sicilians,* Morrow, 1968, 2nd edition retitled *The World around Danilo Dolci,* Harper, 1972; *America is also Italian* (Child Study Association book list), Putnam, 1969; *The Dream and the Deal: Federal Writers' Project, 1935-43,* Little, Brown, 1972.

Writings anthologized in *American Stuff* and *Sidewalks of New York.* Contributor of articles and short stories to *Esquire, Holiday, Saturday Review, Mademoiselle, Harper's Bazaar,* and other magazines. Regular book reviewer for *New York Herald Tribune Books,* 1931-35, *New Republic,* 1931-37, *Pennsylvania Traveler,* 1959-60, and occasional reviewer for other New York newspapers. Editor-in-chief, *WFLN Philadelphia Guide,* 1960-62.

WORK IN PROGRESS: A new novel; a book of memoirs tentatively titled *An Ethnic at Large;* more one-sentence fables of the kind published in *Life Sentences for Everybody.*

SIDELIGHTS: "Except for my more recent experience in the academic world, I have always tried to keep my own writing apart from any I had had to produce as a wage-earner. In short, I write to please myself. For this reason I prefer writing books to short stories and articles, and shun magazine editors as much as possible.

"I like to alternate nonfictional writing with fiction. But whether I am writing a book of nonfiction or fiction I try to stress the element of narrative. I believe that one reason why my books appeal to readers of all ages is that they are written in a strongly narrative style. I suppose my love of narrative can be traced to the days of my childhood when I sat around listening to my Sicilian American relatives, many of whom were born storytellers."

Mount Allegro was published in Argentina and Italy, and *The Ship and the Flame* in Sweden.

FOR MORE INFORMATION SEE: Olga Peragallo, *Italian-American Authors and Their Contributions to American Literature,* 1949; *Saturday Review,* July 1, 1950; *Pennsylvania Gazette* (University of Pennsylvania), December, 1963; "Man About Town" column, *Philadelphia Evening Bulletin,* May 25, 1965; *Delaware Valley Calendar,* Philadelphia, Pa., November, 1965.

MANN, Peggy

PERSONAL: Born in New York, N.Y.; daughter of Harvey T. (a lawyer) and Edna (a psychologist; maiden name Brand) Mann; married William Houlton (in public relations); children: Jenny, Betsy. *Education:* University of Wisconsin, B.A.; graduate study at Columbia University,

He remembered the look on her face when she had first seen her torn-up flower boxes. Somehow he didn't want to ever see her look like that again. ■ (From *The Street of the Flower Boxes* by Peggy Mann. Illustrated by Peter Burchard.)

New School for Social Research, and University of Birmingham, Birmingham, England. *Politics:* Democrat. *Religion:* Jewish. *Home:* 46 West 94th St., New York, N.Y. 10025. *Agent:* Curtis Brown Ltd., 60 East 56th St., New York, N.Y. 10022.

CAREER: Columbia Broadcasting System, New York, N.Y., program writing staff, 1956-58; Doubleday & Co., Inc., New York, N.Y., copy chief of book clubs, 1958-65; author. *Member:* P.E.N., Dramatists Guild, Little Old New York Citizens' Committee (president, 1963—).

WRITINGS—Juvenile books, except as noted: *A Room in Paris* (adult), Doubleday, 1955; *That New Baby,* Coward, 1965; *The Street of the Flower Boxes,* Coward, 1966; *The Boy with a Billion Pets,* Coward, 1968; *Clara Barton: Battlefield Nurse,* Coward, 1969; *When Carlos Closed the Street,* Coward, 1969; *The Clubhouse,* Coward, 1969; *Amelia Earhart: Pioneer of the Skies,* Coward, 1970; *The Twenty-Five Cent Friend,* Coward, 1970; *Golda: The Life of Israel's Prime Minister* (adult), Coward, 1971; *How Juan Got Home,* Coward, 1972; *The Lost Doll,* Random House, 1972; *Whitney Young, Jr.,* Garrard, 1972; *My Dad Lives in a Downtown Hotel,* Doubleday, 1972; *William the Watchcat,* Rand, 1972; *The Last Escape* (Literary Guild alternate), Doubleday, 1973; *A Present for Yanya,* Random House, 1974. Writer for radio and television, including scripts for "Philco Television Playhouse," "Armstrong Circle Theater," "Dr. Christian Prize Plays," "Junior Miss," and other network programs. Contributor to *Cosmopolitan, Harper's Bazaar, Reader's Digest, McCall's, Redbook, Mademoiselle, Saturday Evening Post, Seventeen, Glamour, Holiday, Travel & Leisure, Woman's*

Carlos, Eddie, and Jose in the NBC-TV adaptation, "Street of the Flower Boxes."

Home Companion, *This Week*, *Collier's*, *Parade*, and other periodicals; her articles have appeared in more than twenty-five magazines in the United States, in seven British magazines, and in a number of newspapers.

WORK IN PROGRESS: Ralph Bunche: Citizen of the World.

SIDELIGHTS: Miss Mann's novel, *A Room in Paris*, has been published in England, and in Danish, Swedish, and German translations. She has made more than a dozen trips to Europe, five to Israel, and traveled around the world. She considers Easter Island and Nepal among the more interesting places to visit (and wrote about them for *Harper's Bazaar*), but is most fascinated by Israel because of "the constant dramatic changes in the development of that small nation." She also has written travel articles about Israel and two books for children called *Israel* for Doubleday's Round-the-World-Travel-Program, and for Sterling Publications.

Five of her books are based on her families' experiences when they bought, renovated and moved into a brownstone on a slum street in Manhattan's Upper West Side. The first of these books, *The Street of the Flower Boxes*, was a children's special on NBC-TV in 1973. The others in the series are *The Clubhouse*, *When Carlos Closed the Street*, *How Juan Got Home*, and *The Secret Dog of Little Luis*.

Thanks to Urban Renewal and in large measure to the families dedicated efforts, their block has now been transformed into a showplace side street in Manhattan's West Side Urban Renewal Area—which is now acting as a pilot project for ethnic, economic and architectural integration for other urban renewal areas throughout the nation. In order to encourage families—as opposed to builders and speculators—to renovate the rundown brownstones, Ms. Mann founded and is president of The Little Old New York Citizens Committee. City housing officials, city planners and others have called this committee one of the most important founding cornerstones in the success of the West Side Urban Renewal Plan.

My Dad Lives in a Downtown Hotel was adopted for "A.B.C. Afterschool Special," 1973.

PEGGY MANN

Martha was very fond of making split pea soup. Sometimes she made it all day long. Pots and pots of split pea soup. ■ (From *George and Martha* by James Marshall. Illustrated by the author.)

Something about the Author

JAMES MARSHALL

MARSHALL, James 1942-

PERSONAL: Born October 10, 1942, in San Antonio, Tex.; son of George E. and Cecille (Harrison) Marshall. *Education:* Attended New England Conservatory of Music (Boston) and Trinity College. "No art school (self-taught)." *Home:* 20 Cedar, Charlestown, Mass. 02129.

CAREER: Taught French and Spanish in a high school in Boston; free-lance illustrator. *Awards, honors: New York Times* included *George and Martha* and *George and Martha Encore* on its list of the ten best illustrated children's books of 1972 and 1973; *George and Martha* also selected as a Children's Book Showcase Title, 1973, *All the Way Home,* 1974.

WRITINGS—Author and illustrator: *George and Martha* (ALA Notable Book), Houghton, 1972; *What's the Matter with Carruthers?,* Houghton, 1972; *Yummers!,* Houghton, 1973; *George and Martha Encore,* Houghton, 1973; *Miss Dog's Christmas Treat,* Houghton, 1973.

Illustrator: Byrd Baylor, *Plink, Plink, Plink,* Houghton, 1971; Lore Segal, *All the Way Home,* Farrar, Straus, 1973; Norma Klein, *Dinosaur's Housewarming Party,* Crown, 1974; Harry Allard, *The Stupids Step Out,* Houghton, 1974; Charlotte Pomerantz, *The Piggy in the Puddle,* Macmillan, 1974; Jan Wahl, *Carrot Nose,* Farrar, Straus, 1974.

SIDELIGHTS: Marshall's menage includes an English bulldog and seven cats. He travels often to Europe, speaks French and Italian.

FOR MORE INFORMATION SEE: Horn Book, February, 1970, August, 1972, February, 1973, June, 1973; *New York Times Book Review,* April 30, 1972, November 18, 1973.

MATSUNO, Masako 1935-

PERSONAL: Born July 12, 1935, in Niihama, Japan; daughter of Kiyokoto (a businessman) and Hideko (Nabeshima) Matsuno; married Toshiro Kobayashi (with Sanyo Electric Trading Co. Ltd.), July 12, 1960; children: Ryosaku (son), Satoko (daughter), Kenjiro (son). *Education:* Waseda University, B.A. in Japanese Literature, 1958; Columbia University, M.S., in L.S., 1960. *Home:* 23-1, 1-chome, Furuedai, Suita-shi, Osaka, Japan.

CAREER: Came to United States to study about children's books and libraries in 1958, in line with a plan to translate foreign stories for Japanese children; now writes in both English and Japanese, and also translates stories in English into Japanese and vice versa.

WRITINGS: A Pair of Red Clogs, World Publishing, 1960; *Taro and the Tofu,* World Publishing, 1962; *Fushigina Takenoko,* Fukuinkan, 1963 (published in English as *Taro and the Bamboo Shoot,* Pantheon, 1964); *Chie and the Sports Day,* World Publishing, 1965; *Ryo-chan no Asa,* Fakuinkan, 1968; *Okina Omiyage,* Fukuinkan, 1970; *Boku No Kingyo,* Doshinsha, 1972.

Translator: Eriko Kishida, *Hippopotamus,* World Publishing, 1963; A. H. White, *Junket,* Gakushu-Kenkyusha, 1969; E. Johnson, *The Little Knight,* Gakushu-Kenkyusha, 1969; M. Brown, *Cinderella,* Fukuinkan, 1970.

WORK IN PROGRESS: Stories in English and Japanese.

SIDELIGHTS: "When I was studying at Columbia, I found that there were few books that told about the real Japan and the real Japanese people. The Japanese people may be strange to foreign people in a sense, but at the same time, they are very similar to each other. The Japanese children like playing, eating, singing, and many other things just as foreign children do. I wanted my country and people to be known and understood by young foreign readers. Thus I wrote the stories in English.

"I now write both in English and Japanese hoping that I can tell children what I really want to tell them—about love, beauty, truth, peace, kindness, generosity, gentleness. . . . I would like to write stories for children for my whole life—for it is my life."

HOBBIES AND OTHER INTERESTS: Japanese Noh plays and tea ceremonies, gardening, reading, music, taking a walk.

FOR MORE INFORMATION SEE: Student Times, June 30, 1961; *Japan Times,* September 1, 1963.

MASAKO MATSUNO, with daughter

MAYNE, William (James Carter) 1928-
(Dynely James, a joint pseudonym)

PERSONAL: Born March 16, 1928, in Kingston upon Hull, Yorkshire, England; son of William and Dorothy (Fea) Mayne. *Home:* New House, Thornton Rust, Leyburn, Yorkshire, England. *Agent:* David Higham Associates Ltd., 76 Dean St., London W. 1, England.

CAREER: Writer of children's books. *Awards, honors:* Carnegie Medal of (British) Library Association for best children's book of year, for *The Grass Rope,* 1957.

WRITINGS: Follow the Footprints, Oxford University Press, 1953; *The World Upside Down,* Oxford University Press, 1954; *A Swarm in May,* Oxford University Press, 1955, Bobbs, 1957; *The Member for the Marsh,* Oxford University Press, 1956; *Chorister's Cake,* Oxford University Press, 1956, Bobbs, 1958; *The Blue Boat,* Oxford University Press, 1957, Dutton, 1960; *A Grass Rope* (ALA Notable Book), Oxford University Press, 1957, Dutton, 1962; *Underground Alley,* Oxford University Press, 1958, Dutton, 1961; (with R. D. Caesar under joint pseudonym Dynely James) *Gobbling Billy,* Dutton, 1959, Brockhampton, 1969; *The Thumbstick,* Oxford University Press, 1959.

(Contributor) *Over the Horizon, or Around the World in Fifteen Stories,* Duell, Sloan & Pearce, 1960; *The Rolling Season,* Oxford University Press, 1960; *Cathedral Wednesday,* Oxford University Press, 1960; *The Fishing Party,* Hamish Hamilton, 1960; *Summer Visitors,* Oxford University Press, 1961; *The Changeling,* Oxford University Press, 1961, Dutton, 1963; *The Glass Ball,* Hamish

There was too much noise under the mouth of the bell for him to talk or for Max to hear. ■ (From *The Glass Ball* by William Mayne. Illustrated by Janet Duchesne.)

162

Hamilton, 1961, Dutton, 1962; *The Last Bus,* Hamish Hamilton, 1962; *The Twelve Dancers,* Hamish Hamilton, 1962; *Plot Night,* Hamish Hamilton, 1963, Dutton, 1968; (editor with Eleanor Farjeon) *The Hamish Hamilton Book of Kings,* Hamish Hamilton, 1964 (published in America as *A Cavalcade of Kings),* Walck, 1965; *A Day Without Wind,* Hamish Hamilton, 1964, Dutton, 1964; *Words and Music,* Hamish Hamilton, 1964; *Whistling Rufus,* Hamish Hamilton, 1964, Dutton, 1965; *Sand,* Hamish Hamilton, 1964, Dutton, 1965; (editor with Eleanor Farjeon) *The Hamish Hamilton Book of Queens,* Hamish Hamilton, 1965 (published in America as *A Cavalcade of Queens,* Walck, 1965); *No More School,* Hamish Hamilton, 1965; *Water Boatman,* Hamish Hamilton, 1965; *The Big Wheel and the Little Wheel,* Hamish Hamilton, 1965; *Pig in the Middle,* Hamish Hamilton, 1965, Dutton, 1966; *Rooftops,* Hamish Hamilton, 1966; *Earthfasts,* Hamish Hamilton, 1966, Dutton, 1967; *The Old Zion,* Hamish Hamilton, 1966, Dutton, 1967; (editor) *Hamish Hamilton Book of Heroes,* Hamish Hamilton, 1967 (published in America as *William Mayne's Book of Heroes,* Dutton, 1968); *The Battlefield,* Hamish Hamilton, 1967, Dutton, 1967; *The Big Egg,* Hamish Hamilton, 1967; *The House on Fairmont,* Dutton, 1968; (editor) *The Hamish Hamilton Book of Giants,* Hamish Hamilton, 1968 (published in America as *William Mayne's Book of Giants,* Dutton, 1968); *The Toffee Join,* Hamish Hamilton, 1968; *Over the Hills and Far Away,* Hamish Hamilton, 1968 (published in America as *The Hill Road,* Dutton, 1968); *The Yellow Aeroplane,* Hamish Hamilton, 1968; *Ravensgill* (ALA Notable Book; *Horn Book* Honor List), Hamish Hamilton, 1970, Dutton, 1971; *Royal Harry,*

Hamish Hamilton, 1971, Dutton, 1971; *A Game of Dark,* Dutton, 1971; (editor) *Ghosts,* Nelson, 1971; *The Incline,* Dutton, 1972.

FOR MORE INFORMATION SEE: Wilson Library Bulletin, April, 1963; Roger Lancelyn Green, *Tellers of Tales,* Watts, 1965; *Young Readers' Review,* April, 1966, December, 1968; *Book Week,* March 12, 1967, April 16, 1967; *Christian Science Monitor,* May 4, 1967, August 3, 1967, February 1, 1968; *New York Times Book Review,* May 14, 1967, November 12, 1967; *New Statesman,* November 3, 1967, November, 1968; *The Listener,* November 16, 1967; *Book World,* November 19, 1967, August 18, 1968; *Books and Bookmen,* January, 1968; Brian Doyle, *The Who's Who of Children's Literature,* Schocken, 1968; Eleanor Cameron, *The Green and Burning Tree,* Atlantic-Little, Brown, 1969; *Authors' Choice,* Crowell, 1971; *Horn Book,* February, 1971, October, 1971, February, 1972, August, 1972, April, 1973, December, 1973; John Rowe Townsend, *A Sense of Story,* Lippincott, 1971; *Third Book of Junior Authors,* edited by de Montreville and Hill, H. W. Wilson, 1972; *Washington Post* "Children's Book World," November 5, 1972.

McCALL, Edith S(ansom) 1911-

PERSONAL: Born September 5, 1911, in Charles City, Iowa; daughter of William John and Mary (May) Sansom; married Merle R. McCall, 1935; married Howard C. Worley, 1971; children: Constance (Mrs. David Johnston), Mary (Mrs. Tony Legato). *Education:* Wisconsin Central State College, student, 1928-30; University of Chicago, M.A., 1949. *Address:* P. O. Box 255, Hollister, Mo. 65672.

CAREER: Public school teacher, Elmhurst, Ill., 1930-35, Western Springs, Ill., 1943-47; reading counselor, La Grange, Ill., 1947-55; full-time writer of juveniles and textbooks, 1955—. *Member:* White River Valley Historical Society (secretary, 1961-62), Authors Guild, Missouri Writers Guild (president, 1971-72), International Reading Association, Pi Lambda Theta. *Awards, honors:* Missouri Writers Guild Award, 1960.

WRITINGS—"Butternut Bill" series published by Benefic: *Butternut Bill,* 1965, *Butternut Bill and the Bee Tree,* 1965, *Butternut Bill and the Big Catfish,* 1965, *Butternut Bill and the Bear,* 1965, *Butternut Bill and Little River,* 1966, *Butternut Bill and the Big Pumpkin,* 1966; *Butternut Bill and His Friends,* 1968, *Butternut Bill and the Train,* 1969.

"Button Family" series published by Benefic: *Bucky Button,* 1953, *The Buttons at the Zoo,* 1954, *The Buttons and the Pet Parade,* 1954, *The Buttons at the Farm,* 1955, *The Buttons Go Camping,* 1956, *The Buttons at the Soap Box Derby,* 1957, *The Buttons Take a Boat Ride,* 1957, *The Buttons and Mr. Pete,* 1957, *The Buttons and the Boy Scouts,* 1958, *The Buttons and the Little League,* 1958, *The Buttons and the Whirlybird,* 1959, *The Buttons See Things that Go* (revised editions of all books, 1960-61).

"Frontiers of America" series published by Childrens: *Log Fort Adventures,* 1958; *Steamboats to the West,* 1959, *Hunters Blaze the Trail,* 1959, *Explorers in a New World,* 1960, *Men on Iron Horses,* 1960, *Settlers on a Strange*

WILLIAM MAYNE

163

Behind him, Fitzpatrick heard the yelling Indians draw closer. ■ (From *Hunters Blaze the Trails* by Edith McCall. Illustrated by Carol Rogers.)

Shore, 1960, *Heroes of the Western Outposts,* 1960, *Pioneers on Early Waterways,* 1961, *Wagons over the Mountains,* 1961, *Cumberland Gap and Trails West,* 1961, *Mail Riders,* 1961, *Gold Rush Adventures,* 1962, *Pioneering on the Plains,* 1962, *Pirates and Privateers,* 1963, *Pioneer Show Folk,* 1963, *Pioneer Traders,* 1964, *Cowboys and Cattle Drives,* 1964, *Forts in the Wilderness,* 1968, *Stalwart Men of Early Texas,* 1970.

"Learning for Living in Today's World" series published by Benefic, co-author with Clarence Samford and Ruth Gue: *You are Here,* 1963, *You and the Neighborhood,* 1963, *You and the Community,* 1963. Books in same series, co-author with Clarence Samford and Floyd Cunningham: *You and Regions Near and Far,* 1963, *You and the United States,* 1964, *You and the Americas,* 1965, *You and the World,* 1966. With Mark M. Krug: *You and the Nation,* 1968.

"Man in a World of Change" series published by Benefic, co-author with Muriel Stanek and Evalyn Rapparlie: *Man and His Families,* 1971, *Man and His Community,* 1971, *Man and His Cities,* 1971, *Man and the Regions of the World,* 1971. With Evalyn Rapparlie and Jack B. Spatafora: *Man–United States and Americas,* 1972, *Man–His World and Cultures,* 1972.

Books in other series published by Benefic: (With Charlotte E. Wilcox) *Come On,* 1955; (with Wilcox) *Here We Go,* 1955; (with Wilcox) *Step Lively,* 1955; (with Marjorie Ann Banks) *Where Rivers Meet,* 1958; (with George Crout) *Where the Ohio Flows,* 1960; *How We Get Our Mail,* 1961; *How Airplanes Help Us,* 1961; *How We Get Our Clothing,* 1961; *How We Get Our Cloth,* 1961; (with George Crout) *You and Ohio,* 1971; (with Banks) *Where Rivers Meet,* 1973.

Teacher's guides for 'Button Family Adventures," "Frontiers of America," and for several of other books authored.

Also wrote and published a book for residents of and visitors to the area in which she lives: *English Village in the Ozarks: The Story of Hollister, Missouri,* 1969.

SIDELIGHTS: "To be a writer has been a lifelong ambition, but except for a winning entry in a newspaper contest, my publications were limited to school papers until I was far past my growing-up years. While my children were small, I couldn't afford a typewriter; when I could buy a typewriter, I was too busy raising a family and teaching in the neighborhood school while trying to attain a college degree through evening school, summer sessions, and home study courses.

"In my last years as a teacher, I specialized in helping children who were having difficulty in learning to read. I wrote much of my instructional material then, using the duplicator each day to bring out the next episode of the tale of Punky, a horse who spoke in rhyme and aspired to becoming a detective. In 1952, I was given an opportunity to submit material for books that could be used to help the older child learn to read as well as serving as supplementary reading material in primary classrooms. The 'Button Books' resulted. I drew from my own childhood experiences, such as vacationing on a Wisconsin dairy farm, and from the lives of my children for part of their material, coupling these with imagination. I had always thought it would be fun to be a member of a large family, and truly enjoyed my vicarious life with the Buttons. Their dog, Bumps, was the fictional version of my own family's dachshund.

"Until 1955, I was a city girl, living in Madison and Milwaukee, Wisconsin, and in the suburbs of Chicago, Illinois. But in 1955 I moved to my present home in the beautiful Ozarks of southwestern Missouri. I devoted most of my time to writing from that time on. Learning about my new state for *Where Rivers Meet* revived an old interest in and fascination with the people who built this nation. My research uncovered many true adventure tales. I wanted to write about the pioneers in such a way that the stories would make American history become a living thing to boys and girls. I began the 'Frontiers of America' books, and wrote nineteen of them. I hope to do more stories against historical backgrounds.

"Upon moving to the Ozarks, I developed a deep interest in the folklore of this region. The 'Butternut Bill' stories were written to help keep some of this folklore alive. The background is a real log house and barn, located a few miles from my own home here in Taney County. Our local history, including the tales of the 'Baldknobbers', are a rich field for future writing.

Something about the Author

EDITH S. MC CALL

"My home is just outside the little town of Hollister, on a hilltop. I like working outdoors on the grounds. I also do a little amateur woodcarving and watercolor painting. I have an electronic organ that I have been trying to learn to play, solely for my own amusement. Now and then, I like to go on a trip to other places, but I know I am fortunate always to be able to come home to beautiful surroundings and enough sources of writing ideas to last as long as I shall be able to hit the typewriter keys."

McGEE, Barbara 1943-

PERSONAL: Born February 1, 1943, in Greenbelt, Md.; daughter of John Raphael (a teacher and printer) and Dorothy (Owen) McGee. *Education:* Temple University, student at Tyler School and Fine Arts, 1961-63; Pratt Institute, B.F.A., 1966. *Politics:* Liberal Democrat. *Residence:* New York, N.Y.

CAREER: Illustrator and lithographic artist; assistant teacher in Head Start program, Brooklyn, N.Y., 1966.

WRITINGS—Self-illustrated: (compiler) *Jump-Rope Rhymes*, Viking, 1968.

Illustrator: Siddie Joe Johnson, *Feather in My Hand*, Atheneum, 1967; Shirley Rousseau Murphy, *White Ghost Summer*, Viking, 1967; Elizabeth Witheridge, *And What of You, Josephine Charlotte?*, Atheneum, 1969.

WORK IN PROGRESS: Ms. McGee is currently organizing a greeting card company which will feature her own designs.

SIDELIGHTS: "My mother illustrated children's books years ago and I suppose that was an influence since she was always my best encourager in my art work. But since I was an avid, book-hungry reader as a child, I guess it was only natural for me to try to combine my love for art and literature in one career. I knew in high school I wanted to be an illustrator and I never changed my mind. It's a field I'd like to keep working in all my life. How to write without being corny? It's a simple matter of loving books and drawing and feeling I can make a contribution to life this way."

My mother, your mother,
Live across the way—
Sixteen, Seventeen, Easy Broadway.
■ (From *Jump-Rope Rhymes* by Barbara McGee. Illustrated by the author.)

McGRADY, Mike 1933-

PERSONAL: Born October 4, 1933, in New York, N.Y.; son of Patrick M. and Grace (Robinson) McGrady; married Corinne Young (a designer), November 28, 1958; children: Sean, Siobhan, Liam. *Education:* Yale University, B.A., 1955; Harvard University, further study, 1968-69. *Home:* 95 Eaton's Neck Rd., Northport, N.Y. 11768. *Agent:* Sterling Lord Agency, 660 Madison Ave., New York, N.Y. 10021. *Office: Newsday,* 550 Stewart Ave., Garden City, N.Y. 11530.

CAREER: Fulltime free-lance writer, 1958-62; *Newsday,* Garden City, N.Y., columnist, 1962-74. *Military service:* U.S. Army, 1956-58. *Awards, honors:* Overseas Press Club Award for best interpretive reporting, 1968, for *A Dove in Vietnam;* Nieman fellow at Harvard University, 1968-69; Headliners Award of National Headliners Club for best column in the United States, 1966.

WRITINGS—Adult: *A Dove in Vietnam,* Funk, 1968; (editor with Harvey Aronson) *Naked Came the Stranger* (twenty-five author collaboration), Lyle Stuart, 1971; *Stranger Than Naked or How to Write Dirty Books for Fun & Profit,* Peter H. Wyden, 1972.

Teen books: (With John Floherty) *Youth and the FBI* (foreword by J. Edgar Hoover), Lippincott, 1960; (with Floherty) *Whirling Wings,* Lippincott, 1960; *Crime Scientists,* Lippincott, 1961; *Jungle Doctors,* Lippincott, 1962; (with Floherty) *Skin Diving Adventures,* Lippincott, 1962.

FOR MORE INFORMATION SEE: *Life,* August 22, 1969; *Washington Post,* June 9, 1970; *Esquire,* September, 1970.

McKOWN, Robin

PERSONAL: Born in Denver, Colo.; daughter of George S. and Anna Clason; married Dallas McKown (deceased). *Education:* University of Colorado, B.A.; further studies at University of Illinois and Northwestern University. *Home:* Dry Run Rd., Beaver Dams, N.Y. 14812. *Agent:* Curtis Brown Ltd., 13 King St., Covent Garden, London W.C.2, England.

CAREER: Writer, mainly of books for teen-agers. Worked in New York for several years doing sales promotion for a publicity concern and writing radio scripts and a column on books and authors for the Book-of-the-Month Club. Also worked as a literary agent. *Member:* Authors Guild, Society of Women Geographers. *Awards, honors:* Child Study Association Award, 1961, for *Janine.*

WRITINGS: *Authors' Agent,* Messner, 1957; *Painter of the Wild West–Frederic Remington,* Messner, 1959; *Marie Curie,* Putnam, 1959; *Publicity Girl,* Putnam, 1959; *Foreign Service Girl,* Putnam, 1959; *Janine* (Junior Literary Guild selection), Messner, 1960; *She Lived for Science: Irene Joliot-Curie,* Messner, 1961; *Pioneers of Mental Health* (adult book), Dodd, 1961; *Washington's America,* Grosset, 1961; *Thomas Paine,* Putnam, 1962; *The Fabulous Isotopes,* Holiday, 1962; *The Giant of the Atom* (story of Ernest Rutherford), Messner, 1962; *Roosevelt's America,* Grosset, 1962; *The Ordeal of Anne Devlin,* Messner, 1963;

Peter woke up in Madagascar. He knew that was where he was but he did not know how he knew. ■ (From *The Boy Who Woke up in Madagascar* by Robin McKown. Illustrated by Robert Quackenbush.)

Benjamin Franklin, Putnam, 1963; *Seven Famous Trials,* Vanguard, 1963; *Patriot of the Underground,* Putnam, 1964; *Eleanor Roosevelt's World,* Grosset, 1964; *Mendeleyev,* Messner, 1965; *Story of the Incas,* Putnam, 1966; *Heroic Nurses* (Junior Literary Guild selection), Putnam, 1966; *Rakoto and the Drongo Bird,* Lothrop, 1966; *The Boy Who Woke Up in Madagascar,* Putnam, 1967; *Girl of Madagascar,* Messner, 1967; *The Congo, River of Mystery,* McGraw, 1968; *The American Revolution: The French Allies,* McGraw, 1968; *Horatio Gates and Benedict Arnold,* McGraw, 1969; *Lumumba,* Doubleday, 1969; (with Mary Elting) *The Mongo Homecoming,* M. Evans, 1969; *Colonial Conquest of Africa,* Watts, 1971; *Crisis in South Africa,* Putnam, 1972; *The World of Mary Cassatt,* Crowell, 1972; *Republic of Zaire,* Watts, 1972; *Nkrumah,* Doubleday, 1973; *The Execution of Maximilian,* Watts, 1973; *The Image of Puerto Rico,* McGraw, 1973.

SIDELIGHTS: "My first literary success came at the University of Colorado where my one-act play, 'The King's Enemy,' won first prize and ran for three nights at the University little theatre. Later I did volunteer work for a New York committee that helped the widows and orphans of the French Resistance. In connection with this work, I made a six weeks' tour of France immediately after the war, visiting the families of men who had died in the Resistance.

"Subsequently I spent three years in the mining region of northern France, the setting of *Patriot of the Underground* and *Janine*. In connection with my other books, I have traveled to Peru, Madagascar, North Africa, the Congo, South Africa, Ireland, Italy . . . and in the United States. At present I live on a 100-acre estate, mostly woodland, in western New York State."

FOR MORE INFORMATION SEE: Third Book of Junior Authors, edited by de Montreville and Hill, H. W. Wilson, 1972; *Horn Book,* February, 1973.

ROBIN MC KOWN

MEIGS, Cornelia Lynde   1884-1973
(Adair Aldon)

PERSONAL: Born December 6, 1884, in Rock Island, Ill.; daughter of Montgomery (a civil engineer) and Grace (Lynde) Meigs. *Education:* Bryn Mawr College, A.B., 1908. *Politics:* Republican. *Religion:* Episcopalian. *Home:* Sion Hill, Havre de Grace, Md. 21078; and (summer) Green Pastures, Brandon, Vt. 05733.

CAREER: St. Katharine's School, Davenport, Iowa, teacher of English, 1912-13; Bryn Mawr College, Bryn Mawr, Pa., 1932-50, began as instructor, became professor of English, professor emeritus. Civilian employee, U.S. War Department, Washington, D.C., 1942-45. *Member:* American Association of University Women, Pennsylvania Historical Society, Vermont Historical Society, Hartford County (Md.) Historical Society. *Awards, honors:* Drama League prize, 1915, for "The Steadfast Princess"; Newbery Medal, American Library Association, 1934, for *Invincible Louisa;* Little, Brown & Co. prize for *The Trade Wind;* L.H.D., Plano University, 1967.

WRITINGS: The Kingdom of the Winding Road, Macmillan, 1915; *Master Simon's Garden,* Macmillan, 1916, new edition, 1929; *The Steadfast Princess* (juvenile play), Macmillan, 1916; (under pseudonym Adair Aldon) *The Island of Appledore,* Macmillan, 1917; (under pseudonym Adair Aldon) *The Pirate of Jasper Peak,* Macmillan, 1918; *The Pool of Stars,* Macmillan, 1919, new edition, 1929.

(Under pseudonym Adair Aldon) *At the Sign of the Heroes,* Century, 1920; *The Windy Hill,* Macmillan, 1921; *Helga and the White Peacock* (juvenile play), Macmillan, 1922; (under pseudonym Adair Aldon) *The Hill of Adventure,* Century, 1922; *The New Moon: The Story of Dick Martin's Courage, His Silver Sixpence and His Friends in the New World,* Macmillan, 1924, new edition, 1929; *Rain on the Roof,* Macmillan, 1925; *As the Crow Flies,* Macmillan, 1927; *The Trade Wind,* Little, Brown, 1927; *Clearing Weather,* Little, Brown, 1928; *The Wonderful Locomotive,* Macmillan, 1928; *The Crooked Apple Tree,* Little, Brown, 1929.

The Willow Whistle, Macmillan, 1931; *Swift Rivers,* Little, Brown, 1932; *The Story of the Author of Little Women: Invincible Louisa,* Little, Brown, 1933, reissued with a new introduction, 1968 (published in England as *The Story of Louisa Alcott,* Harrap, 1935); *Wind in the Chimney,* Macmillan, 1934; *The Covered Bridge,* Macmillan, 1936; *Young Americans: How History Looked to Them While It Was in the Making* (stories), Ginn and Junior Literary Guild, 1936; *Railroad West,* Little, Brown, 1937; *The Scarlet Oak,* Macmillan, 1938.

Call of the Mountain, Little, Brown, 1940; *Mother Makes Christmas,* Grosset, 1940; *Vanished Island,* Macmillan, 1941; *Mounted Messenger,* Macmillan, 1943; *The Two Arrows,* Macmillan, 1949; *The Violent Men: A Study of Human Relations in the First American Congress,* Macmillan, 1949.

The Dutch Colt, Macmillan, 1952; (editor and contributor) *A Critical History of Children's Literature: A Survey of Children's Books in English from Earliest Times to the*

Present, Macmillan, 1953, revised edition, 1969; *Fair Wind to Virginia,* Macmillan, 1955; *What Makes a College?: A History of Bryn Mawr,* Macmillan, 1956; *Wild Geese Flying,* Macmillan, 1957; *Saint John's Church, Havre de Grace, Md. 1809-1959,* Democratic Ledger, 1959.

Mystery at the Red House, Macmillan, 1961; *The Great Design: Men and Events in the United Nations from 1945 to 1963,* Little, Brown, 1964; (editor and author of introduction and notes) *Glimpses of Louisa: A Centennial Sampling of the Best Short Stories,* Little, Brown, 1968; *The Dutch Colt,* Macmillan, 1968.

Jane Addams: Pioneer for Social Justice (Junior Literary Guild selection), Little, Brown, 1970; *Louisa M. Alcott and the American Family Story,* Walck, 1971.

SIDELIGHTS: "I grew up in the small and interesting town of Keokuk, Iowa, on the west bank of the Mississippi River where my father was a government engineer in charge of navigation improvements for that many-minded stream. With my sisters I went to a small private school. As may be guessed, we composed the greater part of the student body. It was a long step to the town high school full of a bewildering variety of young persons. It was a longer step still to make my own way through a battery of examinations to Bryn Mawr College.

He came up the little street that led to their house standing big and white with its tall round columns and the great maple trees lifting their branches above the roof, and he felt inside, as he always did, a thump of pleasure over thinking that it was theirs to keep always. ■ (From *Wild Geese Flying* by Cornelia Meigs. Illustrated by Charles Geer.)

CORNELIA LYNDE MEIGS

"It was tolerably plain that I was meant to be a teacher; becoming a writer was not such an evident or easily accomplished process. At an Iowa boarding school where I first began teaching I used to tell stories to the younger children, and found myself experimenting with different kinds of tales and finding quickly just what sort they liked and what they would have none of. It was out of these that my first book came, a collection of stories called *The Kingdom of the Winding Road.*

"I came to realize, in those years just before the First World War, how few good books were being published for children. As time went on and I went more fully into writing, I began to understand that I was at the beginning of a great movement to recognize and remedy that lack. The first publishers' department especially for children was organized. Libraries began to open special rooms for children and to train special librarians for them. I went forward on the wave of that exciting development, finding that teaching and writing went well together and that the American history that I was interested in gave me endless material for stories."

FOR MORE INFORMATION SEE: Junior Book of Authors, edited by Kunitz and Haycraft, H. W. Wilson, 1934, 2nd edition, 1951; *Newbery Medal Books: 1922-1955,* Horn Book, 1955; *Best Sellers,* October 1, 1968, May 1, 1970; *Punch,* November 29, 1967; *Book World,* November 3, 1968; *Horn Book,* April, 1970; *Library Journal,* June 15, 1970; *Publishers Weekly,* October 8, 1973.

(Died September 10, 1973)

MEMLING, Carl   1918-1969

PERSONAL: Born January 18, 1918, in New York, N.Y.; married Pearl Gruber, 1939; children: Lise, Maya. *Education:* Brooklyn College, B.A., 1938. *Home:* 569 Haddon Lane, East Meadow, N.Y.

CAREER: Writer, mainly for children, Bank Street College of Education, New York, N.Y., executive editor, "Bank Street Readers," and program director, publications division. *Military service:* U.S. Army, 1942-45; became sergeant. *Member:* Authors Guild.

WRITINGS: What's in the Dark?, Abelard, 1954; *We Went to the Doctor,* Abelard, 1955; *Little Bear's Mother,* Farrar, Straus, 1959; *Helicopters,* Golden Press, 1959; *Butterflies and Moths,* Golden Press, 1959; *Magic Slate Book,* Golden Press, 1959; *Giant Golden Punch-out Book,* Golden Press, 1960; *Our Flag,* Golden Press, 1960; *Rupert the Rhinoceros,* Golden Press, 1960; *Little Cottontail,* Golden Press, 1960; *My Read & Draw Magic Slate Book,* Golden Press, 1961; *Ten Little Animals,* Golden Press, 1961; *Pony Express,* Parents Institute Press, 1962; *I Have a Secret,* Golden Press, 1962; *Riddles, Riddles from A to Z,* Golden Press, 1962; *Read, Write, and Count,* Golden Press, 1962; *ABC Rhymes,* Golden Press, 1963; *I Can Count,* Golden Press, 1963; *Seals for Sale,* Abelard, 1964; *Gift-Bear for the King,* Dutton, 1966; *Life with Mindy,* Dutton, 1966; *Ten Big Passengers,* Singer, 1969; *Hi, All You Rabbits,* Parents' Magazine Press, 1970; *What's in the Dark,* Parents' Magazine Press, 1970; *Ride, Willy, Ride,* Follett, 1970; *Old Man Riddle,* A. Whitman, 1972.

Stories based on syndicated comics: *Maverick,* Golden Press, 1959; *Captain Kangaroo's Animal Friends,* Golden Press, 1959; *Steve Canyon,* Golden Press, 1959; *Mr. Green Jeans Coloring Book,* Golden Press, 1959; *Chipmunks' Merry Christmas,* Golden Press, 1959; *Dennis the Menace and Ruff,* Golden Press, 1959; *Dennis the Menace,* Golden Press, 1960; *Huckleberry Hound,* Golden Press, 1960; *Quickdraw McGraw,* Golden Press, 1960.

SIDELIGHTS: Memling's wife, Pearl, wrote *SATA:* "He was a vital man who loved children, and so, loved writing for them. Many of his stories were written for his own children, and based on shared experiences with them. *What's in the Dark?* was written for his oldest daughter, Lise, who was afraid of the night. (And, it was, for her, a reassuring tale.)

"For his youngest daughter, Maya, he wrote *Life with Mindy*—which could very well have been called, *Life with Maya.*

"Carl enjoyed tennis, swimming and gardening. And he had a delightful and sharp sense of humor which appealed to his daughters, their many friends, and his wife. Even solemn moments could somehow be turned into moments of fun."

(Died October 16, 1969)

All at once they looked around.
They saw that they were
down, down, down
at the bottom of the mountain. ■ (From *Old Man Riddle* by Carl Memling. Illustrated by Jack Faulkner.)

RENATE MEYER

MEYER, Renate 1930-

PERSONAL: Born March 5, 1930, in Berlin, Germany; daughter of Peter Ferdinand (a cardiologist) and Eva (Tauber) Meyer; married Charles Keeping (a book illustrator), September 20, 1955; children: Jonathan, Vicki, Sean Frank. *Education:* Polytechnic of Central London (better known as Regent Street Polytechnic), National Diploma, 1952. *Home:* 16 Church Rd., Shortlands, Kent BR2 OHP, England. *Agent:* B. L. Kearley, 33 Chiltern St., London W.1, England.

CAREER: Writer and illustrator of books for children.

WRITINGS—Self-illustrated: *Vicki,* Bodley Head, 1968, Atheneum, 1969; *Hide and Seek,* Bodley Head, 1969, Bradbury, 1972; *Let's Play Mums and Dads,* Bodley Head, 1970; *The Story of Little Knittle and Threadle,* Bodley Head, 1971; *Mr. Knitted and the Family Tree,* Bodley Head, 1972; *Susie's Doll's Pram,* Bodley Head, in press.

Illustrator: Helen Cresswell, *The Bird Fancier,* Benn, 1970.

SIDELIGHTS: "I am interested in portraying the sort of situations that children really find themselves in, rather

■ (From *Vicki* by Renate Meyer. Illustrated by the author.)

VICKI
a picture book by
Renate Meyer

than fantasy or cartoon humour. There seem to be so many Victorian settings for children's books. I like to set them in contemporary settings, with the sort of companions they are liable to find themselves with. I agree with the argument that coloured children should be introduced there more, looking like they do, not like white kids with tinted skin. I was never able to identify with fairy princesses as a child, and I still prefer the real life situation. My husband and I discuss this endlessly as we both feel strongly about this sort of thing."

FOR MORE INFORMATION SEE: Saturday Review, May 20, 1972.

NATHAN, Robert (Gruntal) 1894-

PERSONAL: Born January 2, 1894, in New York, N.Y.; son of Harold and Sarah (Gruntal) Nathan; married Dorothy Michaels, 1915 (divorced, 1922); married Nancy Wilson, 1930 (divorced, 1936); married Lucy Lee Hall Skelding, 1936 (divorced, 1939); married Janet McMillen Bingham, 1940 (divorced); married Clara May Blum Burns, 1951 (divorced); married Shirley Keeland, December 14, 1955 (died); married Anna Lee (Joan Boniface Winnefrith of Kent, England; an actress), 1970; children: (first marriage) Joan (Mrs. M. Bergstrom). *Education:* Attended private schools in United States and Switzerland, including Phillips Exeter, 1910-12; Harvard University, student, 1912-15. *Home:* 1240 North Doheny Dr., Los Angeles, Calif. *Agent:* Swanson Agency, 8523 Sunset Blvd., Hollywood, Calif. 90069.

CAREER: Novelist, playwright, and poet. New York University School of Journalism, New York, N.Y., lecturer, 1924-25; Metro-Goldwyn-Mayer, Hollywood, Calif., screen writer, 1943-49. Huntington Hartford Foundation, member of literary committee. *Member:* National Institute of Arts and Letters (vice-president, 1939), Academy of American Poets (chancellor), Dramatists Guild, Writers Guild of America (West), Academy of Motion Picture Arts and Sciences, American Society of Composers, Authors, and Publishers (ASCAP), P.E.N. (charter member; president, 1940-43), Screen Writers Guild. *Awards, honors:* U.S. Treasury Department Silver Medal, World War II; California Writer's Guild Award of Honor.

WRITINGS: The Barly Fields (collection of five earlier novels), Knopf, 1938; *Journey of Tapiola* (juvenile), Knopf, 1938, new edition titled *Tappy,* 1966; *Winter in April,* Knopf, 1938.

Portrait of Jennie, Knopf, 1940; *They Went on Together,* Knopf, 1941; *Tapiola's Brave Regiment* (juvenile), Knopf, 1941; *The Sea-Gull Cry,* Knopf, 1942; *Journal for Josephine,* Knopf, 1943; *Mr. Whittle and the Morning Star,* Knopf, 1947; *The River Journey,* Knopf, 1949.

The Adventures of Tapiola (two juvenile novels, *Journey of Tapiola* and *Tapiola's Brave Regiment*), Knopf, 1952; *Nathan Three* (three novels, *The Sea-Gull Cry, The Innocent Eve,* and *The River Journey*), Staples, 1952; *The Fair,*

Knopf, 1964; *Mallot Diaries,* Knopf, 1965; *Juliet in Mantua* (play), Knopf, 1967; *Stonecliff,* Knopf, 1967; *Mia,* Knopf, 1970; *The Elixir (School Library Journal* book list), Knopf, 1971; *The Summer Meadows,* Delacorte, 1973. (For complete list of writings see *Contemporary Authors,* Volume 15-16.)

Poetry: *Youth Grows Old,* McBride, 1922; *A Cedar Box,* Bobbs, 1929; *Selected Poems of Robert Nathan,* Knopf, 1935; *A Winter Tide,* Knopf, 1940; *Dunkirk,* Knopf, 1942; *Morning in Iowa,* Knopf, 1944; *The Darkening Meadows,* Knopf, 1945; *The Green Leaf: The Collected Poems of Robert Nathan,* Knopf, 1950.

Films: "The White Cliffs of Dover," 1944; "The Clock," 1945; "Pagan Love Song," 1950.

ROBERT NATHAN

Unpublished plays: "Music at Evening," 1935; "A Family Piece," 1947; "Susan and the Stranger," 1954; "Juliet in Mantua," 1965.

Magazine writer in the 1920's and 1930's, contributing to *New Yorker, Atlantic, Harper's, Scribner's, Century, Red Book, Cosmopolitan,* and other periodicals. Writer of songs and a violin sonata. Illustrator of *Tina Mina Tales.*

WORK IN PROGRESS: Plays.

SIDELIGHTS: "I have been devoted to music all my life. If I had had my 'druthers,' I'd have been a great opera singer. As a young man, I was a member of the Fencer's Club of New York, and studied the Italian style of fencing in Florence, Italy. I owned 'The Parsonage' at Truro on Cape Cod for fifteen years. My books have been about New England, New York, Cape Cod, and California. I have also written about Florence, which I knew, and Rome and Israel, which I didn't know.

"I swim every day when I can. I write in pencil, in long hand and then type what I have written, go over it for revisions and corrections, and type it again.

"I have five step-children, and a poodle."

FOR MORE INFORMATION SEE: L. Bromfield, *The Work of Robert Nathan,* Bobbs, circa 1930; *Saturday Review of Literature,* February 2, 1935; *Christian Science Monitor,* November 13, 1935, June 30, 1945; *Springfield Republican,* June 11, 1945; *Catholic World,* October, 1958, January, 1962; *New York Herald Tribune Book Review,* October 5, 1958, November 1, 1959, April 10, 1960; *New York Times Book Review,* December 14, 1958, December 19, 1965; *Booklist,* December 1, 1960, July 1, 1961; Dan H. Laurence, *Robert Nathan: A Bibliography,* Yale University Library, 1961; *Publishers Weekly,* October 8, 1973.

NEEDLEMAN, Jacob 1934-

PERSONAL: Born October 6, 1934, in Philadelphia, Pa.; son of Benjamin and Ida (Seltzer) Needleman; married Carla Satzman (a potter), August 30, 1959; children: Raphael, Eve. *Education:* Harvard University, B.A., 1956; University of Freiburg, graduate study, 1957-58; Yale University, Ph.D., 1961. *Residence:* San Francisco, Calif. *Agent:* Harold Matson Co., Inc., 22 East 40th St., New York, N.Y. 10016. *Office:* Department of Philosophy, San Francisco State College, San Francisco, Calif. 94132.

CAREER: West Haven Veterans Administration Hospital, West Haven, Conn., clinical psychology trainee, 1960-61; Rockefeller Institute, New York, N.Y., research associate, 1961-62; San Francisco State College, San Francisco, Calif., 1962—, began as assistant professor, 1962-66, became associate professor, 1966, now professor of philosophy, chairman of department, 1968—. Union Theological Seminary, visiting scholar, 1967-68. *Member:* American Philosophical Association. *Awards, honors:* Fulbright scholarship in Germany, 1957-58; Fels Foundation fellowship in Munich, 1959; Society for Religion in Higher Education grant, 1967-68; grants from Marsden Foundation and Ella Lyman Cabot Trust for research for *The New Religions.*

WRITINGS: Being in the World, Basic Books, 1963, reissued with new introduction, Torchbooks, 1968; (translator) Erwin Straus, *The Primary World of Senses,* Free Press, 1963; (contributor of translation) *Essays on Ego Psychology,* International Universities Press, 1964; (co-editor) *Care of Patients with Fatal Illness,* New York Academy of Sciences, 1969; (contributor) Austin H. Kutscher, editor,

"I will tell you," said Richard. And he added in hushed tones. "It is Hollywood." ■ (From *Tappy* by Robert Nathan. Illustrated by Doris Burn.)

Death and Bereavement, C. C. Thomas, 1969; *The New Religions,* Doubleday, 1970; *Religion for a New Generation,* Macmillan, 1973. General editor, ''Penguin Metaphysical Library.'' Contributor of articles and reviews to journals in his field.

WORK IN PROGRESS: Man in the Universal World, a book relating modern science to the new mysticism.

SIDELIGHTS: ''I write to people who, like myself, are searching for a way to maintain or return to the questions of the heart that a child puts to the universe: who am I? why am I on earth? how can I find out the meaning of my life? Some time ago I discovered how easy it was to forget these questions when surrounded by sophisticated books and other people's opinions and the promises of clever theorists. I seem to feel my humanity only when I come closer to this search and if anything of that is expressed in my writing I am very glad.''

NEUFELD, John (Arthur) 1938-

PERSONAL: Born December 14, 1938, in Chicago, Ill.; son of Leonard Carl (a manufacturer) and Rhoda (Padway) Neufeld. *Education:* Phillips Exeter Academy, graduate, 1956; Yale University, B.A., 1960. *Residence:* New York, N.Y. *Agent:* William Morris Agency, 1350 Avenue of the Americas, New York, N.Y. 10019.

JOHN NEUFELD

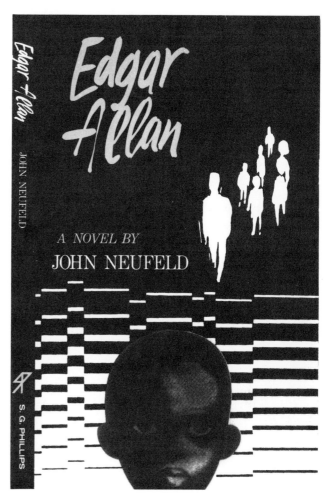

This is a story about my father, and about God. Neither is very easy to understand. ■ (From *Edgar Allan* by John Neufeld. Jacket designed by Simon Jeruchim.)

WRITINGS: Edgar Allan (ALA Notable Book), S. G. Phillips, 1968; *Lisa, Bright and Dark* (juvenile), S. G. Phillips, 1969; *Touching,* S. G. Phillips, 1970; *Sleep Two, Three, Four!,* Harper, 1971; *You Think I'd Go Around Making These Things Up?* (juvenile), Random House, 1973; *For All the Wrong Reasons,* Norton, 1973; *Freddy's Book,* Random House, in press.

WORK IN PROGRESS: I'll Always Love You, Paul Newman and *Charlie Chicago,* both novels; *Twink,* a biographical novel.

SIDELIGHTS: ''As a child, the four books I remember reading at all are *Bartholomew Cubbins, Ferdinand,* Arthur Sziek's Grimm's *Fairy Tales,* and a marvelous story about a turtle, a black duck and a white one, and a strawberry patch. I've never tracked this one down.

''Not being a good child reader, I went straight into adult books when I was twelve or thirteen. I went on week-long binges, reading ten to fifteen books a week. By the time I was fifteen, I had discovered Evelyn Waugh. I read everything he wrote, one book after another, and then went back to start all over again. I have this thing about England.''

Hallmark Hall of Fame filmed *Lisa, Bright and Dark* for a 1973 N.B.C. airing; *Freddy's Book* has been optioned for a TV special.

FOR MORE INFORMATION SEE: New York Times, November 3, 1968; *Best Sellers*, January 1, 1969; *Saturday Review*, January 18, 1969; *New York Times Book Review*, November 16, 1969; *Top of the News*, April, 1970.

NEWLON, Clarke (Michael Clarke)

PERSONAL: Born in Winterset, Iowa; son of an Iowa farming couple; married Betty Sniffen, 1936; children: Michael, Richard. *Education:* Attended Grinnell College. *Politics:* Liberal ·("very"). *Residence:* Washington, D.C. *Agent:* Collins-Knowlton-Wing, Inc., 60 East 56th St., New York, N.Y. 10022.

CLARKE NEWLON

CAREER: Reporter and newspaper editor: *Dallas Dispatch, Chicago Sun Times*, a UPI Syndicate; *Missiles and Rockets*, Washington, D.C., editor, 1958-60. *Military Service:* Retired as United States Air Force Colonel, August 31, 1958. *Member:* National Press Club, International Club.

WRITINGS: 1001 Questions Answered About Space, Dodd, 1962, revised edition published as *1001 Answers to Questions About Space*, Grosset, 1966; *Famous Pioneers in Space*, Dodd, 1963; *L.B.J.: The Man from Johnson City*, Dodd, 1964, revised edition, 1970; *The Fighting Douglas MacArthur*, Dodd, 1965; *The Aerospace Age Dictionary*, Watts, 1965; *Famous Mexican-Americans*, Dodd, 1972; *Men Who Made Mexico*, Dodd, 1973; *Police Dogs in Action* (Junior Literary Guild selection), Dodd, 1974. Contributor, sometimes under the pseudonym Michael Clarke, to magazines, including *Collier's, Saturday Evening Post*, and *Reader's Digest*.

WORK IN PROGRESS: Research for another book.

SIDELIGHTS: Newlon lived abroad for a total of nine years—in England, France, Germany, Norway, and Egypt.

NYE, Robert 1939-

PERSONAL: Born March 15, 1939, in London, England; son of Oswald William and Frances Dorothy (Weller) Nye; married Judith Pratt, 1959; married second wife, Aileen Campbell (an artist), 1968; children (first marriage) Jack, Taliesin, Malory; (second marriage) Owen, Sharon, Rebecca. *Education:* Southend High School, Essex, England, student, 1950-55. *Residence:* Edinburgh, Scotland. *Agent:* Olwyn Hughes, 10B Arkwright Rd., London N.W.3, England.

CAREER: Writer.

WRITINGS: Juvenilia 1 (verse), Scorpion Press, 1961; *Juvenilia 2* (verse), Scorpion Press, 1963; *Taliesin* (children's novel), Faber, 1966, Hill & Wang, 1967; *March Has Horse's Ears* (children's stories), Faber, 1966, Hill & Wang, 1967; *Doubtfire* (novel), Calder & Boyars, 1967, Hill & Wang, 1968; *Darker Ends* (verse), Hill & Wang, 1969; *Tales I Told My Mother* (short stories), Hill & Wang, 1969; *Wishing Gold* (children's novel), Macmillan, 1970, Hill & Wang, 1971; (with William Watson) *Sawney Bean* (play), Calder & Boyars, 1970; *Poor Pumpkin* (children's stories), Macmillan, 1971, Hill & Wang, 1972; (editor) *A Choice of Sir Walter Raleigh's Verse*, Faber, 1972.

WORK IN PROGRESS: Editing *A Choice of Swinburne's Verse*, publication by Faber expected in 1973; editing *William Barnes*, Carcanet Press, 1973; two books of children's stories, *Cricket* and *True Thomas*, both Dent, 1973; a translation of Heinrich von Kleist's play *Penthesilea*, Calder & Boyars, 1973.

FOR MORE INFORMATION SEE: Statesman, February 9, 1968; *Books & Bookmen*, August, 1970.

He hitched up his nightshirt even higher, gave a hop, snatched the maid's hands in his own, and joined in her crazy dance up and down the barcounter, bellowing: "Six and four are ten: Add it up again!" ■ (From *March Has Horse's Ears and Other Stories* by Robert Nye. Illustrated by Dorothy Maas.)

OAKES, Vanya 1909-

PERSONAL: Given name originally Virginia; born September 13, 1909, in Nutley, N.J.; daughter of Herbert Henry (a banker) and Emma (Armstrong) Oakes. *Education:* University of California, Berkeley, B.A., 1932; University of Southern California, M.L.S., 1959. *Home:* 1153 North Vista, Los Angeles, Calif. 90046. *Office:* Hollywood Regional Library of Los Angeles Public Library, 1623 North Ivar, Los Angeles, Calif. 90028.

CAREER: Free-lance writer in China and Southeast Asia for magazines and newspapers, 1932-41; public lecturer, 1941-44; Los Angeles City College, Los Angeles, Calif., instructor in journalism and world affairs, 1945-59; Los Angeles (Calif.) Public Library, reference and young adult librarian, 1959—. *Member:* American Library Association, California Library Association, California Council on Children's Literature, Los Angeles United Nations Association, Common Cause, Beta Phi Mu.

WRITINGS—Juvenile fiction, except as noted: *White Man's Folly* (adult nonfiction), Houghton, 1943; *The Bamboo Gate* (short stories), Macmillan, 1946; *By Sun and Star,* Macmillan, 1948; *Footprints of the Dragon,* Winston, 1949; *Willy Wong, American,* Messner, 1951; *Desert Harvest,* Winston, 1953; *Roy Sato,* Messner, 1955; *Hawaiian Treasure,* Messner, 1957; *Island of Flame,* John Day, 1960; *Challenging Careers in the Library World* (young adult nonfiction), Messner, 1970.

WORK IN PROGRESS: An adult novel, *Bitter Dragon,* planned as the first book of a trilogy.

SIDELIGHTS: "Since the days of the clipper ships my family had been involved with the Far East, so when I graduated from college into a no-job depression it did not seem an outrageous gamble to take a graduation check and hop a freighter. I landed in Shanghai with $100 and no return ticket. My greatest assets were letters of introduction to several Chinese officials.

"One of my first jobs was teaching English and U.S. history to the grandchildren of Sun Yat-sen. Their father taught me far more than I taught them; he became, in effect, my tutor in Chinese history and customs, in the social and political problems of more recent times. One day he announced that it was time for me to become a journalist, and that he had made arrangements for me to work for one of the English language newspapers.

VANYA OAKES

175

Something about the Author

It was a scene of which he never tired; the sturdy outlines of the bay bridges, and the faraway mountain with its halo of early morning fog, so like the paintings of mountains and mist they had in the shop. ■ (From *Willy Wong: American* by Vanya Oakes. Illustrated by Weda Yap.)

"So, to my considerable bewilderment, I became a journalist. In the years that followed I covered the opening stages of the Sino-Japanese conflict in Shanghai. Later, I joined the Chinese on the long trek to the West; and from this experience came *By Sun and Star,* a story about the students who moved their schools away from occupied territory. A trip over the still unfinished Burma Road was to contribute, many years later, scenes for *Footprints of the Dragon,* a novel about the Chinese laborers who built the Southern Pacific railroad.

"The last two years were spent roaming, and reporting, South East Asia. *White Man's Folly* is a journalistic account (adult) of all the years in the Far East. Returning to America shortly before Pearl Harbor, I embarked on a cross-country lecture tour. By this time I knew Asia far better than my own country and the several years I spent crisscrossing the land afforded a rare, and much-needed, opportunity to get acquainted with most of the states. An experience that helped immeasurably when it came to writing about Asians in the United States: *Willy Wong* and *Footprints of the Dragon* (Chinese), *Roy Sato* and *Desert Harvest* (Japanese).

"At the end of World War II, I was asked to teach journalism and world affairs in the evening division of Los Angeles City College. For several years I taught part time and wrote part time, but it became increasingly obvious that I should get a master's degree and, in middle age, settle down. But a degree in what? Teaching at the junior college level was stimulating, but so too were libraries and research. It was a difficult decision to make, but I finally opted for libraries—a decision I have never regretted and which led, eventually, to *Challenging Careers in the Library World.*

"For several years I worked full time, first in the social science department of the Central Library and then at the Hollywood branch. Now I am back to being a part time librarian and a part time writer—an ideal situation. I am also back to jaunting around the world, on what might be termed library-oriented trips; in 1970 the U.S.S.R. and Eastern Europe, and in 1975, back to Asia."

FOR MORE INFORMATION SEE: Wilson Library Bulletin, June, 1972.

O'LEARY, Brian (Todd) 1940-

PERSONAL: Born January 27, 1940, in Boston, Mass.; son of Frederick A. and Mary Mabel (Todd) O'Leary; married Joyce Whitehead, June 20, 1964; children: Brian Todd, Jr., Erin. *Education:* Williams College, B.A., 1961; Georgetown University, M.A., 1964; University of California, Berkeley, Ph.D., 1967. *Home:* 1394 South East St., Amherst, Mass. 01002. *Office:* Hampshire College, Amherst, Mass. 01002.

BRIAN O'LEARY

Something about the Author

CAREER: National Aeronautics and Space Administration, Goddard Space Flight Center, Greenbelt, Md., physicist in Aeronomy and Meteorology Division, 1961-62; high school mathematics teacher in Washington, D.C., 1964; National Aeronautics and Space Administration, Manned Spacecraft Center, Houston, Tex., scientist-astronaut, 1967-68 (on leave from University of Texas, Austin, where he held appointment as assistant professor of astronomy, 1967-68); Cornell University, Ithaca, N.Y., research associate astronomer, Center for Radiophysics and Space Research, 1968-69, assistant professor of astronomy and space sciences, 1969-71; San Francisco State College, San Francisco, Calif., associate professor of astronomy and interdisciplinary sciences, 1971-72; Hampshire College, Amherst, Mass., assistant professor of astronomy and science policy assessment at the college and in five-college astronomy department (the other colleges are Amherst, Smith, Mount Holyoke, and University of Massachusetts), 1972—. University of California, Berkeley, visiting associate professor, School of Law, 1971-72. Principal investigator on Imaging Science Team, 1973 Mariner Venus-Mercury Flyby, 1969-74, deputy team leader, 1971.

MEMBER: International Astronomical Union, American Astronomical Society, American Geophysical Union (secretary of planetology section, 1970-74), American Association for the Advancement of Science (fellow), American Association of University Professors, Western Spectroscopy Association, Astronomical Society of the Pacific. *Awards, honors:* Research grants as principal investigator of Mariner Venus-Mercury Flyby, of observations of Mars, Venus, and the Galilean Satellites of Jupiter, 1971-72, and of other astronomical observations; *The Making of an Ex-Astronaut* was selected by the American Library Association as the best young adult book of 1970.

WRITINGS: *The Making of an Ex-Astronaut* (ALA Notable Book), Houghton, 1970. Contributor of more than thirty articles to *Science, Icarus, Nature,* and other scientific journals and to *New York Times.*

SIDELIGHTS: "I resigned as an astronaut in NASA's manned space program because of overemphasis on test pilots and transportation systems rather than science. . . . The proposed space shuttle might become the nation's costliest boondoggle of all time—extremely wasteful, costing tens of billions of dollars. I have testified before U.S. Senate committees about this issue."

The Making of an Ex-Astronaut was published in London and Paris, in a paperback edition, and is being readied for an Italian edition.

HOBBIES AND OTHER INTERESTS: Hiking, tennis, skiing, and jazz piano.

FOR MORE INFORMATION SEE: *Nation,* May 4, 1970; *New Yorker,* May 30, 1970.

OLSEN, Ib Spang 1921-
(Padre Detine, a joint pseudonym)

PERSONAL: Born June 11, 1921, in Denmark; son of Ole Christian (a gardener) and Soffu (Nielsen) Olsen; married

Grete Geisler, May 3, 1947 (divorced, 1960); married Nulle Oeigaard (an artist), September 8, 1962; children: (first marriage) Tune, Martin, Lasse, Tine (daughter). *Education:* Blaagaards Seminarium, teacher training, 1939-43; Royal Danish Academy of Art, study of graphic art, 1945-49. *Politics:* Democratic Socialist. *Religion:* None. *Home:* Aldershvilevej 193, Bagsvaerd 2880, Denmark. *Agent:* International Children's Book Service, Kildeskovsvej 21, Gentofte 2820, Denmark.

CAREER: Began illustrating for Sunday magazine supplements of Danish newspapers, 1942; schoolteacher in Denmark, 1952-60; full-time illustrator and writer, 1960—. In addition to book illustrating he has done book covers, murals for schools, posters, and ceramic pieces. Began work in Danish television, 1964 and has done numerous programs for young people.

AWARDS, HONORS: Danish Ministry of Culture Award for best illustrated children's book of the year for *Drengen i maanen,* 1962, *Regnen* and *Blaesten,* 1963, *Boernerim,* 1964, and *Mosekonens bryg,* 1966; Danish Society of Bookcraft honor list of year's outstanding books included *Kiosken paa Torvet,* 1964, *Lars Peters cykel,* 1968, *Hokus Pokus og andre boernerim,* 1969, and *Roegen,* 1971; Hendrixen Medal for outstanding bookcraft for *Halfdans abc,* 1967; runner-up for Hans Christian Andersen Medal of International Board on Books for Young People, 1968, and 1970, and winner, 1972; Storm Petersen Legatet for whole

IB SPANG OLSEN

"It would be just like him to go into a shop like this one, full of strange things. He'd look at everything . . . and not buy anything . . . It's embarrassing to be the sister of a boy like that." ■ (From *Cat Alley* by Ib Spang Olsen. Illustrated by the author.)

Something about the Author

body of work, 1971; other awards at Bratislava Biennial, from Organization for Friends of Books, 1966, and from Association of Authors of Juvenile Literature in Finland, 1971.

WRITINGS—Self-illustrated children's books: *Det lille lokomotiv* (title means "The Little Locomotive"), Gad, 1963; *Mosekonens bryg,* Kunst & Kultur, 1957, translation by Virginia Allen Jensen published as *The Marsh Crone's Brew,* Abingdon, 1960; *Boernene paa vejen,* Gjellerup, 1958; *Bedstemors vaegtaeppe,* Kunst & Kultur, 1958; *Drengen i maanen,* Gyldendal, 1962, translation by Virginia Allen Jensen published as *The Boy in the Moon,* Abingdon, 1963; *Regnen* (title means "Rain"), Gyldendal, 1963; *Blaesten* (title means "Wind"), Gyldendal, 1963; *Kiosken paa torvet* (title means "The Kiosk on the Square"), Gyldendal, 1964; *Kattehuset,* Gyldendal, 1968, translation by Virginia Allen Jensen published as *Cat Alley,* Coward, 1971; *Marie-hoenen,* Gyldendal, 1969; *Hvordan vi fik vores naboer,* Gyldendal, 1969; *Roegen,* Gyldendal, 1970, translation by Virginia Allen Jensen published as *Smoke,* Coward, 1972; *Pjer Brumme: Historier em en lille bjoern,* Gyldendal, 1971.

Other books: (With Erik E. Frederiksen, under joint pseudonym Padre Detine) *En Sydamerikaner i Nordsjaelland* (humorous tales), privately printed, 1960; (with Torben Brostroem) *Boern: Det Foerste aar i ord og tegninger,* Hasselbalch, 1962.

Illustrator: *Prinsessen paa glasbjerget,* circa, 1945; *Danish Folk Tales,* J.H. Schultz, 1946; *Danske folkeventyr,* Kunst & Kultur, 1950; Frank Jaeger, *Hverdaghistorier,* Wivel, 1951; Frank Jaeger, *Tune, det foerste aar,* Branner, 1951; *Fem smaa troldeboern,* Danske Forlag, 1952; *Nissen flytter med,* Gyldendal, 1955; *Abrikosia,* Hoest & Soen, 1958; Virginia Allen Jensen, *Lars-Peter's Birthday,* Abingdon, 1959; Jakob J.B. Nygaard, *Tobias tryllemus,* Martins Forlag, 1961, translation by Edith Joan McCormick published as *Tobias, the Magic Mouse,* Harcourt, 1968; Halfdan W. Rasmussen, *Boernerim,* Schoenberg, 1964; Hans Christian Andersen, *Digte,* edited by Bo Groenbech, Dansk Arnkrone, 1966; *Morten poulsens urtehave,* Hoest & Soen, 1967; Halfdan W. Rasmussen, *Halfdans abc,* Illustrationsforlaget, 1967; Halfdan W. Rasmussen, *Den Lille fraekke Frederik og andre boernerim,* Branner & Korch, 1971; *Molbohistorier,* Schoenberg, 1967; Virginia Allen Jensen, *Lars Peters cykel,* Gyldendal, 1968, translation by published as *Lars Peter's Bicycle,* Angus & Robertson, 1970; Lise Soerensen, *Da Lyset gik ud,* Gyldendal, 1968; Halfdan W. Rasmussen, *Hokus Pokus og andre boernerim,* Schoenberg, 1969, published as *Hocus Pocus,* Angus & Robertson, in press; Ole Restrup, *Odin og Tor,* Gad, 1969; *Folkene paa vejen,* Gyldendal, 1972.

Television films: "Hvad bliver det naeste?," "Taarnuret," "Vitaminerne," "Den store krage," "Nikolai," "Stregen der loeb henad," "Stregen der loeb opad."

WORK IN PROGRESS: Illustrations for a three-volume edition of Danish medieval folksongs.

SIDELIGHTS: "Almost all of my picture books have been produced as original lithography in photo offset. The original art work is done directly on film, one separate film for each of the four colours to be used in a single picture. In other words, for each illustration I draw four films, and the colours are then mixed for the first time by the printer cooperating closely with me. The finished books are the originals, they are not reproductions. In this way we can produce original lithography of quality at reasonable prices."

Olsen's books have been published in Finland, Greenland, Netherlands, Australia, Sweden, Germany, Norway, South Africa, and England, in addition to United States. He has given original illustrations for four of the books to the Kerlan Collection at University of Minnesota. Besides the Scandinavian languages, he is competent in English and German.

FOR MORE INFORMATION SEE: Illustrators of Children's Books: 1957-1966, Horn Book, 1968; *Horn Book,* April, 1972, August, 1972; *Bookbird,* Volume X, 1972; *Top of the News,* June, 1972, January, 1973; *Third Book of Junior Authors,* edited by de Montreville and Hill, H. W. Wilson, 1972.

PAULSON, Jack
See JACKSON, C. Paul

EDWIN A. PEEPLES

PEEPLES, Edwin A(ugustus, Jr.) 1915-

PERSONAL: Born March 2, 1915, in Atlanta, Ga.; son of Edwin Augustus (a cotton broker) and Robyn (Young) Peeples; married Malvine Ogle, March 17, 1945; children: Edwin A. III, Charles Lewis, Christopher Cabaniss. *Education:* Georgia Institute of Technology, B.S. in General Engineering, 1936. *Religion:* Episcopal. *Home:* Vixen Hill, R.D. 2, Phoenixville, Pa. 19460. *Agent:* Paul R. Reynolds, Inc., 599 Fifth Ave., New York, N.Y. 10017.

CAREER: James A. Greene, Advertising, Atlanta, Ga., copywriter, 1936-38; Sudite Chemical Manufacturing Corp., Atlanta, Ga., president and general manager, 1938-42; U.S. Army, Ordnance Department, Philadelphia, Pa., civilian associate engineer, 1942-45; *Fortune,* New York, N.Y., member of editorial staff, 1945; Franklin Institute Laboratories for Research and Development, Philadelphia, Pa., research editor, 1946-50; U.S. Army, Corps of Engineers, Philadelphia, Pa., chief procurement officer, 1950-55; Gray & Rogers, Inc. (advertising and public relations), Philadelphia, Pa., senior vice-president and director, 1955-72. McClain-Dorville Advertising, Philadelphia, Pa., technical copy consultant, 1948-50. Lecturer on writing and public relations at Charles Morris Price School, Drexel Library School, and Annenberg School of Communications of University of Pennsylvania. *Member:* Authors Guild of Authors League of America, Philadelphia Children's Reading Round Table (steering committee, 1965—), Tax-Action Committee of Chester County (secretary, 1972—), Phi Gamma Delta.

WRITINGS: Fantasy on an Empty Stage (one act play with music), Walter Baker, 1941; *Swing Low* (novel), Houghton, 1945; *A Professional Storywriter's Handbook,* Doubleday, 1960; *Blue Boy* (juvenile), Houghton, 1964; *A Hole in the Hill* (juvenile), Nelson, 1969. Writer of radio scripts for "Chamber Music Society of Lower Basin Street," 1942, for Jane Cowl's daily comment program, 1946. Contributor of short novel, other stories to *Cosmopolitan,* short stories and articles to magazines and trade journals, including *Good Housekeeping, Collier's, Esquire, Saturday Evening Post, Sports Illustrated, Family Circle, Writer's Digest, Writer, Mademoiselle.*

WORK IN PROGRESS: A novel; a third juvenile.

SIDELIGHTS: "I am a most improbable person to be writing children's novels. I am six-feet-eight-inches tall, weigh 235 pounds and resemble some stray giant or ogre more than I do somebody who would be concerned with animals and children. Just to increase this improbability, I am also a graduate engineer and, according to the Dean of Men at Georgia Tech, I am the only one of what must, by now, be nearly a half million graduates, who ever wrote any fiction.

"Even so, I always wanted to be a writer; I never wanted to be an engineer. I didn't, however, deliberately decide to write books for children. That came by accident.

"From 1944 until 1962, I wrote short stories for most of the major magazines and particularly for the *Saturday Evening Post.* During the fifties, we had a kitten trapped in a wall we were putting into our house on our farm, and we had a lot of trouble getting her out. This suggested a short book

about a cat trapped in a wall. In 1954, I outlined this book and sent the outline to my agent. He said: 'Forget it! You're doing fine with stories; I don't know anything about selling children's books, and, even if I did, I don't like this idea.'

"So I put it aside. But, in 1962, when the *Post* began to fold thus, eliminating the last big market for short stories, I thought I ought to find something else, more modest than a major novel, to take a swing at. So I took out the old outline of the cat in the wall and read it over.

"By now my two youngest sons were seven and eight, and they were doing a lot of interesting things which seemed to go along with the cat in the wall. So, with great misgivings, I began. When I finished a chapter, I would read it to the boys to see if they understood it and liked it. Well, as it was about them, they liked it fine. In two months, I finished the book *Blue Boy.*

"At once, teachers and everyone else said I would never sell it. It had too big a vocabulary; it even had a few foreign words and phrases; the parents drank cocktails, were strict (rather than permissive) people; one of the boys got a severe and unjustified whipping, and I had mixed animals, adults, and children together in the same book. No publisher would buy it and, if one did, no child would like it. All this turned out to be hogwash. Houghton published it, and it has done fine.

"Meanwhile, my two boys discovered a dug cave in a hill across the way. It was a very big cave. It might have been a slave cave; it might have been something from the Whiskey Rebellion. At any rate, it was a very good cave. So I thought up some characters for this cave and put the boys back to work as characters and came up with *A Hole in the Hill.*

"Again trouble. It seems that two thirds of the manuscripts offered as children's novels involve a cave. It also seems that publishers allow themselves only one cave novel per year. Sort of like cutting down on drinking. Well, the first twenty-three publishers had their annual cave novel, among them, Houghton. But Nelson didn't.

"This brings me to some personal philosophy about children's novels, which is in conflict with much prevailing opinion, but which I insist is true. A good children's novel is a good adult novel. A child's novel which bores an adult to death will bore a child to death. This tenet of mine is supported by most of the great children's novels which have endured.

"The adults in a children's novel must behave as rational, quixotic, contemporary adults. They must not be all sweetness and light. They must be as unreasonable and flawed as adults actually are. It is idle to think a child will believe in hokum-type adults. A child sees adults every day. He knows they aren't saints.

"A child's book must first and foremost be an interesting story. It may not be a polemic to promote sex understanding, racial integration, slum clearance, urban renewal, ecology or any other social or political fads. If some aspect of these things are natural parts of the story, they may appear to the extent that they are natural and reasonable. *But no more than that.*

"It is absurd to pander to a child as if he were a halfwit. He is not a halfwit, and he probably knows this better than most adults. Indeed, in a great many ways, a child is far brighter than an adult. He doesn't want to be spoonfed on vocabularies limited to 600 words. Give him the words—make him reach for them—he'll find out what they mean. Also, with every newspaper full of mayhem, riot, murder, war, hard sex and the rest of the cardinal sins—all specifically illustrated with close-up photos in full color—a childrens' author is a fool to try to pretend that death occurs only *in camera* behind the beferned walls of mortuary establishments and is only concerned with the very elderly. Children are touched by death, but are by no means so shocked by it as adults are. Children, not being able to imagine themselves dying, are not morbid about it, unless an author presents it morbidly. Instead, many children are bloodthirsty little beasts and revel in carnage.

"Very well, you may say. If I know all of that, why am I not a foremost author of children's novels. All I can say is, I try. And one day I may be, if I can find a way to bridge the gap from me to the children. A child can scarcely enjoy something, if he can't get his hands on it.

"And today, far too many of the books children do get their hands on are purveyed to them by publishers, parents, teachers, bookstores, libraries and a vast number of other institutions whose concern is what will do the child good or influence his thinking and not what the child may like."

HOBBIES AND OTHER INTERESTS: Managing a sixty-five acre farm he owns; gardening, household repairs and painting, philately, numismatics, reading, playing piano and singing, and dramatic readings.

LILA PERL

PERL, Lila

PERSONAL: Born in New York, N.Y.; daughter of Oscar and Fay (Rosenthal) Perl; married Charles Yerkow (a writer). *Education:* Brooklyn College, B.A.; further study at Teachers College, Columbia University and New York University. *Residence:* Beechhurst, N.Y.

AWARDS, HONORS: American Institute of Graphic Arts award for *Rice, Spice and Bitter Oranges,* 1967.

WRITINGS: What Cooks in Suburbia, Dutton, 1961; *The Delights of Apple Cookery,* Coward, 1963; *The House You Want: How to Find It, How to Buy It,* McKay, 1965; *Red-Flannel Hash and Shoo-Fly Pie: American Regional Foods and Festivals* (ALA Notable Book), World Publishing, 1965; *Rice, Spice and Bitter Oranges: Mediterranean Foods and Festivals,* World Publishing, 1967; *Foods and Festivals of the Danube Lands: Germany, Austria, Czechoslovakia, Hungary, Yugoslavia, Bulgaria, Romania, Russia,* World Publishing, 1969; *No Tears for Rainey* (juvenile), Lippincott, 1969; *Yugoslavia, Romania, Bulgaria: New Era in the Balkans,* Nelson, 1970; *The Finishing Touch: A Book of Desserts,* New American Library, 1970; *Living in Naples,* Nelson, 1970; *Living in Lisbon,* Nelson, 1971; *Me and Fat Glenda* (juvenile; Junior Literary Guild selection), Seabury, 1972; *Ethiopia: Land of the Lion,* Morrow, 1972; *East Africa: Kenya, Tanzania, Uganda,* Morrow, 1973; *The Hamburger Book: All About Hamburgers and Hamburger Cookery,* Seabury, 1973; *That Crazy April* (juvenile), Seabury, 1974.

SIDELIGHTS: Raised in Brooklyn, Ms. Perl had a perfectly ordinary childhood. "I can't honestly praise it or blame it for anything I may be doing today. Oh, I suppose there were 'influences.' I read a lot. Every time I was told to 'go outside and play,' I went off somewhere with a book. During my adolescent years I never thought of being a writer. The idea would have seemed pretentious to me. I didn't know very much, hadn't been anywhere or done anything exciting, and—worse than that—had no perspective on anything."

FOR MORE INFORMATION SEE: Junior Literary Guild Catalogue, March, 1972.

PIENKOWSKI, Jan 1936-

PERSONAL: Born August 8, 1936, in Warsaw, Poland; son of Jerzy Dominik and Wanda (Garlicka) Pienkowski. *Education:* King's College, Cambridge, B.A. (second class honors), 1957, M.A., 1961. *Politics:* None. *Religion:* Roman Catholic. *Home:* 45 Lonsdale Rd., London S.W. 13, England. *Office:* Gallery Five Ltd., 14 Ogle St., London W.1, England.

CAREER: Gallery Five Ltd. (publishers of greeting cards, posters, and printed paper goods), London, England, founder-director, 1961—; graphic designer and illustrator. *Awards, honors:* Kate Greenaway Medal of Library Association (England), 1971, for most distinguished work in illustration, for *The Kingdom Under the Sea.*

ILLUSTRATOR: J.G. Townsend, *Annie, Bridget and Charlie,* Pantheon, 1967; Joan Aiken, *Necklace of Raindrops,* J. Cape, 1968, Doubleday, 1969; Edith Brill, *The*

■ (From *The Kingdom under the Sea* by Joan Aiken. Illustrated by Jan Pienkowski.)

JAN PIENKOWSKI

Golden Bird, Watts, 1970; John Langstaff, compiler, *Jim Along Josie: A Collection of Folk Songs and Singing Games for Young Children,* Harcourt, 1970; Joan Aiken, *Kingdom under the Sea,* J. Cape, 1971; (with Helen Nicoll) *Meg's Eggs,* Heinemann, 1972, Pantheon, 1973; (with Nicoll) *Meg and Mog,* Heinemann, 1972; (with Nicoll) *Meg at Sea,* Heinemann, 1973; (with Nicoll) *Meg on the Moon,* Heinemann, 1973. Did titles and drawings for British Broadcasting Corp. television series, "Watch!," 1969-71.

WORK IN PROGRESS: Educational material for young children; stage designs; three illustrated story books.

SIDELIGHTS: "I enjoy working for and with young children, travel two to three months of the year, speak fluent Polish and French and reasonable Italian . . . , work for local amenity organisations, enjoy gardening. Principal ambition—to learn to do nothing."

PLOWMAN, Stephanie   1922-

PERSONAL: Born December 28, 1922; daughter of Franklyn James (a power station employee) and Violet (Grainger) Plowman; married Arthur Richard Hamilton-Dee (died, 1957). *Education:* University of London, B.A. (honors), 1944, further study, 1948-50, Ph.D. *Religion:* Russian Orthodox Church. *Home:* 2 The Knell, Mathon, Malvern, Worcestershire, England.

CAREER: Teacher and lecturer at various times in England, South Africa, and Ghana; Calouste Gulbenkian research fellow at Lucy Cavendish College, Cambridge University, Cambridge, England.

WRITINGS: Nelson, Methuen, 1955; *Sixteen Sail in Aboukir Bay,* Methuen, 1956; *To Spare the Conquered,* Methuen, 1960; *The Road to Sardis,* Bodley Head, 1965, Houghton, 1966; *Three Lives for the Czar,* Bodley Head, 1969, Houghton, 1970; *My Kingdom for a Grave,* Bodley Head, 1970, Houghton, 1971.

WORK IN PROGRESS: A non-fiction historical book on Anglo-Russian relations 1914-1918, researched under auspices of the Gulbenkian Foundation; a juvenile novel centered on the daughter of Marie Antoinette.

FOR MORE INFORMATION SEE: Horn Book, August, 1971.

Then in the silence, she heard once more the sound which had disturbed her, although it was far and faint, blown in gusts on the night wind; the clear, sweet sound of distant bells. ■ (From *The Queen's Blessing* by Madeliene Polland. Illustrated by Betty Fraser.)

POLLAND, Madeleine A(ngela Cahill) 1918-

PERSONAL: Born May 31, 1918, in Kinsale, County Cork, Ireland; daughter of Patrick Richard (a civil servant) and Christina (Culkin) Cahill; married Arthur Joseph Polland (an accountant), June 10, 1946; children: Charlotte Frances, Fergus Adrian. *Politics:* Conservative. *Religion:* Roman Catholic. *Home:* Newstead, 58 Aldenham Ave., Radlett, Hertfordshire, England.

CAREER: Public library, Letchworth, England, onetime assistant librarian. *Military service:* Women's Auxiliary Air Force, ground controlled interception division of radar, 1942-45. *Awards, honors:* Two books selected as *New York Herald Tribune* honor books, *Children of the Red King,* 1961, and *Beorn the Proud,* 1962.

WRITINGS: Children of the Red King, Constable, 1960, Holt, 1961; *The Town Across the Water,* Constable, 1961, Holt, 1963; *Beorn the Proud* (ALA Notable Book), Con-

stable, 1961, Holt, 1962; *Fingal's Quest,* Doubleday, 1961; *The White Twilight,* Constable, 1962, Holt, 1965; *Chuiraquimba and the Black Robes,* Doubleday, 1962; *The City of the Golden House,* Doubleday, 1963; *The Queen's Blessing,* Constable, 1964; *Flame Over Tara,* Doubleday, 1964; *Mission to Cathay,* Doubleday, 1965; *Queen Without Crown,* Constable, 1965, Holt, 1966; *Thicker Than Water* (adult fiction), Holt, 1966; *Deirdre,* Doubleday, 1967; *Mission to Cathay,* World's Work, 1967; *The Little Spot of Bother,* Hutchinson, 1967; *Minutes of a Murder,* Holt, 1967; *To Tell My People,* Holt, 1968; *Stranger in the Hills,* Doubleday, 1968; *Random Army,* Hutchinson, 1969; *Shattered Summer,* Doubleday, 1970; *Alhambra,* Doubleday, 1970; *To Kill a King,* Holt, 1971; *Daughter of the Sea,* Doubleday, 1973.

WORK IN PROGRESS: A new adult novel.

SIDELIGHTS: Ms. Polland was born in County Cork, Ireland, but she grew up in a small town in Hertfordshire, England, the youngest of five children in an "eventful yet uneventful rough and tumble family with all the freedom and pleasure of country life available."

MADELEINE A. POLLAND

Her early interest was a career as a painter, but family circumstances changed her decision. During World War II, she served with the W.A.A.F. in Ground Controlled Interception on the south coast of England. She married shortly after the war, but it was not until 1958 when her children had reached a manageable age, that a friend suggested she begin writing books.

"I have always been deeply aware of the reality of history, and conscious of the people who made it."

FOR MORE INFORMATION SEE: *Library Journal,* October 15, 1970; *Horn Book,* October, 1970, December, 1970, June, 1971; *Third Book of Junior Authors,* edited by de Montreville and Hill, H.W. Wilson, 1972; *Publishers Weekly,* February, 1973.

PORTAL, Colette 1936-

PERSONAL: Born March 9, 1936, in Paris, France; married Jean Michel Folon, March 20, 1961 (separated); children: Francois. *Education:* Studied four years at art school in Paris. *Politics:* "Love." *Religion:* "Love." *Home:* 65 bis Boulevard Brune, Paris 75014, France. *Agent:* John Locke, 15 East 76th St., New York, N.Y. 10021.

CAREER: Artist and illustrator.

WRITINGS: *Le Premier cri,* Quist, 1973, adaptation by Guy Daniels published as *The Beauty of Birth,* Knopf, 1971.

COLETTE PORTAL

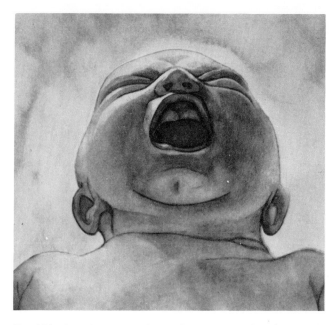

The child is born. It is gasping for air. The chest expands as the lungs fill with air for the first time. ■ (From *The Beauty of Birth* by Colette Portal. Illustrated by the author.)

Illustrator: *La Vie d'une reine,* Hatier, 1964, translation by Marcia Nardi published as *The Life of a Queen,* Braziller, 1964; A.M. Cocagnac, *La Creation du monde,* Editions du Cerf, 1967; Franklin Russell, *The Honeybees,* Knopf, 1967.

WORK IN PROGRESS: Ten books without text, with one theme, "all beginning."

SIDELIGHTS: Colette Portal works in crayon, pastels, water color, gouache, oils, the earth ("the marble that comes from the earth"). In illustrating, she doesn't believe that it is necessary to portray children *for* children. "They love life just as it is, the truth. With each making up their own characters, their dreams, their images.

"The act of drawing, painting, modeling, sculpturing, comes from the senses. They are not a cerebral act. Between the materials and the hand an exchange, a purely sensitive flow, sensual. There is a time for each technique. It is a matter of spirit. One has a crayon, a color, one has the earth."

RADFORD, Ruby L(orraine) 1891-1971 (Matilda Bailey, Marcia Ford)

PERSONAL: Born December 7, 1891, in Augusta, Ga.; daughter of Walter Scott and Elizabeth (Bailey) Radford. *Education:* Teacher's Training School, Augusta, Ga., student, 1911; Columbia University, special courses, 1921. *Religion:* Baptist. *Home and office:* 1422 Johns Rd., Augusta, Ga.

CAREER: Public elementary schools, Augusta, Ga., teacher, 1912-20; free-lance writer, primarily of fiction and biography for young readers, 1921-71. *Member:* Augusta Authors Club (co-founder, former president), Theosophical Society (president), Augusta Art Club, Georgia Writers Association (charter member). *Awards, honors:* Dixie

Council of Authors and Journalists, 1969, chosen "Author of the Year," 1970, second-runner-up in the juvenile division for *Inventor in Industry*.

WRITINGS: *Mystery of the White Knight*, 1927, *Mystery of Adventure Island*, 1928, *Mystery of Palmetto Lodge*, 1929, *Mystery of the Bradley Pearls*, 1930, *Marie of Old New Orleans*, 1931, *Mystery of the Nancy Lee*, 1932, *Mystery of Myrtle Grove*, 1933, *Mystery of Pelican Cove*, 1934, *Rose Colored Glasses*, Theosophical Press, 1939 (all published by Penn, except where noted).

Mystery of Magnolia Beach, McKay, 1942; *Army Nurse*, Whitman, 1944; *Canteen Girl*, Whitman, 1945; *Patty O'Neal on the Airways*, Whitman, 1946; *Secret of the Bay*, Howell, 1946, reissued by Lothrop; *Peggy Parker, Girl Inventor*, Whitman, 1946; *Silver Dunes*, Arcadia, 1946; *Sylvia Saunders and the Tangled Web*, Whitman, 1946; *Highway to Happiness*, Arcadia, 1947; *Sandra of the All Girl Orchestra*, Whitman, 1948; *The Haunted Lighthouse*, Whitman, 1948.

Tomorrow's Promises, Bouregy, 1956; *The Enchanted Cove*, Bouregy, 1957; *Connie Dale, 4-H Leader*, Bouregy, 1958; *Crime and Jury*, Bouregy, 1960; *Once Upon a Spring*, Bouregy, 1961; *Secret of Ocean House*, Abelard, 1961; *Angela's Treasure Chest*, Bouregy, 1962; *Secret of Peach Orchard Plantation*, Abelard, 1963; *Love Finds the Way*, Bouregy, 1964; *Juliette Gordon Low* (biography), Garrard, 1965; (with Charles Graves) *Oglethorpe*, Garrard, 1968; *Sequoya*, Putnam, 1969; *Inventors in Industry*, Messner, 1969; *Robert Fulton*, Putnam, 1970; *Many Paths to God*, Theosophical Publishing House, 1970; *Eisenhower*, Putnam, 1970; *Robert E. Lee*, Putnam, 1973; *Mary McLeod Bethune*, Putnam, in press.

Under pseudonym Matilda Bailey: *Fire Opal of Guatamala*, Whitman, 1948.

Under pseudonym Marcia Ford: *The Sycamores*, 1952, *Dixie Nurse*, 1953, *Peacehaven*, 1954, *Dixie Doctor*, 1955, *Nurse in the Pinelands*, 1955, *Kathy Phillips, Script Writer*, 1956, *Pamela Lee, Home Economist*, 1956, *Ann Fuller, Librarian*, 1957, *A Cruise for Judy*, 1957, *Scout Counselor*, 1958, *Island Nurse*, 1959, *Gail's Golden Filly*, 1960, *Linda's Champion Cocker*, 1961, *Prelude to Love*, Monarch, 1962, *Journey Into Danger*, 1962, *Flying Nurse*, 1971 (all published by Bouregy except where noted).

Contributor of children's short stories to collections and readers, including: *Girl Scout Short Stories*, Doubleday, 1925; *Open Road to Reading*, Ginn, 1928; *Treasure Trove*, John Winston, 1930; *Pioneer Trails*, John Winston, 1930; *Real Life Stories*, Macmillan, 1932; *Child Life Mystery Adventure Book*, Rand McNally, 1936; *Childcraft*, Volume V, Quarrie, 1937; *Childhood Readers*, Scribner, 1938; *Best Short Stories of 1929*, Row, Peterson & Co., 1940; *Echoes of the Southland*, Steck, 1941; *Invitation to Reading*, Harcourt, 1945; *Treasure Trails Parade*, Grosset, 1958.

Short stories and serials in *Child Life*, *Children's Activities*, *American Girl*, *Playmate*, and *Golden* Magazines. Script writer for twenty-six-episode syndicated radio serial.

SIDELIGHTS: Two of her stories have been made into television films and syndicated by Family Films, Hollywood. Two books are being made available to blind children, one in Braille, and one on tape.

HOBBIES AND OTHER INTERESTS: Painting, music.

(Died July 19, 1971)

Then the reaper was driven through into the other field. Before sundown, the reaper had cut six acres of grain. The watching crowd felt as if they had seen a miracle.
■ (From *Inventors in Industry* by Ruby L. Radford. Illustrated by Jim Fox.)

187

RAND, Paul 1914-

PERSONAL: Born August 15, 1914, in Brooklyn, N.Y.; children: Catherine. *Education:* Pratt Institute, graduate 1932; studied at Parsons School of Design, 1932, and Art Student's League of New York (with George Grosz), 1934. *Home and studio:* Goodhill Rd., Weston, Conn. 06880.

CAREER: Designer, typographer, painter, and teacher. Studio of George Switzer, New York, N.Y., apprentice, 1932-35; *Esquire,* art director in New York (N.Y.) office, 1936-41; Cooper Union, Laboratory School of Design, New York, N.Y., instructor in graphic design, 1938-42; Pratt Institute, Brooklyn, N.Y., instructor in postgraduate course, 1946; Yale University, School of Art and Architecture, New Haven, Conn., professor of graphic design, 1956-69. Tama University, Tokyo, Japan, honorary professor, 1958. Design consultant to IBM, Westinghouse, and other corporations. Fulbright scholarship jury, former member; Boston Museum of Fine Arts, visitor at Carnegie-Mellon University School of Art and Design.

MEMBER: Industrial Designers Society of America, Alliance Graphique International (Paris), Royal Society of Arts (London; Benjamin Franklin fellow). *Awards, honors:* American Institute of Graphic Arts Gold Medal, 1966; citation, Philadelphia Museum College of Art, 1964; New York Art Directors' "Hall of Fame," 1972; Honorary Royal Designer for Industry (London), 1973; other awards from New York Art Directors Club, *Financial World* for best design and typography of annual reports, Museum of Modern Art for fabrics design, *New York Times* jury for children's book illustrations, and Society of Typographic Arts for trademarks. Work exhibited in United States, Europe, Japan, and Russia.

PAUL RAND

Oh
I know
such
a
lot
of
things,
but
as
I
grow
I know
I'll
know
much
more.

■ (From *I Know a Lot of Things* by Ann and Paul Rand. Illustrated by Paul Rand.)

WRITINGS: *Thoughts on Design,* Wittenborn, 1946, Van Nostrand, 1970; *The Trademarks of Paul Rand,* Wittenborn, 1960; "Education of Vision" in *Design and Play Instinct,* Braziller, 1965. Contributor of articles on design, advertising, and typography to periodicals.

Illustrator: Ann Rand, *I Know a Lot of Things,* Harcourt, 1956; Ann Rand, *Sparkle and Spin,* Harcourt, 1957; Ann Rand, *Little 1,* Harcourt, 1962; Ann Rand, *Listen, Listen,* Harcourt, 1970.

FOR MORE INFORMATION SEE: Yusaku Kamekura, *Paul Rand: His Work from 1946-58,* Knopf, 1958; Diana Klemin, *The Art of Art for Children's Books,* Clarkson Potter, 1966.

RANNEY, Agnes V.   1916-
(Ruth Ellen Reeves)

PERSONAL: Born May 14, 1916, in Council, Idaho; daughter of Harry (a farmer) and Annie (Reeves) Johnson; married James L. Ranney (an electrician), June 20, 1942; children: Carol, Steve, David, Linda. *Education:* Linfield College, B.S., 1940. *Religion:* Protestant. *Home:* 4318 Southwest Lobelia, Portland, Ore. 97219.

CAREER: High school teacher, Stayton, Ore., 1940-41, Halsey, Ore., 1941-42; Camp Cooke, Calif., secretary, 1943-45; American United Life Insurance Co., Portland, Ore., cashier, 1951-54; high school teacher, Portland, Ore., 1964—.

WRITINGS: *Flash of Phantom Canyon,* Criterion, 1963; *The Valley I Remember,* privately printed, 1973. Contributor of over three hundred short stories and articles to magazines, including *Writer's Digest, Sunday Digest, Jack and Jill,* church youth periodicals.

SIDELIGHTS: Some articles translated and published in book form in Denmark and Sweden.

FOR MORE INFORMATION SEE: *Stayton Mail,* Stayton, Ore., April 11, 1963; *Oregon Journal,* Portland, Ore., April 19, 1963; *Oregonian,* April 28, 1963.

RAPPAPORT, Eva   1924-

PERSONAL: Born April 7, 1924; daughter of Paul (a physician) and Gisela (Jaeger) Stein; married Dov Rappaport (sociologist, director of a sanitarium), January 31, 1945; children: Elana, Leslie Joan, Jesse. *Education:* Cooper Union Art School, Diploma in Fine Arts, 1944; student at New School for Social Research, 1944-46, and Art Students' League, 1945-46; Jewish Theological Seminary of America, Teachers Certificate, 1953. *Politics:* Liberal. *Religion:* Non-affiliated. *Home:* The Kings Valley Animal Family, Route 2, Box 62, Monmouth, Ore. 97361. *Agent:* Barthold Fles, 507 Fifth Ave., New York, N.Y. 10017.

CAREER: Free-lance designer and artist, doing advertising and window display, interior design, graphics, sculpture in hardwoods, and color woodcuts, 1944-66; Forsyte Gallery, Los Angeles, Calif., director, 1948-51; Temple Beth-El, Great Neck, N.Y., art director, 1951-55; free-lance photog-

rapher and writer, 1967—. Exhibitor of slides and speaker on behalf of Guide Dogs for the Blind, Inc., San Rafael, Calif. *Member:* Artists Equity Association, Guide Dogs for the Blind, German Shepherd Dog Club of America, German Shepherd Dog Club of Oregon, American Association of Zoological Parks and Aquariums, American Dairy Goat Association, Collie Club of America, American Smooth Collie Association.

WRITINGS: *Banner, Forward! The Pictorial Biography of a Guide Dog,* Dutton, 1969. Contributor of photographs and articles to periodicals.

WORK IN PROGRESS: Research and photography at the foster care nursery of the Los Angeles Zoo for a fully-illustrated book, *Tender and Tame: Children of the Zoo,* for ages thirteen and up; a book tentatively titled *Living with Animals,* on life with otters, dogs, birds, and other farm animals in the author's collection.

SIDELIGHTS: Ms. Rappaport keeps detailed records and photographs of her own collection of animals, which includes farm animals, and conducts experiments in rearing the young of many "incompatible" species on a 170-acre ranch in Oregon, a setting conducive to peaceful co-existence. She is also concerned with wildlife preservation and aided by her daughter, Leslie, she breeds and exhibits German Shepherd dogs and Smooth Collies and trains these and other dogs for guarding, herding, and guiding of blind or otherwise disabled people.

"We now live in what is virtually a communal behavior laboratory: we observe the animals, and they observe us.

EVA RAPPAPORT

Here, the otters, dogs, cats, rabbits, raven, toucan, rats, chinchillas brought from the city are learning to live with the cows, horses, donkeys, sheep and goats native to the farm. Without fences and restrictions, startling behavior and unusual relationships have developed. The tropical otter turned to a hen for warmth during the cold months; he became attached to her and helped with the hatching of her eggs. The billy goat formed a strong bond with the new-born donkey. The toucan and the raven both fly free and return home for comfort and company. Contrary to expectations, the Golden Retriever protects the ducks and the German Shepherd dogs fondle the goats. The rabbit grazes with the mares and the cats play with a free-living young skunk.

"We have the space now to breed and raise animals, the opportunity to influence their attitudes through constant, personal contact with people and through deliberate exposure to one another. In the back pocket of my jeans I carry a small memo pad in which I record, in short-hand style, revealing incidents and significant behavior. As new patterns of behavior evolve, I shoot a few rolls of film. We compare notes and exchange ideas and experiences, check others' findings, look up references. At that point, I generally begin writing up the scribbled notes. Inevitably, too many characters are doing too many things: superfluous words, isolated episodes, weak descriptions get scissored, the remainder gets re-written, and only the strongest and most expressive paragraphs and photographs survive the process of final editing and selection."

REEVES, Ruth Ellen
See RANNEY, Agnes V.

RICH, Elaine Sommers 1926-

PERSONAL: Born February 8, 1926, in Plevna, Ind.; daughter of Monroe and Effie (Horner) Sommers; married Ronald L. Rich (now a chemistry professor), June 14, 1953; children: Jonathan, Andrew, Miriam, Mark. *Education:* Goshen College, B.A., 1947; Michigan State University, M.A. 1950. *Religion:* Mennonite. *Address:* International Christian University, House 348, 10-3 Osawa, 3-chome, Mitaka, Tokyo 181, Japan.

CAREER: Goshen College, Goshen, Ind., instructor in speech and English, 1947-49, 1950-53; Bethel College, North Newton, Kan., instructor in speech, 1966; Interna-

Banner had to be made aware of the fact that where a dog might manage to slip by, the man next to her often could not. The mastery of such space relationships is the most difficult lesson in the guide dog curriculum. ■ (From *Banner Forward!* by Eva Rappaport. Photos by the author.)

How could she have thought all babies looked alike? She would know this baby in a hundred babies. ■ (From *Hannah Elizabeth* by Elaine Sommers Rich. Illustrated by Paul Edward Kennedy.)

tional Christian University, Tokyo, Japan, lecturer in English, 1971—. *Member:* American Association of University Women (state secretary, Kansas, 1965-66), Women's International League for Peace and Freedom, Speech Communication Association, World Poetry Society.

WRITINGS: (Editor) *Breaking Bread Together,* Herald, 1958; *Hannah Elizabeth,* Harper, 1964; *Tomorrow, Tomorrow, Tomorrow,* Herald, 1966. Contributor to religious journals.

SIDELIGHTS: "C.S. Lewis once said that some of the books he wanted to read did not exist. Therefore he had to write them. I feel that way about my own writing.

"I believe that Jesus Christ is Lord of history. He works in a wonder-inspiring way. (The Pennsylvania Dutch have a saying, 'It wonders me.') Some tremendous things that happen, happen quietly without making big headlines in the world's newspapers. That's exciting to me. Inner growth is exciting. Genuine goodness is exciting, and I'd rather try to portray growth and goodness than to try to write about 'cops 'n robbers and military victories.' *Hannah Elizabeth* tells of how a girl came to glimpse deeply the meaning of her own faith. *Tomorrow, Tomorrow, Tomorrow* shows a tiny seed of love that grew into a tree, improved treatment of the mentally ill. *The Bridge Love Built* (not yet pub-

lished) tells about a boy who came to understand that he belonged to two cultures, not just one, as most people do.

"During the past nineteen years I have lived intimately with our own four children and their many friends, who have been in and out of our home in North Newton, Kansas, and on the campus of International Christian University in Tokyo. I have listened to incredible conversations. One of the most profound philosophical discussions I have ever heard was between two ten-year-old boys about whether and how the universe might end! I have great respect for the intellect and spiritual sensitivity of these children. I write for those of them, their parents and teachers, who wish to read what I have written."

RICHTER, Hans Peter 1925-

PERSONAL: Born April 28, 1925, in Cologne, Germany; son of Peter and Anna (Eckert) Richter; married Elfriede Feldmann, May 10, 1952; children: Ulrike, Claudia, Leonore, Gereon. *Education:* Studied at gymnasium in Cologne after completing military service, and at Universities of Cologne, Bonn, Mainz, and Tuebingen, 1949-54; University of Hannover, Doktor der Staatswissenschaften, 1968. *Home:* 58 Franz-Werfel-Strasse, Mainz 65, Germany.

CAREER: Independent socio-psychologist and writer, 1954—. *Military service:* German Army, 1942-45; became lieutenant; received Iron Cross. *Awards, honors: Friedrich* has received two awards in the United States, the 1971 Woodward School Book Award (shared with Frank Bonham's *Viva Chicano*) as the book best representing significant human relations for elementary or junior high school children, and the 1972 Mildred Batchelder Award of the American Library Association, given for the outstanding children's book originally published in a foreign language and subsequently published in America.

WRITINGS—For children, except as noted: *Karussel und Luftballon,* Obpacher, 1958, published as *Uncle and His Merry-Go-Round,* Bancroft & Co., 1959; *Das Pferd Max,* Obpacher, 1959, published as *Hengist the Horse,* Bancroft & Co., 1960; *Der heilige Martin,* Gruenewald, 1959; *Nikolaus der Gute* (St. Nicholas legends), Gruenewald, 1960; *Wie Heinz und Inge sich verlaufen haben,* Dessart, 1960; *Hans kauft ein,* Scholz, 1961; *Immer ist etwas los!,* Loewe, 1961; *Damals war es Friedrich,* Sebaldus, 1961, abridged edition edited by Ray Milne published in England as textbook under original German title, Oliver & Boyd, 1968, unabridged translation by Edite Kroll published in America as *Friedrich,* Holt, 1970; *Wir waren dabei,* Herder (Freiburg), 1962, revised edition, 1964, translation by Edite Kroll published as *I Was There,* Holt, 1972; *Das war eine Reise!,* Sebaldus, 1962; *Birgitta,* Gruenewald, 1963; *Peter,* Gruenewald, 1963; *Eine Reise um die Erde,* Ueberreuter, 1963; *Eine wahre Baerengeschichte,* Ueberreuter, 1964; *Nikolaus,* Gruenewald, 1965; *Jagd auf Gereon* (St. Gereon legends), Styria, 1967; *Die Zeit der jungen Soldaten,* Verlag Alsatia, 1967; *Ich war kein braves Kind,* Verlag Alsatia, 1967; *Der Hundemord,* Verlag Alsatia, 1968; *Katzen haben Vorfahrt,* Engelbert, 1972; *Kunibert im Schlafanzug,* Engelbert, 1973.

Editor—Collections of stories, except as noted: *Der jungen Leser wegen* (on children's literature), Schwann, 1965;

ELAINE SOMMERS RICH

HANS PETER RICHTER

Schriftsteller antworten jungen Menschen auf die Frage: Wozu leben wir? Verlag Alsatia, 1968; *Schriftsteller erzaehlen vor ihrer Mutter,* Verlag Alsatia, 1968; *Schriftsteller erzaehlen von der Gewalt,* Verlag Alsatia, 1970; *Harte Jugend,* Steyler, 1970; *Schriftsteller erzaehlen aus aller Welt,* Engelbert, 1973.

Scientific and technical publications include: *Hoerermeinungsforschung auf einem Dorf,* Archiv des Suedwestfunk, 1952; *Hausen vor der Hoehe: Eine Rundfunkuntersuchung,* two volumes, Archiv des Nordwestdeutschen Rundfunks, 1954; *Informationsbriefe fuer Fuehrungskraefte,* Industrie-Verlag, 1955; *12 Vorlesungen ueber Marktforschung und Werbung im Aussenhandel* (lectures), Akademie fuer Welthandel, 1957; *Geschichte und Quellensammlung zur Geschichte der Hoererforschung im deutschsprachigen raum,* two volumes, Archiv der Historischen Kommission des Deutschen Rundfunks, 1957; *Die Freizeit deines Kindes,* Verlag Oeffentliches Leben, 1957; *Einfuehrungen zu Fernsehspielen und Spielfilmen,* Archiv des Zweiten Deutschen Fernsehens, 1970.

His fiction has been included in a number of collections, and his articles published in professional journals.

WORK IN PROGRESS: Das Franzoesische Chanson.

SIDELIGHTS: Friedrich, a first-person documentary novel about a boy developing from childhood to maturity in the Germany of 1925-42, is the most widely known of Richter's books. There have been seven printings of the German edition, two editions in Spanish-Castilian in Spain, and translations in Danish, Swedish, Dutch, French, and Italian. Other of Richter's books also touch on the war years. They are "almost biographically stimulated," he says.

HOBBIES AND OTHER INTERESTS: French civilization, traveling in France.

FOR MORE INFORMATION SEE: Horn Book, April, 1971, October, 1971, August, 1972, December, 1972; *Top of the News,* June, 1972.

ROBERTS, Terence
See SANDERSON, Ivan T.

ROBINSON, Charles 1931-

PERSONAL: Born June 25, 1931, in Morristown, N.J.; son of Powell (an investment banker) and Ruth (Wyllis) Taylor; married Cynthia Margetts (a sixth-grade teacher), August 17, 1967; children: Mimi, Charles, Edward. *Education:* Milton Academy, student, 1945-49; Harvard University, A.B., 1953; University of Virginia, LL.B., 1958. *Home and studio:* Millbrook Rd., New Vernon, N.J. 07976.

CAREER: Fiduciary Trust Co. of New York, New York, N.Y., assistant securities analyst, 1954; McCarter & English (law firm), Newark, N.J., associate, 1958-60; Mutual Benefit Life Insurance Co., Newark, N.J., attorney, 1960-68; switched from corporation law to full-time illustrating, 1968. *Military service:* U.S. Army, Signal Corps, 1953-54. *Member:* New Jersey Watercolor Society. *Awards, honors:* Society of Illustrators Gold Medal for cover of *Audubon: The Man Who Painted Birds,* 1971; *The Dead Tree* was nominated for Caldecott Medal of American Library Association, 1972; *The Mountain of Truth* was an Honor Book in *Book World's* Children's Spring Book Festival, 1972.

WRITINGS—Self-illustrated: *Yuri and the Mooneygoats,* Simon & Schuster, 1969.

Illustrator: M. Caporale Schector and Harriet May Savitz, *The Moon Is Mine,* John Day, 1968; Gunilla B. Norris, *The Good Morrow,* Atheneum, 1969; Ruth Philpott Collins, *Mystery of the Giant Giraffe,* Walck, 1969; Betty Horvath, *Will the Real Tommy Wilson Please Stand Up?,* Watts, 1969; Anne Norris Baldwin, *The Sometimes Island,* Norton, 1969; Jean Bothwell, *The Mystery Tunnel,* Dial, 1969.

Jane Louise Curry, *Mindy's Mysterious Miniature,* Harcourt, 1970; Helen Chetin, *Tales of an African Drum,* Harcourt, 1970; Jane Louise Curry, *Daybreakers,* Harcourt, 1970; Barbara Corcoran, *The Long Journey,* Atheneum, 1970; Sonia Levitan, *Journey to America* (Junior Literary Guild selection), Atheneum, 1970; Nathan Kraveta and Muriel Farrell, *Is There a Lion in the House?,* Walck,

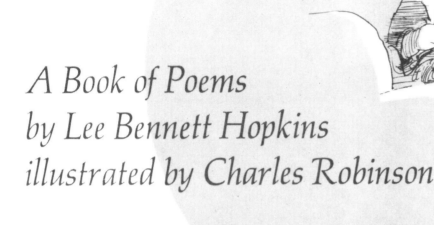

CHARLIE'S WORLD

A Book of Poems
by Lee Bennett Hopkins
illustrated by Charles Robinson

THE BOBBS-MERRILL COMPANY, INC.   **Indianapolis New York**

■ (From *Charlie's World* by Lee Bennett Hopkins. Illustrated by Charles Robinson.)

1970; Florence Parry Heide, *Giants Are Very Brave People,* Parents' Magazine Press, 1970; Norah Smaridge, *Audubon: The Man Who Painted Birds,* World Publishing, 1970; Mattie Lamb Curtis, *Blizzard,* Dutton, 1970; Bronson Potter, *Chibia, the Dhow Boy,* Atheneum, 1971; Gunilla B. Norris, *Green and Something Else,* Simon & Schuster, 1971; Mildred Wilds Willard, *The Luck of Harry Weaver,* Watts, 1971; Winston M. Estes, *Another Part of the House,* Reader's Digest Condensed Books, 1971; Leonore Klein, *Only One Ant,* Hastings House, 1971; Ruth Whitehead, *The Mother Tree,* Seabury, 1971; Arthur Durham Divine, under pseudonym David Divine, *The Stolen Seasons,* Crowell, 1971; Elizabeth Coatsworth, *The Snow Parlour,* Grosset, 1971; Marion Renick, *Take a Long Jump,* Scribner, 1971; Francis Kalnay, *It Happened in Chichipica,* Harcourt, 1971; Jane Louise Curry, *Over the Sea's Edge,* Harcourt, 1971; Adelaide Leitch, *The Blue Roan,* Walck, 1971; Anatolii Aleksin, *A Late Born Child,* World Publishing, 1971; Jack Finney, *Time and Again,* Reader's Digest Condensed Books, 1972; Dale Carlson, *The Mountain of Truth,* Atheneum, 1972; Babbis Friis, *Wanted! A Horse!,* Harcourt, 1972; Maggie Duff, *Jonny and His Drum,* Walck, 1972; Mary Francis Shura, *Topcat of Tam,* Holiday House, 1972; Alvin Tresselt, *The Dead Tree,* Parents' Magazine Press, 1972; Emmy West and Christine Govan, *Danger Downriver,* Viking, 1972; William Corbin, *The Pup With the Up and Down Tail,* Coward, 1972;

Mabel Esther Allen, *Island in a Green Sea,* Atheneum, 1972; Evelyn Sibley Lampman, *Go Up the Road,* Atheneum, 1972; Marden Dahlstedt, *The Terrible Wave* (Junior Literary Guild selection), Coward, 1972; Lee Bennett Hopkins, *Charlie's World,* Bobbs, 1972; Betty Dinneen, *A Lurk of Leopards,* Walck, 1972; Patricia McKillup, *The House on Parchment Street,* Atheneum, 1973; Miriam Young, *A Witches Garden,* Atheneum, 1973; Jean Robinson, *The Secret Life of T.K. Dearing,* Seabury, 1973; Marion Renick, *Five Points for Hockey,* Scribner, 1973; Doris Buchanan Smith, *A Taste of Blackberries,* Crowell, in press; Barbara Corcoran, *All the Summer Voices,* Atheneum, in press; Carol Beach York, *The Midnight Ghost,* Coward, in press.

SIDELIGHTS: "Until I made the switch in mid-career from law to illustrating, my major area of avocational interest was being a 'Sunday painter.' Now that I paint all week I find other pursuits for weekends, i.e., woodworking, gardening. Wish I had made this move fifteen years earlier. Enjoy working in a fairly realistic style—favor watercolors to oils, generally. I have plans for doing a far-out fanciful kind of book one of these days."

FOR MORE INFORMATION SEE: Junior Literary Guild Catalogue, September, 1972, March, 1973.

She landed on her back with the berries clutched in her hands and bumped her head against the trunk of the tree. ■ (From *The December Dog* by Jan M. Robinson. Illustrated by Joan Sandin.)

ROBINSON, Jan M. 1933-
(Flash Flood)

PERSONAL: Born October 30, 1933; daughter of Joseph Edward and Janice (Howes) Lanoue; married Peter D. Robinson, Jr. (a salesman and insurance investigator), November 22, 1952; children: Vickie, Peter, David, Gail. *Education:* Attended business college, one year. *Politics:* Independent ("with Republican tendencies"). *Religion:* Protestant. *Home:* Pumpkin Hollow, Conway, Mass. 01341. *Agent:* Curtis Brown Ltd., 60 East 56th St., New York, N.Y. 10022.

CAREER: Copywriter, typist, and kindergarten teacher in earlier years; teacher of arts and crafts in grammar school enrichment program, Conway, Mass., 1970-71. *Member:* National Wildlife Federation, National Audubon Society.

WRITINGS: The December Dog, Lippincott, 1969. Contributor to *Jack and Jill* and local newspaper.

WORK IN PROGRESS: Two books for children, *Pigpen Poet* and *Mystery Beyond the Hedge.*

SIDELIGHTS: "I have four teenage children, a ten-room house to care for, over forty animals to tend to, and that takes care of most of my time. We also take a Fresh Air child each summer. In the leftover moments when I'm not writing I am active in conservation of wildlife, ecology and the out of doors in general.

"I would like to write something meaningful for children about wildlife conservation. I see a lot of willfull 'destruction of birds and small animals by children. They need to be better educated there.

"I play classical guitar much to the disgust of my children; speak passable French; believe in God and the balance of nature; love living in a rural area and feel close to its growth problems; and am terrified by urban problems. Four of my idols are Thoreau, Jack London, Thornton Burgess, and Paul Newman."

ROLL, Winifred 1909-

PERSONAL: Born March 9, 1909, in Harwood, Lancashire, England; daughter of Elliott and Sophia (Hepworth) Taylor; married Sir Eric Roll (a director of Bank of England), September 22, 1934; children: Joanna (Mrs. Stuart Holland), Elizabeth (Mrs. Robin Greenhill). *Education:* University of Hull, B.A. (honors in English), 1932, Cambridge Diploma in Education, 1933. *Religion:* Church of England. *Home:* D2 Albany, Piccadilly, London W1V 9RG, England.

CAREER: Taught English and Latin in earlier years. Worked in Ministry of Economic Welfare in Washington during World War II.

WRITINGS: Pomegranate and the Rose: The Story of Katherine of Aragon, Prentice-Hall, 1970.

WINIFRED ROLL

194

WORK IN PROGRESS: A book on Mary Tudor.

SIDELIGHTS: "Always interested in art, music, theatre; more recently in English history. This has led to a study of art and topography in relation to the Tudor period in England."

Lady Roll resided for several years in Washington, D.C., and Paris, and has traveled extensively in the United States as well as in Europe.

ROSENBAUM, Maurice 1907-

PERSONAL: Born July 28, 1907, in Leeds, Yorkshire, England; son of Mark Bernard and Amelia (Taylor) Rosenbaum; married Eve Adelaide De Jongh, June 30, 1939; children: Sarah Lucy. *Education:* Attended University of Leeds and Sorbonne, University of Paris, awarded B.A. (with honors in modern languages), 1930. *Politics:* Socialist. *Religion:* "Jewish by birth but no religion practised." *Home:* Flat 2, 74 Elm Park Gardens, London S.W. 10, England.

CAREER—All London, England: Free-lance journalist with occasional temporary staff jobs, 1935-38; Associated Press, desk editor, British section, 1939-45; *Daily Herald,* foreign sub-editor, 1945-50; *News Chronicle,* foreign sub-editor, 1950-52; *Daily Telegraph,* foreign news sub-editor, features sub-editor, and deputy features editor, 1952—.

WRITINGS: (Translator) Klaus Mehnert, *Anatomy of Soviet Man,* Weidenfeld & Nicolson, 1962; *London* (Junior Literary Guild selection), Rand, 1963. Contributor to a wide range of periodicals, including *Lettres Nouvelles* (Paris).

WORK IN PROGRESS: Book on the Anglo-American folk-song revival of the Sixties, with all its implications for popular music, provisionally entitled *Blowing in the Wind.*

SIDELIGHTS: Rosenbaum is fluent in French, has good working knowledge of German, Spanish, and Italian. He considers the life of greatest fulfillment is that of the creative artist—"he [being] the only human being I envy."

ROSENBURG, John M. 1918-

PERSONAL: Born June 2, 1918, in Mountainhome, Pa.; son of Henry H. and Naomie (Frezatt) Rosenburg; married Ursula Donohue, October 8, 1939; children: Gerorda, Hennetta, John J. *Education:* Ithaca College, B.S., 1944. *Home:* 1 Warrior Rd., Malvern, Pa. 19355. *Agent:* Kahn, Lefflander & Rhodes. *Office:* Bell Telephone Co. of Pennsylvania, 1 Pkwy., Philadelphia, Pa.

CAREER: United Press International, New York, N.Y., correspondent, 1945-52; free-lance writer, 1952—; currently doing public relations work for Bell Telephone Co. of Pennsylvania, Philadelphia. *Member:* Overseas Press Club, Dramatists Guild.

WRITINGS: Baseball for Boys, Oceana, 1960; *The Story of Baseball,* Random House, 1962, annual updated editions, 1963—; *Basic Basketball,* Oceana, 1962. Writer of

JOHN M. ROSENBURG

television and radio scripts. Contributor of articles on sports and variety of other subjects to *This Week, Collier's, Pic,* and other magazines and newspaper syndicates.

WORK IN PROGRESS: A juvenile book on George Washington—"the man, not the myth"; four plays.

HOBBIES AND OTHER INTERESTS: Fishing, hunting, bird dogs, horses, and outdoor life in general.

SANDERSON, Ivan T(erence) 1911-1973
(Terence Roberts)

PERSONAL: Born January 30, 1911, in Edinburgh, Scotland; son of Arthur Buchanan (a whiskey manufacturer who founded the first game reserve in Kenya, East Africa, and who was killed there by a rhinoceros while making a film with Martin Johnson in 1924) and Stella W. W. (Robertson) Sanderson; married Alma Viola Guillaume de Veil, February 18, 1934 (died, 1972); married Marion L. Fawcett (an editor and writer), May 4, 1972. *Education:* Educated at Eton College, 1924-27, Trinity College, Cambridge, 1930-32, and Cambridge University and University of London, 1933-34; Cambridge University, M.A. (honors), 1969. *Home and office:* R.D. 1, Ivan Rd., Columbia, N.J. 07832. *Agent:* Paul R. Reynolds, Inc., 599 Fifth Ave., New York, N.Y. 10017.

CAREER: Began animal collecting on his own, 1924, and made a solo trip around the world, 1927-29, collecting for British Museum; leader of Percy Sladen Expedition to Cameroon, West Africa, on behalf of British Museum, Royal Society of London, and other institutions, 1932-33; did research at University of London, 1933-35; collected animals in the West Indies (where he also investigated human rabies carried by bats), 1936-37; led scientific expedition to Dutch Guiana, 1938; made an expedition to Jamaica, British Honduras, and Mexico, 1939-40, doing specialized collecting in Mexico for British Museum and Chicago Museum of Natural History; information and overseas press analyst for British Government in New York, 1945-47; took up residence in United States, 1947, and engaged in television and radio work, lecturing, and writing, 1947-58; retired from regular television programs but continued research and writing, 1958-60; senior trade editor and special science editor, Chilton Book Co., Philadelphia, 1961-65; free-lance writer and editor, 1965-67; science editor of *Argosy*, 1968-70; trustee and administrative director of Society for the Investigation of the Unexplained (non-profit scientific corporation), Columbia, N.J., which he organized in 1965. Did his first radio show for British Broadcasting Corp., 1930; began radio and television series in natural science field for National Broadcasting Co. and local stations, 1948; inaugurated first commercial color television program in history for Columbia Broadcasting System, 1950; featured (with live animals) in weekly spot on "Garry Moore Show," 1951-58. Importer of rare animals, 1950-58, exhibiting them at his private roadside zoo in New Jersey, at sports shows, and on television programs. *Military service:* British Naval Intelligence, 1940-45; became commander. *Member:* Royal Geographical Society (fellow), Zoological Society (London; fellow), Linnean Society (London; fellow).

WRITINGS—Many self-illustrated: *Animal Treasure* (Book-of-the-Month Club selection), Viking, 1937; *Caribbean Treasure*, Viking, 1939.

Animals Nobody Knows (juvenile), Viking, 1940; *Living Treasure*, Viking, 1941; (under pseudonym Terence Roberts) *Mystery Schooner* (Junior Literary Guild selection), Viking, 1941; (editor) *Animal Tales* (anthology), Knopf, 1946.

How to Know the North American Mammals, Little, Brown, 1951; *The Silver Mink* (fiction), 1952; *John and Juan in the Jungle* (juvenile fiction), Dodd, 1953; *Living Mammals of the World,* Hanover House, 1955; (under pseudonym Terence Roberts) *The Status Quo* (fiction), Merlin Press, 1956; *Follow the Whale*, Little, Brown, 1956; *The Monkey Kingdom,* Hanover House, 1957.

Abominable Snowmen: Legend Come to Life, Chilton, 1961, abridged edition, Pyramid Publications, 1968; *The Continent We Live On,* Random House, 1961 (published in England as *The Natural Wonders of North America,* Hamish Hamilton, 1962); *The Dynasty of Abu,* Knopf, 1962; *Ivan Sanderson's Book of Great Jungles,* Messner, 1965; (with editors of *Country Beautiful*) *This Treasured Land,* Putnam, 1966; *Uninvited Visitors: A Biologist Looks at UFO's,* Cowles, 1967; *"Things,"* Pyramid Publications, 1967; *More "Things,"* Pyramid Publications, 1969.

Invisible Residents: A Disquisition upon Certain Matters

Maritime, and the Possibility of Intelligent Life Under the Waters of This Earth, World Publishing, 1970; *Investigating the Unexplained,* Prentice-Hall, 1972; *Green Silence,* McKay, in press.

Contributor to magazines, 1938—, with articles in *Saturday Evening Post, Reader's Digest, American Heritage, Horizon, True, Sports Afield, Saga,* and other periodicals. Feature writer and special reporter for North American Newspaper Alliance.

SIDELIGHTS: Sanderson's bent for travel began as a small child when he accompanied his parents on trips in Europe, the Mediterranean, and North Atlantic. On his last major trek, in 1959, he made a 60,000-mile trip around the North American Continent, examining its phytogeography and basic biotic ecology. Although he continued to import animals for a few years afterwards, his unique collection of wild animals was destroyed by fire in 1953, and a new collection, plus the zoo itself, by floods in 1955.

FOR MORE INFORMATION SEE: Publishers Weekly, April 23, 1973.

(Died February 19, 1973)

VICTOR B. SCHEFFER

196

As in all animals on earth, the body of the whale contains a biological clock, and when the alarm sounds the body tissues respond in predictable ways and their body motions follow suit. ■ (From *Little Calf* by Victor B. Scheffer. Illustrated by Leonard Everett Fisher.)

SCHEFFER, Victor B(lanchard)   1906-

PERSONAL: Born November 27, 1906, in Manhattan, Kan.; son of Theophilus (a biologist) and Celia E. (Blanchard) Scheffer; married Beth MacInnes, October 12, 1935; children: Brian M., Susan E. (Mrs. Robert Irvine), Ann B. (Mrs. William Carlstrom). *Education:* University of Washington, Seattle, B.S., 1930, M.S., 1932, Ph.D., 1936. *Home:* 14806 Southeast 54th St., Bellevue, Wash. 98006.

CAREER: U.S. Fish and Wildlife Service, biologist in Olympia and Seattle, Wash., and Fort Collins, Colo., 1937-69; now retired. University of Washington, Seattle, lecturer, 1966, 1967, 1968, 1971, 1972. *Member:* American Society of Mammalogists, Wildlife Society, Wilderness Society, Nature Conservancy, National Wildlife Foundation, National Audubon Society.

WRITINGS: Seals, Sea Lions, and Walruses, Stanford University Press, 1958; *The Year of the Whale,* Scribner, 1969; *The Year of the Seal,* Scribner, 1970; *The Little Calf,* Scribner, 1970; *The Seeing Eye* (ALA Notable Book), Scribner, 1971.

SIDELIGHTS: During the summers that Scheffer was a student at the University of Washington, he worked as a nature guide at Mount Rainier National Park. After gradua-

tion he joined the United States Fish and Wildlife Service as a biologist. He continued his affiliation with the Wildlife Service until 1969 when he retired to devote himself entirely to his writing. As a member of the Service, he traveled widely and conducted a number of studies. In the summers of 1937 and 1938, he made a wildlife inventory of the Aleutian Islands in Alaska. In the following year, he was sent to the Pribilof Islands to study the life processes of the Alaska fur seal. He was attached to the Rocky Mountain Forest and Range Experiment Station in Fort Collins, Colorado and in 1960 he visited Robben Island in Russia.

FOR MORE INFORMATION SEE: Time, August 15, 1969; *New Yorker,* September 20, 1969; *Horn Book,* August, 1971.

SEIDELMAN, James Edward   1926-

PERSONAL: Born December 7, 1926, in Kansas City, Mo.; son of Ira Clark and Maude Marie (Tilsley) Seidelman; married Shirley Chehey, April 17, 1948; children: Jane Allee, Janice Marie, Joel Craig, Jeffrey Scot. *Education:* Studied at University of Kansas and Colorado State College; Kansas City Art Institute, B.F.A., 1951. *Religion:* Episcopalian.

JAMES EDWARD SEIDELMAN

CAREER: William Rockhill Nelson Gallery of Art and Mary Atkins Museum of Fine Arts (more commonly known as Nelson-Atkins Gallery of Art), Kansas City, Mo., director of education, 1951-68, and director of the junior gallery and creative arts center established under his program for young people; Living Arts and Science Center, Lexington, Ky., director, 1968—. Missouri Council on the Arts, former member of education advisory committee. *Military service:* U.S. Naval Reserve, active duty, 1944-46. *Member:* American Association of Museums (education chairman, 1968-70), International Council of Museums (editorial secretary of U.S. national committee), National Art Education Association, National Society of Arts and Letters, Talent Education of Lexington, Ky., Blue Grass Trust for Historic Preservation (Lexington, Ky.). *Awards, honors:* Named outstanding young man of 1962 by Kansas City Junior Chamber of Commerce.

WRITINGS—"Creating" series, with Grace Mintoyne: *Creating with Clay,* 1967, *Creating with Paper,* 1967, *Creating with Paint,* 1967, *Creating Mosaics,* 1968, *Creating with Wood,* 1969, *Creating with Paper Mache,* 1970, *Shopping Cart Art,* 1970 (all published by Crowell-Collier).

Other children's books with Grace Mintoyne: *The Rub Book,* Crowell-Collier, 1968; *The 14th Dragon,* Harlin Quist Books, 1968. The same writing team is responsible for four gallery films, "Treasures of Time," distributed by International Film Co., Chicago, and a monthly column in *Wee Wisdom* (children's magazine published by Unity School of Christianity).

Sole writer of material for his children's program on KMBC-TV and KCMO-TV, Kansas City. Contributor to museum and art journals.

WORK IN PROGRESS: With Grace Mintoyne, *Gardens from Garbage,* for Harlin Quist Books.

FOR MORE INFORMATION SEE: "Books for Young Created Here," *Kansas City Star,* September 25, 1967.

SHURA, Mary Francis
See CRAIG, Mary Francis

SMARIDGE, Norah (Antoinette) 1903-

PERSONAL: Born March 30, 1903, in England; daughter of Henry and Heloise Smaridge. *Education:* University of London, B.A. (honors), 1923; further courses at Columbia University and Hunter College. *Politics:* Democrat. *Religion:* Catholic. *Home:* 11 Godfrey Rd., Upper Montclair, N.J. 07043.

CAREER: Former advertising writer for St. Anthony Guild Press, Paterson, N.J., for eleven years, and teacher at Marymount High School and Junior College, New York, N.Y. for ten years; professional writer. *Member:* Writers Guild, British Women's Club (Montclair, N.J.).

WRITINGS—Mostly for young people: *Ludi, the Little St. Bernard,* Bruce, 1956; *Nando of the Beach,* Bruce, 1958; *Sunday Best* (poems), Bruce, 1959; *Hands of Mercy: The Story of Sister-Nurses in the Civil War,* Benziger, 1960;

Bernard: A Patron Saint, Sheed, 1960; *Five Gifts from God* (poem), Bruce, 1961, published as *Your Five Gifts,* C. R. Gibson, 1969; *Looking at You,* Abingdon, 1962; *Saint Helena,* St. Anthony Guild Press, 1962; *Pen and Bayonet: The Story of Joyce Kilmer,* Hawthorn, 1962; *The Big Tidy-Up* (poems), Bruce, 1963; *Impatient Jonathan,* Abingdon, 1964; *The Light Within: The Story of Maria Montessori,* Hawthorn, 1965; *Peter's Tent,* Viking, 1965; *A Family Guide to Pets and Hobbies,* Abbey Press, 1965; *Graymoor's Treasury of Meatless Recipes,* Graymoor, 1965; *Watch Out!* Abingdon, 1965; *Master Mariner: The Adventurous Life of Joseph Conrad,* Hawthorn, 1966; *Feast Days and Fun Days,* Guild Press, 1966; *Famous British Women Novelists,* Dodd, 1967; *The Tallest Lady in the World: The Statue of Liberty,* Hawthorn, 1967; *What a Silly Thing to Do,* Abingdon, 1967; *Long Before Forty,* Hawthorn, 1968; *Teacher's Pest* (poems), Hawthorn, 1968; *I Do My Best,* Golden Press, 1968; *Scary Things* (poems), Abingdon, 1969; *Famous Modern Storytellers for Young People,* Dodd, 1969; *Raggedy Ann: A Thank You, Please, and I Love You Book,* Golden Press, 1969; *The World of Chocolate,* Messner, 1969.

The Odds and Ends Playground, Golden Press, 1970; *Audubon: The Man Who Painted Birds,* World Publishing, 1970; *Trailblazers in American Arts,* Messner, 1971; *Where Did Everybody Go? Funny Rhymes About Place Words,*

NORAH SMARIDGE

198

Golden Press, 1971; *Litterbugs Come in Every Size,* Whitman, 1971; (with Hilda Hunter) *Teenager's Guide to Collecting Practically Anything* (Junior Literary Guild selection), Dodd, 1971; *You Know Better Than That,* Abingdon, 1973; *Famous Author-Illustrators for Young People,* Dodd, 1973. (For complete list of writings see *Contemporary Authors,* Volume 37-40.)

Writer of monthly column, "Book Nook," in *Catholic Weekly* and quarterly feature, "Serendipity," in *Mature Years.*

WORK IN PROGRESS: You and Your Potential, a teenage book; a hobby book with Hilda Hunter, for Dodd; researching possible books on organic food, prisons through the centuries, and caves.

HOBBIES AND OTHER INTERESTS: The theater, reading, young people, cats ("I have ten").

FOR MORE INFORMATION SEE: Junior Literary Guild Catalogue, September, 1972.

"No Littering"
The Litter Bug
Drops bits and scraps,
Paper and peel
And bottle caps.
■ (From *Watch Out!* by Norah Smaridge. Illustrated by Susan Perl. Reprinted by permission of Abingdon Press.)

SMITH, Betty (Wehner) 1896-1972

PERSONAL: Born December 15, 1896, in Brooklyn, N.Y.; name originally Elisabeth Keogh; daughter of John and Catherine (Wehner) Keogh; married George H. E. Smith, June, 1924 (divorced, 1938); married Joseph Piper Jones (a newspaperman), 1943 (divorced, 1951); married Robert Finch, June, 1957 (died, 1959); children: (by first marriage) Nancy, Mary. *Education:* Left grammar school, Brooklyn, N.Y., after completing only the eighth grade; attended the University of Michigan, 1927-30, as a special student; attended Yale University Drama School, 1930-34. *Address:* C/o Harper & Row, Publishers, 10 East 53rd St., New York, N.Y. 10022.

CAREER: After leaving school at the age of fourteen, worked in factory, and in retail, and clerical jobs in New York City; later was a reader and editor for Dramatists Play Service, actress and playwright for the Federal Theater project, and a radio actress. While attending the University of Michigan, 1927-30, she began having her one-act plays published, and also worked as a feature writer for NEA (a newspaper syndicate) and wrote columns for the *Detroit Free Press.* She was a member of the faculty of the University of North Carolina, Chapel Hill, 1945-46. *Member:* Authors League, Dramatists Guild. *Awards, honors:* Avery and Jule Hopwood first prize of $1,000, 1931; Rockefeller fellowship in playwriting and Rockefeller Dramatists Guild playwriting fellowship while at Yale; Sir Walter Raleigh award for fiction, 1958, for *Maggie–Now.*

WRITINGS: *A Tree Grows in Brooklyn,* Harper, 1943; *Tomorrow Will Be Better,* Harper, 1948; *Maggie–Now,* Harper, 1958, revised edition, 1966; *Joy in the Morning,* Harper, 1963.

Plays: (With Jay G. Sigmund) *Folk Stuff* (one act), French, 1935; (with Finch) *His Last Skirmish* (one-act), French, 1937; (with Finch) *Naked Angel* (one-act comedy), French, 1937; (compiler, with Finch and Frederick Henry Koch) *Plays for Schools and Little Theatres: A New Descriptive List,* University of North Carolina Extension Division, 1937; (with Finch) *Popecastle Inn* (one-act comedy), French, 1937; (with Sigmund) *Saints Get Together* (one-act), Denison, 1937; (with Sigmund) *Trees of His Father* (one-act), French, 1937; (with Sigmund) *Vine Leaves* (one-act comedy), French, 1937; (with Finch) *The Professor Roars* (one-act comedy), Dramatic Publishing, 1938; (with Finch) *Western Night* (one-act), Dramatists Play Service, 1938; (with Sigmund) *Darkness at the Window* (one-act), Dramatic Publishing, 1938; (with Finch) *Murder in the Snow* (one-act), French, 1938, (with Sigmund) *Silvered Rope* (one-act Biblical), Denison, 1938; (with Finch) *Youth Takes Over; or, When A Man's Sixteen* (three-act comedy), French, 1939; (with Chase Webb) *Lawyer Lincoln* (one-act comedy), Dramatists Play Service, 1939; *Mannequins' Maid* (one-act), Denison, 1939; (with Sigmund) *They*

BETTY SMITH

Released Barabbas (one-act), Eldridge, 1939; (with Finch) *A Night in the Country* (one-act), Row, Peterson, 1939; (with Finch) *Near Closing Time* (one-act comedy), Denison, 1939; (with Finch) *Package for Ponsonby* (one-act comedy); (with Finch) *Western Ghost Town,* Denison, 1939; (with Clemon White) *Bayou Harlequinade,* French, 1940; *Fun After Supper,* French, 1940; (with Finch) *Heroes Just Happen* (three-act comedy), French, 1940; *Room For a King* (one-act Christmas play), Eldredge, 1940; (with Finch) *Summer Comes to the Diamond O* (one-act comedy), Dramatists Play Service, 1940; (with Finch) *To Jenny With Love* (one-act), Eldridge, 1941; (compiler) *25 Non-Royalty One-Act Plays for All-Girl Casts,* Greenberg, 1942; *20 Prize-Winning Non-Royalty One-Act Plays,* Greenberg, 1943; *Boy Abe,* W. H. Baker, 1944; *Young Lincoln,* Dramatists Play Service; (with George Abbott) *A Tree Grows in Brooklyn* (musical), Harper, 1951; (editor, with others) *A Treasury of Non-Royalty One-Act Plays,* Garden City Books, 1958; *Durham Station* (one-act), North Carolina Centennial Commission, 1961. Published or produced many other plays.

SIDELIGHTS: "One night, . . . I, an obscure writer living quietly and on modest means in a small Southern town, went to bed as usual. I woke up the next morning to be informed that I had become a celebrity. My first novel, *A Tree Grows in Brooklyn,* had been published," wrote Betty Smith. With the advent of *Brooklyn,* the main character, Francie Nolan, became almost a national figure. "To this day," continued Miss Smith, "people write or phone me asking where Francie Nolan . . . is living now; has she married, how many children has she, is she happy? . . . One fifth of my letters start out, 'Dear Francie.'"

The book was described as heart-warming, nostalgic, honest, realistic. Orville Prescott commented: "Here is a first novel of uncommon skill, an almost uncontrollable vitality and zest for life, the work of a fresh, original and highly gifted talent. . . . *A Tree Grows in Brooklyn* is a warm, sunny, engaging book as well as a grim one. It is also a rich and rare example of regional, local-color writing, filled to the scuppers with Brooklynese, Brooklyn folk ways, Brooklyn atmosphere. I shouldn't be surprised if Miss Smith had written the best novel of the year." Diana Trilling, however, tried to separate sentiment from literary value: "I am a little bewildered by so much response to so conventional a little book. . . . I have seen [it] compared to the novels of James Farrell, and all to the credit of Miss Smith's novel. This makes me very sad both for the condition of fiction reviewing and for Mr. Farrell, whatever his faults as a novelist of stature. Of course Francie Nolan's story is more cheerful than Danny O'Neill's, and a more popular commodity, but surely popular taste should be allowed to find its emotional level without being encouraged to believe that a 'heart-warming' experience is a serious literary experience."

The setting of Miss Smith's next two books remained Brooklyn. *Tomorrow Will Be Better* was generally a disappointment to the critics, but *Maggie–Now* engendered some guarded enthusiasm. *Newsweek* said of the latter: "The face is familiar, but the charm has faded." *Joy in the Morning,* a strongly autobiographical novel, moved to the Midwest where Miss Smith had attended the University of Michigan with her law student husband. She changed locale because she felt she had exhausted her Brooklyn memories,

Hassler was a fine butcher for bones but a bad butcher for chopped meat because he ground it behind closed doors and God knows what you got. ■ (From the movie "A Tree Grows in Brooklyn," © 1945 by Twentieth-Century Fox.)

but more important, because she was unsure of the connection of the Brooklyn of today and the Brooklyn of her fiction. "An era has come in which little advances aren't important any more. The exhilaration that came to a family when they were able to move from one flat into another flat that cost $5 a month more, the excitement of wanting a $30 coat and finding the price suddenly reduced to $20—these things are no more. Things are too easy to come by now. That's why I can't write about Brooklyn any more. Even with *Maggie-Now*, I kept wondering whether readers will recognize the old ways."

A Tree Grows in Brooklyn, of which 6,000,000 copies have been sold, has been translated into sixteen languages, and was made into a motion picture by 20th Century-Fox in 1945. Miss Smith collaborated with George Abbott in preparing it for production as a musical comedy. Before publication of the book, she had offered to sell it to Hollywood for $5,000 and was refused. Because of its success, the movie offer went up to $50,000 but Miss Smith held out for $55,000. She still wanted that $5,000.

FOR MORE INFORMATION SEE: Yale Review, autumn, 1943; *Nation,* September 4, 1943; *Saturday Review of Literature,* August 21, 1948; *New York Times Book Review,* August 22, 1948; *Life,* June 6, 1949; *Good Housekeeping,* January, 1958; *Newsweek,* February 24, 1958; *New York Times,* January 18, 1972; *Washington Post,* January 19, 1972; *Newsweek,* January 31, 1972; *Publishers Weekly,* January 31, 1972; *Time,* January 31, 1972; *Current Biography,* March, 1972.

(Died January 17, 1972)

SMITH, Dorothy Stafford 1905- (Sarah Stafford Smith)

PERSONAL: Born February 3, 1905, in Hove, Sussex, England; daughter of William (a chief constable) and Mary Jeffares (Cunningham) Stafford; married Percy Heber Smith, March 13, 1943 (deceased). *Education:* Avery Hill

Training College, Teacher's Certificate, 1926; University of London, Certificate in French, 1929. *Home:* 18 The Hermitage, Lewisham Hill, London S.E. 13, England.

CAREER: Teacher of general elementary subjects in London, England, 1926-42; under British Council, teacher of English to Belgians in Alton, Hampshire, England, 1942-45; French and English teacher in London, England, 1945-59; English teacher, both in schools and privately, in Rome, Italy, 1959-64; teacher of English to children of immigrants, London, England, 1964-66; now retired and writing full time. *Member:* Society of Authors, National Book League.

WRITINGS—Under name Sarah (pseudonym) Stafford Smith: *The Ink-bottle Club* (juvenile), Watts, 1967; *The Ink-bottle Club Abroad* (juvenile), Watts, 1969; *The Imperceptible Gate* (poems), Outposts, 1970. Contributor of short stories and poems to *Courier, Outposts, Poetry of Today,* and other periodicals.

WORK IN PROGRESS: Research for a reference book on famous women of this century.

SIDELIGHTS: "My first book, *The Ink-bottle Club,* is largely autobiographical and stems from a holiday spent in Dublin when I was seven. My grandmother did, in fact, teach in a little school called 'The Inkbottle,' but that was many years before, when she was young, so I juggled with

All along the walls of the embankment were little stalls, like school desks, with sloping lids. Some closed but most of them were open and displayed masses of books, some old, some new. ■ (From *The Ink-Bottle Club Abroad* by Sarah Stafford Smith. Illustrated by F. D. Phillips.)

dates and facts a little. I juggled too, for the sake of interest, with the occupations of my father and uncle.

"In the sequel, *The Ink-bottle Club Abroad,* I used my knowledge of France and Paris, acquired much later, to make a story about a holiday which did not, in fact, take place. I spent a fascinating week in Paris in 1968, looking up the back numbers of *Le Figaro* and *Le Temps* for July and August, 1914, to get my details right. This kind of research is, for me, one of the most interesting aspects of the writer's job.

"I should like to spend at least half of every day at my desk, but so many other demands come along that I am not as single-minded as I ought to be. For instance, although retired from regular teaching, I found myself agreeing to teach a four-year-old neighbor to read, helping a little Nigerian boy who missed two years' schooling through the Biafran War and wanted so much to catch up with his brothers in English, and taking over a kindergarten Sunday school. This is probably self-indulgence, because I love children and am always so pleased and more than a little surprised that they seem to like me too. A very successful writer of children's books declared recently that she positively dislikes all children!

"Our local libraries have meetings for children on Saturday mornings at which children's writers and other people concerned with things that interest the young, from puppets to 'Policemen, Past and Present' come and give talks. I am on this panel and tell stories from my books, published and unpublished.

"I read a great deal in English, French, and Italian, but very seldom read children's books!"

DOROTHY STAFFORD SMITH

SMITH, Sarah Stafford
See SMITH, Dorothy Stafford

SORRENTINO, Joseph N.

PERSONAL: Born May 16, in Brooklyn, N.Y.; son of Nicholas (a street sweeper) and Angelina Sorrentino. *Education:* Erasmus Hall High School, graduate (with highest average in the night school's history), 1959; University of California, Santa Barbara, B.A. (magna cum laude), 1963, M.A., 1969; Harvard University, J.D. (and valedictorian of Law School), 1967; Oxford University, further study, 1969. *Religion:* Christianity. *Home:* 12131 Mayfield, Brentwood, Calif. 90291. *Agent:* (Lectures) American Program Bureau. *Office:* 1901 Avenue of Stars, Los Angeles, Calif. 90067.

CAREER: Went to work at fourteen after flunking out of high school four times; failed at about thirty factory and laboring jobs before enlisting in U.S. Marines, 1955; booted out of Marines with a general discharge (as an incorrigible), he went to night school at Erasmus Hall while working days in a supermarket; after graduating with honors from University of California, reenlisted in Marines, 1963-66, to wipe out the general discharge, and became a platoon leader; admitted to California Bar, 1967; practiced law as partner in Olsen & Sorrentino, Los Angeles, Calif., 1967-72. Professor of law at University of California, Santa Barbara, 1970—. Public lecturer, traveling in forty-five states; guest on network television programs, including "Tonight" and "Mike Douglas Show." Active in Sugar Ray Robinson Youth Foundation. *Awards, honors:* Golden Glove finalist, 1954; *Up from Never* was an American Library Association Notable Book, 1971; National University Extension Association Award for outstanding creative program, 1971.

WRITINGS: Up from Never (autobiographical), Prentice-Hall, 1971; *The Moral Revolution,* Nash Publishing, 1972.

WORK IN PROGRESS: New Man for a Better World.

SIDELIGHTS: "My interests are language, love, and learning."

FOR MORE INFORMATION SEE: Time, June 30, 1967.

SPILKA, Arnold   1917-

PERSONAL: Born November 13, 1917, in New York, N.Y.; son of Charles (a designer) and Celia (Altner) Spilka. *Education:* Studied evenings at Art Students' League, New York. *Residence:* New York, N.Y.

CAREER: Sculptor, painter, and writer and illustrator of children's books.

WRITINGS—Author and illustrator: *Whom Shall I Marry?,* Holiday House, 1960; *Aloha from Bobby,* Walck, 1962; *Paint All Kinds of Pictures,* Walck, 1963; *A Lion I Can Do Without* (nonsense poems), Walck, 1964; *Little Birds Don't Cry,* Viking, 1965; *Once Upon a Horse* (nonsense poems), Walck, 1966; *A Rumbudgin of Nonsense* (nonsense poems), Scribner, 1970; *. . . And the Frog Went "BLAH"* (nonsense poems), Scribner, 1972.

Illustrator: Beman Lord, *The Trouble With Francis,* Walck, 1958; Michael Sage, *If You Talk to a Boar,* Lippin-

cott, 1960; Beman Lord, *Quarterback's Aim,* Walck, 1960; Michael Sage, *Words Inside Words,* Lippincott, 1961; Beman Lord, *Guards for Matt,* Walck, 1961; Beman Lord, *Bats and Balls,* Walck, 1962; Don Lang and Michael Sage, *New Star in the Big Cage,* Lippincott, 1963; Beman Lord, *Rough Ice,* Walck, 1963; Beman Lord, *Mystery Guard at Left End,* Walck, 1964; Adele and Cateau De Leeuw, *The Salty Skinners,* Little, Brown, 1964; Robert Froman, *Faster and Faster* (Junior Literary Guild selection), Viking, 1965; Solveig Paulson Russell, *Lines and Shapes,* Walck, 1965; John Lawson, *You Better Come Home With Me,* Crowell, 1966; Aileen Fisher, *Best Little House,* Crowell, 1966; Michael Sage, *Deep in a Haystack,* Viking, 1966; Michael Sage, *Careful Carlos,* Holiday House, 1967; Michael Sage, *Dippy Dos and Don'ts,* Viking, 1967; Ann McGovern, reteller, *Robin Hood of Sherwood Forest,* Crowell, 1968; Michael Sage, *The Tree and Me,* Walck, 1970; Lee Bennett Hopkins, compiler, *Poems to Remember,* Scholastic Book Services, 1973.

SIDELIGHTS: "The opportunity to strive for creativity is a fine one in doing books for children. The opportunity is all. As for my writing nonsense poems—it's good to know that no reason is needed."

FOR MORE INFORMATION SEE: Book World, December 17, 1967; *Library Journal,* October 15, 1970.

ARNOLD SPILKA

The Tree is the tree—and I am me. ■ (From *The Tree and Me* by Michael Sage. Illustrated by Arnold Spilka.)

STARBIRD, Kaye 1916-
(C.S. Jennison)

PERSONAL: Born June 3, 1916, at Fort Sill, Okla.; daughter of Alfred A. (a general, U.S. Army) and Ethel (Dodd) Starbird; married James Dalton (deceased); second husband, N. E. Jennison (also deceased); children: (first marriage) Kit (Mrs. Wayne Slawson), Beth (Mrs. Peter Snyder); (second marriage) Lee (Mrs. Robert Bergman). *Education:* University of Vermont, student, four years. *Address:* General Delivery, Peterborough, N.H.

CAREER: Professional writer. *Awards, honors:* Bread Loaf Writers' Conference fellowship, 1961; seven fellowships to MacDowell Colony, two to Helene Wurlitzer Foundation in Taos, N.M., four to Wavertree in Greenwood, Va., four to Ossabaw Island Project; awarded a grant for writing serious adult poetry, Elly Lyman Cabot Trust, 1971.

WRITINGS: Speaking of Cows (juvenile), Lippincott, 1960; *Don't Ever Cross a Crocodile* (juvenile), Lippincott, 1963; *A Snail's a Failure Socially* (juvenile), Lippincott, 1966; *The Pheasant on Route Seven* (juvenile), Lippincott, 1968; *Watch Out for the Mules* (adult), Harcourt, 1968; *The Lion in the Lei Shop* (adult), Harcourt, 1970. Contributor, at times under name C. S. Jennison, of satirical verse, poems, essays, and short stories to magazines.

WORK IN PROGRESS: A book of adult poetry entitled, *Don't Hurry Home, Ulysses.*

SIDELIGHTS: "As for how I write, I just decide on a book and write eight hours a day until it is completed. Throwing away a lot at the beginning and rewriting until I turn the manuscript in to the publisher. I started writing when I was eight and started selling verse to magazines like *Good Housekeeping* while I was in college, going on to magazines like the old *American Mercury* and then satirical verse and essays for the *Atlantic.* After that I changed to writing books.

"I derive material from experience and also from a galloping imagination that I was born with and for which I claim no credit. In my latest book of poems, *The Tower,* I have given the imagination free rein, although of course, I discipline the form and content. As any writer does. Writing is hard work but I am happier doing it than not doing it. I never Set Out to Be a Writer. I just started writing."

And raising his eyes
From his four-foot size,
He'll chuckle, perhaps, and say:
"Now you'd have to stoop to a job like mine,
But I'm always down here, anyway."
■ (From *The Pheasant on Route Seven* by Kaye Starbird. Illustrated by Victoria de Larrea.)

Something about the Author

STARK, James
    See GOLDSTON, Robert

STEIN, M(eyer) L(ewis)

PERSONAL: Born in Escanaba, Mich.; son of Alexander (a merchant) and Fannie (Joseph) Stein; married Irene Noshlen, September 10, 1949; children: Gregory, Andrea, Jeannine. *Education:* University of Missouri, B.J., 1942; Wayne State University, graduate student, 1951; Stanford University, M.A., 1961. *Home:* 1 Morewood Oaks, Port Washington, N.Y. 11050.

CAREER: Royal Oak Daily Tribune, Royal Oak, Mich., reporter and telegraph editor, 1946-51; *San Francisco Examiner,* San Francisco, Calif., staff reporter and rewrite man, 1951-61; New York University, New York, N.Y., assistant professor, 1961-64, associate professor of journalism and chairman of department, 1965—. *Military service:* U.S. Army, 1942-45; served in Italy; became sergeant. *Member:* Association for Education in Journalism, American Association of University Professors, Society of Magazine Writers, Sigma Delta Chi, Kappa Tau Alpha.

WRITINGS: Your Career in Journalism, Messner, 1965; *Freedom of the Press–A Continuing Struggle,* Messner, 1966; *Write Clearly ... Speak Effectively,* Cornerstone Library, 1967; *Under Fire: The Story of American War Correspondents,* Messner, 1968; *When Presidents Meet the Press,* Messner, 1969; *How to Write High School and College Papers,* Cornerstone Library, 1969; *Reporting Today,* Cornerstone Library, 1971; *Blacks in Communication,* Messner, 1972. Contributor to business, technical, and general consumer magazines, and trade and journalism publications.

M. L. STEIN

STERNE, Emma Gelders   1894-1971
(Emily Broun, Josephine James [joint pseudonym])

PERSONAL: Born May 13, 1894, in Birmingham, Ala.; daughter of Louis (a businessman) and Blanche (Loeb) Gelders; married Roy M. Sterne, March 17, 1917; children: Ann Copperman, Barbara Lindsay. *Education:* Smith College, A.B., 1916; advanced study at Columbia University, 1923-24, New School for Social Research, 1925-27. *Politics:* Democrat. *Religion:* Atheist. *Home:* 1125 Carolyn Ave., San Jose, Calif. *Agent:* Edith Margolis, 11 West 42nd St., New York, N.Y. 10036.

CAREER: English teacher, Rowayton, Conn., 1946-50; American Book Co., New York, N.Y., editor, 1950-56; Haar Wagner (textbooks), San Francisco, Calif., editor, 1956-57; free-lance writer. *Member:* American Civil Liberties Union, Emergency Civil Liberties Committee, National Association for the Advancement of Colored People, Congress of Racial Equality, Southern Educational Fund, Women for Peace, San Jose (Calif.) Peace Center, Women's International League for Peace and Freedom, Student Nonviolent Coordinating Committee, San Jose Committee for Defense of Soledad Brothers (steering committee), San Jose Committee for Defense of Angela Davis and All Political Prisoners (steering committee).

WRITINGS: White Swallow, Cadmus, 1928; *Blue Pigeons,* Duffield & Green, 1929; *Loud Sing Cuckoo,* Dodd, 1930; *No Surrender,* Dodd, 1931; *Amarantha Gay, M.D.,* Dodd, 1932; *Calico Ball,* Dodd, 1933; *Drums of Monmouth,* Dodd, 1935; *Miranda Was a Princess,* Dodd, 1936; *Far Town Road,* Dodd, 1937; *Some Plant Olive Trees,* Dodd, 1937; *European Summer,* Dodd, 1938; *Pirate of Chatham Square,* Dodd, 1939.

America Was Like This, Dodd, 1940; *We Live to Be Free,* Farrar & Rinehart, 1942; *Incident in Yorkville,* Farrar & Rinehart, 1943; *Printer's Devil,* Aladdin, 1951; *Long Black Schooner,* Aladdin, 1953; *Let the Moon Go By,* Aladdin, 1954; (editor) *Moby Dick,* Golden Books, 1954; *Mary McLeod Bethune,* Knopf, 1956; (editor) *Little Women,* Golden Books, 1957; *Blood Brothers,* Knopf, 1958; (with daughter, Barbara Lindsay) *The Sea,* Golden Books, 1958; *Balboa,* Knopf, 1960; (with daughter, Barbara Lindsay) *King Arthur and the Knights of the Round Table,* Golden Books, 1962; *I Have a Dream,* Knopf, 1965; *They Took Their Stand,* Macmillan, 1966; *Benito Juarez* (biography), Knopf, 1967; *His Was the Voice: The Story of Dr. W.E.B. Du Bois,* Macmillan, 1971.

With Barbara Lindsay under pseudonym Josephine James: "Kathy Martin" Series, twelve volumes, Golden Press, 1959-66.

Editor, "American Heritage" Series, Aladdin; "Blue Print for Tomorrow," International Business and Professional Women pamphlet series for Office of War Information, United Nations.

(Died August 29, 1971)

STEVENS, Franklin 1933-
(Steve Franklin)

PERSONAL: Born October 31, 1933, in Camden, N.J.; son of Franklin P. and Virginia (Mitchell) Stevens. *Education:* Attended public schools in Summit, N.J. *Home:* Old Kings Hwy., Stone Ridge, N.Y. 12484. *Agent:* Mary Yost Associates, 141 East 55th St., New York, N.Y. 10022.

CAREER: Writer.

WRITINGS: (Under pseudonym Steve Franklin) *The Malcontents,* Doubleday, 1970; *If This Be Treason: Your Sons Tell Their Own Stories of Why They Won't Fight for Their Country,* Peter H. Wyden, 1970; (under pseudonym of Steve Franklin) *The Chickens in the Airshaft,* Doubleday, 1972.

WORK IN PROGRESS: A serio-comic love story, *In Chinese Soup;* a psychological thriller, *I Am Harry Bates.*

SIDELIGHTS: "I live, at present, in a rather rickety old house one-hundred miles upstate from New York City, with an unpredictable Puerto-Rican-American wife, an irritable Maine Coon cat, and a water pump which blew up recently while I was reading threatening letters from the Irving Trust Company, Mastercharge, American Express, and the people who, reluctantly, deliver fuel oil.

"In spite of such financial hassles, it occurs to me that I am a very lucky man: at the age of thirty-nine I'm still doing work which becomes, more, not less, exciting and meaningful to me as time passes. Why does it? A sense of catharsis, for one thing, and certainly a sense of power. But also, a sense of discovery. For no matter how detailed the outline I prepare, each book undergoes a sea-change as it is being written; each book is a journey of exploration and discovery. I discover the book in the writing of it, and rediscover the world."

Stevens has lived in Paris and has traveled in Europe, Morocco, most of the United States, and Martinique.

FOR MORE INFORMATION SEE: Library Journal, June 15, 1970; *Best Sellers,* December 15, 1970.

STEWART, Elizabeth Laing 1907-

PERSONAL: Born September 1, 1907, in Colorado Springs, Colo.; daughter of Herbert Greyson and Della (Mann) Laing; married Donald M. Stewart (an editor and writer), 1938 (divorced, 1947); married Charles Sweetland (an editor and writer), 1958 (divorced, 1960); children: (first marriage) Robert Laing Stewart. *Education:* Barnard College, A.B., 1929. *Politics:* Democrat or independent. *Religion:* "Attend Quaker meetings (not member)." *Home:* 238 Lee St., Evanston, Ill. 60202.

CAREER: Columbia University, New York, N.Y., secretary in Spanish department, 1933-34; Bobbs-Merrill Co., Inc., Indianapolis, Ind., associate editor, 1934-38; Reilly & Lee Co., Chicago, Ill., editor, 1938-41, 1946-49; Scott, Foresman & Co., Glenview, Ill., editor, 1950-72, and editorial consultant in driver education, 1972-75.

ELIZABETH LAING STEWART

WRITINGS—Picture books with vocabulary for beginning readers: *Billy Buys a Dog,* Reilly & Lee, 1950; *Funny Squirrel,* Reilly & Lee, 1952; *Patch, You Just Be You,* Reilly & Lee, 1953; *Little Dog Tim,* Reilly & Lee, 1959; *See Our Pony Farm,* Reilly & Lee, 1960; *Kim the Kitten,* Reilly & Lee, 1961; *Mogul Finds a Friend,* Reilly & Lee, 1962; *The Lion Twins,* Atheneum, 1964.

Directing editor, Maxwell Halsey and Richard Kaywood, *Let's Drive Right,* 3rd edition (she was not associated with the first edition), Scott, Foresman, 1964, 5th edition (with Richard Meyerhoff as additional author), 1972.

WORK IN PROGRESS: Keeping up with driver education field to prepare for any changes in next edition of *Let's Drive Right.*

SIDELIGHTS: "For many years, my chief avocational interest has been in organizations that promote peace in world affairs. Currently I do volunteer work for the Peace Center of Evanston. Though I'm sure it isn't obvious, the point I wanted to get across to children in *Little Dog Tim,* the favorite of my own books, was to help children live at peace with their fellow-beings and promote peace in the world. For all of my picture books except one or two, I collected the pictures first and let them suggest the story to me."

STILES, Martha Bennett

PERSONAL: Born in Manila, Philippine Islands; daughter of Forrest Hampton and Jane (Bennett) Wells; married Martin Stiles; children: John Martin. *Education:* Studied at College of William and Mary; University of Michigan, B.S., 1954. *Religion:* Episcopalian. *Residence:* Ann Arbor, Mich.

CAREER: Writer. *Member:* National Audubon Society, South Carolina Historical Society, Clements Library Associates, Phi Beta Kappa. *Awards, honors:* Avery and Jule Hopwood Awards (both major and minor) at University of Michigan.

WRITINGS—For young people: *One Among the Indians,* Dial, 1962; *The Strange House at Newburyport,* Dial, 1963; *Darkness Over the Land,* Dial, 1966; *Dougal Looks for Birds,* Four Winds, 1972. Contributor to *Virginia Cavalcade, Ingenue, Four Quarters, Thoroughbred Record, Stereo Review, Seventeen, Virginia Quarterly Review, Brigitte, Maryland Horse,* and other magazines and newspapers.

WORK IN PROGRESS: Research on eighteenth-century South Carolina and sixth-century Gaul.

Mr. MacDougal found an empty oriole's nest. Mrs. MacDougal found an empty pheasant's nest. Dougal MacDougal found a full hornet's nest. ■ (From *Dougal Looks for Birds* by Martha Bennett Stiles. Illustrated by Iris Schweitzer.)

MARTHA BENNETT STILES

STODDARD, Hope   1900-

PERSONAL: Born March 31, 1900; daughter of Bode Moseley and Rosa Lee Stoddard; married Hermann Johns (separated). *Education:* Studied violin at Juilliard School of Music in earlier years; University of Michigan, B.A., 1923. *Home:* 4 Peter Cooper Rd., New York, N.Y. 10010.

CAREER: Etude, Philadelphia, Pa., editorial staff, 1924-32; then went to Europe and taught for two years at Berlitz schools in Copenhagen, Denmark, and Hamburg, Germany; on her return her joint interest in music and writing led to her becoming an editor of the *International Musician,* Newark, N.J., 1940-65.

WRITINGS: From These Comes Music: Instruments of the Band and Orchestra (young adult book), Crowell, 1952; *Symphony Conductors of the U.S.A.* (young adult), Crowell, 1957; *Subsidy Makes Sense,* International Press (Newark), 1960; *The Noon Answer* (poems), Humphries, 1965; *Famous American Women* (young adult), Crowell, 1970.

SIDELIGHTS: "I wrote *Famous American Women* because I felt there was an imbalance in the man-woman relationship—an imbalance not caused by any particular unfairness exercised by either sex, but one built up by customs and attitudes over the years. I felt, for instance, that it is harder for a woman to achieve in what we call the 'outside world' and harder for a man to become involved creatively in personal relationships in the home. I thought of ways I might help to right this imbalance. Reading many books, it seemed to me there was a conspiracy of silence in regard to what women have actually achieved in the outside world. It was just as though it was thought slightly anti-social for her to be anything but background. It seemed just and reasonable, to me, therefore, that women's achieve-

HOPE STODDARD

ments be recorded—particularly here in America where women have had so much to do with the development of the country.

"Dorothea Dix revolutionized the treatment of the mentally ill. Clara Barton founded the Red Cross in America. Lillian Gilbreth pioneered in the field of motion study. Susanne Langer has broadened the field of philosophy, as has Dr. Margaret Mead that of anthropology. It seemed only sensible to me that the contributions of women to the development of our country be set down. So I wrote the book."

STONE, Helen V(irginia)

PERSONAL: Born in Philadelphia, Pa.; daughter of Raymond D. and Eliza (Olivit) Stone. *Education:* Pennsylvania Academy of the Fine Arts, courses in painting and illustration; Germantown Friends' Adult School, courses in creative writing; Mexican-North American Institute of Cultural Relations, Diploma in Spanish, 1965. *Home:* Apartment 513, 5457 Wayne Ave., Philadelphia, Pa. 19144.

CAREER: Endres Associates (management consultants and manufacturers representatives), Flourtown, Pa., part-time secretary, 1962—. *Awards, honors:* Pennsylvania Academy of the Fine Arts traveling scholarship, 1943; named distinguished daughter of Pennsylvania, 1956; first prize in short story contest sponsored by Junto Writers of Philadelphia, 1957.

WRITINGS: Pablo the Potter (juvenile fiction), Lantern Press, 1969. Contributor of articles and self-illustrated stories for children to *Presbyterian Life,* 1962—.

WORK IN PROGRESS: Writing and illustrating humorous verses for a children's book, *With a Grain of Salt;* translating Latin-American legends into English.

SIDELIGHTS: "Having had fragile bones from birth, I spent my days in casts, braces, and a wheel chair. The reality of a permanent orthopedic disability had to be faced but never subdued a tremendous zest for living. Books, paints, friends, and understanding parents added to the joys of a happy childhood.

"Gradually drawing and painting came to be great sources of delight, but not until some time after art school did my serious writing begin to develop. Writing for children has always captured my imagination. For such a demanding audience the author must be completely honest and direct, a challenge which sometimes brings out the most inspired work. To put into words something meaningful and appealing to the adult as well as juvenile reader is my earnest intention.

"My material comes mainly from personal experience and aims to point out that a disability can actually be an incentive toward fulfillment in life rather than a limitation, that no matter what the circumstances, living can be a joyful adventure.

HELEN V. STONE

Something about the Author

■ (From "Pablo the Potter" by Helen V. Stone. Illustrated by the author.)

"Until recently I lived with my mother but now have a small apartment geared to my needs directly across the hall so that we can easily visit back and forth. Writing, illustrating, and secretarial work keep me busy at home. I enjoy cooking and find it great fun to experiment with exotic flavored herbs. In the apartment I use crutches and outside a folding wheel chair where necessary. My greatest problem seems to be the days are never long enough!"

Ms. Stone assists a blind teacher by reading and helping with research. An extended visit in Mexico, 1964-65, provided background material for her first book.

ROSEMARY SUTCLIFF

SUTCLIFF, Rosemary 1920-

PERSONAL: Born December 14, 1920, in West Clanden, Surrey, England; daughter of George Ernest (Royal Navy) and Nessie Elizabeth (Lawton) Sutcliff. *Education:* Educated privately and at Bideford Art School in Devonshire, England. *Politics:* "Vaguely Conservative." *Religion:* Unorthodox Church of England. *Home:* Swallowshaw, Walberton, Arundel, Sussex, England.

MEMBER: P.E.N., National Book League, Society of Authors. *Awards, honors:* Carnegie Medal for *The Lantern-Bearers,* 1959; placed on Honours List of Hans Christian Andersen Award for *Warrior Scarlet,* 1959; *New York Times* Spring Book Festival Prize for *Dawn Wind,* 1962; Lewis Carroll Shelf Award, 1971, for *The Witch's Brat; Tristan and Iseult* won the *Boston Globe*-Horn Book Award and was runner-up for the Carnegie Medal, 1972.

WRITINGS—All children's books except as noted: *The Chronicles of Robin Hood,* Walck, 1950; *The Queen Elizabeth Story,* Walck, 1950; *The Armourer's House,* Walck, 1951; *Brother Dusty-Feet,* Walck, 1952; *Simon,* Walck, 1953; *The Eagle of the Ninth,* Walck, 1954; *Outcast,* Walck, 1955; *The Shield-Ring* (ALA Notable Book), Walck, 1956, new edition, 1972; *Lady in Waiting* (adult novel), Coward, 1956; *The Silver Branch,* Walck, 1957; *Warrior Scarlet,* Walck, 1958, new edition, 1966; *The Lantern-Bearers,* Walck, 1959.

Knight's Fee, Walck, 1960; *The Rider of the White Horse* (adult novel), Coward, 1960; *Houses and History,* Bats-

The scent of incense drifted on the air, and the chanting voices of the Brothers rose and hung high under the shadowy roof. ■ (From *The Witch's Brat* by Rosemary Sutcliff. Illustrated by Richard Lebenson.)

ford, 1960; *Dawn Wind* (ALA Notable Book), Walck, 1961; *Beowulf* (ALA Notable Book), Bodley Head, 1962; *Rudyard Kipling* (adult), Bodley Head, 1962; *Sword at Sunset* (adult novel; Literary Guild selection), Coward, 1963; *The Hound of Ulster* (retelling; ALA Notable Book), Bodley Head, 1963, Dutton, 1964; *Heroes and History*, Batsford, 1965, Putnam, 1966; *The Mask of the Horse Lord*, Walck, 1965; *The High Deeds of Finn MacCool* (*Horn Book* Honor List), Dutton, 1967; *The Chief's Daughter*, Hamish Hamilton, 1967; *A Circlet of Oak Leaves*, Hamish Hamilton, 1968; *The Witch's Brat* (*Horn Book* Honor List; ALA Notable Book), Walck, 1970; *Tristan and Iseult* (ALA Notable Book), Dutton, 1971; *Heather, Oak, and Olive: Three Stories*, Dutton, 1972.

HOBBIES AND OTHER INTERESTS: Archaeology, anthropology, primitive religion; making collages and costume jewelry.

FOR MORE INFORMATION SEE: More Junior Authors, edited by Muriel Fuller, H. W. Wilson, 1963; Roger Lancelyn Green, *Tellers of Tales*, Watts, 1965; Brian Doyle, *The Who's Who of Children's Literature*, Schocken, 1968; Eleanor Cameron, *The Green and Burning Tree*, Atlantic-Little, Brown, 1969; *Horn Book*, December, 1970, December 1971, October, 1972; John Rowe Townsend, *A Sense of Story*, Lippincott, 1971; *Author's Choice*, Crowell, 1971.

TENNANT, Kylie   1912-

PERSONAL: Born March 12, 1912, in Sydney, Australia; daughter of Thomas Walter and Kathleen (Tolhurst) Tennant; married Lewis Charles Rodd, November 21, 1932; children: Benison, John Laurence. *Education:* Attended Brighton College and University of Sydney. *Religion:* Church of England. *Home:* 5 Garrick Ave., Hunter's Hill, New South Wales 2110, Australia. *Agent:* A. P. Watt, 10 Norfolk St., London W.C. 2, England; Willis Wing, 24 East 38th St., New York, N.Y. 10016.

CAREER: Macmillan and Co., London, England, Australian literary adviser; member of board, Australian Aborigines Co-operatives Ltd.; Commonwealth Literary Fund Fellowship, 1951; lecturer for Commonwealth Literary Fund, 1957-58, member of advisory board, 1961-72. Has made appearances on Australian television and radio. *Member:* Australian Fellowship of Writers (life patron), Australian Society of Authors. *Awards, honors:* S. H. Prior Memorial Prize for best Australian novel, 1935, for *Tiburon*, 1941, for *The Battlers;* Australian Literary Society's Gold Medal, 1941, for *The Battlers;* Commonwealth Jubilee Stage Play Award, 1952, for *Tether a Dragon;* Children's Book Award, 1960, for *All the Proud Tribesmen.*

WRITINGS: Tiburon (novel), Endeavor Press, 1935, Angus & Robertson, 1973; *Foveaux* (novel), Gollancz, 1939; *The Battlers* (novel), Macmillan, 1941, new edition, Angus & Robertson, 1973; *Ride On, Stranger* (novel), Macmillan, 1943, new edition, 1965; *Time Enough Later* (novel), Macmillan, 1943; *Lost Haven* (novel), Macmillan, 1946, new edition, 1965; *John o' the Forest, and Other Plays* (plays for children), Macmillan, 1950; *Tether a Dragon* (play), Associated General Publications, 1952; *Australia: Her Story* (history), Macmillan, 1953, Pan, 1971; *The Joyful Condemned* (novel), Macmillan, 1953; *Long*

John Silver (fiction for children), Associated General Publications, 1954; *The Bells of the City, and Other Plays,* Macmillan, 1955; *The Honey Flow* (novel), Macmillan, 1956, Angus & Robertson, 1973; *The Bushranger's Christmas Eve, and Other Plays,* Macmillan, 1959; *Speak You So Gently* (travel), Gollancz, 1959; *All the Proud Tribesmen* (fiction for children), Macmillan, 1959, Piccolo, 1971; *Trail Blazers of the Air* (fiction for children), Macmillan, 1966; *Ma Jones and the Little White Cannibals,* Macmillan, 1967; *Tell Morning This,* Angus & Robertson, 1967; *Evatt: Politics and Justice,* Angus & Robertson, 1973; *The Man on the Headland,* Angus & Robertson, 1973. Critic for *Sydney Morning Herald.* General editor of *Great Stories of Australia* and *Summer's Tales,* Macmillan, 1964-66.

WORK IN PROGRESS: A novel.

SIDELIGHTS: "'Go and find out,' brings with it so much fun that some is sure to brim over into a book. In the 1930's everyone was talking about the 'traveling unemployed' going from town to town looking for work, but there was no-one recording what their lives were really like in Australia. So I tramped around, a few hundred miles here, six hundred there, camping and meeting people. Later, I bought an old laundry cart and a bad-tempered horse and went pea-picking and packing cherries. At one camp the drinking water came from a pond where the dogs, men and horses swam. You boiled it with a handful of tea to help the taste.

KYLIE TENNANT

"*The Battlers* was the novel telling of people 'on the track.' *Tiburon,* which I wrote when I was twenty-one, is about a country town; and for *Lost Haven,* which tells about life in a fishing village, I worked helping to build a snapper boat. For three books about Sydney, *Foveaux, Ride On Stranger,* and *Tell Morning This,* I lived in slum areas, and had jobs ranging from social worker to barmaid. A hard book to write and one which caused me to make many journeys was *The Honey Flow,* a novel about the migratory apiarists who take their bees on huge trucks hundreds of miles following the flowering of the eucalypt tree blossoms.

"The native children on a mission station near the tip of Cape York and, later, in the Torres Strait Islands, were struggling to learn to read English out of books in which the little white boy was always the hero. So I wrote another book, for children, *All the Proud Tribesmen,* with a brown boy as the chief character. It received the Australian Children's Book Award, but I was better pleased to learn that children in Papua-New Guinea read it and loved it.

"When we studied Australian history at school it was always dull, and it was not until I came to write a popular history, *Australia: Her Story,* that I found how exciting it could be. This book has gone through many editions and led me on to write a play about an early Australian Prime Minister, Alfred Deakin, called *Tether a Dragon.* Later I spent four years writing a large book, *Evatt,* the life of a great Australian statesman and first President of the United Nations Assembly, whose last years were marked by misunderstanding and were very tragic.

"*The Man on the Headland,* was about an old bushman who let me build a tiny shack on his farm, a sanctuary for wild animals, wallabies, goannas, hares, cassowaries, because he was too kind to kill anything.

"I should not forget the three books of plays for children. My husband was a headmaster and could not find suitable plays for his pupils so I would write plays according to the number of characters that he wanted and after the children had acted them and tried them out, they were published.

"I want to write another novel about life around Sydney Harbour but too often find myself tending to the ducks and fowls, the cats and horses, on a little farm in the Blue Mountains where my daughter has a wonderful time painting pictures and riding her horse, Peppi."

HOBBIES AND OTHER INTERESTS: The welfare of the Aborigines.

FOR MORE INFORMATION SEE: New York Times, November 8, 1941; *Meanjin Quarterly,* Number 4, 1953; Margaret Dick, *The Novels of Kylie Tennant,* Rigby, 1966.

ter HAAR, Jaap 1922-

PERSONAL: Born March 25, 1922, in Hilversum, Netherlands; son of Jacob E. (a businessman) and Mieke (van Hengel) ter Haar; married Rudi Schurink, November, 1945; children: Jaap, Bart, Saskia and Jeroen (twins). *Education:* Attended schools in Netherlands. *Politics:* "Not much." *Religion:* "Not much either." *Home:* Eikenlaan 57, Hilversum, Netherlands.

CAREER: War correspondent with Royal Netherlands Marines in United States and Indonesia, 1945-47; head of transcription service, Radio Netherlands, 1947-55; professional writer, 1955—. *Member:* Dutch Writers Union. *Awards, honors:* City of Rotterdam Award (juvenile jury), 1958, for *Noodweer op de weisshorn;* Bijenkorf Award, 1961, for total work; City of Rotterdam Award (critics jury), 1966, for best book of the year, *Boris;* Sonderpreis for German edition of *De Geschiedenis van Noord Amerika;* Jan Campert Foundation Award, 1972, for *Geschiedenis van de lage landen.*

WRITINGS—Young adult: *Nordweer op de weisshorn,* van Holkema & Warendorf, 1957, translation by Barrows Mussey published as *Danger on the Mountain,* Duell, Sloan & Pearce, 1960; *De Geschiedenis van Noord-Amerika,* van Dishoeck, 1959, translation by Marieke Clarke published as *The Story of America,* Thomas Nelson, 1967; *De Franse Revolutie,* Fibula-van Dishoeck, 1961; (with K. Sprey) *Het romeinse Keizerrijk,* Fibula-van Dishoeck, 1961; *De Geschiedenis van Napoleon,* Fibula-van Dishoeck, 1963; *De Grote sagen van de donkere middeleeuwen,* Fibula-van Dishoeck, 1963; *De Geschiedenis van Rusland,* Fibula-van Dishoeck, 1965; *Koning Arthur,* van Holkema & Warendorf, 1967, translation published as *King Arthur,* Lutterworth, 1971; *Boris* (Child Study Association book list), van Holkema & Warendorf, circa 1967, translation by Martha Mearns published under same title, Blackie & Son, 1969, Delacorte, 1970; *Altijd, overal, iedereen: Het Nederlandsche Roode Kruis 100 jaar* (history of Netherlands Red Cross), Callenbach, 1967; *Bart: Lumberjack in Canada,* van Holkema & Warendorf, 1968; *Bart met geologen naar de Yukon,* van Holkema & Warendorf, 1968; *De zes Falken,* Callenbach, 1968.

JAAP TER HAAR

[Boris] wanted to fight the Germans who had killed his father; it was their fault that thousands of people were dying in Leningrad; that the cheerful houses were lying in ruins . . . ■ (From *Boris* by Jaap ter Haar. Illustrated by Rien Poortvliet.)

Juvenile: "Saskia en Jeroen" series, ten books, van Holkema & Warendorf; "Ernstjan en Snabbeltje" series, nine books, van Holkema & Warendorf, one title in series, translated by Barrows Mussey, published in America as *Duck Dutch,* Duell, Sloan & Pearce, 1962; "Eelke" series, nine books, van Holkema & Warendorf; "Lotje" series, twelve books, van Holkema & Warendorf, two titles in series, translated by Martha Mearns, published in England as *Judy at the Zoo,* Blackie & Son, 1969, and *Judy and the Baby Elephant,* Blackie & Son, 1970; (with Rien Poortvliet) *Het Sinterklaasboek,* van Holkema & Warendorf, 1969; (with Poortvliet) *Het Kerstboek,* van Holkema & Warendorf, 1970; *The Little World of Beer Ligthart,* van Holkema & Warendorf, 1973.

Adult: *Geschiedenis van de lage landen,* four volumes, Fibula-van Dishoeck, 1970; *Jacob Simonsz: De rijk, watergeus,* van Holkema & Warendorf, 1972.

Writer of films and radio and television plays.

SIDELIGHTS: "Even as a young child I wanted to become a writer, but as I got older I thought this quite impossible, as I appeared very unintelligent at school, at least not above average.

"However, as a war-correspondent and later as producer at the Dutch Radio, I began to understand that intelligence is not so much needed for writing as imagination, feeling, and above all, an intense interest and knowledge of people. And so, by way of this growing insight, I started my first book at the age of twenty-seven and was able to quit my job and become a full-time writer at the age of thirty-two.

"For me, writing is not so much a gift, but a profession. The harder you work at it, the better you learn your trade. (I probably work harder than most people in offices.)

"The biggest problem about writing a book, at least for me, is the first chapter. I rewrite the first ten pages, twenty, sometimes thirty times. Not because they are badly written, but because I need a certain amount of time to get fully acquainted with my characters. After a week or two (and those are miserable weeks!) I suddenly feel that I know the persons in my book completely: I know how they look, how they dress, how they think, feel, worry, etc. And having reached that point, the book takes its course without many problems and the characters go their own way to the last chapter."

Ter Haar's books for young people have been translated into ten languages, *Boris* into nine, including Afrikaans, and the "Lotje" series into six (as "Lisbeth" series in France, "Lotti" in Sweden, "Lotte" in Denmark, and "Conny" series in Germany). The Dutch author has visited America at the invitation of the Department of State and Russia as a guest of the Soviet Writers Union.

HOBBIES AND OTHER INTERESTS: Gardening, the theater, films.

TRAHERNE, Michael
See WATKINS-PITCHFORD, D. J.

Van LEEUWEN, Jean 1937-

PERSONAL: Surname pronounced Van *Loo*-en; born December 26, 1937, in Glen Ridge, N.J.; daughter of Cornelius (a clergyman) and Dorothy (Charlton) Van Leeuwen; married Bruce David Gavril (a digital computer systems designer), July 7, 1968; children: David Andrew, Elizabeth Eva. *Education:* Syracuse University, B.A., 1959. *Home:* 444 East 75th St., New York, N.Y. 10021.

CAREER: Random House, Inc., New York, N.Y., assistant editor and then associate editor of juvenile books, 1963-68; Viking Press, Inc., New York, N.Y., associate editor of juvenile books, 1968-70; Dial Press, New York, N.Y., senior editor of juvenile books, 1971-73.

WRITINGS—For young people: (Editor) *A Time of Growing,* Random House, 1967; *Timothy's Flower,* Random House, 1967; *One Day in Summer,* Random House, 1969; *The Great Cheese Conspiracy,* Random House, 1969; *I Was a 98-Pound Duckling,* Dial, 1972.

SIDELIGHTS: "I have written four books to date, each quite different from the others, and each with a different genesis. My first book was a realistic picture book story based on characters and incidents I observed on the block in which I lived in New York City. My second was an attempt to capture for very young children, from my own memories of childhood, the feeling of a perfect day spent on the beach. The next book was a complete change of pace—a far-out fantasy about a gang of mice plotting to rob a cheese store. It was completely imaginary, but had its basis in my life in New York. Most recently I've written a humorous book for girls which has its roots in my own experiences in adolescence.

"Trying to find some common denominator in my writing, I guess I would say that more and more I am trying to do two

Here, under one roof, are all the cheeses of my dreams. To be on the safe side, I pinch myself to make sure I'm awake. I am. ■ (From *The Great Cheese Conspiracy* by Jean Van Leeuwen. Illustrated by Imero Gobbato.)

things—to use humor to put across something serious that I want to say, and to recreate certain remembered turning points in my own life in terms that will be meaningful to readers of today.

"I started writing books for very young children, then moved to the middle range, and my latest is for girls going into their teens. Despite this pattern, I don't think that I'm heading for an adult novel next. My interest is in books for children, and I expect to keep writing them, for all ages, as long as I have something to say. When I don't, I hope I'll stop.

"My only comment about my way of working is that it's slow—achingly, frustratingly, agonizingly slow."

The Great Cheese Conspiracy has been optioned for a TV special.

HOBBIES AND OTHER INTERESTS: Photography, reading, travel, music.

FOR MORE INFORMATION SEE: New York Times Book Review, November 5, 1967.

JEAN VAN LEEUWEN

VIGUERS, Ruth Hill 1903-1971
(Ruth A. Hill)

PERSONAL: Born July 24, 1903, in Oakland, Calif.; daughter of Everett Merrill (a clergyman) and Alfarata (Kimball) Hill; married Richard Thomson Viguers (now a hospital administrator), June 2, 1937; children: Deborah Hill (Mrs. Norman L. Buttrick), Susan Thomson and Doris Kimball (twins). *Education:* Willamette University, A.B., 1924; University of Washington, Seattle, B.S. in L.S., 1926. *Politics:* Democrat. *Religion:* Methodist. *Home:* 110 Cliff Rd., Wellesley, Mass. 02181. *Office:* Horn Book, 585 Boylston St., Boston, Mass. 02116.

CAREER: Children's librarian at Seattle (Wash.) Public Library, 1926-27, New York (N.Y.) Public Library, 1927-29; International Institute for Girls, Madrid, Spain, organizer of library and librarian, 1929-31; American Library, Paris, France, head of children's department, 1931-32; New York Public Library, children's librarian, 1932-36; Boone Library School, Wuchang, China, instructor in library science, 1936-37; New York Public Library, assistant superintendent of work with children, 1937-43; Simmons College, School of Publication, Boston, Mass., lecturer in children's literature, 1949-71, also instructor in School of Library Science; *Horn Book* (magazine), Boston, Mass., editor, 1958-67. Lecturer and storyteller. *New York Herald Tribune* Children's Spring Book Festival, judge, 1958; White House Conference on Children and Youth, delegate, 1960; Friends of the Wellesley Free Library, member of board. *Member:* American Library Association, Women's National Book Association, New England Library Association, Massachusetts Library Association. *Awards, honors:* Ed.D. from Portia Law School, 1965; Women's National Book Association Constance Lindsay Skinner Award, 1968.

WRITINGS: (Under name Ruth A. Hill, with Elsa de Bondelli) *Children's Books from Foreign Languages,* Wilson, 1936; (with Cornelia Meigs, Anne Eaton, and Elizabeth Nesbitt) *A Critical History of Children's Literature,* Macmillan, 1953; (with Marcia Dalphin and Bertha Mahony Miller) *Illustrators of Children's Books 1946-1956,* Horn Book, 1958; *Margin for Surprise,* Little, Brown, 1964.

FOR MORE INFORMATION SEE: Horn Book, October, 1967, April, 1971, June, 1971; Elinor W. Field, *Horn Book Reflections,* Horn Book, 1969; *The Writer,* December, 1969; *Publishers Weekly,* March 1, 1971; *Antiquarian Bookmen,* June 24, 1971.

(Died February 2, 1971)

VINING, Elizabeth Gray
See GRAY, Elizabeth Janet

WATKINS-PITCHFORD, D(enys) J(ames) 1905-
(BB, Michael Traherne)

PERSONAL: Born July 25, 1905, in Lamport, Northamptonshire, England; son of Walter and Edith Elizabeth (Wilson) Watkins-Pitchford; married Cecily Mary Adnitt, August 10, 1939; children: Angela June, Robin John (deceased). *Education:* Privately educated; Royal College of Art, A.R.C.A. *Home:* The Round House, Sudborough, Kettering, England. *Agent:* David Higham Associates Ltd., 5-8 Lower John St., Golden Square, London W1R 3PE, England.

CAREER: Rugby School, Warwickshire, England, art master, 1934-49; retired to devote full time to writing and illustrating. Illustrator of other books besides his own. *Military service:* Royal Horse Artillery territorial army, 1925-29; King's Prize, 1928; Home Guard, World War II; became captain. *Awards, honors:* British Library Association Carnegie Medal for *The Little Grey Men* as outstanding children's book of the year.

WRITINGS—Mainly self-illustrated, all written under pseudonym BB: *Wild Lone,* Eyre & Spottiswoode, 1938; *Manka,* Scribner, 1939; *Countryman's Bedside Book,* Eyre & Spottiswoode, 1941; *Idle Countryman,* Eyre & Spottiswoode, 1943; *The Wayfaring Tree,* Hollis & Carter, 1945; *The Fisherman's Bedside Book,* Scribner, 1945, revised edition, 1960; *Brendon Chase,* Hollis & Carter, 1946; *Shooting Man's Bedside Book,* Eyre & Spottiswoode, 1946; *The Sportsman's Bedside Book,* Eyre & Spottiswoode, 1947; (under pseudonym Michael Traherne) *Be Quiet and Go A-Angling,* Lutterworth, 1949.

Confessions of a Carp Fisher, Eyre & Spottiswoode, 1950; *Tides Ending,* Hollis & Carter, 1950; *A Stream in Your Garden,* Eyre & Spottiswoode, 1950; *Letters from Compton Deverell,* Eyre & Spottiswoode, 1950; *The Wind*

RUTH HILL VIGUERS

in the Wood, Hollis & Carter, 1952; *Dark Estuary,* Hollis & Carter, 1953; *A Carp Water,* Putnam, 1958; *The Autumn Road to the Isles,* Nicholas Kaye, 1960; *The White Road Westwards,* Nicholas Kaye, 1961; *September Road to Caithness,* Nicholas Kaye, 1962; *The Spring Road to Wales,* Nicholas Kaye, in press.

Juveniles: *Meeting Hill,* Hollis & Carter, 1948; *Little Grey Men,* Scribner, 1949; *Down the Bright Stream,* Eyre & Spottiswoode, 1950; *Forest of Boland Light Railway,* Eyre & Spottiswoode, 1955; *Monty Woodpig's Caravan,* Edmund Ward, 1957; *Monty Woodpig and His Bubblebuzz Car,* Edmund Ward, 1958; *Mr. Bumstead,* Eyre & Spottiswoode, 1958; *Ben the Bullfinch,* Hamish Hamilton, 1958; *Wandering Wind,* Hamish Hamilton, 1959; *The Wizard of Boland,* Edmund Ward, 1959.

Bill Badger and the Pirates, Hamish Hamilton, 1960; *Bill Badger's Winter Cruise,* Hamish Hamilton, 1960; *Bill Badger's Finest Hour,* Hamish Hamilton, 1961; *Bill Badger's Whispering Reeds Adventure,* Hamish Hamilton, 1962; *The Badgers of Bearshanks,* Hamish Hamilton, 1962; *Bill Badger's Big Mistake,* Hamish Hamilton, 1963; *Lepus the Brown Hare,* Benn, 1963; *The Real Book of the Countryside,* Dobson, 1964; *At the Back o'Ben Dee,* Benn, 1965; *The Whopper,* Benn, 1967, published in America under title *The Monster Fish,* Scholastic, 1972; *The Tyger Tray,* Methuen, 1970.

D. J. WATKINS-PITCHFORD

Illustrator: M. C. Carey, *Fairy Tales of Long Ago,* Dutton, 1952; Andrew Lang, *Prince Prigio and Prince Ricardo,* Dutton, 1961; Frances Browne, *Granny's Wonderful Chair,* Dutton, 1963; George MacDonald, *The Lost Princess,* Dutton, 1966; A. R. Channel, *Jungle Rescue,* S. G. Phillips, 1968.

Contributor to *Country Life, Field,* and *Shooting Times.*

SIDELIGHTS: "I think I began writing at an early age (about ten), illustrating the stories with my own drawings. I cannot write to set times. To do so would be to destroy any enjoyment and once that is lost your work will die.

"I find that the people who enjoyed my books as children now buy them for their own and hence the success of stories like *The Little Grey Men, Down the Bright Stream* and *Brendon Chase.* The latter, especially, has great appeal to children because it fulfills the idea of rebellion against the authority of grown ups. This story has sold many thousands of copies and is perhaps my own favorite for, strange as it may seem, I like to re-read my own books—the better ones! As a boy with my brother, we used to lead a Huckleberry Finn type of existence during the holidays and *Brendon Chase* is based on these experiences.

"I have a great love of sports—shooting and fishing—things which seem odd to those who like my accounts of birds and beasts and nature. I do not attempt to reconcile these things in myself. I have the hunting instinct and that's that. I live in the country adjoining a great forest—part of the old Royal Forest of Rockingham—and the deer there, still wild and free, are the descendants of those hunted by the Kings of England and King John. My house, the ''Round House'', was built ten years after Shakespeare died, and it *is* quite round.

"I have an enormous amount of hobbies: Bonzai trees, gardening—especially water gardening, painting (portraits and landscapes), etchings and engraving, horse riding, shooting, fishing, reading of autobiographies and nature books, Hudson and Jefferies. (Seldom novels save those of Thomas Hardy whom I admire enormously, and Conrad.) I also find the opposite sex marvelous.

"Life, I find, is an enormous adventure, and I never cease to marvel at the fact but for mere chance I might have been a spider or a butterfly, an earthworm or any living thing, or simply nothing at all. I am in despair about mankind. How he is polluting this lovely planet, at his greed and hatred of his fellows and above all at the terrible prospects of overpopulation. He seems hell bent on his own destruction. That is how I see it. The miracle of the passing moment—each pump of one's heart—I have not lost my sense of wonder and gratitude to Someone for this.

"My attitude toward religion has undergone a change. I rarely go to church yet I am not an atheist by any means. Anyone who has studied nature cannot be, for there is that sense of great beauty everywhere in the design of flowers and birds and fishes, etc. A wonderful storehouse of treasures which a lifetime is too short for exploration.

"I write only when the spirit moves me and then my hand cannot keep pace with my thoughts. I start a book with

■ (From *The Lost Princess* by George MacDonald. Illustrated by D. J. Watkins-Pitchford.)

hardly any idea how it is to end. I think this must be unusual. The story unfolds as I go along almost as if I had inspiration from outside myself, which of course, I don't believe.

"I do not 'write for children,' I write to please myself and never think of how the reader will react or what age he (or she) is. I try to use simple words and short sentences simply because I find that this is the best form of expressing myself. I do not consider 'style'—to be conscious of 'writing a book' is fatal. I try to write with honesty. I do not write about anything with which I am not familiar.

"I prefer animals and birds to many of the human species, for in them one senses the complete absence of evil and only man is evil (as well, of course, as being good). The only thing that depresses me is that nothing is permanent and that at some time in the future this world and all that is in it will 'be' as if it had never been."

Watkins-Pitchford's books have been translated for publication in Germany, Holland, Yugoslavia, Israel, and Switzerland. They have also been adapted for television.

FOR MORE INFORMATION SEE: Illustrators of Children's Books: 1946-1956, Horn Book, 1958; Roger Lancelyn Green, *Tellers of Tales*, Watts, 1965; Brian Doyle, *The Who's Who of Children's Literature*, Schocken, 1968; *Third Book of Junior Authors*, edited by de Montreville and Hill, H. W. Wilson, 1972.

WELLMAN, Manly Wade 1903-

PERSONAL: Born May 21, 1903, in Angola (Portuguese West Africa); son of Frederick Creighton (a medical missionary and scientist) and Lydia (Isely) Wellman (American citizens); married Frances Obrist, 1930; children: Wade. *Education:* University of Wichita, A.B., 1926; Columbia University, B.Litt., 1927. *Politics:* Democrat. *Religion:* Episcopalian. *Home and office address:* P.O. Box 744, Chapel Hill, N.C. *Agent:* McIntosh & Otis, Inc., 18 East 41st St., New York, N.Y. 10017.

CAREER: Kansas newspapers, worked as reporter, book and motion picture reviewer, feature writer, 1927-34; freelance writer, 1934—. *Awards, honors:* Ellery Queen Award, 1946; Mystery Writers of America Edgar Allen Poe Award for best non-fiction study of crime, 1955.; Association for State and Local History award of merit, 1973.

WRITINGS—Novels: *Find My Killer,* Farrar, Straus, 1948; *Fort Sun Dance: Candle of the Wicked,* Putnam, 1960; *Not at These Hands,* Putnam, 1961.

American history: *Giant in Gray,* Charles Scribner's Sons, 1949; *Dead and Gone,* University of North Carolina Press, 1954; *Rebel Boast,* Holt, 1955; *Fastest on the River,* Holt, 1957; (with Elizabeth Amis Blanchard) *The Life and Times of Sir Archie,* University of North Carolina Press, 1958; *The County of Warren,* University of North Carolina Press, 1959; *They Took Their Stand,* Putnam, 1959; (with Frances Wellman) *The Rebel Songster,* Heritage House, 1959; *Harpers Ferry: Prize of War,* McNally & Loftin, 1960; (with Robert F. Cope) *The County of Gaston,* Heritage House, 1961; *The County of Moore,* Moore County Historical Association, 1962; *Winston-Salem in History, Part I: The Founders,* J. F. Blair, 1966; *The Kingdom of Madison: A Southern Mountain Fastness and Its Peoples,* University of North Carolina Press, 1973.

Science fiction: *Twice in Time,* Avalon, 1957; *Giants From Eternity,* Avalon, 1959; *The Dark Destroyers,* Avalon, 1959; *Island in the Sky,* Avalon, 1961; *Who Fears the Devil?,* Arkham House, 1963.

Novels for young readers: *The Sleuth Patrol,* Nelson, 1947; *The Mystery of Lost Valley,* Nelson, 1948; *The Haunts of Drowning Creek,* Nelson, 1951; *Wild Dogs of Drowning Creek,* Holiday, 1952; *The Last Mammoth,* Holiday, 1953; *Gray Riders,* Aladdin, 1954; *Rebel Mail Runner,* Holiday, 1954; *Flag on the Levee,* Washburn, 1955; *To Unknown Lands,* Holiday, 1956; *Young Squire Morgan,* Washburn, 1956; *Lights on Skeleton Ridge,* Washburn, 1957; *The Ghost Batallion,* Washburn, 1958; *Ride, Rebels!,* Washburn, 1959; *Appomattox Road,* Washburn, 1960; *Third String Center,* Washburn, 1960; *Rifles at Ramsour's Mill,* Washburn, 1961; *Battle for King's Mountain,* Washburn, 1962; *Clash on the Catawba,* Washburn, 1962; *The South Fork Rangers,* Washburn, 1963; *The Master of Scate Hollow,* Washburn, 1964; *The Specter of Bear Paw Gap,* Washburn, 1966; *Battle at Bear Paw Gap,* Washburn, 1966; *Jamestown Adventure,* Washburn, 1967; *Carolina Pirate,* Washburn, 1968; *Brave Horse,* Colonial Williamsburg, 1968; *Mountain Feud,* Washburn, 1969; *Napoleon of the West,* Washburn, 1970; *Fast Break Five,* Washburn,

There was only a scrap of moon to give him light, but he put Circe to the half-seen road and she galloped boldly upon it. ■ (From *Brave Horse: The Story of Janus* by Manly Wade Wellman. Illustrated by Peter Burchard.)

1971. Stories in eighteen anthologies, more than 500 short stories and articles, mostly of fantasy, mystery and historical adventure, in national magazines.

SIDELIGHTS: "I was six when my parents returned to America. Both my father and mother were published authors. My oldest brother, the late Paul I. Wellman, was an author of substantial reputation. My second brother, Frederick L. Wellman, a plant pathologist, has contributed importantly to the literature of his scientific calling. My sister, Alice Wellman, has published books of both fiction and nonfiction, and my son, Wade, has published a volume of poetry, besides seeing many poems into print in national magazines. But none of this heritage and environment must be supposed to make writing easier or more certain of success. Any writer, under any conditions, must write alone if he will succeed. Getting into print was a formidable task, and today I find it as hard to write as ever, however, more sensibly and skillfully I may work.

"Though born abroad, I am from old American stock, and my soul's roots are deeply driven into the rock of whatever may constitute America. I do not think I represent a particular school or preach a particular cult, unless I might be called a minor and modest figure among Southern regionalists."

HOBBIES AND OTHER INTERESTS: American history, American folklore and folkways, sports, travel.

WILSON, Carter 1941-

PERSONAL: Born December 27, 1941, in Washington, D.C.; son of George Wood (a lawyer) and Harriet (Fort) Wilson. *Education:* Harvard University, A.B., 1963; Syracuse University, M.A., 1965. *Residence:* Santa Cruz, Calif. *Agent:* Candida Donadio, Candida Donadio, Inc., 111 West 57th St., New York, N.Y. *Office:* Board of Community Studies, University of California, Santa Cruz, Calif. 95064.

CAREER: Stanford University, Palo Alto, Calif., lecturer in English, 1965-66; Harvard University, Cambridge,

CARTER WILSON

218

Mass., teacher of creative writing, 1966-69; Tufts University, Medford, Mass., assistant professor of English, 1969-72; University of California, Santa Cruz, assistant professor of community studies, 1972—.

WRITINGS: Crazy February (novel), Lippincott, 1966; *I Have Fought the Good Fight* (novel), Lippincott, 1967; *On Firm Ice* (children's stories), Crowell, 1970; *A Green Tree and a Dry Tree* (novel), Macmillan, 1972. Also co-produced and wrote a documentary film about a fiesta in southern Mexico, "Appeals to Santiago," released through Contemporary-McGraw Hill.

WORK IN PROGRESS: A novel; a feature film, "Shadow Catcher," with Tim Hunter.

SIDELIGHTS: Lived for a year among the Mayan Indians in the mountains of southern Mexico, the setting for his first novel which was called "anything but run-of-the-mill" in the *New York Times Book Review.* Thè reviewer found the characters of the Indians and Mexicans of the region "more subtly penetrated by Carter Wilson . . . than were the famous 'Children of Sanchez,' as tape-recorded by Oscar Lewis." Wilson speaks Spanish and a Mayan Indian dialect, Tzotzil.

FOR MORE INFORMATION SEE: New York Times Book Review, February 27, 1966.

Samik had begun to believe that he had been waiting at the same breathing hole his entire life. ■ (From *On Firm Ice* by Carter Wilson. Illustrated by William A. Berry. Reprinted by permission of Thomas Y. Crowell.)

WILLIAM WONDRISKA

WONDRISKA, William   1931-

PERSONAL: Born June 29, 1931, in Chicago, Ill.; son of William Charles and Ruth Marie (Zavodsky) Wondriska; married Rebecca Jane Shoemaker, August 27, 1955; children: Alison Elizabeth, Stefanie Ann, Jana Margret. *Education:* School of the Art Institute of Chicago, B.A.E., 1953; Yale University, B.F.A., 1954, M.F.A., 1955. *Religion:* Protestant. *Home:* 239 Ridgewood Rd., West Hartford, Conn. 06107.

CAREER: Lester Beall, Brookfield Center, Conn., designer, 1957-58; University of Hartford, Conn., instructor in art, 1958-61; self-employed as designer, 1961—. *Military service:* U.S. Army, 1955-57. *Awards, honors:* Books included in American Institute of Graphic Arts Children's Book Show, 1957, 1960, 1964, 1968, and 50 Books Exhibit, 1959, 1964, 1970.

WRITINGS: The Sound of Things, privately printed, 1955, published by Pantheon, 1958; *1, 2, 3, A Book to See,* Pantheon, 1959; *Puff* (Junior Literary Guild selection), Pantheon, 1960; *Which Way to the Zoo?,* Holt, 1962; (designer, illustrator) *A Cat Can't Count,* Lothrop, 1962; *A Long Piece of String,* Holt, 1963; *All by Myself,* Holt, 1963; *The Tomato Patch,* Holt, 1964; *John John Twilliger,* Holt, 1966; *Mr. Brown and Mr. Gray,* Holt, 1968; *All the Animals Were Angry,* Holt, 1970; *The Stop,* Holt, 1972.

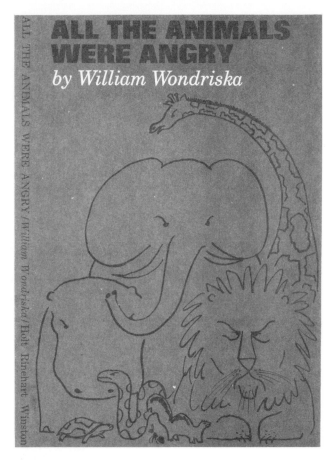

"All the animals were so angry they were ready to tear each other to pieces." ■ (From *All the Animals Were Angry* by William Wondriska. Illustrated by the author.)

This child goes where the four hills of life
And the Four Winds are standing.
■ (From *Hollering Sun* by Nancy Wood. Photographs by Myron Wood.)

SIDELIGHTS: "Too frequently too many people are involved in giving birth to a book. . . . As a result not many beautiful books are produced. A book is such a personal statement that it should reflect more of the human and less of the machine. As a designer and author, I am completely responsible for all the functions. If the result is not beautiful I am responsible, but the satisfactions of creating a book that is beautiful are overwhelming."

FOR MORE INFORMATION SEE: Graphic Design, Tokyo, Japan, No. 1, 1959; *The Penrose Annual,* London, England, Volume 56, 1962.

WOOD, Nancy 1936-

PERSONAL: Born June 20, 1936, in Trenton, N.J.; daughter of Harold William (a businessman) and Eleanor (Green) Clopp; married Myron Gilmore Wood (a photographer), March 1, 1961 (divorced); children: Karen Alison, Christopher Keith, Eleanor Kathryn, India Hart. *Education:* Studied at Bucknell University, 1955-56, and University of Colorado Extension, 1958-59. *Politics:* Democrat. *Religion:* Congregational. *Home:* 825 Paseo, Colorado Springs, Colo. 80907. *Agent:* Marie Rodell, 141 East 55th St., New York, N.Y. 10022.

CAREER: Writer.

WRITINGS—With former husband, Myron Wood, as photographic illustrator: *Central City,* Chaparral Press, 1963; *West to Durango,* Chaparral Press, 1964; *Little Wrangler,* Doubleday, 1966; *Colorado,* Doubleday, 1969; *The Last Five Dollar Baby,* Harper, 1972; *Clearcut: The Deforestation of America,* Sierra Club, 1972; *Hollering Sun,* Simon & Schuster, 1972; *In This Proud Land,* New York Graphic Society, 1973; *Many Winters,* Doubleday, 1974.

WORK IN PROGRESS: Two children's books; a novel; poetry collection.

WRIGHT, R(obert) H(amilton) 1906-

PERSONAL: Born December 26, 1906, in Vancouver, British Columbia, Canada; son of Leslie Havelock (an insurance agent) and Clare DuPuy (Rogers) Wright; married Kathleen Joan Creer, September 9, 1931; children: R.L.D., I.G., Kathleen Jennifer. *Education:* University of British Columbia, B.A., 1928; McGill University, M. Sc., 1930, Ph.D., 1931; University of New Brunswick, D.Sc., 1973. *Office:* 6822 Blenheim St., Vancouver 13, British Columbia, Canada.

CAREER: University of New Brunswick, Fredericton, 1931-46, started as assistant professor, became professor of physical chemistry; British Columbia Research Council,

R. H. WRIGHT

Vancouver, head of Division of Chemistry, 1946-62, head of olfactory response investigation, 1962-71; Food and Agriculture Organization of the United Nations and other organizations, private consultant, 1972—. Holder of several U.S. and Canadian patents. *Member:* Chemical Institute (Canada; fellow), Entomological Society of America, Entomological Society of Canada.

WRITINGS: Manual of Laboratory Glass Blowing, Chemical Publishing Co., 1943; *The Science of Smell,* Basic Books, 1964. Contributor of about one hundred articles to *Nature* and to technical journals.

WORK IN PROGRESS: Studies in insect attraction and repulsion, infrared spectroscopy of perfumes, and substances that influence insect behavior.

YORK, Carol Beach 1928-

PERSONAL: Born January 21, 1928, in Chicago, Ill.; daughter of Harold and Mary (Cantwell) Beach; married Richard Marten York, 1947; children: Diana Carol. *Education:* Attended Thornton Junior College. *Religion:* Christian Scientist. *Home:* 14839 Main St., Harvey, Ill. 60426.

WRITINGS: Sparrow Lake, Coward, 1962; (with Mary Beach) *One Summer,* Coward, 1963; *Where Love Begins,* Coward, 1963; *The Doll in the Bake Shop,* Watts, 1965; *Ghost of the Isherwoods,* Watts, 1966; *Miss Know It All,* Watts, 1966; *Until We Fall in Love Again,* Watts, 1967; *The Christmas Dolls,* Watts, 1967; *The Blue Umbrella,* Watts, 1968; *The Good Day Mice,* Watts, 1968; *The Mystery of the Diamond Cat,* Watts, 1969; *Good Charlotte,* Watts, 1969; *The Ten O'Clock Club,* Watts, 1970; *Nothing Ever Happens Here,* Hawthorn, 1970; *Mystery at Dark Wood,* Watts, 1972; *Miss Know It All Returns,* Watts, 1972; *Dead Man's Cat,* Nelson, 1972; *The Tree House Mystery,* Coward, 1973; *Mystery of the Spider Doll,* Watts, 1973; *Takers and Returners,* Nelson, 1973; *The Midnight Ghost,* Coward, 1973. Author of short stories and nonfiction for women's and children's magazines.

SIDELIGHTS: "I began to write when I was about seven years old. I wrote poems and short stories in spiral notebooks that sold (then) for ten cents apiece. My mother was my only reader.

"When I was in my twenties I began to write and submit short stories for women's and children's magazines, and then to write books for children. I enjoy 'elaborating' more than one can in short stories, so once I started on books I never went back to short stories. I love typing 'Chapter One' at the head of a page.

"*Where Love Begins* is based on a real true experience from my high school days, when, like the girls in the story, my girlfriend and I fell in love with two trapeze performers at a circus. *Until We Fall in Love* again is also based largely on experiences from my own teenage years.

"Lately I have been writing mostly mysteries. They are fun to write. It is fun to decide exactly how many clues to give the reader without giving the final conclusion away.

"I live with my daughter, Diana, in a rambling old house constantly in need of repairs (which I am totally inadequate about). Besides writing, reading is my most favorite occupation. I am also extremely interested in art, history, and philosophy. My New Year's resolutions included a resolution to begin practicing the piano again—after about a ten year's holiday!"

FOR MORE INFORMATION SEE: Young Reader's Review, March, 1967; *New York Times Book Review,* December 3, 1967; *Library Journal,* September, 1968.

SOMETHING ABOUT THE AUTHOR

CUMULATIVE INDEXES, VOLUMES 1-6
Illustrators and Authors

ILLUSTRATIONS INDEX

(In the following index, the number of the volume in which an illustrator's work appears is given *before* the colon, and the page on which it appears is given *after* the colon. For example, a drawing by Adams, Adrienne appears in Volume 2 on page 6, and another drawing by her appears in Volume 3 on page 80.)

AUTHORS INDEX

(In the following index, the number of the volume in which an author's sketch appears is given *before* the colon, and the page on which it appears is given *after* the colon. For example, the sketch of Aardema, Verna, appears in Volume 4 on page 1).